MASSIMO D'AZEGLIO

THINGS I REMEMBER

(I miei ricordi)

MASSIMO D'AZEGLIO

Things I Remember
(I miei ricordi)

Translated with an Introduction by
E. R. VINCENT

LONDON
OXFORD UNIVERSITY PRESS
NEW YORK   TORONTO
1966

Oxford University Press, Ely House, London W. 1

GLASGOW NEW YORK TORONTO MELBOURNE WELLINGTON
BOMBAY CALCUTTA MADRAS KARACHI LAHORE DACCA KUALA LUMPUR HONG KONG
CAPE TOWN SALISBURY IBADAN NAIROBI LUSAKA ADDIS ABABA

Printed in Great Britain by Richard Clay (The Chaucer Press), Ltd.,
Bungay, Suffolk

CONTENTS

Contents

PART II

INTRODUCTION

UNLIKE Winston Churchill, Massimo d'Azeglio was painter long before he was Prime Minister. The two activities are not often combined; nor can it be common that painter-statesmen have also been professional soldiers and professional authors. In d'Azeglio's case there are further attainments to record. He was an excellent horseman, musician (vocal and instrumental), fencer, gymnast, and billiards player. There is evidence that he appreciated his own versatility. On the eve of setting out in February 1853 for London, where he was to dine with Queen Victoria and the Prince Consort and win their, and everybody else's, hearts, he wrote to his wife as follows:

I am in the middle of the troublesome business of packing. My luggage is a real epitome of my fairly varied life: in the same valise there is a helmet; a palette; medals and decorations; painting brushes; a uniform; sketches; writings and—forgive my bluntness—vests, pants, and similar gear. There is enough to arouse the gravest suspicions in the minds of the customs people, who will suppose I have robbed artists, officers, and ministers and am now making off with the spoil.

The writer of this letter was a tall, fair, blue-eyed, handsome man of very great charm. There is no doubt that women found him irresistible. His first wife was Giulia, daughter of the great novelist Alessandro Manzoni. On her early death, in 1834, he married her aunt, Luisa Blondel, much to the family's dismay. Although a love-match, the second marriage was a failure owing to incompatibility of temperament, for the couple found they could not happily live together. Despite this, d'Azeglio wrote long, intimate letters to Luisa until the day of his death.

Apart from marriage, d'Azeglio had very numerous love-affairs, but the reader will find little about this side of his life in his autobiography. The Countess Morici, however, the *femme fatale* of his Roman days, haunts the pages, unnamed but insistent. She had a daughter by d'Azeglio, named Bice, of whom he was very fond, but of whose existence no hint is here dropped. Nor is his legitimate daughter Rina, Giulia's child, introduced to the reader. This was due to d'Azeglio's belief that, although a man may reveal everything about himself, he has no right to implicate the private lives of others.

D'Azeglio's life (1798–1866) spans a fascinating period in the history of Italy and Europe: childhood under Napoleon in Turin and Tuscany; youth as an art-student in and around Papal Rome; maturity in the artistic circles of Austrian Milan; middle age as the Prime Minister of an independent Piedmont. His experience of society was equally varied. A member of one of the ancient Piedmontese noble families, he could converse easily with Kings, Popes, and Princes. At the same time, as one of the classless fraternity of artists, he was on familiar terms with peasants, inn-keepers, adventurers and bandits. Although a rebel against the conventions in which he had been brought up, he held moderate liberal views in politics. Having won a wide popularity through his patriotically inspired novels, he was known to all and seemed chosen by fate to lead Italians to the liberal-monarchical solution of their constitutional problem. He who witnessed the birth-pangs of the new Italy was not the least of her accoucheurs.

Although we get little, or nothing, of d'Azeglio the active politician in this book, it reflects much of his political experience. By nature a man of sanguine, optimistic temperament, his views of Italy and Italians ended by being, on the whole, pessimistic. As a pragmatist he deplored the idealistic excesses of Mazzini and his followers; as a simple moralist he disliked the opportunism of Cavour, his associate and successor. In retirement at Cannero on Lake Maggiore his views hardened and he grew out of touch with the rapidly evolving events of his later days. Like so many others of those prominent in bringing about the liberation and independence of Italy, he felt it was happening in the wrong way. He was against the hastily achieved inclusion of the South and he was against Rome as capital. Some historians have been inclined to take an unduly simplified view of the *risorgimento*, which such books as this serve to correct. It was, on the whole, a painful process.

Constantly in the following pages we find the idea that, Italy being made, it was now necessary to make Italians. Young Italians must be taught the simple virtues of truth and self-sacrifice, which alone can make a nation great. These virtues he recognizes in the peoples of Piedmont and the Romagna, but hardly elsewhere in Italy. It is to this end he thinks the relation of his own experiences may serve a useful purpose.

In his Preface d'Azeglio explains his motives for writing an autobiography; the first was didactic; the second, commemorative. He did not mention what was obviously more important still, namely his relish for life and the pleasure he felt in expressing it in words. The reader will be delighted to find that the pious, pedagogic themes are constantly being overwhelmed in the rush of d'Azeglio's creative vitality. He was far more than a Samuel Smiles and his artistic sense would not let the commemorative element encroach too much.

The typical Italian attitude towards parents, especially mothers, is something they have perhaps inherited from the Roman cult of ancestors. Women, to judge from d'Azeglio, may be angels until they marry, but then almost immediately become very far from angelic. After they have produced sons, they evolve, through matriarchy, to the angel status once more. At their death, all the bells of Heaven ring, and ever afterwards their names are only mentioned in hushed tones of profound veneration or accompanied by the rhetoric of an eighteenth-century tombstone.

It is in this tradition that d'Azeglio gives us the portrait of his mother as a hypochondriacal angel. This is unfair to a woman who was obviously far more than that.

That gallant, splendid, impossible man, his father, largely escapes the necrological treatment and comes to life for us. It is moving to recognize the struggle in d'Azeglio between the natural antipathy a man of his temperament felt for an ultra-conservative father, and his admiration for the latter's sterling virtues. He knew he ought to love him, but he obviously found it very difficult to do so.

D'Azeglio had a good deal of material already collected by the time he finally decided to write his autobiography in February 1863, at the age of sixty-five. This consisted of family papers, including his mother's little biography of his father, copies of his own letters, and many letters written by others. Particularly important for his art-student period were the Roman stories he had already published in 1856 in the Turin periodical *Il Cronista* under the title of *Racconti, leggende, ricordi della vita italiana.*

He never intended to carry his autobiography as far as the period of his entry into the Piedmontese Government in 1849. In point of fact his death cut the book short before the story had reached that point. He had, however, left a number of disconnected writings, which his friend Giuseppe Torelli subsequently added to the published version of the work. The present English translation contains some, but not all, of this additional matter.[1] Much of this posthumous appendix is chronologically misplaced, but we must be grateful to Torelli for having saved the description of the political tour of Romagna, and d'Azeglio's

[1] After Part II, p. 320 as indicated.

account of his wonderfully dramatic interview with King Carlo Alberto.

Even though the avowed object of his book is pedagogic—however far he strays from it in the enjoyment of his reminiscences—d'Azeglio finds it a little difficult to see himself as an exemplary model for the young. At sixty-five he still revels in the escapades of his youth, and what was perhaps first intended as a horrid warning turns out, to the reader's delight, to be still riotous fun. D'Azeglio is much too fond of life to moralize all his experiences. This brave, true, honest gentleman has nothing of the prig about him.

It is really amusing, for example, to see (in Chapter 15 of Part I) an inveterate amorist attempting to draw up Queensberry rules for the pursuit of illicit love. Here we find a surprising confusion of thought, with God and Louis XIV in the same paragraph; Turkish harems; African kraals; and erotic French novels. His deductions are: tell as few lies as possible; don't make friends with the husband of the woman you are courting; if you can't be good, be careful. It is entertaining to see this honest Latin trying to moralize in a field where those with a puritan heritage will be hard put to it to find room for any morals at all!

D'Azeglio is a simple empiricist; no philosopher. His ideas sometimes strike one as surprisingly naïve, although there is a basis of sound sense in nearly all he says. His views on art and education will appeal to the elderly reader; hardly to the young.

Even within the chronological limits he proposed, d'Azeglio has omitted much; for example, his visit to the Paris Salon Exhibition of 1836, and his various trips to Sicily. It is sad that he did not continue the story to contain an account of his adventures as a colonel in the Papal army in the war of 1848, when he saw action and was wounded. Perhaps, however, it is for the best that he has not given us a connected narrative account of his political life, written in the disillusioned mood of his retirement. For this we have to consult his numerous political pamphlets and letters.

As for his paintings, he has told us a good deal about his methods and intentions in this book, and many of his pictures can be seen in galleries in Turin, Milan, Rome, and elsewhere.[2] They will seem romantically old-fashioned to the present generation, though they were appreciated during his lifetime and found ready buyers. He has also told us much about his two published historical novels, but they too belong to a genre now out of favour. He was neither a great painter nor a great novelist.

Perhaps he came nearest to successful artistic achievement in the

---

[2] See Appendix, p. 347.

brilliant descriptions of places and people which abound in this book. He saw everything vividly and distinctly with a painter's eye. Few writers, for example, would have noticed and remembered the colour and design of the upholstery of the chair he sat on during his historic interview with Carlo Alberto.

D'Azeglio informs us in his Preface that his style is deliberately colloquial and familiar and, as translator, I have attempted to keep it so in English.

*   *   *

Since d'Azeglio's *I miei ricordi* was translated into English as *Recollections* in 1868 by Count Maffei, the text has been radically revised (in 1949) by Professor A. M. Ghisalberti from the original manuscript. The present translation is of the complete Ghisalberti text (as published by Giangiacomo Feltrinelli, edited by Massimo Legnani, Milan, 1963) with the following omissions: Part I, pp. 8–10; 47–49; 50–51; 100–1; Part II, pp. 370–6; 403–14; 478–505; 508–14. The reason for these omissions will be plain to those who consult the original text. The minor omissions in Part I have been made in order to spare the reader either questions of Italian linguistic style or the sort of digression which the author himself advises us to skip. The first two omissions in Part II are of extracts from the author's brother Enrico's Diary, and from a long Essay by his father, neither of which seems likely to please or instruct the English reader. Omissions after p. 478 are of material supplied after the author's death by Giuseppe Torelli, which did not receive the approval of Alessandrina d'Azeglio. Some of this would have been included had space permitted, but much of it is fragmentary and chronologically confusing. The description of the political tour of Romagna and the interview with Carlo Alberto, however, had been seen in manuscript by Alessandrina and was originally published with her full approval.

Corpus Christi College   E. R. VINCENT
   Cambridge

AUTHOR'S PREFACE

I HAVE been planning to write the story of my life for several years now. Whenever I considered the idea, however, I was assailed by innumerable doubts. I felt discouraged, and my determination came to nothing. Is my life worth telling? Why do I feel this urge to write an autobiography? Am I prompted by a worthy motive, or is this a snare set by a vulgar, inappropriate egotism?

Everyone can silence such doubts by affirming the persuasion of his friends. But, to tell the truth, I cannot accuse mine of any special insistence in the matter. In such cases, too, I think one would get better advice from one's enemies. I will not pursue the subject.

The following are the real motives which have induced me to write this book.

I have all of a sudden, it seems, reached the age of sixty-four without having had time to look back. It behoves me now to give a glance at the road I have travelled. It is a healthy thing and a good thing to judge the actions of youth and manhood by the dispassionate criterion of maturity. If such a consideration is, to some extent, useful to oneself, why should it not be equally so to others; always provided the judge be fair, sensible, and sincere? It remains to be seen whether I can be so. Without replying too positively in the affirmative, I shall not say more than that I hope so and that I shall try as hard as I can.

It will not be a bad thing, as a first proof of my sincerity, if I give this advice to the reader. When I speak ill of myself, follow me blindly; when I speak well of myself, keep your eyes wide open.

Very well then! To be of some use to others, and above all to the new generation, I have decided to compose my book as follows. My intention is not so much to narrate the events of my life, as to treat myself as a subject for moral and psychological study. I shall attempt to know myself and describe my inner nature and character in its successive changes. At the same time I shall point out the causes, both objective and subjective, which have led to my improvement or deterioration. Unless I am mistaken, this kind of moral autopsy will be far from useless for those who have to educate others, as well as for those who understand that everyone, to his last day, must be concerned with self-education.

It will not be enough to analyse myself so that I may deduce useful lessons from the study. I hope to offer the reader better provender than myself.

It has fallen to my lot to meet a very large number of people during my life; among these are men of the highest calibre, great intelligence, rare spirit, and lofty character. I hope that by portraying these I can provide a rich gallery of noble examples. I only wish that it could result in another equally rich, that of their imitators!

I have met authentic heroes during my career. By heroes, I mean those who sacrifice themselves for others; not those who sacrifice others for their own advantage. Not for me to offer as models men in the smallest degree similar to those great oppressors of mankind, who are worshipped and admired in direct proportion to the harm they do. No! My heroes, mostly unknown, victims rather than butchers, belonged to every class; for God be praised, even though men are not as they should be, they are not all dolts or criminals, as the pessimists of all periods believe.

I have been singularly fortunate in this: to find elect souls, worthy to be put forward as models of noble sacrifice and unblemished life, I need go no farther than my own home. I do not know how better to begin this critical study of many lives, among which my own appears merely as a thread to bind up the others into a richer fabric; I do not know how better to begin, I say, than with my own father and mother.

I should like to inscribe their names on a far more lasting and honourable memorial than these poor pages, which I dedicate to their cherished and revered memory; but to do more is beyond me.

I know very well that the reader cannot entirely share my sentiments, but this is no reason why I should withhold what I have to say. Should I do this, I would be false to my heart and conscience; I should violate the rule I have imposed on myself to tell the whole truth. I should seem to deny the piety I feel towards those who gave me birth and—what is more—everything of good there may be in me. They never let me see an act or hear a word that was not exemplary. Is there a man of feeling who would say I was wrong in my sentiments?

Another word of warning! I do not want this to be a political book or one written for our own day only; and if I succeed in doing what I want to do, it will certainly not turn out to be so. I well know how difficult it is for an author not to take on the colour of his period, to a greater or lesser extent. One can say it is impossible to be quite free of it. But I have done my utmost during my political career to recognize and follow only what is true and just, without party passion and without worrying if what I did were popular or not. I have the inveterate habit of calling a man an honest fellow or a rascal according as I find him, and not because he belongs to one party rather than another. This used to annoy everybody. I have tried hard to discover and apply, whenever I could, the great elementary laws, which serve to found, maintain, and prosper nations, without heeding interests, petty passions, and vulgar trivialities. So much so that I almost hope I can attain my purpose of handing down to posterity a few pages which can be read without too much trouble, even in circumstances and in times far different from the present.

At the same time, I should also like my book to be, in a sense, useful to our own age. Let me explain myself.

For half a century Italy has been in travail to become one people, a nation. To a large extent she has won back her territory. The struggle against the foreigner has been successfully ended; but this has not been our greatest problem. The real difficulty and the greatest, that which keeps us in a state of uncertainty, is the internal conflict. The worst of Italy's enemies are not Teutons, but Italians.

Why is this? The reason is because the Italians have wanted to make a new Italy, but themselves to remain the old Italians, with all the worthlessness and moral poverty that have been their undoing for ages past; because they think they can reform Italy, and yet not one has appreciated that to do this it is necessary for Italians to reform themselves. Italy, as all other peoples, cannot become a nation, cannot be well organized, well governed, strong against foreign foes and domestic plotters, free in her own right, until everybody, great, middling, and small, each in his sphere, does his duty and does it well, or at least as well as he can. But to do one's duty—usually troublesome, commonplace, and inconspicuous as it is—one needs strength of will and a realization that duty must be done, not because it is amusing or advantageous, but because it is duty. This strength of will, this realization, is the precious heritage known by the single word 'character'. So we simply say that Italy's prime need is to educate Italians who know how to do their duty, that is to say Italians with strong, lofty characters. Alas! Every day we are going in the opposite direction.

Should the subject matter of this book, the anecdotes and the examples it contains, help to contribute to the formation of just one good man, I should consider I had done a great service to my country. If the proverb be true which tells us that one fool makes a hundred (we see notable examples of this every day), it is equally true that a strong, elevated character can make one thousand one hundred similar and give life, warmth, and, so to say, a worthier and more generous tone to an entire country, for years and years.

I now have to proclaim the last of my motives in writing this book; it is the least important as it is entirely personal. I must therefore beg the reader to be patient with me.

In all probability my family will shortly die out. I am far from considering this a national disaster. In fact, as far as my own wishes are concerned, I prefer to see it finish honourably now, than later with inept—and quite likely worse than inept—successors; seeing that the last three generations, I can frankly say, have been honest, respected folk.

Dante himself says in his *Purgatory*:

> O Ugolin de' Fantolin, thy name
> Is safe; it cannot look for heirs again
> To grow debased and blacken it with shame.[3]

So I am in good company.

True it is, however, that we have an inherent dislike of destruction and, still more, of oblivion. I can't bear the idea that, in a country I have loved so much and which my people have loved and served so well, within a few years there will be no one left who even knows we have existed.

It is therefore my purpose to narrate the events of my own life and of those worthy people to whom I was related or with whom I was acquainted. Finally, this book is to be a kind of short history of our family, so that its memory may not so quickly fade from the minds of my fellow-countrymen.

Alas! I know I am not one of those swans described by Ariosto, who alone can save the names of the deserving from the waters of oblivion. But what I cannot do, why should not the kindness I have found in so many of my contemporaries perform for me, and this history become a legacy, I hope, for their children and grandchildren.

So much for the spirit of my work; I shall now speak of its form.

As I am writing about myself, I must show myself as I am. I must really be myself and no other. Therefore I must not only relate facts accurately and express my thoughts and opinions without circumlocution, but I must adopt the words, phrases, and expressions I habitually use, those which spring from my individual character.

My view is that to write well, one must in all circumstances write as though one were speaking to a group of cultured friends, in which the men are worthy of respect and the women modest.

[3] *Purgatorio* XIV, 121–3, transl. Dorothy L. Sayers.

As long as one avoids certain trivialities and improprieties of diction, one can express oneself frankly, with the same words and in the same style as though speaking.

If only this method were followed in Italy; if only so many authors did not feel obliged to change their language directly they have a pen in their hands! If only—if I may make use of a rather daring metaphor— they would put their pen in their mouth, so many books would not be such an immense toil to read, almost impossible to get through, whether the reader be an Italian or a foreigner.

Is this not true? Italy is one of the countries abounding in fluent, easy speakers and, at the same time, in unreadable writers. Let them write as though they were speaking in good company, and they will be read with the same pleasure as they are listened to.

One last remark. Since they have invented the *homme sérieux* in France; since children have taken up smoking; youths of eighteen have stopped going to dances; men of thirty marry for the dowry; fifteen-year-old girls marry millionaires of fifty; since finally the most tedious of the seven capital sins—pride, envy, and avarice—have got the better of the other four; all languages, more or less, have adopted a pedantic, magisterial, solemn tone, which produces a most boring impression on me. I mean to avoid it.

It is my nature, when any problem arises, to consider at once all its aspects and consequences. I immediately see the ridiculous side of serious matters, and the serious side of trifles.

So I am, and so I shall reveal myself in my book. Life, thank goodness, is not always sad and tragic; it is sometimes gay and sometimes ridiculously solemn, which is the cream of humour. Writing about a single life or many, why should I deal with only one aspect of things and not with all the various sides that naturally follow one another?

My intention is, then, to let myself be carried along by the subject matter as it comes. Should food for thought or instruction arise, why should I omit it?

Here, my dear readers, is the menu. If you think it promising, come along! If you don't like the sound of it, we must meet again on a more suitable occasion. *Au revoir* and good luck to you!

PART I

1

Up to three months ago I knew nothing about my family except for scraps of information picked up from an old bailiff. Neither my father nor my mother ever spoke of it. I do remember, however, that one day there was talk of the nobility in the family circle, a few friends being present. I was then a child of perhaps not more than twelve and asked in all innocence: 'Are we of the nobility, father?' As they all laughed, I realized I had asked a foolish question. My father replied with a smile: 'If you're good you will be noble', and I asked no more. It was a long time before I re-opened the subject. For some reason our name of Taparelli has always been disagreeable to me and I have invariably used the name Azeglio and signed myself so.

Three months ago on a sad occasion for us—the death of my elder brother Robert—I had to examine family papers and documents. In this way my archaeological knowledge of the history of our house reached farther back than my grandfather's day, my previous limit. This is what I learnt.

Our people came from Brittany and probably that is why we are all rather obstinate. The old records speak of a family and a castle of that province called Brenier Chapel or Capel. The castle had the same crest carved on it we have borne to this day. When the building was destroyed the family disappeared. Later it turned up in the Dauphiné. Its existence is proved by numerous documents in the Grenoble archives.

When Charles of Anjou came down to conquer the kingdom of Naples, or perhaps somewhat earlier, a member of the family settled and took a wife at Savigliano, how or why I do not know. From him sprang a certain George whose name Chapel or Capel had, in some curious way, changed to Taparel. This man and his children are the first properly-documented persons of our family. As for our previous history I have reported what I found written, and those who doubt may go and look it up themselves.

Monsignor Agostino della Chiesa, in his description of Piedmont, tells a different story and says—I give the sense rather than his actual words for the sake of brevity: The Taparella family is very old-established in Savigliano, prominent on the Guelph side in politics. In the parchment statutes of the people of Savigliano we find a William and an Oddo, together with their children, mentioned, even before 1240, as owners of mills and other water-driven machinery, of fishing rights, lands, and villages of this commune.

George of the other version now reappears. Monsignor della Chiesa adds that when Queen Joanna's seneschal and Captain General, Ruperto di Leonardo, was in Cuneo in 1344 he invested Geoffrey, Leone, and Petrino, sons of George, with the fief of Genola with the right of building a castle there to oppose the enemies of the Angevins. This was given in acknowledgement of the numerous services the family Taparella of Savigliano had performed for that Queen. A few years before this (1341) the family came into possession of the fief of Lagnasco, bought for 25,000 gold *florins* by Geoffrey Taparelli and Petrino Falletti d'Alba from Thomas, Marquis of Saluzzo, who needed money to help pay a ransom of 80,000 *florins* to his uncles. The latter, with the support of Bertram del Balzo, seneschal of Charles II of Anjou, and other allies, had seized his state and made him prisoner.

The family has always held the castles of Lagnasco and Genola and still does.

As our family, though ancient, has not been distinguished for great deeds or historic personages such as might have made a detailed account valuable, I will spare the reader the trouble of reading it and me of writing it. I will only say that both versions of our origins can be reconciled. It can be that our ancestors, before they were Guelphs of Savigliano, had come down from France on one of those regrettably numerous northern invasions.

There is certain information about one Brenier, man-at-arms in M. de Thermes' company, who came to Savigliano during the war between France and the Empire—Montluc speaks of his being in garrison in Savigliano at that period. I find that this gentleman recognized us as kin after making inquiries, on seeing his own coat-of-arms displayed in our house. For his better assurance he inquired to which of the saints we paid most devotion. On learning that it was St. Mary Magdalene he declared that his family too was specially devoted to her. It would seem unlikely that these circumstances should be fortuitous. If this man-at-arms was right in his surmise I should be a barbarian myself after having so often cried 'Out with the barbarians!' It's a funny world!

Instead, therefore, of relating the history of a succession of obscure lordlings, and goodness knows what worthless rubbish would turn up on trying to verify the true facts, I shall stick to the anecdotes I have come across in my rummaging. These should be of some interest, not so much because they concern the Taparella family, but because they illustrate human nature in general, and the offspring of father Adam can never be studied enough.

My grandfather was Count Roberto di Lagnasco, who married Cristina, Countess of Genola, both descended from two different branches of our family. They had two sons, the Marquis of Montenera, who died young after a fall, and Cesare, my father.

A few days after giving birth to my father, his mother died. Some years later Count Roberto married Matilde Caissotti di Casal Grasso, from whom he had an only daughter, who married Count Prospero Balbo, father of Cesare the author, who was therefore my step-cousin and also one of my dearest, most excellent, and respected friends.

I know little enough of this grandfather, but what I learnt from my father. He was a man of lively intelligence, not without that touch of eccentricity which is said to be habitual in our family. In fact, in the Piedmont of bygone days, I have to admit that the race of the Taparelli was reputed not to keep their wits in the usual place. Without entering into any argument about that, it is only fair to say that this old Piedmont, full as it was of sterling qualities, was also notorious for never changing anything, for love of tradition, and for fear of novelty: characteristics of all strong races who know how to preserve their individuality over long periods. Therefore anything out of the ordinary, however trifling, was frowned on by the majority and rejected out of hand. Without further consideration it was written off as madness.

Take my grandfather, for instance, who was a great cultivator of the English language and literature. I seem to hear his acquaintances saying: 'What an odd fellow that Count of Lagnasco with his English! What an idea to learn English!' And from that it would not be long before they concluded: 'Ah well, all the Taparellis have a bee in their bonnet!'

I know from experience (as I shall tell presently) that from having wished to do something different from all the other sprigs of nobility when I was young, I was unanimously pronounced mad.

However that may be, my grandfather followed a military career, then went to Court and was a friend (as far as Kings can have friends) with the King Vittorio of the period. Even though at Court, he had the reputation of being an honest man. However, as no one in that profession can sit so secure in the saddle or contrive things so ably that he does not often risk a somersault, or at least have to swallow many bitter mouthfuls, my grandfather wanted to forearm himself and stuck up prominently in his study a Piedmontese inscription: '*Ai fa pa nen*', that is to say, 'It doesn't matter'. The dialect is really more pungent than the Italian and, if you will pardon me, really means: 'I don't care a hoot.' So when he came back from Court with a bitter taste in his mouth owing to some dirty trick played on him, he would see the motto, shrug his shoulders, and sit down to his supper with his usual excellent appetite. This was told me by Cesare Balbo.

My grandfather died when he was fifty-seven, just when he was arranging for the marriage of his only surviving son, the engagement having been already announced.

Coming now to Cesare, my father, I have the best and most precious evidence, a manuscript about him written by my mother. Now that I have reached the point where I have to speak of my mother, quote her words, penetrate the veil with which she studiously tried to conceal all her acts and all her goodness, I must admit to my reader that I feel most uncertain and that I experience sentiments I cannot clearly define. Should I not be guilty of a kind of profanation? Even though I have only to reveal the most perfect beauty of which a human soul is capable, is there not an instinct in every civilized being that prompts him to recognize that a mother's life, even her memory and praise of her virtues, should be jealously guarded within the home? Such things should be impressed on the minds of children and grandchildren, be kept as a hidden family treasure, and not be thrown into the great stream of publicity for strangers and those who care nothing. I confess to this feeling, though I resolve to ignore it. I yield to the wish to depict the beloved features of that noble being, endowed not only with grace, candour, and feminine beauty, but also (as we shall see) with virile strength. For twenty-five years she has been at rest beside my father in the humble Capuchin church at Genoa. She belongs to an age that has gone. This fact, surely, could permit, justly and reasonably, modification of the strict principles to which I have referred. Can it be right and proper that such noble models of feminine virtue should never be revealed for the imitation of later ages? Who, if not a mother, has had the charge from God to impress the first most indelible traits of character on man? Must those who so well knew how to create strong men, and therefore great epochs of history, remain unknown, when Italy's first need is to find men and those who can educate them and form strong, generous characters? What is more, have I the right to deprive my own offspring of the most precious of inheritances, that of noble and virtuous examples? Such reflections have decided me and I write on. But first a few words to describe my father. Here I quote my mother's manuscript: 'Young, handsome, charming manners, talented, vivacious without shallowness, cultured, excellent in music and singing, etc., etc.' Let me round off the portrait by adding that he was considered one of the best soldiers of our army, that he was a man of the strictest principles and, at the same time, of indescribable goodness of heart. He would have shed his blood to spare his family grief, but rather than betray honour or duty he would have let us all perish before his very eyes. He was such a man to die, according to period, under the tortures suffered by Regulus, or rather as a Christian martyr, torn to pieces by lions in the arena, upholding his faith. He never in all his life flinched from duty, and such are the martyrs, whatever age they live in and whatever their circumstances.

Duty and love, sentiments almost always opposed and often mutually exclusive, made his life a constant struggle. Suspicious of the promptings of his own heart, he was always on the watch to restrain possible acts of weakness. So much so that he sometimes went to the opposite extreme and appeared gruff and severe. We young people at home were incredibly scared of him and fear, alas, clouds judgement. It is among my bitterest regrets that I have only learnt to know and appreciate him as he deserved when he is no longer with us. What a loss there is in such misunderstandings and how important it is to avoid them always.

He was born on February 10th, 1763. At the age of eleven his father brought him up before the magistrate, then called Uffizio del Soldo, in charge of voluntary army enrolment, a bad system (although the English and Americans think otherwise) that has made the name of recruiting sergeant notorious and which now, thank goodness, has been abolished on the adoption of conscription.

There was so much military spirit among the nobles—arms and the army being the basis of the Savoyard monarchy—that, despite their privileged position, they did not consider it demeaning to serve as common soldiers in the ranks. However graded in the military hierarchy, it was accepted by everyone that honour was equal; be one ranker, general, or even the King.

With us it would be impossible to witness that curious phenomenon of a child going for a walk with his nurse, dressed as a major or a colonel.

True it is that, though our gentry joined the army by the street door, they soon received different treatment, for they became cadets and there was certainly privilege in that. My father, ranker, cadet, and officer in the Queen's regiment, served in the garrisons, finally at Cagliari. He was specially commended to the Colonel and superiors:

who [I quote the manuscript] in those days were really fathers to the young men, inspiring them with a sense of true honour, based on faith in God and loyalty to King, probity and loftiness of soul. This was the general tone of the Piedmontese nobility, nearly all of whom were serving with the colours. Pay in the army was very low, much below that of those who served at Court, so that it nearly all went in tips and subscriptions. Honour was our motto in those days. . . .

The royal family played their part in this; they treated their nobles with respect and only relied on them to shed their blood when the occasion demanded.

Between the ages of eleven and seventeen he trained and became proficient in handling arms and in military science and, so writes my mother, 'this was the *unhappiest* (so he says himself) time of his life' and this because, as a lively youth with hot passions, he sowed his wild oats.

At seventeen he was appointed equerry to the Duke of Aosta and was then recalled for service in Turin by King Vittorio Emanuele, the father of the Duke and of Carlo Felice. This is how the manuscript describes the young man who judged himself at that period of his life with such severity: . . . 'it was not long before he became known in the highest society and by the most brilliant hostesses; he was adored in the family circle, the closest friend of his elder brother, most affectionate towards his sister and step-mother, in fact much more a real mother in her love for her husband's children.'

One sees that his conduct did not appear so dissipated, either to his family or to the high society of the time. It was a very odd sort of society of which we now have little notion. I certainly should not like to see it re-established as it was, but, although we have changed so much and are so alien to the ideas of those days, it can still provide matter for interesting reflections and unexpected conclusions.

The Piedmontese nobility of the last and the early part of the present century was, rather than tyrannical, fastidious. My dear reader, I feel sure that more than once it has fallen to your lot to have to do with someone who, in his attitude towards you, failed in nothing due to courtesy, who uttered no word to which you could object without being ridiculous or absurdly punctilious, and yet at the same time gave forth from his whole person such a clear 'keep your distance', such an obvious 'I'm what I am and you don't count', that, as there was no reason for getting angry and no possibility of putting up with it, one simply longed to get out of range and, if possible, never let oneself be caught again.

Such was the effect produced by the Piedmontese nobility, and hence the class division that is hardly now beginning to disappear. But despite their defects, they had great qualities and preserved themselves active and energetic while their peers in Italy were faithfully depicted in the effete characters of Goldoni's plays. And the reason? Because there was constant warfare (Piedmont took part in three wars in the last century alone) and because war is morally more salutary than long periods of peace to populations. Character is tempered by devotion to difficult and dangerous duties. Also war fits men to act well and courageously in other matters besides fighting. Alfieri, for example, tells us that he attacked Greek grammar as he would have stormed a breach when he was a soldier.

From this arises a very curious consequence, namely that to preserve the virtues which save it from decadence a people must, of necessity, from time to time, kill a certain number of its neighbours. The reader should ponder this problem and I shall too. In the meantime let us proceed.

When he was twenty-four my father underwent one of those intimate transformations that change and renew a man, but which are only possible with upright, strong, passionate natures.

Throughout the world at that time, but chiefly in France, there was a burning fever in men to destroy the established order of things, so much so that many thought creation was returning to chaos. It was, however, leading us, with horrible crimes it is true, but in the direction of *coelum novum et terram novam,* as the Bible puts it.

Italy is the ancient land of *Doubt*. The Reformation could effect little there, not so much owing to the authority of the Inquisition, but because we paid very little attention to Rome and still less to Wittenberg. It is in our nature not to believe more than the priests believe, and the priests of Rome gave every indication of believing in very little indeed. Consequently Italians never took matters of dogma very seriously, and from the time of Guido Cavalcanti onwards we have been guided by that melancholy phrase 'who knows if it's true?' Italy, therefore, was a somewhat indifferent spectator in the struggle between Rome and Wittenburg, caring little for either. It was the disbelief, derision, and sarcasm of Voltaire that proved more to her taste, and she turned a

smiling face to French scepticism as to a familiar old friend. But if this
were the case in the rest of Italy it was quite different in Piedmont. In
opposition to a handful of innovators, the ancient faith of the people
stood steady on its foundations. Today, after so many tempests have
passed over this harassed land, we see little or nothing changed in its
traditional character. We can imagine how it must have been in those
earlier days when the country had barely lost its medieval atmosphere.
The feeling for religion was in most people true and profound and
there were certainly more wrong-doers than disbelievers among those
who opposed Catholicism. In the cathedral of Turin, San Giovanni, in
the year 1784 the lenten sermons were preached, so the manuscript informs me, by one of the two friars, Father Denobili or Father Casati.
My father listened and became convinced that it was his imperative
duty absolutely to change his way of life. For him, as we know, to
recognize a duty and follow it at whatever sacrifice was one and the
same thing. Without letting a day pass, caring nothing for criticism,
mockery, reproof, and personal anguish, he gave himself up to the most
strict church observances, adhering to Catholic morality and the
Christian cult, even in the minutest detail. So he persisted, firm and
constant to his dying day.

With such a resolute character, unvacillating in all things, faith soon
became absolute certainty. He was thus provided with the most valid
comfort in all the bitter troubles that awaited him; namely, a belief that
for the true Christian the ills of this world provide the best entry into
the infinite good of the world to come. Happy the man who feels
certain of such an excellent arrangement. But alas, in matters of faith,
wishes and hopes do not suffice. One believes what one can, not what
one would like to. God who knows all will not demand the impossible
as men do, nor will he be as cruel as they.

Today the word 'conversion' sounds as though it belonged to the old
legends of the Saints. Where nowadays does one meet or hear about
one of those famous public conversions associated with St. Francis,
St. Benedict, St. Jerome, etc.? Religious exaltation, however, is common
enough among the Anglo-Saxon and Germanic peoples. Conversions
are frequent. Every seer, real or feigned, soon finds devotees and will
undergo sacrifices and privations for his particular dogma. Let such
a one come to Italy, however. Let him start preaching in the public
square and he will attract the same audience that listens to the mounte-
banks. The sermon over, they'll disperse, shrugging their shoulders,
saying in Piedmontese: *'A l'a bon temp'*, in Italian, *'È matto'*, 'He's
daft!'

At first sight it seems we should say: 'We're worth more, as no one can pull the wool over our eyes'; but on considering the matter closer what must we conclude? Only that it is not the Latin race, clever as it is, that is the stronger, more moral, more dominant, but the Anglo-Saxon. That proves that nations are not founded on cleverness (*l'esprit*), but by people of strong austere characters prepared to die for their faith, however odd or twisted. You can deal with such folk, but in whose name and for what cause can you rouse those who believe in absolutely nothing? Doubt is a splendid let-out, in fact the only true begetter of the Italian *Dolce far niente*.

At this point we run our ship on the rock mentioned previously. Can a nation, any more than an individual, say: 'I want to have faith'? And if it can't, chiding is useless. I don't want to imitate those who blame Rome and the priests, for every misfortune and everything that offends them. Let's be tolerant to all, even to priests! In the Middle Ages the priesthood was subjected to such terrific temptations that to resist them would perhaps have been beyond human capacity. To have the cross in one's hand and with a single word be able to change it into the sceptre of world dominion and to leave that word unspoken! Let the man who feels capable of that, cast the first stone!

Tolerance, however, should be used towards men, not towards logic nor to historical truth. The latter tells us what Machiavelli said three centuries ago, that it is the spectacle of Papal Rome that has extinguished religion in Italy. And if it is true, as I believe undeniable, that a nation without religion cannot be disciplined or strong (consider the ancient Romans, the modern Anglo-Saxons, and, alas, ourselves), we have to conclude that Italy will never be a nation until she holds fast to principles of religion. These cannot come by decree or command or by an act of will, but may appear when they are seen to be, not an instrument of power, and evil power at that, but as a beneficent emanation from above. The ultimate and natural conclusion is then that, if Rome, if Catholicism, does not reform, if the priest does not succeed in convincing us that he believes what he preaches, if he believes that riches are not too desirable and poverty not so frightening, that it is good to be meek and humble and bad to be cruel and arrogant, that love and pardon are good and hate and vengeance bad; until he can persuade us by his actions that he believes all that, there is no hope of a spread of true religion among Italians. Without that we shall for ever be, as now, a spineless people of little character with small hope of internal cohesion.

2

My father's conversion made a great stir in Court circles and beyond. But the young man who was so bright and agreeable, so full of health and strength, began gradually to give the impression of fading away. One could say that his iron will had grappled with his flesh and bones and that he was collapsing in the struggle.

From the battles between will and natural inclinations one does not come out unscathed. After some months the family began to feel very apprehensive, seeing their only surviving son showing ever plainer signs of prostration. He had to have extensive medical treatment, which, thanks to his youth, had the happiest results. His constitution, however, had received a great shock and, although his illness had been routed for the moment, the treatment could not restore his previous health and strength. Never again was my father really robust.

In those days the extinction of a family was not taken so philosophically as at the present, when, for example, I foresee the extinction of ours without any loss of appetite or sleep.

Questioned by my grandfather, the doctors told him without mincing matters that as the Marquis Cesare was an only son it was high time he should be set to breed. My father related this anecdote later, much amused that the excellent doctor had put him on a level with a King Charles spaniel or an Arab horse.

In any case they soon set about finding him a wife. Cristina, daughter of the Marquis Morozzo di Bianzè, appeared to be eligible; her hand was sought, it was granted, and the match was made.

My mother, who could never say enough in praise of her husband's sentiments of delicacy, told me that, on his first visit as a fiancé, instead of dressing up as was usual on such occasions, that is to say of showing himself in as good a light as possible, he appeared so carelessly got up (and everyone knows what kind of fashions were then the mode) that his fiancée, and her family too, were bewildered, not knowing what to make of it. He had done so on the excellent principle that he did not wish to create any illusions, but appear as any husband would later, in the privacy of the family circle.

'This was only the beginning,' added my mother. After a few polite words my father produced a sheet of paper from his pocket, turned to his fiancée, and said: 'Madam, here you will find a description of my character that you cannot judge at a glance, as you can my appearance.'

Having handed her the paper, he courteously took his leave, saying as he left that should she still be of the same mind, after having known his real character, he would consider himself happy to devote the rest of his life to her as her wedded husband.

My mother told me that, with the artless inexperience of a girl of eighteen, and in her ignorance of the world after a most restricted education, she was in two minds, on reading the long list of defects which her suitor attributed to himself, whether she ought not to produce a similar one to give him, so seriously had she taken the matter. But her people knew what weight should be given to such a confession, laughed at the document and at her. The self-confessed sinner was recalled, received with acclamation, and told that they had complete faith in his future conversion. And so the marriage came off after all!

Here my mother's manuscript continues: 'This was the first link in a golden chain that bound us indissolubly in faith and married love for forty-two years. Fortunate Cristina, until that day, November 26, 1830, when death took him, or rather set him in Heaven above, immortal!'

On their marriage the disturbances that preceded revolution were already reported from France, although the outbreak itself came later. My parents enjoyed three years of peace and happiness and I think they were the only happy years of their life. Two male children were born, one after the other. The first died in the cradle, the second, Roberto, lived for seventy-two years. Four more boys and two girls followed. Of the latter, Metilde was as lovely as an angel and as good; she married Count Rinco and died of consumption when she was twenty-two; the other, Melania, also died very young, unmarried. Enrico, a captain in the Gunners, died aged twenty-nine in 1824. The only surviving members of the family were Roberto, the Jesuit Prospero, and myself. Now in the year 1862, barely a month since, they have gone and I am left alone; the last.

It was 1788 and '89. Society was being transformed. The age of legalized *cavalieri serventi*,[1] persons even sometimes specified in marriage contracts, was coming to an end. Such a practice was itself an indication of the need for reform in society. Let the reader imagine if my father, fashion or no fashion, would have been the man to conform to such a ridiculous practice. Even could he have brought himself to adopt it, my mother would never have allowed it. In her manuscript I find a few words on the subject which depict the age, and still more the charm of her wit and the maturity of her judgement.

[1] The Italian practice of extra-conjugal attachments has nowhere been better described than by Byron in *Beppo*, Stanza XXXVI et seq. (tr.).

'Now came that fortunate period when it became modish for husbands to dance attendance on their own wives. What yawns, what long faces were to be seen when certain couples sacrificed liberty and inclination on the altar of fashion.' One seems to see them!

The happy days of tranquillity did not last long. My father, staghunting with the Duke of Aosta, whose equerry he was, in order to recall some distant huntsmen, gave a great hallo. The effort burst a vein in his chest and he suffered a rush of blood from the mouth. He was in danger of his life and had to receive treatment for a considerable period, so that he was forced to give up his Court appointment. A horse at Court, even a delicate one, gets plenty of care and attention so that he can carry on. If you're a man you must keep well!

My father's medical treatment was once again successful and he recovered. He got well in time to participate in the long wars and the various political vicissitudes, that only in 1814 gave us some respite. Now from '21 onwards it all started again and so it will continue until God thinks good to give us an established régime. As it is not my purpose to write a history book, especially when the events are well-known and have already been described, I shall say nothing of the wars fought by Piedmont against the French invaders. I have to say Piedmont, alas! as I cannot say 'together with the other Italian States', although they shared the same fears, hopes, and perils. All refused an alliance, when offered. Only Naples showed some inclination to come in, but it ended in nothing. The governments who had refused to unite spontaneously against the danger were, in fact, forcibly united in one common ruin.

How many times did I not hear in childhood my father tell how Piedmont was left without support to rely on her own strength alone. No one more than he hated the foreign invasion and therefore no one more than he hated the age-old Italian discord.

When war broke out in the Nice region, Count di Sant' Andrea, whose family was from those parts, had command of that army corps and appointed my father his aide-de-camp. He fought two campaigns with the Count and was then posted to the Val d'Aosta, where he had the rank of Lieutenant Colonel in the Vercelli regiment. I must admit at this point in shame that I know very little about my father's military exploits, except for the final one of which I shall presently speak. I only know that on the whole he was reputed, as I've said before, to be a very great soldier. He never spoke of himself or boasted and I've only very occasionally heard him tell of some experience of those days. I could have found out more from his contemporaries or comrades, but, owing to youthful negligence, I never did. What would I not give now to call back and question their ghosts! Let this serve as a warning to those who still have time, if they desire, to spare themselves such reproaches.

I do remember one anecdote told me by a friend of the family. When the war of the revolution started, our army had been at peace since the war of the Polish Succession. Forty-six or forty-seven years of peace means a complete lack of practical training in the field, from general to drummer boy. What is more, the territorial organization, by which the men spent a very short time under arms, was not such as to remedy the lack of experience. One of the officers' difficult duties was to habituate their subordinates to that severe, detailed, and continuous sacrifice of self, that is known as discipline. Without this you can have a host of brave men, but not an army, not even a regiment.

One day in the Val d'Aosta my father had to lead his battalion across a long stretch of plain in the face of the enemy and under direct fire from a battery. It was a good opportunity to inure his provincial troops to real war. He was one of those men who prefer to risk their own skins rather than those of others. Out of bravado he could have formed them up by sections in column order, thus presenting his flank to the enemy, fifteen or twenty ranks deep, adding to the men's danger rather than his own. Instead of this, he ordered line ahead in two ranks, took the lead himself, and advanced at a slow march, drums to the front. There was no question of hurry-skurry and they kept formation until they reached cover. One curious fact was that only one of the enemy's shots told, and that hit the tip of the standard pole! Which only goes to prove the truth of that famous proverb of the Piedmontese mask Gianduia: *La paura l'è faita d'nen* (Fear's made of nothing), a saying that, if not absolutely accurate (for example under machine-gun fire), is a true image of our people, who dislike seeing danger where there is none, and sometimes even when there is.

I don't mean to give greater importance to this episode than it had, and which was certainly not attributed to it by my father. There is no doubt that his military career could provide matters much worthier of remembrance!

I now come to the action in which he was made prisoner. It happened in the Little St. Bernard pass between Thuile and the Hospice, fighting having continued only along those heights. He and his corps occupied the place called Terre Rosse. It turned out badly for our side and the regiment commanded by my father was cut to pieces or scattered, you could say destroyed. He, of course, never turned his back to the enemy, but, completely surrounded, was captured, roughly handled, and robbed of anything he had of value. Nowadays things aren't so bad in that respect, thank goodness!

At the moment of capture he glanced over his shoulder to see if any of his men had stayed there. He told me as follows: 'I turned about, but saw no one except a drummer boy of about fourteen years of age. I said to him with a gesture of impatience, thinking that might make him clear out and avoid capture: "What are you doing here?" The boy answered: "As long as my colonel stands his ground, I stay too." '

It is a pity that one doesn't know what became of the excellent youth. My father knew nothing more. But another of his men had stayed with him and I'm glad to say I do know all about him.

I said a few pages back that I should be able to tell you about true heroes from all social classes. Here is one and of the best; a poor peasant from the Lanzo valley, ignorant, lumpish, unable to read or write, with no idea what heroes were, ancient or modern, no inkling of the offspring of Atreus, of Agamemnon, of Orestes, so that he could never understand why my father called him Pylades ever afterwards. Still less could he fathom what a glorious title he had acquired by this classical, semi-mythological baptism.

The population of the Lanzo valley, by long tradition, has undertaken the mission of providing Turin with servants and wine porters, known, in Piedmontese, as *brindour*. They wear blue blouses of much older origin than those of their rivals, the carters and workmen.

From a little hamlet on the Colle San Giovanni in that valley, Giovanni Drovetti came to take service in our house. He was a young mountaineer, who looked as if he had been hewed out with an axe. Finding him robust, my father took him to war with him as a batman. He never let his master out of his sight and so, at this time of peril, he was at his heels as usual. 'Be off, don't get yourself captured!' said my father just as he had to the drummer boy, but the mountaineer looked him in the face, showing such shocked amazement that a proposition of this kind should be addressed to him, Giovanni Drovetti, that my father accepted the sacrifice of his devoted servant without another word.

The look that passed between them at that moment bound them together for evermore.

They were both taken behind the front line, where my father was surrounded by a clamorous crowd who accused him of being an emigré. They heaped insults on him and even went so far as to make a cut at him with a sabre, shouting out 'Bloody emigré'. 'Non, je ne suis pas un emigré,' said my father without losing his composure. At last an officer appeared in their midst, put an end to this scene, unworthy of regular soldiers, and took him away.

From here he was escorted via Moutiers and Vienne to Montbrison, then to Feurs in the department of Forez. Robespierre and his minions were still in power, for in that small town, madder and more ferocious than other places, the Terror lasted for some time after the ninth of Thermidor, when it came to an end in Paris.

Ten *sous* a day in *assignats* were given to prisoners of war for their keep, but as these lost 80 per cent. of their value, the ten were only worth two. Master and batman both were supposed to live on this, which meant that they could only subsist on alms. One can guess what this meant under the Terror when helping *royalists* was frowned on and to be frowned on was fatal. So these poor waifs tried not to compromise their benefactors. The mountaineer, then known by his real name Giovanni, used to beg and receive alms secretly. My mother's manuscript records as follows: 'My husband found much comfort in the charity of good-hearted people of whom there has never been a lack in France, especially in those days and amongst the gentler sex. These good ladies used to wait for Giovanni after nightfall and give him bread, eggs, and butter for his master. One peasant woman wanted to lend Cesare six hundred francs without any security.' There's another virtuous soul, whose very name I shall never know, and to whose children and grandchildren I can never express my gratitude.

I have often heard my father give details of his life as a beggar. 'One day,' he said, 'we were being taken down the Rhône in a barge, together with some horses and mules. Hunger forced us to beg from the other passengers. They threw us some onions as we stood in the bows with the animals. They fell amongst the dung, but we soon rinsed them and made our meal of them.' It was a good thing that my father was such a man as to consider it rather an honour than otherwise to share his befouled onions with a poor mountain peasant. The highest honour is surely to merit that others should be ready to sacrifice themselves for you.

Sometimes he was secretly advised that Mass was to be celebrated at a certain hour of the night in some out-of-the-way spot. In snow and ice, darkness and danger (to be discovered was to lose your life, such was the liberty of conscience of the time) he used to make his way to the meeting place, just like the early Christians in the first centuries of the Church.

At last Robespierre died, the Terror ended, and even in terrorist

c

Montbrison reaction came, hardly less cruel than that of the previous régime. My father was no longer hated and repulsed as formerly. A *royalist* could now be tolerated, if only because under Robespierre it had been suggested that prisoners might be executed in order to save the two daily *sous* for their keep. The relations and children of Jacobin victims were overcome by a fever of savage vengeance and sought for the previous butchers to kill them. My father told me about a young man, whom he had known as honest and religious, who appeared one day with staring eyes and bristling hair shouting out: 'Monsieur, je viens de tuer celui qui a fait guillotiner mon père!' 'Monsieur, vous n'êtes pas chrétien,' said my father to the demented youth.

While my father was living in dire want, my mother was even more miserable in Turin, for she mourned her husband as dead.

In the action in which he was captured our troops had yielded ground to the advancing French. There was therefore no chance to verify our dead and wounded. The evidence of those present, or who should have been present, during the fighting had to be relied on. Unfortunately (and I deplore having to report this of a Piedmontese officer) there was a certain man who, in order to make it appear that he was as forward in the fight as my father, asserted that the latter had been struck in the chest by a bullet and that, while he was supporting him, he received another in the forehead and fell dead to the ground.

As it was impossible to credit such wickedness in an officer, he was implicitly believed. The name of Colonel Cesare d'Azeglio appeared in the list of fallen and my mother was informed that her husband had died honourably fighting at the head of his men.

When his three sons, Roberto, Enrico, and I, joined the army, our father made us give our word of honour that we would never try to trace that wretched man nor inquire his name, which he would never reveal. At that time my mother was big with my brother Enrico and the effect of the news was one of the reasons for undermining her health. Subsequently she was always rather an invalid.

My father's will, which he had left when he went to the front, was opened and it was found that a large income had been left to my mother which was to continue *even if she married again*. One article of the will was as follows: 'Should I die in battle, I beg my wife not to wear the customary mourning, but to put on her most splendid attire, because once she has mastered her grief due to the love she bears me, she must consider it great good fortune for herself and for me that I have been permitted to give my life for King and Country.'

Nearly two months passed without any news of her husband and then she heard that he was alive, unhurt, a prisoner in France. The joy of this unexpected good fortune was a new blow to her already debilitated constitution. Through the King's minister in Switzerland she succeeded in getting permission for her husband's repatriation on parole. She and the family were hoping to welcome him quite soon, but there was a condition attached to his release: 'not to bear arms against the French Republic until a mutual exchange of prisoners', and my father insisted that he would never sign a promise not to fight for his country or against his country's foes. He preferred to stay in that bitter captivity, barely subsisting, far from his beloved wife and children, and he put up with these hard conditions for a further six months rather than fail in what he believed to be his duty. He had, however, a satisfaction far from common in those days. When, after the armistice of Cherasco (21 April '96) and the hard peace of the 15th of May, he finally had leave to return home, the very men then at the head of affairs in France, and history will judge them, would not let him go without honourable mention of Colonel d'Azeglio's noble conduct. In his new permit to leave there is mention of the 'louable délicatesse du citoyen d'Azeglio en refusant sa liberté sous la condition de ne pas porter les armes contre les ennemis de son souverain, etc., etc.'.

I ask the reader to think of all the men he has known during his life and to consider how many he has found of this calibre. Should he have found few or none he can understand my feelings as I pen these words.

Here it is suitable to repeat, and repeat again, how powerful is the influence of men of strong and lofty characters on their nation, their country, and their age. I can only speak for us, his children, and say that, although we are a thousand miles behind our father in power of sacrifice and generosity of sentiment, yet if during our life we have at any time managed to achieve anything good and honourable, we all of us owe it to his noble example.

I can feel in myself the indestructible force of first ideas and impressions. If, indeed, one opens one's eyes and draws one's first breath in an atmosphere of truth, good faith, and honour, and if one grows up in such an environment from infancy to adolescence, from youth to manhood, one absorbs it into one's very marrow, so that despite all errors, sins, and back-slidings, the basis of one's character maintains its instinctive feeling for duty and honour. When the test comes it is almost impossible to bring shame on oneself and one's family, in fact the contrary is possible. Thus the country gets served well, defended well, and grows strong and respected.

It was precisely for this reason that Washington, whom I consider one of those rare individuals, a true father of his country who gave it spiritual rather than material life—it was for this reason that he wrote to the governors after he had retired to Mount Vernon, 'for your officers, choose *gentlemen*'. He had no aristocratic arrogance nor democratic envy. He had his head screwed on straight and he loved his country. By 'gentlemen' he certainly did not mean exclusively men of rank, but all those who had had a liberal education and were probably in an independent position.

It is certainly not my intention to belittle those in a humbler situation, but society apportions its gifts as is most beneficial to it. On board ship everyone's qualities are reckoned as is best for navigation, the men who know, command, those who don't, obey orders. If ships normally get on better than states, it is solely due to the fact that all on board accept the job for which they are fit, while in the state the less people know, the more, generally speaking, they are ambitious to command. It is not sufficient, either, to say, 'Let the man who knows, command', unless you add, 'and let him who commands have the strength to sacrifice himself for his duty', which means give up his personal interest in the interests of all. Now I ask, which of the two will be readier for such a sacrifice, the man who from childhood has learnt that it is honourable and liberal to acquire honestly and give *gratis*, or he who from everything he has seen and heard from his earliest years must imagine that one's mission on earth is to buy cheap and sell dear.

Washington's democracy was a triumph of the common good over privilege. What we see now is the triumph of another sort of privilege over the common good. The realistic school does not only flourish in literature and painting, indeed one can say that its cradle is in the field of politics. (If you want to be clever and look for remote origins, study Hegel, Schelling, and the Pantheists, etc. but let's leave Germans in their clouds.) This school, who only recognize the real in what is ugly and foul, has given us, in literature, kept women for heroines and pimps for heroes; in painting, canvases which only look like pictures if you gallop past them on horseback. Good Lord! What could such a manner of thinking give us in politics? The abuse of words has reached such a pitch that a dirty torn coat is called 'a democratic coat', a house unswept and full of filth 'a democratic house'. A lot of people end up by seriously persuading themselves that democracy is the cult of what is ugly, ignoble, soiled; both materially and spiritually.

I wish Washington and his 'gentlemen' could arrive here, he would soon show his indignation at this sort of democracy.

I myself am an aristocrat by birth, but a democrat by choice (but mind you, I refer to a true, holy, Christian democracy that holds all men equal before the law, be it political, social, civil, or religious), and I will now ask permission to utter a prophecy and say that Italy, Europe, and the world will never find tranquillity, not even that relative tranquillity consonant with human passions and our life here below, until true democracy reigns undisputed on the ruins of privilege, old and new. There will be no peace until democracy can extirpate the two parasites gnawing at the leaves and roots of the great plant of human society, nor until the persuasion is assimilated and drawn into general circulation of the body politic, that there can be no government, no liberty, no independence unless every power, party, association, and indeed individual shares in a law-sanctioned responsibility; and this given a real concrete actuality, only as rarely as possible permitting of exceptions.

But as long as society swings, like a pendulum rocked by a rude hand, between two extremes, the despotism from above of Russia, and the despotism from below of the United (now Dis-united!) States, the poor offspring of Adam will look in vain for settled convictions.

I must in justice ask pardon of Russia for having compared her despotism with that of America, for whereas Alexander Romanoff breaks the chains from off his own serfs, Abraham Lincoln only breaks the chains from off the slaves of his opponents. What are we to divine from all this? Which is the worse of the two tyrannies? But I shall never have done! I've strayed too far from my path and the reader will be saying: 'He's certainly got enough courage to digress!' True enough! But from my side I must ask him not to pay too much attention to my book as literature; I offer it as a sort of portfolio in which I throw any idea that comes to me that can be of some use to the rising generation. I may be mistaken, but I can't help it. It will be the fault of my capacity and not my will. I now continue my tale.

The blessed day of their reunion came at last for my parents. The meeting took place at the Mont Cenis Hospice, where my mother fell into my father's arms. As I am writing of true events and not a novel, it is not my purpose to describe affecting scenes, so I leave to the reader's imagination the joyful meeting of these two young people, who loved each other so ardently, who had believed themselves parted for ever, and who yet found themselves together again after so much anxiety, so much sorrow, of which nothing remained but an aureole of glory round my father's brow for the firmness and generosity of his behaviour.

Providence reserves exceptional rewards for those souls who constantly sacrifice themselves for the good of others. There are certainly moments in life that would suffice to make up for an eternity of suffering.

My father did not return from captivity unaccompanied. The poor batman came with him, the man who had freely chosen to remain to be taken and who had freely chosen to beg. He wept, overcome, at seeing his master and mistress once again united. My father introduced him to his wife, no longer as Giovanni Drovetti but as Pylades. He presented him as a friend, and as a friend he lived in our home to the last. I still have the pleasure of paying his pension to his heirs, whom may God preserve, multiply, and bless. The only thing was that the other servants could not get hold of that poetic classical name, and they sometimes called him, rather unfortunately, not Pylades, but Pilate. But that made no difference to the love and respect everyone gave to that honoured, faithful peasant who had such a happily constituted character that, without the liberal education we have mentioned, he had enough courage and sensibility for a hundred 'gentlemen'. The exception proves the rule.

One of the earliest impressions of my infancy is of him, but when I first got to know him I did not understand, and hadn't the capacity to appreciate, how worthy he was; the old servant, sturdy and solid, always dressed in short breeches which displayed a pair of tubby muscular legs, rather like those of caryatids who have the function of propping up cornices and balconies.

He died in our house at an advanced age, always performing the same lowly tasks, without presuming in the least on the service he had rendered, and without any awareness that he was anything more than the poor peasant servant in Casa Azeglio, like all the rest.

Poor Pylades. I would wish that there were enough virtue in these pages that they might live for a little. In that case you would not suffer the fate of so many poor obscure men who, without any inspiration from books or personal example, find within themselves the seeds of heroism that lead to their making the greatest sacrifices that no one knows about, and no one dreams exist. You would at any rate escape total oblivion.

Enough! Providence will give him a better reward. What is certain is that, believing in justice, I could not imagine that in that secret, mysterious place that awaits our souls and rewards them according to their merits, if there exist, humanly speaking, ranks, hierarchies, crowns, thrones of greater or lesser eminence, I could not, I say,

imagine, if God's grace permits me entry, that I should suffer the morti-
fication of seeing Pylades seated lower, for example, than Alexander
the Great. I feel quite sure that I should find Pylades installed very
much higher, and that would be no more than justice for both of them.

It would be a fine thing indeed if the man who caused such desperation and desolation in so many human souls, merely that he alone
should usurp what Providence intended for the happiness of many;
the man who, when drunk, killed his best friend; who died of over-
drinking, leaving so many nations to be torn to pieces by his ruffians:
it would indeed be a fine thing if eternal Justice should prefer
Alexander the Great to Giovanni Drovetti. I should indeed like to
see it!

3

MY parents' domestic happiness was soon turned to grief by public
disasters. Piedmont and Italy for several years became a battlefield for
two powerful nations and we were forced to give blood and treasure
to both sides, the only possible outcome being to become the slaves of
one or the other of them.

No one paid any attention to the grand truths of the revolution, the
so-called true beneficent principles of '89. The principles that did
flourish were those of '99, which can all be summed up in a simple
formula, 'Fill your pockets'. In those days we had not seen so much,
and experience had not yet taught us what is now so well known by
babes and sucklings; namely, that big heroic-sounding words are very
helpful in attaining that happy result.

Many then still believed that liberty could be imported from abroad
like other Parisian *nouveautés*, and that to follow the trade of a free
man, be one, and stay one, was something that any nincompoop could
accomplish without qualities of personal character. So many people
were tired and disgusted, rightly, with the antiquated ways of previous
governments, which the French revolution came to reform, that there
were those who were happy to be its apostles. All their promises
were later faithfully kept, as history relates and we all know! But this
is beside the point and I proceed.

When my father was a prisoner of war my mother was pregnant.
She gave birth to a boy, my brother Enrico. The terrible perturbations

experienced by the mother during the period of gestation had a fatal influence on the constitution and character of the child. He had special ability in the exact sciences, but he was mentally slow. Loving study and wishing to distinguish himself, he was downcast by finding his mental equipment insufficient. He lost faith in himself, became melancholic, and led a short, sad, troubled life. He died of consumption before he was thirty. I shall have more to say of him later, as one can consider his character with advantage. He was frank, affectionate and unhappy, and can provide a useful example to the young, and to do this is my most important object.

Enrico was not the youngest of the family, for I was born afterwards. I have now reached the point at which I have to talk of myself and be ready to repeat endlessly that boring pronoun 'I', which refers to that person always most difficult to handle. But if I am to do what I set out to do, I must confront this difficulty; so let's face it without further ado!

I was born on the 24th of October 1798 in our house in Turin, in the same street as the Angennes Theatre, in the yellow room on the first floor, where many generations of my people have been born. My Godfather was Cardinal Giuseppe Morozzo, then a Monsignore. I was given the following string of names; Giuseppe, Maria, Crisostomo or Gerolamo, Raffaelle, Massimo; the last of which has stuck.

My mother nursed me herself and this was the first of the great benefits she lavished on me with constant unwearying solicitude as long as she lived.

After the treaty of Paris of May '96 my father retired from public life, dedicating himself to his family and the family property, which during the wars of recent years had fallen much in value. We had once been very well off, but we were now in straits. I have often heard us Piedmontese, especially gentry, derided because we're poor. But one must remember two things. First that ill-gotten gains cannot be imputed to people without gains, secondly that in every war—and there were many in which Piedmont took part—the first thing done by the gentry, the King giving the example, was to make a clean sweep of all the valuables in the house in order to contribute to the costs. How can one grow rich when, at least twice in a century, every gentleman's house underwent this sort of pillage?

Don't imagine for a moment that they were the only ones to make sacrifices. The Government, the Treasury, that is to say the whole community, made them too. Coins of eight, four, and one *sou* are still in circulation, which were then worth twenty, ten, and five (values stated on coins minted in 1796). This was really all fake coinage, recognized as such by everybody, but which everybody accepted; and why? Because the Piedmontese are austere towards themselves, put up with all hardships (*malo assuetus Ligus*, was said at the time of the Romans), and do not shrink from dangers or difficulties, when it is for the sake of Country, their House of Savoy, and their honour.

This is why they have remained masters in their own house, never having been resigned to foreign dominion. When Piedmont fell into the power of Charles V, Francis I, and Napoleon, she acted in such a way, so tossed and struggled, that she succeeded in freeing herself from her oppressors and regaining her pristine independence.

Here it is well to say that the Piedmontese were, and are, very far from having more cleverness or ability than other Italians; it is simply that they have a rather stronger character, hence their good fortune in being in a position to initiate the total (let us hope) emancipation of the whole peninsula, and as a reward to be unpopular with all other Italians.

But as we have never thought of patriotism as a speculation, nor the liberation of our country as a limited liability company paying interest or dividend, and as we are still the same race *malo assueti* as our ancestors were, we are prepared to put up with this inconvenience, just as they did with so many others in years gone by. When Italians, perhaps, have become men and the nation strong and united, the greater or lesser degree of sacrifice entailed in achieving such a glorious object will be of very little consequence.

But wait, let us be fair all round! If Piedmont has got herself disliked by other Italians, the latter are partly to blame but, I must admit, so are the Piedmontese, or rather, as the poor Piedmontese have nothing to do with it, the Piedmontese Government owing to their marvellous stupidities. I shall have to deal with these as I proceed, as I have, and shall continue to have, a reputation for plain speaking. But this is not yet the time or place to do so.

Very well then, my father, back at home, attended to his family and occupied himself in straightening out family affairs. All this rumpus had cost him altogether 400,000 *francs* in hard cash; without reckoning the impoverishment of his land due to the incredible lack of labour; or the value of silver, jewels, etc., donated at the outbreak of war, similar offerings having been made by the Court and all the nobility.

As well as acting the part of steward of estates he had the habit of devoting all his spare time to study. My mother had had an excellent basic education, as was the custom in well-to-do families, but it was not then usual to attend to the higher education of girls, who could talk French well, Italian very little or not at all, had read Rollin and Télémaque, and that completed their education.

My father took up the intellectual training of his young wife, who by nature had a keen, bright mind, which could grasp ideas and express them equally well. Her style was flowing and natural and her writing full of acute observations and generous sentiments. Listen to how she describes her intimate life:

Cesare's delight was in family life and the few trusted friends he loved having at his table ... his day was a full one. After his devotions, he gave up several hours to perfecting his young wife's education by reading good authors, translating, and other suitable tasks. What little she knows, she owes to the loving care and instruction of such a teacher. Four hours a day were generally set aside for such studies over a period of four or five years. In this way preparation was made too for the education of the children, as the mother was able to take her husband's place when he was called away on civil or military duty. The rest of his time he used in the study of literature, general and ecclesiastical history, etc.

This comfortable family life, these days of studious ease, were peaceful enough in appearance, but really disturbed by gloomy presentiments. For the man who truly loves his country and sees it little by little decay and slide down the fatal slope that leads to ruin, or at least to long, terrible misfortune; to observe such a spectacle and to be powerless to prevent it; to see all that and then to ignore it or console himself with literature and art! Anyone who believes it possible has not had the painful experience. My poor father had such an experience, and it was protracted and bitter.

Piedmont, thank God, only fell twice and twice recovered. She waged war for four years against the best soldiers in Europe and only yielded ground to Napoleon, who took fewer months and weeks to reach Vienna, Berlin, and Madrid than he, or the Republican generals, took years to enter Turin. This was not an ignoble defeat! One must, however, admit that our last two Kings had neither the resolution nor the talent of many others of their house.

At the beginning of the century the indomitable Vittorio Amadeo II, despoiled of all, ranged through Piedmont, no longer his, with a troop of horse. Without a *sou*, with nothing but his sword and pistols, he snapped the chain of an order he wore round his neck, to present it to some poor peasants who had been pillaged and driven from their burnt cottages. But his bones now rest in the burial place of the Superga and on a tottering throne fate placed Carlo Emanuele and Vittorio Emanuele, honest, as all princes of their house, but incapable of either strong resolutions or bold rapid action.

The Savoyard monarchy was overthrown owing to the strength, and still more the perfidy, of the French Government. At the same time it was undermined by the Piedmontese republican party, which made up for lack of numbers by its activity and boldness. And as though this were not enough, the princes of the dynasty and their natural supporters diminished its reputation and hastened its fall, through blind obstinacy in striving for the impossible; that sort of obstinacy shortens the agony of systems doomed to perish.

My father was a witness of these irreparable misfortunes and was helpless to avert the destruction of all that he loved and revered most on this earth and, what was a thousand times worse, the shame of it all. At every opportunity that presented itself for him to make himself heard, he came forward. Twice he offered himself as hostage for the King; when Napoleon sailed off to Egypt with all the luck of the French army, and when in Europe they were beaten by Suvarow and the allies, he was sent to the island of Sardinia by Count Sant' André to invite the King to return to Turin. In the end, when, on the plain of Marengo, victory once more favoured the French standards, and all hope was lost, he left the place associated with such misery and decided to establish himself with his family in Florence. In his study over his writing desk he placed a gouache painting of Turin in a carved wood frame, underneath was inscribed *Fuit*. In my early childhood I used to spell out that motto letter by letter, little knowing what glories, what misfortunes, what long obstinate struggles, what griefs, what anxieties, what ardent desires and immortal hopes were summed up in that single word *Fuit*, for that noble spirit who had set it up before his eyes in the land of exile.

Was Florence really a land of exile for one from Turin? Yes! today it must be so described, as it is only pure truth.

If my father then thought of Piedmont rather than of Italy (every single state, as we saw, thought, or supposed it thought, of its own interests when there was a question of uniting for the common defence), the error was not his, but of the time. But it was to his personal credit that he opposed the foreigners with all the means in his power; that he never demeaned himself by serving them; that, during his whole life, he maintained that political and religious faith he believed, in conscience, to be true; that he was never persuaded by fear or hope to waver from the straight path; that he died without having ever once

hesitated for a moment wherever he could recognize a duty. He therefore gained the honourable distinction of being sometimes described
as an exaggerated fanatic by the sceptical, spineless generation with
whom he had to spend his life.

Revolutions, however, even those most stained by every sort of crime
and violence, sometimes have a way of finally producing political benefits and also, by a strange antithesis, a moral regeneration among men.
They are jolted, roused, forced to seek in themselves a support and an
inner strength; they have to show qualities, talents, and dispositions
for good, of which they did not suppose themselves capable.

After certain political tempests, it seems that people, as after real
storms, breathe better and with distended lungs take (in Manzoni's
words) a *potente anelito*. I should not, myself, wish to unleash such
storms for such a purpose. I don't like revolutions, but sometimes it
seems that Providence does, and I restrict myself to trying to explain
their effects.

What a great number of effeminate characters were re-tempered by
persecution and martyrdom! How many victims in the terrible days
of '93 conquered the ferocity of judges and executioners by their
fortitude? Among the clergy of Courts and boudoirs, who no longer
knew in what, or in whom, they believed, what power of faith, what
invincible characters unexpectedly arose under the fulminations of those
new despots who outlawed Christ and had a strumpet personify the
Goddess of Reason!

Europe was full of those among the persecuted who had managed
to escape the executioner's axe. A contingent of exiles was to be found,
as elsewhere, in Florence, and those who had sacrificed their all for
duty became, as is easily to be imagined, the close friends of my father
and constituted his social milieu.

Among them was a Bishop d'Alby, a Bishop of Béziers (they haunt
my memory like ghosts), an elderly couple named Sessolles. Refugees,
like us, were Prospero Balbo with his family, a Baron Di Perrone,
the Delborgos, the Marquise de Prié with her sons, a certain Scarampi;
all from Turin.

In Florence too was that famous voluntary expatriate Count Vittorio
Alfieri, who greatly admired my father, not so much for his behaviour
and learning, but for the strength of character he had shown in not
flinching before the French revolutionaries.

My family consorted with this honoured group of people. We lived
in a miserable house in the Mercato Nuovo, of which I have no
recollection, as we left it when I was still a babe in arms. We then

went to the Casin de' Nerli beyond the Arno, and of this I have some memory, so I can now start to record my earliest impressions of the world.

4

'FOR goodness sake keep still, my little pet!'

These words were addressed in a deep voice to a four-year-old child, stark naked, seated on his mother's knee, by a tall man dressed in black. His face was pale, his eyes were blue. His somewhat reddish hair was thrown back from his brow. He was frowning. The baby, scared and anxious to obey the terrible black figure of a man, stopped kicking and sat as still as a statue, so that an impatient painter, seated in front of a large canvas depicting the Holy Family, could more easily portray him as the infant Jesus.

The scene was the studio of the painter Fabre; the man in black was Vittorio Alfieri, and the 'little pet' was I.

The picture, destined for Montpellier, still exists, as far as I know, in one of the churches of that town and consequently my portrait is to be found there too. I should be very glad to know if there are any votive offerings lying before it.

This episode is one of the first of which I have any clear recollection. I remember too that I often went to the Countess of Albany's house. They took me there on Sunday mornings and the Countess used to hear me recite verses I had learnt during the week. After the recitation I was immediately given my reward. I can still see the ample circumference of that celebrated lady, all in white with an enormous cambric fichu à la Marie Antoinette, as she climbed on a chair in order to reach down a box of nougat from the top shelf of her bookcase.

After the nougat came the stump of a pencil and a sheet of paper for scribbling. I remember (happy memory!) a drawing I made of the Greek fleet leaving for Troy. It was much admired. If I have not turned out a great poet or a great painter, it's not for lack of patrons or of precocious encouragement.

Subsequently the Countess organized a children's party every Saturday evening. Besides ourselves, there were the Balbos, the Ricasolis from the Ponte alla Carraia, the Antinori boys and their sister, who was a beauty. She later married one of the Rinuccini and became the mother of the present Marquis Laiatico and Marquis Trivulzio. The Prié boys, and the Torrigiani, Santini, and Del Borgo girls also came. If I close my eyes I see, as though it were now, the fire-place opposite the windows, and seated near it in a big old arm-chair the Countess of Albany in her usual Marie Antoinette attire. On the walls are two paintings by Fabre, one of the ghost of Samuel with the witch of Endor and Saul; the other a subject taken from the excavations of Pompeii. I can see the round-arch windows looking over the Arno, with three steps up to them; on the top one I am sitting nibbling an ice and a couple of wafers, which was the invariable ration allowed by the Countess. I see my father talking politics in a group consisting of M. Lagensverd, the Swedish Minister, Carletti, and Libri. I see two large sofas, one on each side under the pictures, their wooden framework white and gold and their covers of red morocco. I see them, almost indeed feel them, because the two youngest Del Borgo girls, who were always teasing me, used to amuse themselves by seating me on a sofa, and, while one held my legs, the other pulled the sofa back from underneath me so that I could not fall on my feet. These young ladies subsequently became the Marchesa Passalacqua and the Marchesa Pamparà. Let posterity judge between them and me!

The house in which the Countess of Albany lived with Count Alfieri is completely transparent, as some ancient philosopher said houses should be. Thanks to his *Autobiography* and the self-revelations it contains, thanks to the learned investigations of the searchers for spicy anecdotes, and, let us admit it, thanks to the very slight importance given in that age to the concealment of human and feminine frailties, we now know everything about these now historic figures. And we must link them with the painter Fabre, heir to the affections of a heart, which, according to the fashion of high society of the time, felt an uncontrollable need of continuous occupation. It is therefore no violation of a domestic secret to give a few more details about that already well-known scandal. Every evening at nine o'clock Count Alfieri went out to visit a lady with a French name which I have forgotten. Was she a rival of the Countess? Was it a cause or an excuse for her relationship with Fabre? God knows! When he came back late, there was the devil to pay if the servants closed the front door and shot the bolt so that he could hear the noise they made. 'I'm quite enough of a slave as it is,' he shouted. 'I don't want to hear myself being locked up in prison as well.'

The Marchesa di Prié, my aunt, a charming, active, witty woman, well in with society and politics, a great opponent of all the French innovations, so much so that Napoleon thought good to restrain her and had her clapped into the Fenestrelle prison—this aunt of mine, who was the most amusing creature in conversation and her anecdotes, told me once after I was grown up: 'I had been aware for some time of the intrigue between the Countess and Fabre. I told Madame Santini and she said I was mad. Once they were having theatricals in Alfieri's house and he was himself acting in one of his tragedies. I happened to be in the front row at one of these performances; in the midst of a group of men on my left was Fabre, leaning against one of the door-posts. I thought he was staring at me. Every now and then he put his lips to the back of his hand. "What ever does that fellow want from me?" I thought. Then something struck me—I glanced in the same direction to the left and there sat the Countess. Aha! I understood! I then whispered to Madame Santini to look round and see if I was as mad as she supposed. So she too saw Fabre making eyes at the Countess, while he kissed a ring he had on his finger.

'When poor Vittorio died the Countess was in a dreadful state, but Fabre didn't lose his head. He took the dead man's keys and brought them to her, etc.' In fact the relationship between these two only ceased at death.

To finish the story about these people as far as I know it, I must tell you that in gratitude for those early pieces of nougat I always made a point of calling on the Countess whenever I passed through Florence. I also used to visit Fabre in memory of my apotheosis in his picture. I sometimes found him ill with gout with the Countess at his bed-side. But little by little they had become very tart, especially the lady. I don't know whether it was due to politics or old age or chagrin at seeing me still young. I therefore called less often, until a final catastrophe caused a definite breach. This is how it happened:

The Albany receptions still took place every Saturday and everybody who was anybody went; foreigners, diplomats, Florentines. The Robillant brothers, friends of mine, had just arrived in Florence and we proposed to go to the At Home, where I was to introduce them. There was a performance at the Pergola theatre that night and we were tempted to go. Let's visit the Countess after the theatre, said I with my passion for arranging things, and that's what we did. When we arrived at her door, people were already leaving and there were not many left. I advanced in somewhat of a flutter, and introduced my friends with good grace. The Countess barely nodded and then turned to Prince Borghese, who stood next to her, saying in a barely subdued voice: '*A quelle heure viennent ces Messieurs!!!*'

We retreated, shrivelled by this thunderbolt, to find sanctuary among the groups of people still there. Fortunately I spotted Count Castell-alfero, the Sardinian Minister in Tuscany, a courteous old gentleman, a born diplomat, and man of the world, who felt no antipathy towards youth because he was no longer young himself.

As it was a gala evening he was in full fig, Minister's embroidered uniform with insignia, medals, and diamond 'gongs'. He welcomed me heartily, as usual. Reassured by his kindness, I now had the unlucky idea of taking an ice from a tray before me. This was in the shape of a peach and was globular and hard. I stood directly opposite the Count as I was trying to break into my ice peach with a little spoon. All of a sudden it slipped away as a cherry stone does when you pinch the fruit; I saw it land full on the Minister's decorations and from there to the carpet, where it rolled to the feet of the Countess of Albany.

How I ran! I still seem to be bolting! That was my last visit to that house.

My father, who had the precious gift of activity and a hatred of inaction (Heaven help us children if he caught us idle), used his enforced leisure in study. He started a little newspaper, *The Bee*, with a literary, philosophic bias, which found favour and continued to be published. He printed a little work, *I Trattenimenti all' Elceto,* and he wrote various literary, political, and controversial compositions, always with the object of being useful and doing some small thing now he was prevented from doing anything more important.

Nowadays when there is a constant open battle being waged between good and bad principles, his is a precious example to be noted and imitated by the young. One day he wrote a sonnet for Alfieri, in order to thank him for some kindness. Alfieri approved it and corrected it for him. This was a very great favour and one accorded only to his closest friends. Another of his poems was also revised by Alfieri. My father told me it finished with an *arietta* in the manner of Metastasio. When Alfieri had read so far he threw it down on his desk, exclaiming: 'Metastasian stuff!'

One of the merits of that noble spirit was, in fact, to have found a Metastasian Italy and to have left it Alfierian. What is more, his first and greatest merit was to have discovered Italy, as Columbus discovered America, and to have started the idea of Italy a Nation. I rate this a higher achievement than his poetry and tragedies. For style, propriety, precision, and felicity of expression, he was a hundred miles behind the despised poet-laureate Metastasio. If the latter was soft, was not Alfieri perhaps not too hard? There comes to my mind, apropos of this, a Piedmontese dialect sonnet with which he meant to counter a similar criticism and, in fairness, I quote the last line which is the only one I remember. After having talked of the accusation of 'hardness' brought against him by his peers, the gentry of Turin, he finished by saying that it remains to be seen *'se me i sonn dur, o s'i se voui d' polenta'*.[1]

As I have renewed the same criticism, it will be well for me to pull myself together and examine my own conscience to see whether his reply cannot be applied to me.

I've just remembered another anecdote, and as it's about such a great man I think any of my readers will be glad to hear it.

Alfieri himself read his tragedies, *Alceste* and *Mirra*, to my parents. The first drew tears from my mother's eyes, but the second had greater success and one of which the author was well able to appreciate the sincerity and importance. My mother's education had been so carefully guided by her husband that anything less than pure was avoided. She was ignorant of the story of Myrrha (I must confess that I have always found it odd that the classical writers, under the pretext of a vengeance of Venus, have foisted that shameful story on us. Today we understand but one thing by a Venereal attack and that is hardly a subject fit for the stage). Therefore, as Alfieri read on, first act, second act, third act, and to nearly the end, my mother kept staring at her husband, then at Alfieri, while expressing amazement by such phrases as 'What ever's happening? What's the matter with the woman?' Only right at the end when Myrrha says, if I remember right, speaking of her mother, *'Felice lei che può morirti accanto*[2] when everyone understands the situation, because the author wishes them to; then and only then my mother understood. Alfieri was delighted, and it was certainly a great satisfaction to him and quite unexpected.

The friendship between my father and Alfieri was perfect except in the point of religion. All know Alfieri's views on that subject, and those who have had the goodness to follow me so far will know my father's. Here were two characters not likely to make concessions, so they avoided useless disputation on the subject that has created such divisions among men and made them so cruel and inexorable towards each other since the days of Christ up to the present time.

But every sincere faith, ardently believed, leads to proselytism or it would be illogical. In the privacy of his family circle my father used to grieve over the spiritual condition of his friend. The less it seemed

---

[1] This could be freely rendered as: 'If I am hard or you made of porridge.'
[2] Happy she who can die beside thee.

D

likely that he would change his attitude, the more he grieved. My
parents were not the only ones to feel bitterly regretful about it, the
whole emigré colony shared their views, especially the women, who
were more sympathetic and more devout.

One day a great piece of news fell into the middle of this pious group
and filled them with amazement and joy. The Marchesa di Prié had
a daughter, Clementina, who married the Marchese Incontri and became the mother of the present Marchese Attilio. During one Easter
week she came back from Mass to find her mother at breakfast
in the parlour with her sons Curzio and Demetrio (the latter died
young and the former was implicated in the revolution of '21 and was
noted for his trick of the fifteen wigs to simulate the growth of his
hair), and a few friends were there too. I don't know if my father was
there, but I think not. He certainly told me the story so that it must be
true.

'Mother,' exclaimed Clementina, as she took off her veil, 'who do
you think took communion with me this morning? Count Alfieri, who
was next to me at the rail.'

You can imagine the joy, consolation, and amazement of all
those excellent folk. I must say, in repeating the story, that I am filled
with astonishment too. So much so that, as I cannot doubt my father,
I could almost believe that Clementina had confused Alfieri with someone else. . . . But, after all, the thing is not impossible. What is certain
is that if Alfieri wanted to go to Easter communion he was more than
capable of doing so, despite the whole of the French Encyclopaedia,
with Voltaire himself at their head. That's what having a character
means!

During his last brief illness Father Canovai of the Scuole Pie was
called in. He imagined he had to bear a grave responsibility and would
go first to the Bishop for instructions. He delayed too long. When at
last he entered the sick man's room he saw him bow his head. He
thought it was a greeting, but it was death. Vittorio Alfieri had gone.
My father told me this.

I find the following in my mother's manuscript: 'It was a great grief
to him [my father] to be in Alfieri's rooms and not to be able to prove
his Christian friendship during his last days on earth. Alfieri would
certainly have been grateful to him for all eternity but . . . God's
decisions are profoundly inscrutable.'

5

Now that my father had been deprived of all opportunity of serving King and Country, his first and most important preoccupation was the education of us children. As the Tolomei college of Siena had the reputation of being a good one, my three elder brothers, Roberto, Prospero, and Enrico, were sent there, whereas I myself, being too young, stayed at home. My sister Melania was in Turin with our grandmother; Metilde went to school at Ripoli, but soon left and came home again. The daughter of an old employé from Nice, the Cavalier Biscarra, came to live with us as companion and governess. Her name was Teresina and she later married one of the Rimediotti family. She is still alive and is one of my oldest friends as she was particularly fond of me as a child.

Our parents' concern therefore was all for my sister and me. She had a docile, gentle, sweet nature. I was equally good, but much livelier. Neither then, nor for years and years afterwards, did I feel any sort of resentment against any living person. Nor should I ever, had it not been for these cursed politics. I can however honestly claim that although in politics I have sometimes felt indignation and hostility, thanks to those who use Italy as a cloak for their greed, avarice, ambition, and vanity; I can say, on my honour, that I have never felt hatred against any individual, although there has been no lack of those who have given me just cause for what they have done against me. I claim not the slightest merit for this, for so I was made.

Our two characters were, as you see, not the most difficult in the world to guide. Things at home went smoothly between Metilde and me and, despite her five or six years' advantage in age, perfect harmony prevailed.

The only circumstance to disturb our happiness at home was my mother's indifferent health. The blows of fate had been too severe for such a delicate constitution. Her nervous system had suffered permanent harm, and, as is always so in such a case, this led to strange inexplicable symptoms. Sometimes she had convulsions and frenzies, now cramps and muscular spasms; sometimes she couldn't utter a word for months on end, so that she had to communicate by gestures or the deaf and dumb alphabet; there were times when the slightest noise or the smallest vibration in the room caused acute pain in her chest.

She was hardly able to look after us or contribute towards our education, but fortunately such a mother, by precept and example, could give us something more valuable than formal instruction; namely the true guidance of our sentiments and affections. She, no less than her husband, had too much good sense to fall into the common error of parents who educate their children at home, that is to say of thinking more of their own convenience and vanity than of their pupil's welfare. I never had to undergo any of those inflictions which the pride of fond mammas so often impose on their unfortunate children, who have to play the role of infant prodigies. Except for the few verses from Ossian, which I learnt willingly enough with an eye to the Sunday nougat, I do not ever remember having been obliged to perform in front of my parents' visitors. Nor was I ever dressed up as a Highlander, a Zouave, or the like. I never wore fashionable hats or smart boots. I was never an object of admiration on the part of either father or mother; neither did I ever hear the exclamations, 'Oh what a little dear! Oh how sweet he is!' although, with the mug I've got now, I can say that I think I really was! In fact I well remember—for children heed such words more than one supposes—that strangers used to pay me any amount of compliments and used to eat me up with kisses and pet me; I rather liked it.

But my own people, before all, wanted to turn me into a man and they knew that education starts at birth and that it should be, so to say, childish in childhood and manly when one is a man. They knew that the germs of the future adult are in the first childish impressions and that adulation and stimulation to pride and vanity can, in parents, be ill-considered fondness, but provide a bad lesson and a bad legacy to the children themselves. Nor were they ignorant of the fact that we are all made of a stuff in which the first crease endures.

They therefore never displayed admiration for me, never flattered me, so that I was saved from presumptuous vanity. They never dressed me up in finery so that I should not have any pretensions to thinking myself beautiful, a particularly silly thing in men. Nor was I made soft or timid with too much: 'Be careful! Mind! Or you'll tumble and hurt yourself!' If I did fall and bump myself, they didn't get agitated or show over-much sympathy. They used to say, not harshly, but smiling affectionately, 'Run along, run along, it's nothing!' One day I scratched myself and cried. I remember my mother saying 'You'd better look out or your inside will get to hear of it and pop out!' I saw I was being teased, took affront, and was so cross I stopped crying.

In one word, my parents' object was to accustom me to life such as

I was to find it later. This training was all directed at acquiring the strength to make sacrifices and to learn how to suffer.

It is true that, if the faults of an undue affection were not so attractive, one should severely blame parents who train their children to withstand heat, cold, and bad weather, knowing they will inevitably have to endure burning sun, snow, rain, etc., and then, although they cannot fail to know that they will with equal certainty have to suffer disappointments, misfortunes, and the inexorable claims of honour and duty, don't give a thought to teaching them how to suffer.

One must also reflect that natural rights exist even for children, and that they should not be corrupted, deceived, or misguided. They have the right not to be sacrificed to inopportune, harmful affection. They have the right to be directed in the speediest, surest way towards the moral and material well-being that is their own capital, so to say, their heritage on this earth, held directly from the goodness of Providence.

No good can follow if a man be not trained to suffer, as well as to obey, when duty and circumstances require. What then is the first and greatest good? That a man should be virtuous and free. To be the first he must obey the moral law, to be the second, obey the laws of the State. Can he do this without sacrifice, without some degree of suffering? I know only too well that in present-day Italy not all accept this definition in practice; that liberty is to be found in obedience. In fact there is an opposite assumption, namely, that liberty means disobedience to all laws. Up to a point those who think like this are to be pitied. The long, hateful despotisms of the past had to be succeeded by a violent reaction. But to pass from one arbitrary rule to another does not resolve the problem and one can never be free, strong, or independent until, instead of the rule of one man or many, only the law is supreme. The basis of this manly obedience, however, must be laid through early education. By the law of nature, children must be moulded by authority and not through independent discovery of their own. I challenge any father, still more any mother, to reply to all their children's whys? except with the phrase 'because I say so!' But this authority must be reinforced in the child's little brain by love and deep respect for his parents.

It is therefore as nonsensical as any false idea of children themselves to treat them as equals, to put father and sons on the same level of intimacy, to permit the young to have their say about everything and to ask for explanations of everything. There is no sort of equality between the adult and the child, between father and son, and if their relationship infers it, it is false. But here, too, the old despotism and the new licence in the matter of education were cause and effect, as in politics. Shall we, after experience, find a rational method? Let's hope so!

It seems to me that my people had almost discovered such a rational method. Let me explain the 'almost'. Despite the profound veneration I feel for my father, I think I can be allowed respectfully to voice certain doubts about some of his actions and opinions. In fact should I avoid all criticism my praises might ring false. I must say, then, that in following his excellent authoritarian methods with us, sometimes his quick impetuous nature carried him too far. There was too that constant diffidence towards the promptings of his own heart, mentioned before, which caused him to go to the opposite extreme, so that sometimes he was perhaps inordinately severe. But I really bless this fault in him. A momentary severity is a hundred times better than its opposite. In all cases a weak government is the worst of all.

Such were the principles which guided my parents in our education. A few anecdotes will show how they worked in practice. They will naturally be childish trifles. It is not a trifling matter, however, but the most important and difficult of all undertakings, to train children in the way they should go from the start. Should my book be not quite useless in helping the reader to such an object, my warmest wishes will be fulfilled.

The organization of our daily occupations was fixed for Metilde and me according to a written time-table that was not lightly to be varied. In this way we became accustomed to routine and to not keeping people waiting for our convenience, one of the most annoying defects both in children and grown-ups. I remember one day when Metilde, out with Miss Teresina, came in late, after luncheon was well under way. It was winter and snowing. The two malefactors sat down nervously while soup was served to them in two bowls which had been kept hot (guess where?) out on the terrace! They were therefore not only at zero temperature on the Réaumur scale, but they had a covering of snow an inch thick.

At table, of course, neither she nor I ever uttered a word, receiving what was provided without right of question or comment. In regard to sitting straight, cleanliness, not making a noise with one's mouth when eating, or indeed any sound whatever, we well knew that the slightest failure in any of these things meant immediate banishment at least. Our every effort was, therefore, to pretend we didn't exist. This system, I can assure you, never allowed us to imagine that we were the centre of things and everyone else at the circumference, which is a notion almost forced on poor little minds by the stupid grimaces and flattery of elders, whereas if they had been left to their natural simplicity they would have behaved quite reasonably.

Lessons in good behaviour were not restricted to mealtimes. Even out of doors we were forbidden to shout, interrupt, and especially to lay hands on each other on any pretext. If I chanced to run in front of Metilde in going into the dining room, my father would take me by the arm and lead me to the rear of everybody, saying: 'There's no need to be rude because she's your sister.'

In many parts of Italy the older generation had the habit of bawling as though their listener were deaf, of interrupting him as though he had no right to speak, of laying hold of him in all sorts of ways as though there were no other way of dealing with him except by corporal punishment. Don't therefore tell me that our discipline was a superfluous pedantry; I only wish it could be the general rule throughout Italy.

On another occasion my excellent mother gave me a lesson about thinking myself a superior person. I have never forgotten it, nor the place where it happened. It was in the big meadow of the Cascine park in Florence, the one with the old oak tree in the middle where they ran the horse races, as you go in on the right of the Piazzone flower-bed, where there's a path along the wood. I was in the corner just by the entrance, accompanied by my mother and an old servant, who hailed from the same region as Pylades, although not such a hero, but all the same an excellent person. I don't remember why, but for some reason or other, I struck him with a little stick I was carrying, may I be forgiven!

My mother forced me to go down on my knees and beg his pardon in full sight of the crowd of by-standers. I can still see poor Hodge's look of consternation as he stood, hat in hand, unable to take in the fact that, kneeling before him, was the Cavalier Massimo Taparelli d'Azeglio.

Not to mind pain was another lesson most assiduously taught by our father; whenever the occasion presented itself, by example. If we ever complained of a pain, he would say in joke, but fundamentally in earnest: 'A Piedmontese, after his arms and legs are broken and he has been run through the body twice, then, and not till then, may say, "Yes, I really think I am a little unwell." '

Such was the moral authority that he had over my mind that there could never have been any occasion when I should not have obeyed him implicitly, even if he had told me to jump out of the window.

I remember when I had my first tooth pulled out and how, on the way to the dentist Campana, who lived in the Square where the Palazzo Vecchio is, I felt simply awful inside, though I put a brave face on it and tried to show indifference.

There came a rather more serious occasion which was to test my childish courage and equally, as you will see, that of my father himself. He had rented a little villa a musket-shot from San Domenico at Fiesole, on the right as you go up-hill. It was called Villa Billi. I went back there two years ago, and I found the same family of peasants with their two sons, my play-fellows of that time, now more decrepit than I am, Nando and Sandro their names, and we fell on each other's necks.

When we were up at the villa, it was my father's habit to take us for long walks which had their own special rules. It was absolutely forbidden to ask: 'How much further is it?' 'What's the time?' or to say, 'I'm thirsty, or hungry, or tired.' Otherwise we could do or say what we pleased.

On the way home one day from one of these trips, we were coming down steep stony ways under Castel di Poggio, going towards Vincigliata. I had picked a great bunch of broom and other flowers and I had a stick in my hand; somehow or other I got caught up and fell heavily. My father ran to me, picked me up, and examined me. As I complained of pain in my arm, he stripped it bare and saw that it was somewhat dislocated; in fact I had broken an ulna bone of one of my forearms.

I was watching his face and I saw his expression change to one of deep sympathy and concern, so that he seemed a different man. He made me as comfortable as he could with a sling and we set off once more. After a short time he regained his usual mien and said: 'Listen, dear boy, your mother is not at all well. She might be very upset if she finds out you've hurt yourself. You must bear up and tomorrow we'll go to Florence and have you attended to, but this evening you must not let her know you have been hurt. Do you understand?'

He said this in his usual severe tone, but most affectionately. I was delighted to have this important and difficult charge. The whole evening, in fact, I sat in a corner holding my poor broken arm as well as I could. My mother, who thought I was tired after our long expedition, noticed nothing wrong.

The next day I was escorted to Florence and the arm was attended to, but the complete cure had to wait some years until I went to the mud baths of Vinai.

Perhaps some may say here that my father was a barbarian. I remember the episode as though it had just happened, and I also remember that I felt no shadow of such a criticism towards him. I was so happy at witnessing the infinite tenderness reflected in his face, and I also considered it most reasonable not to alarm my mother, that I looked on the difficult injunction as an opportunity to acquire honour. All this arose from the fact that I had not been spoilt and had already some soundness of character. Now that I'm old and have seen the world, I bless my father's strictness and I wish Italian children of today could have similar fathers and could benefit more than I did, so that, thirty years hence, Italy would be the first among the nations.

You must also appreciate that children have more discrimination than appears and do not resent a just, but affectionate, strictness. I have always found them disposed to prefer those who keep them up to the mark rather than those who give in to them. Soldiers are just the same.

Here is something more to show whether my father deserves to be called a barbarian. He held the view that it was bad to wake children suddenly, disturbing them brusquely from their sleep. When we had to rise early for a journey he would approach my cot and begin to sing a little song—I can hear it now. It began :

> *Chi vuol veder l'aurora*
> *Lasci le molli piume.*[1]

As he gradually sang louder I found myself awake without the slightest shock.

God knows I loved him deeply, despite his severity. He never failed to show when he was pleased with me, sometimes indeed beyond what I deserved. When the family went to the Bagni di Lucca, which we did on two occasions, we lodged in the house of the Abbé Lena. He was an original, very tall, always dressed in a flowered dust-coat; a man never at a loss, whatever the difficulty. Years after, he had the notion one day of going to Paris. He climbed into a one-horse shay he owned and off he went, even though it had no hood. Passing through Turin he called on us for hospitality so that he could rest himself and his beast. Then off again, quite alone, and I don't know how many months later he reappeared once more and, after the same procedure, left for home.

There are lots of snakes at the Bagni di Lucca, harmless enough, but a nuisance, as they get into the rooms. One evening I was in a little garden close to the house and, finding some snakes there, I managed to kill several with a stick I picked up.

There was no merit in this since at that time—I was only some six or seven years old—I was completely ignorant of the fact that snakes

---

[1] He who would see the dawn
Must quit his soft pillows (feathers).

were poisonous and that their bite could be mortal. As for the antipathy some people feel for snakes, I felt none and never have, so that there was no question of being brave in beating those unfortunate creatures to death.

So when I took them in to my father, who was in the company of our Osasco uncles, ex-officers, I was pleasantly surprised to be received by them with loud acclaim for my success. Even my father, with less fuss, praised me, so that my reputation for courage was established on small foundations; as indeed often happens, not only with children.

One of my father's principal ideas was to impress on my mind, and Metilde's too, that fear is an unlovely thing and, still more, to show it and be overcome by it. Sometimes he put us to a test suitable for our age. One such was to take us into the woods at night, just him and us two. In the dark, as everyone knows, objects such as rocks and tree-trunks take on strange appearances. When our father noticed such an object he would stop and make us look at it from afar, saying: 'Look over there, doesn't it look like an animal, or a devil with horns!' Then he would take us by the hand and lead us to it so that it appeared strange no longer. Then he would repeat our dialect proverb I mentioned before: *La paura l'è faita d'nen*, fear is made of nothing.

If my victory over the snakes had little real credit, I did deserve some praise for a victory I won over myself.

It is a practice in families to give so many toys to the elder children that, after experience, such gifts turn out to be excessive and the younger ones get nothing. I, who was the *eighth*, never had a toy and amused myself with chairs and brooms; whatever came along. A solitary exception to this general rule did occur at the Bagni di Lucca. Going down to the village one day for a walk, we saw in a shop-window a number of toy carts, some with one horse, some with two, some with four. I don't know if it was in honour of some saint or other, but in any case I was given one of the humblest of the carts. I'd never had such a wonderful thing and I was in ecstasies.

There was another little boy, son of Count Cinzano, who used to come and romp with me, and he too had never been spoilt in the matter of playthings—you must remember that all our families at that period were stony-broke—and his mouth fairly watered at the sight of my cart; he was dying to have it.

I felt so sorry for him, as he had nothing to play with, that I gave it to him. Overjoyed and without waiting a second he ran off with the little cart. I was rather glum and almost repented what I had done, but when my people heard about it they made such a fuss of me that

I began to think I had done something rather grand. That was not the end of the story; the next day there arrived for me the finest cart in the shop from where we had bought the first one.

I still think my sacrifice praiseworthy, as it was made out of pure sympathy. I have never been able to agree with the theories of M. de la Rochefoucault, who claims that he does not in any way admire the sentiment of pity. It is true that, in his day, a gentleman's headache was of concern, but no one paid any attention to the torture meted out to a labouring man who went home crippled for life. Pity was then relative.

Nevertheless, the Gospel says 'Blessed are the merciful', and the Gospel was there even then. This only shows for how long Christians in name have stayed pagan, and worse than pagan, in fact. If we consider the world today with this in mind, we might discover that Christian civilization has many miles to go before it deserves such a title.

As an example, let us imagine one of those enormous tenement buildings such as one finds at Genoa, with eight or ten floors, divided into flats occupied by different families. Should we see these people busy inventing locks, bolts, and iron-clad doors, never going out of their premises or down the stairs without daggers and swords and pistols, even though they sometimes called on each other and, when meeting, were full of compliments, would you say such a house had reached the peak of Christian civilization?

Isn't modern Europe in precisely the same state?

6

As I have strayed into a digression, I had better finish what I was saying. If the tenants who occupy their family apartments in the great house called Europe had had, as children, teachers, not only to instruct and train their intelligence, but to educate them, to open their minds to an appreciation of truth, goodness, and justice, do you mean to tell me that there would have been no saving of armour-plating, of big guns, and better still of prisons and gallows?

I'm no Quaker, I do not believe in the rule of the Saints, I do not belong to the Society for Everlasting Peace. I cannot do otherwise than accept men as they are, with all their seven deadly sins upon them, and

I expect there will always be, more or less, crimes, quarrels, and violence. Our argument hinges on that 'more or less'. Perfect peace is a dream and is a return to the Golden Age. I admit that. But is this a good reason to call a man mad who tries to lessen the causes of those manifold evils that are let loose on mankind, owing to the grave discrepancy that exists between the training of their intellects and the education of their characters?

One way would be to set up a Ministry for Real Education instead of those Ministries of Public Instruction that are to be found in all constitutional governments. The latter would train good technicians; the former, good men. But, you will object, it is moral training that makes good men, and morality is a branch of theology, and theology is the science of the Church. Do you really want a government department of priests? Well, I appreciate the difficulty, but let us look closer. I do not want a clerical Ministry of Education, especially as in nearly all Christian nations there is one already. The teaching of morality is everywhere the function of the clergy. On the other hand, it is obvious that it is insufficient. Men pay little heed to it. It is therefore indispensable to find something better or, at least, something more. Would it be impossible to try? To put the idea into practice?

I am not only addressing priests, in fact I don't want to mention them, because I have attacked the Roman clergy when no one else dared. Now it is respectable to go for the priests I want to let them be. Let them alone, then, and let us speak of governments, be they monarchies, republics, of whatever shape or size or influence, not forgetting parties and factions. Let us for once speak clearly. We have a government, let it take power to set up a Ministry of Real Public Education, and this should be the proper function of all authorities. Let it promote the work of this ministry by its own example, the only efficacious method. Can it be that the morality of official utterances differs from that of official actions? What government, what party, faction, public body, what authority of any kind does in fact fulfil the first and most important of duties due from those above, namely to set a good example to those below? Montesquieu says, 'There are bad examples worse than crimes. More states have perished through disregard of morality than disregard of the law.'

Without making a case against the authorities, I will cite only one instance. Since the time of the Reformation, there have been several occasions when a ruler has renounced his own religion to adopt that of another country, which had offered him the crown under those conditions.

What can the public deduce from that? Either you believe in your religion, and in that case you barter your conscience for a throne; or you believe in none, and, if so, you are a vile hypocrite who simulates a faith you do not believe in, for the same motive. You, my dear prince, give a lesson to all beneath you that what counts is to get on, and that *Paris vaut bien une Messe.*

Can you, afterwards, complain of the man who, to serve his own ends, betrays you? In that case you complain of a man who merely looks after his own interest; at your expense, however.

Let us therefore set up a Ministry of Real Public Education, which could be called the Ministry of Good Example, whose portfolio is given to the whole government and to all those set in authority over us. Then, and not before, you can talk of Christian civilization.

Such conclusions have all started from the episode of the little toy cart of the Bagni di Lucca! Now let us pick up the thread of our story.

My childhood passed very happily and peacefully in the charming city of Florence, which, therefore, has always seemed to be my native place rather than Turin.

When they began to teach me to read and write I wouldn't have anything to do with it. I was therefore sent to the Scolopian School of St. Giovannino at the end of Via Larga. My first teacher, humble enough and completely in accord with his pupil, was the porter.

Signor Piacenti had three pupils, of whom I was one. I spent the whole day long putting up a show of study. I remember those friars: a Father Mauro and a Father Bertinelli, who gave me grapes and made a fuss of me and of whom I can only speak well.

I learnt most, however, from what I got orally at home. I furnished my mind with all sorts of ideas, historical, geographical, mythological, as well as with French, by following, with my sister, the lessons of the excellent Signora Teresa Biscarra.

While my family was living obscurely in happy tranquillity in Florence as I have described; while my father, after having witnessed the collapse of all he most loved in the world, the independence and dignity of Piedmont, was hoping to remain undisturbed in his Tuscan refuge, the hand of Napoleon, which had abased the proudest brows in Europe, succeeded in discovering his humble person and teaching him how powerful it was. As all know, Napoleon the First had no respect for universal suffrage and saw no point in permitting individuals to choose their own master. It was therefore forbidden for the Piedmontese, those Frenchmen of Turin, to have their children educated abroad, and Siena was 'abroad'. My father, therefore, had to remove my three brothers, Roberto, Prospero, and Enrico, from the Tolomei college and bring them back home.

They continued their studies under the Scolopian friars, while I went on with the porter. Life at home became much livelier, although discipline and order were in no way relaxed, only applied to a greater number of persons.

Meantime, in the north of Europe, the great events of the Napoleonic wars were taking place, to be followed by strange reorganizations of states and unlikely annexations of peoples, forced to put up with alliances contrary to their traditions, wishes, and interests.

Napoleon I was not politically-minded, and of his political creations nothing remains.

The definite annexation of Piedmont to France was decreed. Hard on the heels of the first order forbidding the sending of children *abroad* to be educated, came another, still more painful, that forced the new subjects to swear allegiance to their new master and to return home. My father, who had already sworn such an oath to his King Vittorio Emanuele, then on the island of Sardinia, wrote to him as follows (I quote the manuscript verbatim): 'to offer his services and to share his misfortunes, ready to abandon for ever country, wife, and children'.

He left Florence by himself and travelled as far as Parma, where he waited for forty days, the period taken by the reply to his letter to reach him there.

Vittorio Emanuele 'replied in the most affable manner and with a deep sense of obligation, but he absolutely refused to add to the number of the victims of his own misfortune. He told him to swear the oath demanded, as he had no wish to separate him from his wife and young children, now, more than ever, in need of such an excellent father. Further, he was no longer sure of bread for himself and his faithful followers.'

This sensible, affectionate reply pained my father, but decided his course of action. He had done all he could, and more, for his King, his allegiance, and his Country, and he had gone to the ultimate extent of self-sacrifice, until he found the way blocked by a wall of bronze. Now he thought of his family. He returned to Turin and swore fealty to Napoleon I, who discovered five years later what such oaths are worth when extracted by force and not given of free will.

But my father was not one of those who taught him that lesson. However, he had been made to give his word, he had given it, and that was enough.

There was a term fixed for the return of the emigrés and time
pressed. My mother received a message from her husband that she
must return to Turin with the family. It was late in December and our
caravan was to be seen as it left Casa Pitti-Gaddi, our most recent home,
wending its way through the San Gallo gate and then up the Pellegrino
road towards the high ground. There were two carriages, one with our
mother and Metilde, the other larger vehicle with all the rest of us under
the eye of a certain Abbé Moni from Lucca, recently taken into employment by my father. All noble families who were religious had to have
their domestic chaplains.

Today travelling by diligence is a thing of the past. At that period
we had not yet arrived at the point of imagining such luxury. Those
who couldn't afford post-horses travelled with Pollastri's drivers, the
man whose name and whose mules were so well known throughout
Europe. To give some idea of their speed, I remember once leaving
Pisa in the morning and sleeping at the Osteria Bianca at Empoli, and
the day after, *before night*, we reached Florence. On we journeyed at
the pace enjoyed by sacks of rice, maize, and the like, where there is
no railway, our ears full of the jingle-jangle of the mule bells; through
Bologna, Piacenza, Milan, until, after a fortnight or so, in God's good
time, at long last we pulled into the courtyard of the Azeglio house,
Via d'Angennes, Number 19, in Turin.

The bad weather, the cold, the fogs of Lombardy, and, more than all
else, the grief of having to go where we didn't want to; to put ourselves
under the claws of a foreign ruler in our own country; all in all this
had made the journey a great ordeal for my mother and, on arrival,
she was at the end of her tether.

For me and the other boys this unknown Turin, this family mansion, hitherto seen but dimly through the elegant descriptions of the
Piedmontese man-servant, kindled our fancy to such an extent that we
were filled with impatient longing. When at last, on getting out of
the carriage, I found myself in a magnificent vestibule, met by servants
and the secretary, the lawyer Cappello; when to cap all I heard: 'Have
you had a good journey, Signor Cavaliere?', I leave you to imagine
my excitement. I had never been aware that I was a Cavaliere and to
find myself so unexpectedly promoted to such a rank!

Nowadays, it is fortunate that very many find themselves turned into
Cavalieri, expecting it as little as I did. I say it is fortunate, because
only they can fully appreciate my delight at that solemn moment.

I became more and more ecstatic as I found my way into a magnificent apartment hung with silk, with balconies overlooking a garden,

shining parquet floor, etc. This was one of the few occasions when I realized a feeling of satisfied ambition. Not that I have lacked ambition, but, as will be seen if I am granted enough time to continue writing, my ambition had nothing to do with titles, palaces, promotions, and such trifles.

We found the Countess of Casal Grasso, our old grandmother, much enfeebled by a chronic disease which soon carried her off. We were taken to her bedside and she welcomed us and embraced us and it was plain that the good soul was overjoyed to see us.

Such was her fondness for us that at the approach of spring when we went off on an expedition to Stupinigi she wanted us to visit the Castle of Millefiori on the banks of the river Sangone, which was her property and which she was determined to leave to us. The history of this castle is as romantic as that of Woodstock, but I will pass on as it is not my purpose to write about the days of yore.

Now a new epoch of my life began. After the thrifty emigré existence I found myself in richer, easier surroundings. I had a decent room and a plot of my own in the garden. Little by little I was introduced to my relations of all ages and sexes, beginning with an old great-grandmother, whose huge white bonnet, with a diamond brooch all a-sparkle in the middle, made a great impression on me.

When Napoleon passed through Turin (I think on his way back from his coronation at Milan) this lady went, willy-nilly, to his Court. The hero of the hour, as everyone knows, never found it necessary to be polite, and certainly no one in Europe was in a position to teach him manners. As he went from one lady to another, as was his wont, snapping out one remark to each, he came before my great-grandmother and asked her curtly,

'How many children have you?'

'One hundred and seven, Sire,' she answered. Napoleon took a step back and gazed fixedly at her with his eagle eyes, while the old Countess, not at all dismayed, explained that she had had nine daughters, who were all of them mothers and grandmothers, and some, I believe, great-grandmothers, so that the number of her offspring living was one hundred and seven. She had seen the fifth generation!

Napoleon (Madame de Staël knew it well) was all for a high birth-rate, and he had good reasons! so was quite mollified and said:

'Well, Madame, I congratulate you', and passed on.

The priest from Lucca, who was in charge of us children and had escorted us on our journey, did not give satisfaction, so my father sent him back to his native city. But we had to have a clerical tutor; such was the custom. The previous one had been engaged before his abilities had been tested, so, in looking for another, much more trouble was taken. At last one was found of whom all his references spoke well. In fact Don Andrea di Dronero was a candid soul as virtuous as anyone could desire, but he fell short in everything else. He hardly seemed to know he was alive!

I had to put up with this excellent priest for five years. In regard to any sort of education, tact, or knowledge of the time or way to tackle me, he simply hadn't a clue. I was aware of his stupidities and I led him on every day with a hundred sly tricks in order to produce more. You can imagine how much respect I felt for him, or what moral authority he could impose on my mind. He was of the Jesuit order and he oppressed me with the devotions he made me perform. The following was my religious time-table. In the morning (before daylight in winter) he said Mass and I served for him; half-way through the morning, devotional reading; before lunch, examination of conscience; after lunch, visit to church or Benediction; usually in the evening some *triduum* or *novena*; finally prayers before bed. Thank goodness he then left me in peace till the morrow. I had forgotten that, in a particularly fervid phase, one had to find time during the day for half-an-hour's meditation. The object of all this was to make me partial to religious practices!

When one wants to accustom horses to the noise of fire-arms one sometimes fires a pistol near them at the moment they get their oats. My priest had different tactics; to make me love Mass he made me get up by candle-light, chilled and sleepy, and act as server to him in a dark, gloomy chapel. You can imagine how agreeable I found it!

For some time he added another tribulation. There was a priest in Turin, I believe not a bad man at heart, who daily thought out some new form of devotion in order to collect children and teach them to be pioneers in pious exercises, and perhaps, via the children, to get his foot in with the parents; but this last is only my supposition and perhaps not true in regard to Father Polan, ex-friar though he certainly was. In his oratory he collected about thirty children, among whom was I, thanks to my tutor. He made us perform all sorts of ritual with prayers and meditations in the dark, then from time to time there were picnics in the country. I must say there was nothing improper, or worse, in any of the ex-friar's activities, so far as I observed. But it was, to say the least, inopportune and unsuitable to cram a lively and quite intelligent child into a monkish hood that would have been too heavy for a grown man.

E

To conclude the religious history of my childhood, I shall only add that my saintly priest was quite desperate when he saw that his method, instead of making me more pious as he had hoped, produced the exactly opposite effect, as was inevitable.

I have never succeeded, at any time in my life, in concealing boredom. Anyone who looks me in the face is at once aware if I am bored. My face spoke clearly enough how impressed I was by all his holy goings-on. Sometimes I burst out laughing at certain of his stories; where he dug them up I can't imagine! They were all about apparitions of damned souls, visions, and miracles.

One day, and this was a serious matter, we made a kind of pilgrimage to the Madonna of Oropa, where they worship an ancient image of black wood, stuck in a niche, possibly Byzantine. Below the head of a woman there is a bell-shaped affair to represent the body. The infant, of course, is similar in form, and both were loaded with crowns, jewels, necklaces, and much else of value, left by several generations of the devout. In God's good time I reached this marvel, after a journey of many miles, mostly on foot; but instead of being overcome with emotion, I said that I respected the Madonna in heaven, but I didn't care a fig for that ugly, black Madonna and I didn't believe she could do me any good or harm.

These ideas of mine, as you will easily imagine, stirred up a hornet's nest. I was treated like a heretic, an atheist; I should come to a bad end, etc., etc. How often shouldn't we spank the teachers rather than the pupils!

As a final test they thought it a good idea to put me through what was known as the 'Exercises'. There's no mention of such things today. I think it was a Jesuit invention. Certainly they were organized by members of that order and in a convent or sanctuary, once their property. A few miles from Lanzo in the Dora Valley there is a mountain-top on which certain shepherds (the usual story!) had one day seen St. Ignatius appear. The top of this mountain was a bare, sharp rock which was soon, thanks to the apparition, enclosed by a fine church of which it remained the central feature. Around the church they built a convent. A corridor ran all round with access to rooms on both sides. Some of the rooms faced out to a magnificent open view of the mountains, the others looked inwards to the church, with not quite such a magnificent view of a coloured gesso St. Ignatius standing up on the top of the rock.

It was in one of these latter rooms (so that I should have less opportunity for distraction) that I was ensconced by my priest one fine summer day in the year 1813; and I ask you to imagine how I enjoyed such a country holiday!

There were forty or fifty people living in this house of 'Exercises', as in a boarding establishment. My brothers Prospero and Enrico were among them, but they were considered worthy of a room with a view. The principal was a certain Abbé Guala, well-known in Turin and famous for his priestly intrigues. It was said he had made a special study of Horace's Satire in which he writes of the art of getting legacies, and that he had outdone his master. I have no proof of this and it is my maxim not to affirm anything I don't know for certain. But I have first-hand evidence to state that he was an unintelligent fanatic, without a shred of judgement as to how to attain the good results which, I should like to think, was his objective. What I know even better, is that he made me endure a week that I shall never forget, should I live a thousand years.

Except for mealtimes, I spent my waking hours either listening to sermons in church or stuck in my room to meditate on what I had heard. If I woke up in the night I could see St. Ignatius watching me. That dark, motionless figure in the semi-darkness, lit only by the pale little altar lamp, seemed little like a visitor from Paradise.

The result was, not knowing how to pass the long hours of the day and in part to vent my spleen, I wrote a sonnet, which could truly be called a 'sonnet of occasion'. I wrote it up on a door in pencil. I remember the first quatrain which ran as follows:

> *Volendo far veder la Seccatura*
> *Quanto tremenda sia sua potestà*
> *Fece dar gli Esercizi di pietà*
> *Da un prete seccator senza misura.*[1]

I don't know how, but my priest discovered the sonnet. I only found this out later, for he said nothing at the time. He must really have felt dreadful to see the fine result of his most recent efforts!

My father was told, but I had no reproof from him. He will probably have said to the priest: 'It serves you right.' The fact remains that from then on I had fewer boring devotional exercises and was allowed to breathe more freely.

---

[1] If you want to see Boredom in person
In its horrid monotonous might,
Take a look at a boring old parson
Who troubles me morning and night.

7

RELIGIOUS instruction is one of the biggest problems in education. It opens the field to some of the subtlest metaphysical arguments. I shall take good care not to enter the labyrinth, for which there is no Ariadne to give you a thread which does not snap directly you want to use it.

From the beginning of time every generation of men ask themselves as follows: 'Where have I come from? What must I do? Where am I going?' Human reason, never yet having given the real answer, which is 'I don't know', has found hundreds of ways of replying, according to the fashion of the times, one more attractive than the other. Men will continue to find answers, I suppose, as long as God gives them the right to inhabit this planet.

If one can defend oneself from metaphysics one cannot so easily discard real practical life, with all its inevitable exigencies. To guide men through these, without tormenting his reason with metaphysics, there is something available, namely, Faith. Faith gives a firm answer to man's three questions and points the way to go to those who will follow. But, as I said much earlier, a man believes only what he can, not what he would like to. In these modern days, if one wants to examine and fruitfully discuss practical social problems, among these education is fundamental, it is absolutely essential to start from a basis acceptable to all, or nearly all; that is if one wants to be listened to.

I will only say that I don't want anything to do with atheists, pantheists, or materialists. Atheism, if logical, reduces the problem of life to a very simple formula: 'Help yourself how and when you like, short of running the risk of the gallows.' As it is impossible to conceive the existence of a social order without continuous, willing, reciprocal sacrifice, there is no possibility of agreeing with atheism.

This, however, does not simplify the problem very much. Between my poor priest's method of turning education into a Capuchin novitiate, and that of Rousseau, who would wait thirty years before broaching the question of religion, there is plenty of room. I shall restrict myself to a few brief observations which, I think, may be acceptable to all.

Every single educator, whatever his religious opinions, must set himself the aim of making his pupil a good man. To be such, one must first learn to do things which one often dislikes. I should be curious to hear why I should do things I don't like, unless for the sake of reward or punishment in the future.

Apart from this idea it all comes down to impunity, that is to say, to learn to do what one likes in such a way as to avoid other unpleasantness. What could I then say and what reason could I give to my pupil, to prevent him from always doing what he likes, so that he may become a good man? Must I say that he must be good in order to make a success of life? He would laugh in my face, even as an infant. Must I bring up the Socratic thesis, that justice is the only good and injustice the only evil? If I therefore do what is unjust, it would only be right and proper, *even for me*, that they chop off my head to vindicate justice. He would laugh more than ever. It is essential, therefore, to base morality on dogma.

If you agree so far, I suppose that any educator among us, however much a sceptic, would choose the dogma of the Gospels rather than the Islamic or Brahminical. In general I seem to see that we should all agree in taking the ten commandments as a far from despicable basis for morality. The sceptical educationalist will say: I cannot teach and affirm what I do not recognize as certainly true. I reply and ask if he is absolutely certain of the contrary. If he assumes the responsibility of making a choice on behalf of his pupil, is he not running the risk of claiming infallibility for himself; of which, too, I suppose, he is not quite certain.

In my opinion, doubt itself should lead to the consolidation of the pupil's morality. It should instil into his heart, by means of dogma, that Christian feeling for right and wrong which is the basis of modern society and the sole guarantee of a fairly equal distribution of wealth, which is itself the most reasonable and the most general application of the first of the Gospel precepts—charity.

The age of doubt will come soon enough, do not let us hasten it. God has spared childhood and youth from doubt and we should not alter what, of his goodness, he has decreed.

I know that my arguments will not satisfy the theologian or even the philosopher, but perhaps they will have some effect on sincere minds who are so often reduced to rest content with moral probabilism.

In life, many problems demand immediate solutions, and one has no time to indulge in the luxury of metaphysics, or of a fully convinced understanding; one such is the question of religious instruction in childhood and youth.

One of the worst evils arising from the religious instruction given to me was to rob me of all respect for very respectable matters, such as a true and sincere belief in the supernatural and in morality itself. How could I feel any respect for the cult of the black Madonna of Oropa or for my priest, who was a fanatic for her?

He had the same effect on me in miniature, that Rome has had on whole generations of men. That is to say, in making reverence impossible by an abuse of it.

The religious authority and political authority today dominant in Europe, by making it impossible for men to respect them, have brought about that profound, unrestrainable renewal of ideas and things in general which, in so far as it is a revolution, we can describe as a locomotive, while the general good sense of the population is the brake which prevents us all from breaking our necks.

However, in this great seething of everything that makes society, the feeling of respect, considered in the abstract, has gone up in smoke. The new generations feel enthusiasm, passion, fashionable crazes, for men and for things, but, one can say, they feel no respect for anybody or anything. When one considers the past, and in some degree the present, one understands why.

Now it is up to education (if you really want to return the world to order and normality) to bring back this fecund, noble sentiment into men's hearts—*respect for what is worthy of respect*. Without this, one of the greatest instruments for good—example—becomes useless, nor can any well-established legal order exist.

One is very ready to refer to the Romans and Greeks. To praise to the skies some assassin or some ambitious thruster, out come the Gracchi, the Brutuses, Cassius, and so on. But let us pay more heed to those laws and customs which prove the importance given by the Romans to *respect for what deserves respect*. The treaty which put an end to the war between Romans and Sabines contained a clause that no Roman should appear naked before a Sabine woman. A salutation was due by all who met a pregnant woman, and so on. The respect for religion, the city, the law, paternal authority, the consular fasces, the magistrates, and tribunes is confirmed by hundreds of examples. Nasica as consul, accompanied by the lictors, meets his father on horseback and makes him dismount out of respect for the first magistrate.

When, on the contrary, Duilius before battle took the augury and the chickens wouldn't pick up any grain, he said: 'Let's see if they'll drink', and had them thrown into the sea. Such was not the act of a wise man nor of a statesman.

After the time of the Gracchi, the Romans gradually lost their respect for all these things until they became so decadent that they had to respect Tiberius, Nero, and men like that. Should any forget, there was the *Lex Majestatis* to refresh their memory.

Now, recapitulating all the facts and reflections I have placed before the reader, cannot we conclude that *respect for what is worthy of respect* is the third element in a good education, to be added to the other two we have already indicated; namely, obedience to legally-constituted authority and strength of will?

Thanks to my father, I was not deficient in strength of will at the age of about twelve; I had also learnt to obey; but, owing to the limitations and misplaced zeal of my priest, all sense of respect had been stifled in me, which meant that I had more than my fair share of presumption.

The scholastic education I got from him was worth little more than the religious. When I think that I spent five or six years learning Latin at an age most suitable for the acquisition of languages, and that instead of knowing inadequately Greek and Latin, which really are of no use to me, I could know German and English, that would be of the greatest use to me!

My education was founded on Jesuit principles, and the Jesuits have resolved the problem extremely well; that is to say, they bring up a youth to the age of twenty, forcing him to the constant study of things of absolutely no use in forming character, intelligence, and mature judgement. In fact my education and the little knowledge I have managed to acquire I've had to get myself, working twice as hard alone, at an age in which one should be applying what one has already learnt, rather than gathering knowledge.

As far as history is concerned, which, equally with languages, is the most fruitful study for all classes of men, I was handed ancient history and I got to know fairly well what had happened in Rome, Athens, Memphis, and Babylon before the Christian era, but I knew absolutely nothing about medieval Italy. And the reason? Because I ought to know nothing about Theodora or Marozia, about Alexander VI and the ambitions, meannesses, violence, and fraud of the Popes.

I even got little good from my study of that blessed Latin, so I was sent as an external pupil to the grammar school, where the Military Academy now stands, to study under Signor Bertone, the rhetoric master.

It was obvious that Napoleon was not interested in producing rhetoricians, as there were only three in the class! Perrier, a Frenchman; Fascine, a Piedmontese; and myself! I have never since met my fellow-pupils, of whom I have the best of memories. Should they read these pages their old comrade sends them warm greetings.

I was always the most asinine of the class. It may be due to my faulty character, or to a spirit of contradiction, but it is only too true that I never did any good as long as they stood over me forcing me to study, but when left in peace I swotted away like anything, and I've more or less done so up to this day. Examinations approached, and one fine day I found myself in the school-room with my two companions, seated at separate desks, writing essays. I had to write one in Greek! I sweated away with the help of the Greek–Latin dictionary of Scheravelio and a grammar book; squeezing out my composition, word by word. The *maître d'études* paid us a visit from time to time. He gave a glance at Perrier and Fascine and I could see that he was pleased. Then he came to my desk, but at the sight of my Greek his face clouded. Goodness knows what kind of schismatic Greek I was fabricating!

The reader will at once appreciate the anxiety of the *maître d'études* on my behalf. You see, I was the nephew of Prospero Balbo, the president of the University! It was as clear as daylight that the nephew of the man who ruled over the careers of so many *maîtres d'études* must simply not be a dunce.

For half an hour our mentor vanished and then reappeared. He had made one of those decisions that are the saving of nephews and sometimes even of those set in authority over them. He had decided to do himself what I couldn't do and leave the honour to me.

With an agility worthy of Bosco, the conjurer, he removed my work, without my companions noticing, and left in its place a sheet of paper on which was a ready-made Greek essay. All I had to do was to copy it!

I must say to my credit that, having understood the dodge and, in a flash, the motive behind it, I felt bitterly humiliated and very loath to avail myself of the deception. But to my shame, I must add that I lacked the courage to let my praiseworthy sentiments influence my action. They had instilled obedience into me and my judgement on right and wrong was not sufficiently well founded to let me act on my own decisions. I therefore followed authority and barefacedly copied the Greek essay, which, naturally enough, was pronounced excellent. I heard my uncle Balbo, in conversation with my father, say that he could hardly believe I had such a remarkable leaning towards the dead languages. Imagine whether I could believe it either!

Prize-giving day came and I received in public from the hands of Count Balbo a fine well-bound folio volume, *Homeri Opera Omnia*,

with a compliment on my erudition. I still have it among my books
and I intend to leave it to a public library as restitution (the phrase is
not easy to pen, but I must do it) of stolen property.

I was certainly in the wrong, but that *maître d'études*! God forgive
him, he was worse than I was and he set me a very bad example. Bad
examples set by adults to children are real crimes.

The child's divine innocence really seems to suggest that the human
soul does come from the lap of the angels to be clothed in flesh. The
man who first stains it, who first defiles it with fraud, is guilty indeed.

I must confess that this episode, together with several others, and
perhaps too the over-severe pressure exerted on my mind, especially
with regard to religious matters, gave a bad slant to my character. All
forms of oppression, be they great or small, are the ruin of character.
Little by little I began to dissimulate and then, what is worse, to deceive,
and I told lies with ease. Later on, I cured myself of this defect and I
do believe that, for the last forty years, I am one of those in Europe who
have told fewer deliberate falsehoods than any of my contemporaries,
including my period as minister and diplomat, professions in which it is
supremely important not to lie, because the general public believes the
contrary. Men will finally be persuaded when they have grown to
understand that the most irresistible of forces is that based on the trust
you have been able to inspire.

Having concluded my classical studies with such success, I passed,
as is normal, to so-called philosophy, which I began at the age of about
thirteen at Turin University. Don Baruc taught logic and Vassalli Eandi
physics, Carena being his deputy. At this period my mind was beginning to develop and store things up. While the tutor-priest taught us
brothers Latin, the only thing he knew, our father spent time with us
in order to give us some variety by exploring the many varied branches
of learning. With him, we read literary works, poetry and the romantic
epics. Dante, Tasso, Pulci, Ariosto, etc., etc. were introduced to us.
Of course we were not allowed all they wrote; but the parts suitable
for young people were enough to give us an idea of their style, to train
our taste, and to provide matter for our father's comments. He was
widely read and had a most retentive memory. I preferred Dante and
Ariosto to all the rest and still do.

In this way I began to form my taste and get the habit of application and of reading, which I still have. It was a bad day for us if our
father caught us indulging in that Italian *dolce far niente*. Fortunately
the Piedmontese have never been very partial to such a habit.

We were gradually introduced to another occupation, that of writing stories and descriptions, real or imaginary, in our own words. One of us was often deputed to describe what we had seen after a walk or a visit to a beauty-spot, some country house or castle. This is a most useful practice for young people and I have mentioned it so that teachers may consider it.

So that children should have enough subject matter for their descriptions, it is well to get them to observe a variety of objects and places they see on their excursions. Our father took the opportunity to speak to us about the military possibilities of the features of the landscape. He trained us to find the way, to guess the points of the compass, to recognize places already passed; to judge the probability of finding water, the vicinity of built-up areas, the distance of peaks we were scaling, to gauge distances by eye, to appreciate the lie of the land, etc., etc. All these things can be very useful on innumerable occasions, not only in war, but in normal circumstances too.

In any case these were real soldiers' marches of eight, ten, or twelve Piedmontese miles.[1] I remember the longest, which lasted from the evening to two o'clock next day and was of twenty-five of our miles, that is to say some thirty-six ordinary Italian miles : I was under fourteen and, at the end, I was dead-beat and slept twenty hours without a break. What with our father, the priest, a servant, and us boys, all tall, proceeding one after the other in line through woods, over the hills, sometimes on roads, sometimes across country, we were not infrequently at night taken for robbers. I well remember on our famous pilgrimage to Oropa that at two o'clock in the morning we found we had lost our way not far from Serra, on the mountain-side near Ivrea. My father heard passers-by and said to me and another of us : 'Go and ask those people the way.' I ran down, but, when they saw us galloping towards them, they took to flight and wouldn't stop, however much I shouted.

You can see from this that our father wanted to have us grow up real men, in body as in mind. He therefore took pains to see we exercised ourselves in every possible way, to make us strong and agile. At that period there were no gymnasia, but, thanks to his loving care, we had them all the same, as he invented them. Before I was ten I was taught fencing and dancing; later, swimming and riding. Then he made us learn how to turn somersaults on the ground and from the spring-board, and to dance on a tight rope. My brother, the Jesuit, was then a novice and I well remember him turning somersaults in his long black priest's robe. Anyone seeing him turning on his own axis in this

[1] A Piedmontese mile was 2,466 metres.

sack-like garment would hardly have prophesied that one day he would be Father Taparelli, editor of the periodical *Civiltà Cattolica* and one of the big-wigs of the Jesuit order.

8

LIKE to like is not always a true proverb. I think that it would be difficult to find two men more completely opposite in political and religious opinions than my Jesuit brother and I. And it would be equally difficult to find two so fond of each other from childhood up to his death last year (1862). Since infancy, I always got on better with him than with my other two brothers. He was cleverer than I was and than all the others; he was far readier to sacrifice himself, and he had an unshakeable strength of character. He can be summed up in three simple little words: ability, goodness, character. Very simple, aren't they?

If only he had remained in the world, even as a priest, who knows what high destiny his happy disposition and strong character would not have prepared for him! Who can tell in what way he could have been useful to his Country, to society, and to his own religious and philosophical opinions! But in the strait-jacket of a monkish order, just see if you can be a great man! I know, because I have spent hours and hours in his cell with him, where no half-hour passed without a tiresome interruption. Imagine some excellent person writing, for example, on the subject of natural law. Tinkle, tinkle, tinkle, goes the bell. What is it? I have to teach the boys French grammar for a short period. *Amen.* Off he goes to teach French. He comes back and picks up the thread of an idea about natural law. After three quarters of an hour, Tinkle, tinkle, tinkle, once more. Oh! it's the triduum or the novena in chapel for St. Stanislaus Kostka or someone. *Amen.* To the novena he must go. Then he comes back and attacks natural law. After ten minutes, rap rap at the door. *Deo Gratias*, whines a nasal voice. Come in! A novice asking for guidance about some distraction during Mass, or a pupil who asks if Ancona is spelt with or without an H. Is it possible that a man forced to work under such difficult circumstances, both physical and moral, however strong his will and powerful his intellect, can achieve one quarter of what he would, free from such interruptions? It would be mad to suppose any such thing.

Indeed the Jesuits have distinguished and meritorious men among them (God knows what torture they have had to put up with) but none of the first class.

However, if my brother failed to reach that intellectual supremacy for which he was born; if he did not make an impression such as is the legacy of the truly great, as he might have done; he did bequeath to us a wonderful example of sacrifice and virtue which is worth more and serves a higher purpose for those able to discern it, than all the marvels of the intellect.

Please understand that I do not mean that we should all imitate him and become Jesuits, but here is where we could and should do so. He was a youth of fiery temperament, of impetuous passions, sometimes overwhelmed by outbursts of furious rage; he felt all the aspirations and desires implanted by God in human nature. He tamed and conquered them all. Before he was thirty he had attained such a sweet serenity of temper that I never again saw him angered. His mind and heart in harmony had conquered, one could say destroyed, what was material in him; indeed by his continual, inexorable, severity towards himself he ruined his health, which never recovered. He believed strongly in religion, in philosophy, and in politics, and during his entire life he sacrificed every convenience to the triumph of what he believed to be the truth. He had the good fortune, given to few, not to have even a shadow of doubt about religion; he had absolute certainty as to the truth he aspired to. His truth was certainly not my truth, nor the truth of many today. But as Pilate said: What is truth?

Let the man who has the answer to this step forward. If none can answer without reserve, let us at least respect all beliefs sincerely held and sacrifice ourselves for that truth vouchsafed to us, and for what our conscience bids us. In this my brother can be an example to anyone. He was born to a position that could have given him anything he wanted, yet he renounced everything. I have watched his life closely. I can affirm that, except for that intimate and, certainly, very great satisfaction that derives from doing one's duty, he never gratified himself during his whole life. His room had no comforts, no fire-place, no carpet, it was poorly furnished. He lay on a pallet bed which he made himself. His food was simple though appropriate, but without luxuries of any kind. There was continuous obedience, prolonged study, preaching, the carrying out of his ministry. Every night, summer and winter, he rose at three o'clock. If this is not self-sacrifice I do not know what else to call it.

I, for sure, am no Jesuit; I remember all the harm caused by some of their principles and machinations, but so much the more do I marvel when I observe them as individuals and see the kind of abnegation to which they condemn themselves. And what comes of all this? Either they do harm or get nowhere.

I do not, on the other hand, belong to the opposite party, which for me is the living image of the first, I mean the revolutionary extreme left. But I must say that the latter, although also leading to harm or ineffectiveness, yet in regard to the individuals concerned, have a long way to go before they reach the level of abnegation of my brother and his fellows.

On careful consideration one can find very odd parallels here. I restrict myself to pointing out the fact and leave its further treatment to those who like analysing human misery and folly. I must, however, make one parallel, and that is that I recognize one similarity between the Jesuits and the English. As individuals they are all excellent persons, but taken *en masse* they would cut the throats of their own parents for the sake of Old England or of the Society of Jesus. As they normally hate each other, I make my apologies to both for having drawn such a parallel.

To return to my brother; he very nearly had to adopt another walk in life. Napoleon had nominated him for the military academy of St. Cyr, via the Prefect of Turin, A. Lameth. It was a bomb-shell for my father and the whole family. A man such as my father to feel wounded in the most hallowed of his rights, his authority as a father, something acknowledged by all at all times, the right to educate and direct his own children as he thought best, and to see two of them snatched away (Roberto was nominated at the same time a probationer clerk in the Magistrate's department of the Council of State) by the enemy of his country, by the man who had plucked Pius VII from the Quirinal, he whose ambition and insensate pride was now intoxicating him, as was becoming clearer than ever after the treachery of Bayonne; and to have no means of defence against him! It was enough to break his heart.

I was not of an age to appreciate such things to the full, but I well remember the gloom that overshadowed the house for a time. This is what I thought then, and still do: Napoleon was a tyrant, and ten Austerlitzes and twenty Wagrams are not enough to excuse a single act of violence, or one natural right trampled under foot.

Yet, thanks to the good sense of mankind, Napoleon, who for his own satisfaction caused a million men to be slaughtered, and broke the hearts of countless fathers and mothers; Napoleon is famous even among remote peoples; while the man who has saved millions from death and dried the tears of their parents, the inventor of vaccine, I wager my reader doesn't even know his name. Well, he was called Edward Jenner, and was born on the seventeenth of May 1749 at Berkeley in Gloucestershire. And I, who am preaching to you, have had to look him up in the *Dictionnaire de la conversation*, to remind myself about him. Reader, let us at any rate remember his name!

Now let us return to my family. My brother Roberto was eighteen years old when he had to go to Paris to take up his new appointment. He was accompanied by Cesare Balbo, Prié, Guasco, and Collegno, who had all been posted as he had. Giacinto Collegno went to the St. Cyr military academy. All these men, in various roles, achieved distinction and many of them played a major part in the political affairs of Piedmont and Italy. Owing to my father's exertions, the government postponed for a year Prospero's enrolment at St. Cyr. He was then barely sixteen. Roberto, however, had to go at once, and my father accompanied him to Paris. The year's grace soon passed and my father had, once more, to take the dreary road through Savoy, Lyonnais, and Burgundy, with the second victim of Napoleon's despotism. However, he worked to such purpose that, by the help of friends and, if I recall aright, of Monsignor della Torre, Archbishop of Turin (pro-French and Count of the Empire, etc.), he succeeded in bringing back his son to Turin, free to follow the profession of his choice, that of the Church. He received his first ordination at the hand of the Archbishop, began his ecclesiastical studies, and started on the road which he followed all the days of his life.

Of my two sisters, Melania, who had stayed with our grandmother in Turin while we were in Tuscany, died when she was twelve. Metilde, who married Count Pallio di Rinco, was a beauty. Thanks to an excellent education and the good examples she had had, no less than through her own angelic nature, she turned out a real treasure.

It is a commonplace for all elegiac poets to say: 'Such and such were too good, too angelic; the world was unworthy of them; God wanted them in Heaven.' Yet, in sober truth, experience sometimes bears out what the poets say. There are people so perfect, with such heavenly natures, that they seem to have come to earth by mistake, to have strayed here. They soon pass on and are mourned and no one marvels at their disappearance.

So it was with Metilde, companion of my boyhood. I have her portrait with clasped hands, as in prayer, with a blue veil over her head, just as Carlo Dolci used to paint his young Madonnas, and in truth she resembled them. She died of consumption before she was twenty-two, at the Castle of Rinco near Asti. I never think of her without calling to mind her close resemblance to those charming angels of Fra Angelico, dressed in fluttering robes down to their feet, with their blue, delicate, pointed wings!

The reader must forgive me for these dreams of long ago. All but a few have now forgotten her, poor little girl, and I have wanted to commemorate her once more, while I am still alive to do so.

Her death was an unspeakable grief to us. But nature, which allots a dawn, noon, and night to each generation, sees to it that childhood is incapable of those long, intense, conscious sorrows, which shake the grown man and shorten the last span of old age. My age at that time lessened and made supportable the grief I have since felt on looking back when grown up. But our parents can be said to have died with her.

Years after, I recall, they could not listen to the music of Paer's *Agnese,* and especially the duet between the distracted father and Agnese:

> That sepulchre encloses
> My daughter's last remains.

My poor mother's constitution was still more shaken, after so many agitations, by this new blow.

We have now reached August 1813, the date of Metilde's death. My education had dragged on indifferently at the University, where I argued in syllogisms under Don Barucchi and wrote my physics notes in Latin under dictation by the well-known and esteemed Vassalli Eandi. In order that I should get some idea into my head of arithmetic, algebra, and geometry, my father put me under Professor Giorgio Bidone, who afterwards made a name for himself in pure mathematics and hydraulics.

As will presently be seen, I was to owe so much to this man that I ought to kiss the ground on which he trod. After my father and mother, there is no one in the world who has put me under such obligations, but this is not the moment to speak of them.

He toiled and sweated to teach me arithmetic, algebra, and the rest, but all to no purpose. Heaven had not granted me an aptitude for figures. It is very odd that my mind is always, quite naturally, calculating causes, consequences, probabilities, etc., of events, but immediately figures appear it jibs and that's the end of the matter.

Despite my mental inertia and the little good I derived from his teaching, my tutor gradually grew very fond of me. Rather than from his scientific instruction, I drew the greatest advantage from discussing things with him. This was something my poor priest had never been able to provide, although it is one of the foundations of a good educational system. Little by little I learnt how to think, reflect, discard false ideas and discover truer ones. Bidone, one could say, was reshaping my brain, rather as the surgeon and midwife do to a newborn baby, in an attempt to give a better shape to the soft parietal sides of the cranium. From then on I began to judge men by their honesty and knowledge, and things by their real utility. According to this method you can, if opportunity offers, do noble, great, and useful things, but you must appreciate from the start that it is not the way to get on in the world. This is fair warning to anyone who complains later that by following my ideas he is on the way to starve to death.

Since coming back from Florence, my father and the whole family had led a very retired life. The only people who came to the house were a few old, tried friends. They all belonged, of course, to the so-called Branda movement (named after Branda Lucioni, a royalist partisan leader of the republican era), men who have now no such appellation, as they are no longer a factor in politics. Those who are dubbed Codini by our young men of today would have been considered as so many Marats by the members of the Branda movement. My father did not agree with their foolishness and laughed at them. We boys, who knew all about their stupid goings-on, spoke out so frankly about them that we gradually grew into liberals to prove the truth of the law of opposites. It all ended in smoke. My father and most of his friends had sworn to do nothing against Napoleon and, even to see the most ardent of their hopes realized, the liberation of Piedmont from foreign rule, they would not break their oath.

Then came the time of the persecutions of the Pope, cardinals, bishops, etc., and their notorious consequences. Piedmont, being on the road between Rome and Paris, saw a constant coming and going of all kinds of clergy, blown hither and thither like dead leaves by that whirlwind mind, which lacked judgement, but still kept its brilliance.

Napoleon III would never have been so childish.

My father's constant preoccupation was to help these victims of persecution in every way he could. When Napoleon, having failed in his machinations, had recourse to violence, and the prisons, specially the fortress of Fenestrelle, were filled with cardinals and bishops, my father, who had sworn not to oppose Napoleon, but not to help him persecute others, became most active in bringing assistance, comfort, and hope to the poor captives.

We used to see him continually on the go; in town and country; now here, now there; always alone (a good way to avoid spies) in his one-horse gig (you don't see them now, but they were known as Padovanelli). He went wherever the work demanded, without a fear in the world, because it was a matter of his religion, and for that he would have sacrificed himself, us, and everything else.

He became at that time a close friend of Cardinal Gregorio, then imprisoned in Fenestrelle. He succeeded in getting to see him and other cardinals and priests. All of them were suffering for conscience sake and they were all, on that account, worthy of respect. To think what these priests had been a few years before, and what they had become! From out of that ignoble quagmire of corruption and trickery such as was the old Roman Curia, to see so many noble, strong, fine characters appear, who had dared to say no to Napoleon, then considered as powerful and eternal as fate itself! They had left their fine palaces and the mild climate of Rome and tranquilly took up their abode in the cells of a fortress where it snowed even in June. Could they know when they would ever get out? Who could have dreamed then of Moscow and Napoleon's defeat on the Beresina?

The power of self-sacrifice can renew and ennoble human nature to such an extent! But another idea strikes me at once. Must the mysterious decree be immutable that says that all that is good, grand, and noble in the world derives from suffering? But I really mustn't go on like this or goodness knows where I shall finish! I am half afraid I shall be growing too much of a Jeremiah with my continual philosophizing. However, the reader can always skip the pages that bore him, so he's the only one to blame if he gets bored.

I have just said that Napoleon gave the impression to men of that age of a fate impossible to resist. It was true. Imagine the bewilderment of all those people who felt crushed under that enormous weight, without hope of salvation, loathing their disaster and shame, when there came a first gleam of a possible deliverance! Borne on the wind, one can say, there came a rumour: Napoleon has been beaten! Napoleon is in retreat!

I have been through a time of reaction; I know what it means; but not even that experience can ever make me regret (that blessed French word *regretter* has no Italian equivalent) Napoleon and French rule in Italy, although true it is that we were losing a government which, when all's said and done, was eventually to lead to the triumph of principles

F

which are the very life of human society; to go back once more to an inept government of bemused, prejudiced, ignoramuses. Nobody considered this at the time, and even had they done so, I think that all of us—certainly my father and I—would have said: 'Let the Devil himself come, but out with the French.' And because we feel like that in Piedmont, foreigners have had short shrift with us.

The vague rumour, meanwhile, had become certain, beyond all doubt. The famous communiqué Number 29 announced a great disaster, and who could doubt its truth?

There was a stirring among the people, a feeling of coming to life, a deep agitation of hopes, fears, unlooked-for joy and unlooked for terror, because after all *he* was still alive. Moments so well described by Manzoni in the chorus of his tragedy *Adelchi*:

> *Un volgo sprezzato repente si desta,*
> *protende l'orecchio, solleva la testa.*[1]

Meanwhile the flood of good news kept pouring in. The whole of Europe, not Italy alone, awoke to the great discovery that Napoleon could be beaten.

The peoples called to one another like soldiers waking in a camp; they stretched out their hands; they banded together, keeping close, in order to rush on the wounded lion. The year 1813 passed in the anxiety of continuous possible alternatives. Meanwhile there began to appear those long processions of employés, both civil and military, last disintegration of a failing power; people uprooted by the enemy, who drove them in flocks before his advance. Troops began to pass, ragged, wan, tragic, downcast (no longer those threatening looks!). Then came ambulances, waggons, carts full of wounded. New hospitals were made ready. There were not enough beds, so they had to make do with straw, first in one line, then in two, then strewn along just as it came. Then there was no more room and the wounded were laid under gateways, under any sort of projection, in the snow, in the rain; they died from their hardships. So many died along the road, after God knows what suffering. Shaken in rude waggons, crushed under heaps of their comrades, I saw them as they were unloaded! How many poor youths, boys almost, lifted up by those unloading and found to be dead and dropped back again. Then they lugged them out by the feet and threw them down for the grave-diggers. How many fathers without a prop for their old age, how many mothers without support, how many

---

[1] A people scorned is suddenly roused,
listens intent, raises its head.

desolate widows, how many ruined families were not represented by only a single one of those cartloads! Why? For whom?

It was from these early impressions, I think, that I have fixed and riveted in my mind the profound hatred I feel for conquerors, for ambitious men, for all that evil crew, who, had they only drunk the blood of 200,000 men for a whim, all right! but they have also contrived to get themselves celebrated, admired, I almost said adored, by all the silly fools whose blood they have spilled!

You can well believe that my father rejoiced with all his soul, certainly not at the suffering to be seen on all sides, but at the immense collapse of the greatest and most invincible of tyrannies. It provided also a rare opportunity to instil sound ideas and virtuous principles in us young people, and he was not the man to let it slip.

Under more normal circumstances my brother Enrico and I, the two youngest, had been taken by the priest to visit the sick poor in the garrets they inhabit in Turin. (This is an excellent practice. For many reasons it is good that the rich should get to know the poor and the poor the rich.) We used to take comforts and sympathy to these unfortunates. Let those with young people to educate imitate my father's practice in this. One quickly learns that all do not find their dinner ready for them when the bell rings, and that is all to the good.

Now in this great calamity, in this flood of new suffering, he sent us to visit the hospital of St. John and other military hospitals, without being too particular about the prevalent typhus and other epidemic fevers. I still recall the sad spectacle of those poor wounded soldiers lying on stinking chopped straw, in filthy rags, to whom we brought what few restoratives we could, seeing the great number of sufferers. In this way our father taught us that for a miserable, beaten, wounded, human being, there is no such word as foreigner; Frenchman, German, or Chinese. He is a brother, or better still a fellow-man (the word brother seems now rather a debased coin!) whom one must succour for the love of Christ, if one is a Christian; if not, for the love of God; and should you be an atheist for love of yourself, confound you!

I thank God I have never forgotten what I learnt then, and when later I had enemy prisoners under me, wounded and in a bad way, I do not think they could have had any complaint against me.

9

At long last that blessed day came when we had the great news that Napoleon was no longer our master and we were about to be free and independent.

Those who did not see Turin on that day, do not know what a people is like in a delirium of joy. I do not say this without some regret, because no one more than I recognizes the enormous debt of gratitude we owe to the Napoleonic family. No one more than I knows the value of every drop of generous French blood spilled on Italian soil, for the redemption of Italy in 1859. But all the same, it is true and must be said, there was immense satisfaction at seeing the French go.

I add at once, however, that there was as great a difference as between day and night, between the French army of those earlier days and that of the present. I do not speak of military skill and valour. There was no lack of both, then as now; what I refer to is the spirit, the habits, the sentiments and conscience of the two armies. From this point of view, all the advantage belongs to the army of today.

It is said that the French know how to make conquests, but not keep them, and it is a true saying. It is also claimed that the Teutons find it difficult to capture what belongs to others, but once they get their claws on it they do not lose their grip, which in general terms is also true enough. Yet which of the two peoples has a better character? Without doubt the French are immeasurably superior. How do we explain this phenomenon then?

It is to be explained by the fact that the French carry the full weight of their vanity like Simon the Cyrenian who bore Christ's cross; the Teutons, on the contrary, are quite ready to hoist your cross on their shoulders, provided they are masters in your house! Men are generally so made that a master who robs them with a modest air, humbly, almost begging pardon for his presumption, is more tolerable than a master who may rob them of less, but who makes them feel, by his words, acts, gestures, and looks, that he is everything and you are not worth a fig.

If the great, noble, generous, agreeable French nation could only exchange its vanity for an equal quantity of real honest pride, such as that of its neighbours over the Channel, it would then really be the first among all other nations, past, present, and to come.

I have such a high opinion of that nation that I have no doubt that, one day or other, it will be prepared to make such an exchange. It is certain that not only the army, as I have said, but also the civilian employees and ordinary citizens, are progressing since the fall of the first Empire, and we all know what grateful memories the army of occupation left behind when it went back over the mountains three years ago.

It was otherwise under the first Empire, when we called after them, 'Don't come back', as the toad said to the harrow in the Tuscan proverb. Not to mince matters: the military insolence and the civilian *hauteur* of those days was quite intolerable and I have a vivid recollection of it. I shall never forget something that happened in our house, when the French army was in full retreat towards Mont Cenis. Some major or colonel or other had a billeting ticket for the Azeglio mansion. That was quite in order, for at such times of crisis all must help the town authorities. My father, however, had rented decent quarters in an inn for the officer so as not to disturb the household, seeing that my mother was still an invalid and we were all, more or less, children. The officer was not satisfied and, what was less in order, tried to storm the very part of our house where we were living ourselves, shouting and swearing as he did so.

The good man, one well understands, was in a bad temper at the time, but he was in the wrong.

I can still see my father, not famous for his patience, facing him at the top of the staircase, seizing him by the lapel of his coat, and forcing him to beat a retreat. The Frenchman broke out into oaths; my father, furious, was raging with clenched teeth; Don Andreis, the family chaplain, was protesting; we children, like small dogs who start barking if they have someone to back them up, followed him calling out rude names in French; Giacolin, Pilade, and the chamber-maids, in a compact group all together, made such a din about the poor officer's ears that he could stand no more and turned tail.

We all trooped downstairs after him; then into the courtyard; then hatless into the street. As was to be expected, people started coming out from the workshops and quite a crowd assembled from the neighbourhood.

This was enough, for it was plain that a riot might develop, so of one accord we quietened things down. The good colonel went off to his inn and we returned home to rest on our laurels.

Our joy at seeing the French go was soon followed by another, not quite so great, that of *seeing the Austrians arrive*.

I have to pinch myself, my dear reader, to make sure that it is really I who have penned the above words. And I find I am that person, body and soul. But the reader doesn't require me to explain what Austrians meant for us then, and what they have come to mean later.

A change of masters is always, and at all periods, a glorious time for rascals of all kinds. To prevent pillage a national guard was quickly formed, the so-called Guardia Urbana.

At sixteen I was as tall and robust as though I were twenty. I was wild to see everything, to do things, to run about; I was so full of life that I seemed to have a very devil inside me, and I had an irresistible longing to kick over the traces. The conditions were favourable, the whole place being upside down in holiday mood; my father, as you can imagine, had so many thoughts, so much business, so many interests, desires, and hopes to keep him fully occupied, that he had little time to spare for attending to the family. I only had to overcome my poor Don Andreis and my victory was full, complete, and absolute.

We have reached the moment when we must say farewell to that good priest, whose only fault was lack of intelligence, but who otherwise was an excellent soul and conscientiously did all he thought would do me good. I recognize my debt to him and I preserve an affectionate memory of him and sincerely respect him. So much the more, as the boring things he made me do prevented me from appreciating his good qualities, and I was therefore unjust to him. It's incredible the harm bores do without meaning it!

Here I must steel myself to make a confession and tell a story, which although not precisely about our last parting, certainly only shortly preceded it, and is therefore appropriate.

We used to spend our school holidays in a villa on the hill behind Moncaliari, near a village called Revigliasco. There we did enough work to prevent us from forgetting our past studies; otherwise we concentrated on physical activities; running about, jumping, and going out shooting, etc., etc. In an attic I had discovered an old gun which must have been used during the war of the Polish Succession. By dint of much labour with emery powder, alburnum, oil, and especially elbow grease, I had got it into a state where it could be fired. At first secretly, then, finding I was tolerated, half openly, I used to go shooting with the priest and my brothers, without my father hearing anything about it. I don't know what was wrong with the works of that blessed gun, but I do know what it used to do every time I fired it—give a terrible kick! That is what gave me away, because I developed an obstinate bruise on my right cheek-bone which finally caught my father's attention. There were no ill consequences from the discovery and all finished in a scolding. What is more, he was so sympathetic about my cheek, that he gave me a nice little gun in good order on my birthday, so that at least my cheek-bone suffered no more.

During one of those shooting expeditions, when I was alone with Don Andreis, I started to pick a quarrel with him for some trifling reason I have forgotten. Little by little I warmed up; we raised our voices, started to shout, then to get really angry, finally—I really don't know who began it, probably I—we were all at once punching and kicking each other; using, thank goodness, only those arms provided by nature and not man-made weapons. As I was tall, strong, fit, and nimble as a cat, and what is more as every one of my blows represented the breaking of a five-year-long patience, you can imagine what a blind fury I was in and how I pummelled him. I was out of my mind! The poor priest got away bedraggled, torn, and bleeding, with half his lip severed in the scuffle. Naturally enough he reported what had happened.

I expected to be annihilated! That very evening the rural dean from Revigliasco, a certain Don Rinaldi, often in our house, called me on one side and told me that my father was very angry and considered me unworthy of his presence, and that, having the care of souls of the parish, he had to inform me that I had deserved excommunication as one who, at the prompting of the devil, had struck a priest—*qui percutiet clericum, suadente diabolo*, etc. I listened with hanging head, as modest as could be, waiting for what was to come, but as nothing much seemed to be happening, I looked up and asked, as meek as a lamb, what precisely excommunication meant, so that I could act accordingly.

'You', pronounced the rural dean, 'are cut off from membership of the Church Militant and can therefore take no part in Church services until it pleases the bishop to absolve you.'

You must know that the villa had a chapel where we all forgathered every evening to repeat the prayers of the rosary together. A special rosary interspersed with lots of *oremus*, litanies, and other prayers which seemed endless; absolute torture for me. The first thing that came into my mind, therefore, was the rosary service. With tearful voice I said: 'Not even the rosary?' 'Certainly, you are forbidden all services of the Church.' Well, I thought, it's an ill wind that blows nobody any good and I do believe that, *suadente diabolo*, I really blessed the pounding I had given the priest.

From next day there was an end of Masses, prayers, novenas, and tapers! At rosary times I went off to the meadows to catch crickets. It really was a restful period.

Unfortunately the Archbishop of Turin spoilt it all. After a few days the rural dean called me into the sacristy, pulled out a letter, and read it to me. It was a long whitewashing rigmarole written by the Superior of the Order about my crime, giving me absolution from all excommunication and censure on condition, etc., provided that, etc., etc., as long as, etc., etc., etc.

I put on the most relieved air I could manage and was readmitted into the, not very joyful, embrace of the evening service, to the greater glory, quiet, and satisfaction of the meadow crickets.

Ever since then, however, I had doubts, later turned to certainty, that the whole business of the excommunication, bishop's letter, and so on was a put-up job, intended to make a deep impression on my mind and cure me from any inclination to hit priests, should I live a hundred years.

It was, in fact, a pious fraud, own sister to the admonition *pie credendum*, and like all frauds, pious or not, it had the great fault of being subject to being found out, as they always are. They then make things worse instead of better.

I compare fraud to brandy; at the moment it gives you strength, but afterwards it leaves you more feeble than before.

When I joined the National Guard, for which I easily got permission, I made the first step of my military career, and my education came to a full stop. It was only later, after I had got a little more judgement, that I began to educate myself from the beginning. My father was not displeased at the martial ardour I displayed at that time, but in order not to give me free rein—I was not yet sixteen—he had the patience to take service himself and mount guard, go on patrol, and drill on the square, etc., along with us.

King Vittorio Emanuele I had meanwhile left Cagliari and was due to arrive. There were no native national troops, so that the National Guard had to do service for the royal entry into Turin. All of us, officers and men, were busily occupied in learning, at least, how to parade and form column, without getting into a jumble.

On May 20 (1814) this longed-for and much invoked King at last arrived. I was lined up in Piazza Castello and I well remember the King and his entourage. They were all dressed in antiquated style, with powdered hair in pigtails, and eighteenth-century tricorn hats à la Federico II. They made a very odd picture, but everything seemed lovely to me and to all the rest of us; just as it should be. The customary *cris mille fois répétés* greeted the good monarch, so that he can have had no doubts about the affection and sympathy of his faithful inhabitants of Turin.

That evening, of course, there was a grand illumination, as spontaneous as it was splendid. The Court came out to see it, that is to say the King, the Queen, and their daughters, just a family party, unless I am wrong, without any suite. I don't know if the horses and carriages of Prince Borghese (the ex-governor of Turin) had disappeared, or if, probably enough, the royal family did not wish to use them. I well know that His Majesty did not own a single carriage or a pair of horses, so that my father presented him with a big old ceremonial coach that he had used at his wedding, all gilt and glass, with dropsical cupids on the doors.

In this very coach, the good King, with that sawney face of his, let's admit it, but honest enough—the proof came in 1821—rode through the streets of Turin up to one o'clock in the morning, amid the hurrahs of the crowd, scattering smiles and bows to right and left as he went, which consequently meant that his pigtail wagged from side to side too, an extraordinary sight for boys of my age.

This was the time when all rulers were returning to their capitals. It was known that the Pope would soon be back, so the King wished to send his felicitations as quickly as possible; it being as traditional in the House of Savoy to pay respect to the Pope as it had been to be firm with the Roman curia.

My father was chosen to be the envoy, and it was certainly impossible to find a more suitable representative of the political principles, as well as of the religious faith, of the two Princes.

The nomination having been made and conveyed to him, he had to leave without delay. My poor mother was still ailing, despite her happiness about the recent events, and took fright at the idea that I, in my boisterous mood, should stay in her charge. She easily persuaded my father to take me with him.

We went off in two carriages, he, and I, and Prospero, who had decided to join the newly re-established company of Jesuits. The whole of Italy was upside-down. Italians, employees and soldiers, were pouring back; the French were departing. The roads were swarming like an ant heap with these two currents of traffic.

Before we reached the Appenines, I remember we met a poor youth returning from the army, half crippled. I fell into talk with him at a place where our horses had to go at walking pace; it was a piece of good luck for him. I invited him into the carriage and he got home in no time, instead of dragging along on foot for goodness knows how many days.

We reached Rome late at night. It was half-way through June and

the plaster triumphal arches were still standing in the streets, put up
for Pope Giulio and, at Ponte Molle, for the return of Pope Pio VII,
who had arrived a few days before. We got down at the palace at the
end of Piazza Mignanelli, then an inn. Next morning early (typical of
Rome) there was a band blowing trumpets and beating drums outside
our windows. What ever's this? Oh, papal retainers come to welcome
your excellency! Anyone with any feeling realizes he must respond to
such cordiality with a handful of coins.

Rome, as indeed the whole of Europe, presented the appearance of a
tract of country, or some quarter of a city, just visited by a violent
hurricane, which the wind had swept away elsewhere. People stare
at each other, happy to be still alive as they gaze at the landslides,
mounds of gravel, collapsed buildings, floods, uprooted trees, roofs
blown off, and chimneys tumbled. But they are still alive and the tempest has gone, so it isn't so bad and they feel happy. It's only a question
of time and money. To it! All to work, singing and congratulating
themselves; some to mend, others to hoist, protect, renew, re-build—
such was Europe, such was Rome.

The Romans had not yet experienced a *Papa neto* (an absolute Pope)
such as the *Rey neto* of the Spaniards. Everyone knows that the previous temporal governments, as bad as they were, had been restrained
by agreements, contracts, provincial and communal rights, customs,
and traditions; therefore much less bad than the one established by
Cardinal Consalvi and his officials, apeing Napoleon. The latter had
left to Europe, as a souvenir, the legacy of the most ingenious instruments ever invented by despotism, that is to say, police and bureaucracy.

The Romans, as indeed the rest of Europe, could not foresee that
the leaders and gentry, representing the restored governments, would
be so foolish as not to understand how different people were in 1814
from what they had been in 1789. They could not persuade themselves
that under no circumstances would men renounce those benefits
created by the genius of Napoleon and the march of time, to which they
had grown accustomed.

Rulers and ministers, back from exile, found it convenient to accept
Napoleon's legacy, disclaiming liability. They kept police, bureaucracy,
taxes, disproportionately large armies, etc.; but the good legal and
administrative system, the stimulation given to merit and the sciences,
class equality, the improvement and extension of communications,
liberty of conscience, and so many other excellent features of the rule
of the great warrior they threw out of the window.

In Italy, especially, the political state, the new despotism, could be defined as: Napoleon dressed as a Jesuit. The spear of Achilles in the hand of Thersites!

Two States specially distinguished themselves by this far-seeing, intelligent political attitude: Rome and Piedmont.

We shall speak of Turin presently. Meanwhile I can say of Rome that all was put back as before, *in primis et ante omnia.* I saw the return of the court of summary jurisdiction, police spies, instruments of torture, etc., etc., etc., and everything of that sort.

The Romans were not then thinking of political questions, neither was I, so I only saw a city full of life and happiness, and I enjoyed all this splendid novelty with the vivacious ardour of youth.

Pius VII soon granted my father an audience, and received him as deserved such a constant devotee of the Papacy, who had so recently given such courageous assistance to persecuted cardinals and bishops, and now came in the name of the pious, devoted King of Sardinia.

My father's instructions were, first to congratulate the Pope on his return, then to remain provisionally in Rome as minister, until the arrival of the Marquis di San Saturnino, the permanent representative of Sardinia attached to the Holy See.

We therefore took an apartment in the Fiano palace on the Corso in order to have what was requisite for a short period as representative. So there I was, almost without realizing it, a diplomat, an attaché, almost half an embassy secretary. In one month, from university student I had become a member of the Diplomatic Corps, with a uniform of the guards established on the King's arrival and given to me on my release from the previous civic guard.

Was it perhaps a foretaste of the numerous transformations and metamorphoses that were to come during my long career?

Thanks to my position, I found myself at the centre of the high society of Rome, both clerical and lay, not to speak of the Diplomatic Corps, then only in process of formation. All governments had so much business on their hands that they found it difficult to do anything systematically. Count von Lebzeltern soon appeared for Austria. An Abbé Sambucy, if my memory serves me, represented the provisional government of France; there were others I don't remember. Cardinal Consalvi was at the Congress of Vienna. Cardinals Pacca, Somaglia, De Gregorio were very intimate with my father; as were Monsignor Morozzo, my great-uncle, Riario, Frosini, Ugolini, all cardinals later, and many others. We often saw members of the Massimo, Patrizio, Torlonia, and Piccolomini families. As I always liked to associate with good, simple people, and had no ambitions to mix with the great, I saw a good deal of the Orengos. Of Piedmontese extraction, they had been settled for a century in Rome, where, from father to son, they had filled the office of Sardinian expeditor or official forwarding agent.

Then, and always, they treated me with most affectionate consideration and I shall always be happy to express publicly the gratitude I feel towards them.

There were many distinguished men in arts and letters living at Rome at the time. I knew Canova; Thorwaldsen; Rauch; Camuccini; Landi; Chauvin; Marianna Dionigi; the latter's daughter Orfei; Ferretti, poet and author of many of Rossini's libretti; the Abbé Coppi; Gherardo de' Rossi, writer of comedies.

All this group formed a gay society, full of life and animation. Napoleon had inspired that generation and they were not in the least like the snail-like creatures who flourished later for so long, under the protection of Jesuits, of big thrones, little thrones, usurped thrones, and of the Austro-Bourbon-Italic princelings. God rest their souls!

In this lively environment I drank greedily, as some poet or other puts it, the breath of a new life of the imagination, so that at last I felt I was living.

10

ACCORDING to my father's educational system one should never waste time. In making the best use of it, one should always take all opportunities that offer. In our situation, the best thing to do was, undoubtedly, to seize the chance of getting to know Rome. We therefore went the rounds; first with Signor Visconti, son or nephew of Ennio Quirino Visconti the antiquarian; then with Signor Malvotti, a painter.

Roman history was then accepted by all just as the ancient historians had handed it down. The splendid modern works of Niebuhr and other Germans, of Thierry, Ampère, Micali, and many others on the origins of Italy, had not yet, I will not say discovered all the true facts, but at least demonstrated with how much reserve we must accept the mass of previous history. We therefore only got from Signor Visconti the confirmation of what we already knew. We had the whole repertory of antiquity displayed before us, spun out in detail, far more than was necessary, for the benefit of guides, custodians, *laquais de place*, attendants, vinedressers, and such like, who keep one as long as possible in order to deserve a larger tip from the visitor. We had the whole stock-in-trade, without leaving out a single brick, and we had to swallow, with the faith of Moslems, Romulus, Clelia, Scaevola, Horace, and the Pons Sublicius: the entire cast of that ancient drama.

Antiquarianism is one of the few subjects possible under priestly rule. It would indeed be difficult to discover subversive tendencies in it. I must, however, admit that the venerable relics of ancient Rome which stimulated the minds of Gibbon and Goethe did not produce a great impression on my own poor little brain.

It was novelty I loved, not antiquity, at that time, and Signor Malvotti was just the man for me. I began to explore Rome and its environs from the point of view of art. With him, I visited the sculpture museums, the picture galleries, all the churches, palaces, and buildings that contained important objects, or claimed to do so. This second series of visits interested me far more than the first, and I must admit that the personality of my guide had a lot to do with it.

Visconti was an old man with white hair, all in black with knee-breeches and an enormous three-cornered hat, who never wandered from the subject he was expounding. Malvotti, on the other hand, was a debonair fellow, about thirty, gay, crazy as all artists were before the invention of *serious men*. He talked about everything under the sun, all that could be seen and, when my clerical brother was out of earshot, enjoyed. Rascals recognize each other at first sight and Signor Malvotti and I understood one another before we had scarcely exchanged a word.

The second tour over, Prospero began to frequent the Jesuits in preparation for taking the habit. Having seen the pictures and the statues with the gay Malvotti, I now began to study the living models. Here begins one of the most unsatisfactory periods of my life; I am ashamed of it and wish I could forget it. Instead of which I remember it as though it were yesterday, except that, thinking of myself as I then was, I seem to be seeing another person altogether, some bad lot I had casually met and with whom I later broke as bad company.

That is really so, thank God; four or five years later I discarded the Massimo of those days like a soiled garment. I should willingly skip that period, but it can't be done! I must play fair, not only with my reader, but with myself, otherwise I should treat my story like a pear with a worm in it, cut away the bad and present the good. I might also make a mistake in doing so.

If I early began to break loose, too early, it was due to Signor Malvotti. However was it that my father had not chosen a more reliable man? The fact was that a Monsignore had recommended him and a Monsignore cannot err through malice, ignorance, or carelessness. My father's profound sincerity in religion, his unshakeable faith, had led him to have a kind of exalted love for the Pope, above all, but also for the whole Church hierarchy. The rogues in the clerical party, lay or ecclesiastic, abused his loyal, noble nature on several occasions, and I shall speak of this later.

A very useful lesson is to be learnt here. When party feeling runs high, as today, it is a common affectation to call our side the good, and the opponents the bad. As though it were in the realm of possibility to divide a country in this way; let us say five million honest folk here and five million rogues there! Anyone whose mind works like that is, naturally, easily taken in or swindled by someone believed honest only because he belongs to your party. So that this should not occur, beware of choosing friends and confidants only because of the colour of their favour. Bear in mind also that two opposite opinions held by two parties cannot both be equally true, good, and logical; but two men belonging to two such opposed parties can either be two arrant rogues or two honest men.

It was during my stay in Rome in 1814 that I developed that decided inclination for painting that has remained with me until today. Although the antiquities and remains of Roman grandeur failed to attract me, I was enormously impressed by the still greater and more permanent grandeur of the Campagna, 'that vast unhealthy region that calls itself a State'. True enough, but it is a region that will always be the love, poetry, and desperation of artists, just like certain *femmes fatales*. One doesn't know why, but once you have seen and been in the company of such women, their presence fascinates and their absence afflicts you.

The usual school drawing lessons, with the usual *fricassée* of ears, noses, mouths, etc., had wearied me with their boring pedantry. It is true enough that I used to dash off horses, knights, and thousands of other things, defacing my school texts and exercise books in the process, but Heaven defend us from taking this habit for a prognostic of future artistic ability. Let fathers and mothers bear this in mind and save themselves sad disappointments!

In Rome, however, I really felt a flame kindle within me, presage and motive force of that long-drawn struggle with oneself and with the perplexities of technique and art. I told my father all about it and, with his usual intelligent affection, he gave me every assistance.

My first master was a Calabrian called Don Ciccio de Capo. Despite his babyish name, Don Ciccio was eighty and he belonged to the old school, put into the shade during the Empire period by Woogd, Verstappen, Bassi, and Therlink. The previous school was mannerist, the new one meticulously realist.

Anyone who knows Rome will remember several large landscapes which used to adorn the Caffè del Veneziano in Piazza Sciarra. They were compositions of large masses and very effective. They were the work of my old master, whom I remember with affection for his rare modesty. He often said when I praised his painting: 'Nowadays the landscape painters are so good, I can't paint as well any longer.'

Under his guidance I began to daub canvas with oil and get some practice with palette and paints, covering myself with splashes as always at first attempts, but immersing myself up to the neck in the task.

Besides painting, I took up music once more and with greater gusto than before when, as part of my educational plan, I studied under the maestro Tagliabò of Turin. He never succeeded in getting me to repeat the notes of the scale without several mistakes. In Rome, however, I began to feel enthusiastic for this lovely art, and I took it up with great keenness.

Ever afterwards, and to an increasing extent, I have been passionately fond of music. My father was most proficient in it, he read music with ease, and as it was not then usual to have a piece transposed for violin, cello, and piano, he accompanied from the full score. This is a very difficult thing to do as one has to be familiar with all keys. He had a rich, expressive bass voice, not very varied, but most suitable for the ancient music, which he loved.

My Jesuit brother, however, was better than any of us. He knew counterpoint and composed. He wrote pieces of sacred music and could be said to be a first-rate performer on the piano—for those days at any rate, because there has been enormous progress in this, as in so much else nowadays.

What is more he invented a new instrument, which he called a *violicembalo*. In this, by means of the normal keyboard, mechanism is set in motion by which notes are sounded by the vibration of strings obtained by the rubbing of hairs as by a violin bow. As notes can be held on this instrument and expression thus obtained, the slow passages are more effective than the quick light ones. The Emperor of Russia acquired one of these instruments.

As far as I was concerned I never learnt music thoroughly, though, by nature, I had a not unpleasing flexible voice and some taste in singing, if I do not deceive myself. There was a time when I only thought of semi-quavers, but, having realized that they were the cause of much waste of time, I sent them to the devil, together with the gay troop of friends who helped me spend my life warbling. This was one of my few righteous acts.

Yet, of all human creations, the most marvellous, and the only inexplicable one for me, is music. I understand poetry; I understand painting and sculpture; the imitative arts in fact. Their very names reveal their origin. Models existed and men spent centuries in trying to imitate them, and finally succeeded.

I understand the exact sciences. Given the power of ratiocination, I do not find it hard to comprehend that, by each age reflecting and, as it were, climbing on the shoulders of the previous age, the human race has reached its present high level.

But from where the deuce did we get music? That's what I fail to understand. Music is a mystery and I think it must be considered in the same way as language. Yet music exists, it is part of our nature. However, it is not part of everyone's nature, for I well remember once, at a concert, Cobden leant over me and whispered: 'I have never understood the meaning of that noise they call music.' Experiments with the monochord and the prism to demonstrate the relations which exist in the distances between notes and colours prove that harmony and discord are no arbitrary facts or acoustic conventions. But what does this explain? Even if you say I am venturing into a cloud-cuckoo-land, I want to give you my ideas.

Have you never, on hearing certain melodies, felt tears come to your eyes as though you heard a beloved voice, or as though some sweet forgotten memory had been evoked. At the sound of another, felt a better man, truer, suddenly ennobled? Your heart more generous? Your will more steadfast? How do you explain the influence of melody and harmony on moral sentiment? What can those notes have said, what reasons communicated to inspire you with a feeling for what is beautiful, good, and great?

Is music a forgotten tongue? A tongue whose meaning we have lost, but whose sweetness remains? Could it be a reminiscence? Is it a language of what was before? Or perhaps of what is to come?

Let me leave the clouds and return to solid earth.

Poor human mind! Bound to a fixed point with only a restricted range in which to live and explore; to see beyond but not to be able to progress further! That is the fate of man. I had this idea the other day in seeing a poor little kid tethered to a tree. She too had only a certain length of rope, only a limited extent of grazing; she too complained with a piteous bleating, her only means of expression; she too could see further and tugged and struggled to increase her range; she too tugged and struggled in vain. Let us put vain regrets behind us and get on with our story.

Not all my Roman occupations were in the fields of poetry and imagination. Do not forget I was a diplomat and, as such, I had office work as well as social studies.

The Holy Alliance had been so kind as to accept the confession and repentance of Murat. They had not denied him absolution, but as they did not trust the new convert, they kept their eye on him; waiting and hoping, I believe, for the opportunity to crown the good work by setting him a penance. The penance, of course, would be to relieve him of crown and sceptre and fling him out of doors.

As all other resident diplomats in Rome, we kept our Court informed about everything we could know, suppose, or disbelieve about the affairs of the Court of Naples. I had the charming task of copying pages and pages of cypher for our new Legation archives. Such was my life at that time and, despite the cypher work, I had very easily got accustomed to it. Dinner parties, balls, soirées, the smart set did not then fill me with the holy horror which now keeps me aloof from such activities. I had never experienced such things before nor enjoyed myself so much, and I was well content. But just as we were getting on famously, our successor, the Marquis of San Saturnino, arrived and we had to think of packing up. There was one consolation for me: I had been appointed a second lieutenant in the royal cavalry regiment, the Piemonte Reale Cavalleria. I didn't know the uniform, but I nourished a faint hope that beneficent fortune had decreed that I should realize my boyish dreams and be entitled to wear a helmet. This splendid future saved me from shedding too many tears on leaving the friends I had made in Rome.

The Jesuits, meanwhile, had been re-established. My brother was now in the order and was about to take the habit. He made use of the few days still remaining to him before the ceremony in having his portrait painted by Landi.

It turned out one of the best works of that artist, who, poor fellow, didn't paint many good ones. My nephew Emanuele now has the portrait. At last the day of the novitiation ceremony arrived and I attended the service at Monte Cavallo. All the Jesuits were rejoicing, as was only natural, at their re-establishment and, as was also natural, they were all old men, except for a few very youthful novices.

We went into an oratory, scented with new-washed napery and

G

flowers on an altar, crowded with silver, saints, and lighted candles. Myrtle branches strewed the floor; the windows were half shut and the curtains drawn. It is a fact, although inexplicable, that people feel more devotional in the dark than in the light; at night rather than by day; with eyes shut rather than open.

We were received by the General of the order, old Father Panizzoni. He was a little bowed man, with red-rimmed eyes, half-blind, and I think entering on his second childhood. He wept with emotion, while we stood there modest and demure as befitted the occasion. At a certain moment, when the postulant had to step forward, Father Panizzoni turned to me with open arms and the tenderest of welcomes, mistaking me for my brother. It was a blunder that went some way towards lightening the gravity of the assembled congregation.

If I had taken advantage of Father Panizzoni's embrace, it would indeed have been a fine business for both of us! His was not the only invitation I had, to embark on a clerical career. Monsignor Morozzo, my great-uncle and godfather, then secretary of the Bishops and Clerks Regular, asked me one day if I would like to enter the Church Academy and continue in the priesthood under his patronage. I burst out laughing, the idea seemed so absurd, and nothing further was said about it.

If I had said *yes,* in course of time I might have become a cardinal and after some years even Pope! If so, I should like to lead the world after me like a lamb running after salt. Was I perhaps wrong to say *no*?

True enough, with my habit of saying what I mean always, to all men, on all subjects, I should have got into hot water. Either my character would have changed, or I should have expired in a couple of years.

At last we left Rome; in an open carriage, in the depth of winter, travelling more by night than by day, as was my father's custom. As the horses trot on I will give you the impressions of Rome and Roman society I took away with me.

The simplest idea was that the priests of Rome and their religion had very little in common, either with my father, or with Don Andreis, or with their religion, or with the dedicated priests of Turin. What in the ascetic vocabulary is called, I don't know why, unction; the demure demeanour, always mournful, unless very occasionally cheered up by some rare sacristy witticism; the environment that weighs you down like Horace's *plumbeus Auster,* and in which I had lived and grown up under the ferule of my priest—there was absolutely no trace of any of this in Rome.

There was not a Monsignore, not a priest, who did not step out bravely, with head up, without exaggerated humility, showing a pretty leg, and turned out more than sprucely. They discussed everything, the affairs of the day, and *de quibusdam aliis* as well, so much so that my father, as I noticed, was on tenterhooks. I well remember a particular prelate, whose name I will not mention, and who was, I think, pretty free in his habits. One day, at a dinner party in a villa beyond Porta Pia, he laughingly related some matrimonial anecdotes that I didn't even understand at the time, but which so upset my excellent father that he seemed to be on the rack, as he tried in every possible way to interrupt and change the subject.

The prelates and priests I used to meet in company not quite so orthodox as that frequented by my father seemed to me still more emancipated. Either in the present or the past, either in theory or in practice, with some veil of discretion, with little, or with none, all of them without exception were sailing, or had once sailed, on the sweet waters of the *pays de Tendre*.

I came across an ancient canon, for example, linked by an ancient chain of love to an old lady; I met a young pink and white prelate, who darted hardly chaste glances from his eye, mad for the fair sex, going all the way with some and giving promises to others. Just imagine it! This gay young apostle comes to me one day and informs me that there is a girl in the Tor di Specchi nunnery who has fallen in love with me. I wanted nothing better and took the hook and asked for particulars. Then began a childish interchange of notes and messages, then of tender glances and a hundred absurdities of the same nature, all cut short by the pair of post-horses which dragged us away from Rome through the Porta del Popolo.

All these discoveries—they were really new for me—with others of the same kind, constituted the matter of my cogitations, as I sat huddled up in my cloak in the corner of the carriage bowling along the road to Tuscany.

My father's view of the Roman curia and clergy was certainly exclusive and definite, but, with his sound judgement, he simply must have observed what was obvious, even to the blind. During our journey he kept hinting, without laying stress on it, that it would only be good manners, and indeed our duty, to speak with due circumspection, should we have noticed abuses and things not quite in order in a country where we had been so hospitably received. Such a maxim, if discreetly understood, is not to be condemned.

He certainly must have been pained by the behaviour of a section of

Roman society, by its lack of 'respectability', in present-day slang. But he found comfort, no doubt, in the point of view of Abraham the Jew of the *Decameron* story, that is to say that the best proof of the truth of the religion professed by Rome lies in the fact that it still goes on, even in such hands.

The reasoning is good up to a point, but if Boccaccio had had the patience to wait another forty years, he would have learnt from John Hus first, and then from Luther and his companions, that things only last in certain hands until they are snatched from them. I make no comment as to what Boccaccio and his Jew would think if they came back to the world today!

11

AT about two or three o'clock a.m. I at last found myself at home, groping for my bed, which was in the same room as that of my brother Enrico, whom I woke up.

'Who is it? Who is it?' 'Massimo just back from Rome', and I was under the covers in a flash. My first question was: 'Do Piemonte Reale wear helmets?' 'Yes, they do.' I breathed again, and after a few more questions we were both fast asleep.

Hardly a week passed and one splendid, fine, sunshiny Sunday I at last tried on that wonderful helmet. I viewed myself in the glass in the glory of full uniform and, according to feminine flatteries, really cut a fine figure. I could taste the unutterable joy of being saluted by sentries and of strolling up and down along the arcades of Via Po, until dinner time, so that no single inhabitant of Turin should be deprived of the chance of having a look at me.

The regiment was in process of being formed and I believe only one squadron had its horses. They collected all those men returned from serving in the French army, appointing officers by pulling ex-officers out of retirement. The way they filled administrative and military posts is notorious. They consulted the Court Almanac and *Palmaverde* for the year of the King's departure. Everyone was to occupy the post he held at that time, except those who had died meanwhile. (I might have left this last observation to the reader's intelligence!) But the old, quite apart from the dead, weren't enough, and they had to call in the young. I was one of these and had my epaulettes, all in a flash. And why? Only because, if the reader remembers, in 1240 or '60 or '80 (odd that I have forgotten the date) a certain man-at-arms of the family of Brenier Capel happened to take a wife from Savigliano and had the good fortune to be the actual progenitor of that long line of Taparellis, of which I have the honour to be the last but one.

Those who had returned from the French army were accepted, but they all lost a rank; corporals became rankers, sergeants, corporals, and so on up to the captains and colonels. This is a topsy-turvy state of affairs! We stripling cavaliers had a free gift without deserving it; those who had deserved their ranks, owing to their valour and the blood they had shed, were demoted.

We shall soon see how that injustice affected my way of thinking.

I must not omit to record that they offered to take back my father into the regular army, for which he had always felt inclined. He refused, however, excusing himself by saying that after eighteen years he considered that he would be more of a burden than a help to the country by returning to the colours. He therefore remained a retired general. He was made a commendatore of the order of San Maurizio e Lazzaro, which was worth something in those days; the two brave Tribunes of the Theban Legion had not become bus drivers,[1] as they did later on; a year later he was appointed Governor of Casale.

But, despite his past conduct, his merits, and the qualities of which the reader has heard (provided he has not skipped too much), my father never found much favour at Court or in high government circles.

The King was an honest man, and those about him were not evilly inclined. The gentlemen who had stayed in Piedmont and had more or less bowed low before Napoleon obtained posts and employment without too much difficulty. They too were, in general, honourable, civilized persons, and they all esteemed my father; they admired his talents and his culture; no one was hostile—but in their heart of hearts none of these people really liked him. It's no good! There are some honest men who simply do not suit certain situations. The effect that paddy-fields have on the physique of the workers is exactly what Courts do to men's souls and characters. Bad atmosphere! I make no pretence at saying anything original, the phrase *inique corti* (iniquitous Courts) has become common currency. To find a remedy, that would be something new! But as it is the rulers who would have to apply it, and they are those who have suffered most from the contagion, we are in a vicious circle. Yet who are those who have always toppled the crowns

[1] D'Azeglio refers to the indiscriminate bestowal of this order in his day (tr.).

from off Kings' heads? Not hosts of rebels—Courts! It would therefore be to the interest of rulers, no less than of subjects, to purify the air. I know how it could be done, but I do not wish to reveal it. My reticence, however, is not due to any republican ideas! That would be a fine exchange indeed! One would still have a King, chamberlains, *les marquis de la république*! Thank you very much!

My father, like all men of lofty character, did not push himself and, while others elbowed their way to the front, he stayed back. This will always be so at all times with men of his stamp.

My regiment was ordered to the Veneria, an old royal castle, three miles from Turin, in part destroyed during the wars in which Marshal Catinat commanded the French army at the end of the seventeenth century; then granted by the royal family to the army as a cavalry garrison. I was one of the first fully-equipped officers when the day of our departure from Turin was fixed.

This was the last definite break with home and schooling. It was rather early considering my character, seeing that I was only fifteen and a half. I took a last farewell of Don Andreis. To finish his history I must record that, freed from the task of educating me, and perhaps realizing that his pupil had not turned out the pious young gentleman he had aimed at, he became a Capuchin monk. He died, poor fellow, in 1830 or '31, always praying, I think, for my conversion. I, in my turn, pray most sincerely that God may grant peace to that honest soul, for such he was, who really strove after good.

There are five or six occasions in my life when I tasted joy; a happiness so complete, so—if I dare misuse a word where there is none adequate—intrinsic, that I cannot express it and hardly, I was going to say, had a heart capacious enough to contain it.

One of these occasions, one of the days that I shall make a point of recording as they come along, was when I came to our quarters in the Bastion Verde. I was in uniform, with that famous helmet on my head, mounted on a first-rate horse as frisky as his master, a good devil like me without vice, and one I could handle very well. What with my youth and the excellent condition I was in owing to all those somersaults, fencing, swimming, riding, etc., I was as nimble as could be and a real madcap on a horse.

As I was the first fully-equipped officer, even down to the harness, I was warmly welcomed by my superiors and comrades. The trumpet sounded and off we went through Porta Palazzo to my new destiny, happy as a Pope, and perhaps rather more so.

It was a queer way of forming a regiment! The senior officers, old-

timers, had forgotten everything; we juniors had not yet learnt anything. Don Andreis had given me no lessons on military theory. The
other ranks, quartermasters, non-commissioned officers, and soldiers,
nearly all of them trained in the finest school in the world, knew their
job thoroughly. They laughed at us in their hearts, both in our presence
and in our absence.

I shall never forget the first time that I appeared as a second lieutenant
with the regiment on parade, and what I felt when I glanced to right
and left and saw all those martial, bronzed, bearded faces, looking even
more severe owing to the shadow thrown by the peaks of their helmets.
They were men fit for any hazards; they had experienced the snows of
Moscow and the burning heats of Andalusia, they had come through
innumerable battles unscathed and here they were under the command
of beardless boys such as myself. I felt so small, so humble, so nothing—
much worse—so ridiculous! The absurdity became real torture when I
thought, 'The only reason for this situation is because, by the grace of
God, I'm a young gentleman.' Every time I saw the eyes in those
haughty faces directed on me, I felt as though I had received a slap,
such as one gives to tiresome children when one wants to get rid of
them.

I was still more upset to see that, whereas I felt the situation so
deeply as to make my life bitter, my superiors, who should have felt
ashamed, behaved as though it was they who had conquered Napoleon.

Among the captains and subalterns, however, there were several who
had themselves come from various French regiments. The adjutant
major, the Marquis Doria Cavaglià, had been in the Cuirassiers. He
had come straight from Moscow, having forded the Beresina and not
on the pontoons; he was as tough as anyone. Cavalier Gazelli, now a
general; cavalier d'Albrione; a certain Lombardi; a cavalier Lovera
and a few others had only just come from taking part in those great
epic events. They spoke of nothing else and I listened avidly, with
open mouth, drinking it all in and kindling my imagination with the
tales of those tremendous human sacrifices and immense devastations. I
was greedy to hear all facts, names, anecdotes, as well as to learn of
orgies, crazy acts, smashing of property, soldiers' excesses, songs of the
tavern and the camp, and all the rest. With this, I pieced together some
idea of an epoch; of a world so different from ours; more splendid,
grander, worthier of soldiers and men. Every day my sense of humiliation grew, as I looked around me at many of my comrades, especially
those set in authority over us.

With my head stuffed with Napoleonic reviews, parades, and drill, it was certainly bitter to watch our major, one Sunday at a church parade, bungle his orders to file off; to see our colonel on the square search through his pockets for his notes—owing to his poor memory he had notes of all the commands and drill movements and he'd left them on his desk—and shout out to those near him, 'Gentlemen, where's my piece of paper? Wherever's my piece of paper?' He felt no shame at knowing nothing of the military art and most of my comrades showed no interest in it either. But some of us studied as hard as we could under the adjutant major, who held classes for us. After a month we knew more than the colonel, the major, and quite a few captains, and I was soon considered capable, not only of drilling, but of instructing, both mounted and dismounted, the squadron to which I belonged.

Theory and drill were the same as in the French army, but of course the noodles of our Court had not returned from the island of Sardinia to bow to the whims of the usurper! They composed a new drill manual in Italian; so far so good, but their innovations and inventions had to be seen to be believed. I will give you one example.

The orders for the leading rank in a charge were the same as today. This is known, but what is not known is what was laid down for us to do when we arrived at the enemy square. This is the happy invention which was to ensure victory. I quote the exact words: 'Every rider when he reaches the infantry will give a blow with his sabre in an upwards sweep, *in order to try to unfix the enemy's bayonets.*'

There is nothing that makes one more annoyed with people than having to make a fool of oneself for their sake. It was due to this piling up of injustice, stupidities, and petty vexations to which we were subjected, the fruit of the exaggeration of the principle of monarchy, or rather bigotry, that my enthusiasm for the King when I saw him appear that day in Piazza Castello had very much cooled down, and my sympathy for the system had vanished. That was not all. The final result was that I conceived a violent hatred for the nobility, who took the leading part in the government. I wager that all the middle class of the time in Turin didn't hate them half as much as I did.

Not only did I hate the nobility, but I was in despair that I was a noble myself, I was ashamed of it and, whenever possible, concealed the fact. At Fossano one day I was happy to pass myself off as the son of Monsú Aragn, our Lagnasco bailiff.

Here I must state that God, of his goodness, has planted in my heart a love of justice and a hatred of injustice and domineering. He gave me a love of justice, just as he gave me a highly-strung sanguine temperament, a fair skin (*quondam*), and blue eyes. I have no merit in this, for I couldn't be otherwise if I wanted to. I can therefore claim quite freely that I hate injustice always, in all circumstances and whoever benefits, whoever suffers from it. I hate it, if it is to the advantage of my enemies, my friends, myself; I should still hate it if it brought a benefit to those I love most in the world, if it should lead to my most ardent desire, to see Italy *really* made.

Having said that, you will understand my profound chagrin in being noble, knowing only too well that no power in the world could ever alter this fact. My misfortune was therefore beyond repair. I envied those who had not been cursed with this disadvantage, reckoning their happiness immense.

The reader will perhaps think I am amusing myself by exaggerating. Nothing of the sort, I pledge my word that I do not exaggerate by one iota. At that time I really believed that the nobility were justly hated for their domineering and that they were the only class capable of tyranny. I really believed that those who railed against them would lose their lives rather than become Cavalieri and Counts themselves. How shrewd I was! If only I had known then what I discovered later, that the democratic egg hatches out a Count, I should not have got so worked up!

These exaggerations of mine were based on a worthy sentiment, an aversion to myself and undeserved privilege. It was only my lack of experience that caused me to believe that the vice of domineering was restricted to the nobility. As time went on I began to see that it is a vice inherent in human nature and that man, as man, when he has the knife by the handle without anyone to restrain him and keep him sane, will use it to subjugate his equal and make him unequal. The consequence must be that no one under a well-run government must be irresponsible, no individual and no class; therefore no privileges, therefore perfect equality before the law.

But the King, you will say, is and must be responsible to no one. That is so. But I should rather say that in his person he is inviolate. Suppose a conflict to arise between the Crown and the other two powers, legislative and judicial, what finally must the sovereign do if the latter do not yield and are probably in the right. He can certainly send down a battalion of soldiers to shut parliament and put the keys in his pocket. But what next? Isn't that a responsibility?

Although my scorn for the government of that day and my hatred for the nobility were based on a sound principle, they produced bad consequences. Owing to my youthful tendency to go to extremes, and by force of contrast, I gradually drifted into the worst company and associated with the dregs of society. It wasn't sufficient for me if a man was not a noble, he had to be a rogue.

I said that this was the period of my life I should like to forget and which makes me blush. I can hardly believe that afterwards, and to an increasing extent, I have felt an invincible repugnance for all that is ugly, foul, and impure; both physical and moral. In fact I have often to accuse myself of intolerance in that respect, but after all men aren't angels and we are all in need of forgiveness, I more than anybody. But in those days, I cannot explain how, I mixed with the scum and took to them like a fish to water.

Let this be an example for parents not to despair when they see their sons going the same way, and for those in similar circumstances to appreciate that all bad habits can be broken, *if only the will is there.*

In any case I did not neglect my military duties, in fact I performed them zealously and was never punished for service irregularities. I was, however, often punished for mad pranks, nocturnal brawls, fights, and all sorts of escapades.

I once had a quarrel with a comrade and we got as far as the duelling field. I was not yet sixteen and my opponent was little older, so that our seconds, who were much senior officers, as soon as we had taken up positions, intervened. I am very rarely angered, not even at that period, but on this occasion I was furious, and having got back and the others having gone about their business, I ran after my comrade and said: 'Let's go somewhere by ourselves where we shan't be disturbed.'

Luckily, General Count Richelmi had arrived that day to inspect the regiment. I was free at the time of our appointment. I turned up and waited and waited, but no one came. My adversary had been delayed on service, and afterwards was immediately arrested and therefore could not come. I say 'luckily', because a duel between two angry boys, each of whom wanted to prove himself a man, could have had serious results.

Having found the field mine, I returned to quarters at sunset. The adjutant told me that I had behaved very well and that I was under arrest. A premise followed by a logical conclusion, as is obvious to all.

My father knew of the affair and I was told to expect a visit from him. I did not realize he knew the facts, and I thought: 'If he finds me under arrest, he will ask why. Whatever shall I say?' The only thing to do is to be ill. When I heard his carriage stop outside my door and recognized him, I jumped into bed without even undressing.

He came in, but didn't look too grumpy. He approached the bed and I told him I had a pain somewhere. He made no reply and, after a short stay, he went off with my sister-in-law, who had accompanied him and was laughing like anything at my illness.

Had I got into trouble on account of this visit, it was owing to the fact that the Church had precise precepts about duelling and treated it as a matter for excommunication. My father's strict religious views were such that he would not hesitate in such a case, even though he was a soldier of high repute and though, in his youth, he too had met his man on the field of honour. I was not yet sixteen, and he must have thought I was making a fine start by being about to be excommunicated for the second time!

Some days later I received a letter from him, in which he discussed, with his usual typically lucid reasoning, the whole question of duelling and the religious and philosophic aspects concerned. The letter was a kind of résumé of everything he had previously told us about the matter, whenever duelling had been mentioned. He was much concerned to convince us.

Unfortunately duelling, which is really a practice of nordic nations and not of Graeco-Latins, has its roots in a sentiment in human nature not easy to eradicate—vanity! How many things in the world would go better if vanity could be changed for proper pride. Only public opinion can effect such a change. When it is no longer applauded, there will be no more duelling. It disappeared in England when opinion turned against it.

Without entering into the question of the rationality or morality of duelling, which would be rather too much, there is one good piece of practical advice I can give to young men.

Always treat a duel as a very serious matter. You can kill a man or make him an unhappy cripple for the rest of his life and bring sorrow to many others. A time can come when such a memory could be a millstone round your neck. I refer to real duels; ceremonious duels are absurd. It's a bad business however you look at it. Avoid it as far as you can.

12

THE creation of a cavalry regiment is indeed a task! According to my rank, I worked hard, and what is more I had the strain of a life of dissipation. After a day's drill, I used to mount my horse at sunset and make off along by-roads to Turin, where I spent a reckless night. At half past three next morning, however, at réveillé, I was back punctually in quarters. You can imagine that after a few months I had to consider my health.

I also began to feel how empty is the life of a garrison officer in peacetime, and there now seemed no likelihood of a war.

Napoleon had escaped and landed, there was a general *sauve qui peut* of the diplomats from the Congress of Vienna. Once more the man of destiny spread terror, and many of the restored rulers trembled in their shoes. Not all, however, for Vittorio Emanuele, old and ailing as he was, proved from what stock he came; he was ready to mount his horse and he gave orders to our small army to advance.

You can imagine our joy, and mine in particular, when we heard we were to go to war. Young, fit, used to excess, what could I wish for better? Cesare Balbo, austere as he was, has said: 'There are two pleasures in the world; making war and making love.' I should, however, add, 'both are occupations for young men'.

But things go contrariwise; when young, I had to stay at home; when I began to feel the burden of my years, I had to face the wind and the rain and go to war. Then came the defeat of Waterloo and the arch-disturber of the world was sent to St. Helena. It did not need great intelligence to appreciate that to belong to the profession of arms, especially of the non-specialist branches, would for a very long time be as important and amusing as to belong to a brotherhood of penitents.

My friend Bidone, whom I saw from time to time, frequently dropped a little word, some ironic remark or joke on my fate as a regular officer; he used to say: 'What a fine career in which your two arms take the place of your head!' To be honest it did sometimes occur to me, when duty forced me to spend hours giving strict surveillance over the grooming of horses; making certain that the curry-comb, the brush, and the wisp of straw were used according to the best methods; when I had to keep an eye, hour after hour, to see that the men did not use the curry-comb on the mane, and washed out the eyes and nostrils of their faithful friends; or when I had to be present at feeding-time so that the oats were served precisely as laid down by the Ministry of War; on such occasions, I say, it did occur to me that this sort of nonsense could go on for thirty years of my life.

At first the idea was fleeting, a mere flash, but it gradually became more stable and finally continuous and daily more powerful. When you add to this my impaired health that I referred to before; when every evening I had a temperature and a cough fit to burst my tonsils; when, notwithstanding, I never gave up my usual pranks and escapades; my parents appreciated that I couldn't go on like this and decided to look after me.

They got me sick-leave whether I wanted or not, and nursed me at home. Meanwhile my friend Bidone continued to press his point of view and I began to think he was right, especially when I remembered that damned grooming. On the other hand, I didn't really see what I could do about it. Finally, still having kept my taste for painting while in the regiment and even, on rare occasions, having attempted some sketches from nature, I expressed the desire to retire from the cavalry and join the territorial army. The latter service gave one four months under arms, followed by twelve months free, and therefore much more time for study.

In view of the state of my health, and so as not to impede a half-inclination I showed towards settling down and working, my father was prepared to satisfy me. He applied and received permission for me to join the territorials and I joined the guards brigade, and was attached to the company commanded by Captain Santarosa, the same man who soon became famous in the revolution of 1821.

The fox may change his skin, but not his tricks. I was now a scape-grace on foot instead of a scapegrace on horseback! I kept on consorting with bad company, both military and civilian. It must be confessed that ex-soldiers from the French armies, who were used to conquering the world, continued to behave as though they were still in a conquered country. It was a disaster when a regiment marched in; the cafés and inns they frequented were soon emptied of other customers. The din, the breakages, the staring of civilians out of countenance made us thoroughly disliked. The officers of the present-day army are perfect lambs in comparison with us.

One evening, just imagine, there was a masked ball at the Carignano theatre, attended, however, by very few people. All of a sudden our famous garrison decided to expel the dancers, such as they were, turn out the lights, and close the theatre. A programme immediately and punctually carried out. It needs a Muse to describe the pushing and shoving, the screams, insults, and hullaballoo produced by this fine exploit, which seemed a bit too much of a good thing, even to me. Our commanding officers thought the same, and gave us what we deserved in the order of the day. They should have done twice as much.

On another occasion the public of Turin was treated to a spectacle of which I was the sole inventor and author. The company in which I found my pleasure included persons of both sexes, politely described as *demi-monde* and which we, being less polite, called by another name. We often used to go out to dinner in the country (to 'go junketing' in barracks slang), or to some tavern in the suburbs, to speak more precisely. I owned two horses and a gig. One Sunday when the afternoon stroll was in full swing, behold me accompanied by two young ladies notorious for their generous natures, driving a pair of horses at full gallop, *alla Daumont*, that is to say, each mounted by a postilion!

The sight created much talk in the town and among my relations, and my reputation as a ne'er-do-well reached the highest point yet. This was exactly what I wanted. I loved distinction!

My confession is nearly over and I shall soon have done with it. I simply mustn't omit, however, one last anecdote which created a good deal of unfavourable comment at the time. I shall say as Brantôme: *encore celle-ci et puis encore!*

I, with several of my scapegrace friends, had the idea of going to Milan. We were, however, all stony-broke, and between the lot of us we could only raise a miserable sum to spend on our revels at the *cassina d'ij pomm* and other such taverns. What could we do? I searched the whole house to see if I could find any booty. It was no good, 'not a fly in the air' as we used to say in our slang. But we simply had to go to Milan.

One day, alone in my room, deeply pondering the problem, my eye was attracted by two oil portraits hung on the wall facing me.

It was a piece of good luck for me, that a Count of Lagnasco had had the excellent idea of seeking his fortune in Germany. This was quite usual in the seventeenth century for gentlemen who could not find an opening at home. He had served King Augustus III and commanded the royal guard in Poland. One of the Wallenstein ladies, of the family of the famous Duke of Friedland, had found him attractive and married him. What was more to my purpose, however, was that both of them had had themselves painted by Rigault, a well-known painter of the time, who had a charming style.

Their two portraits (he in armour with a huge powdered Louis XIV wig, she with hair à la Sévigné, and her dress open and décolleté in the fashion of that day), in handsome old frames, adorned the wall opposite where I sat cogitating. Casting my gaze, as I said, on the handsome visage of my great-great-grandfather, it seemed as though he regarded me sympathetically as though *non ignarus mali*, as though he understood my quandary, and was inviting me to throw myself into his arms in my difficulty.

I did not wait for him to speak twice, but caught on at once and accepted his polite invitation, as you shall see.

Two days later at dawn there could have been seen a two-wheeled gig pulled by one horse (the days for two were over!) trotting along the road to Milan. The gig was a two-seater, but there were five persons in it; myself, two friends, and the Count of Lagnasco on one side with his wife the Countess of Lagnasco-Wallenstein on the other. They were like two large screens which prevented any enjoyment of the beauties of the countryside to right or left, but gave us a clear view along the straight road to our longed-for Milan. I remember it was a tight squeeze.

Why did that worthy couple accompany us? I do not say it without a blush, because they were destined to be sold to a picture dealer and thus help pay the expenses of our trip.

After all, the Circassians and the Georgians sell their daughters and little sons all alive-oh; is it after all such a great crime to sell a couple of old, painted ancestors?

I won't record all the mad pranks we played in Milan, except to relate that the city's future governor was arrested for failure to produce identity papers. I will say, however, that my idea of absconding with the ancestors seemed so original to everybody that the escapade was forgiven, and the affair was ever afterwards known in the family and by all the relations as the 'trip with the ancestors'.

Many years later they were at last brought back home, so that the service they were able to do me only cost them a stay of a round dozen years in Milan.

My dissipation, fatal to both body and mind of a young man, caused grave anxiety to my father and mother and even today in writing these lines I feel a stab in my heart thinking of the trouble I gave them in those days. I wish to God they had been the only anxieties I provoked.

I really was going to the bad, for I have not related everything about my life then; not all, and not the worst. I give notice of this as, after so many protestations of sincerity, if I am permitted to leave things out, I am not permitted to pretend that all has been said, when that is not so.

My mother, poor soul, often went alone, closely veiled, to knock at my friend Professor Bidone's door; to unburden her heart about me; to seek comfort and advice; sometimes to pay back small sums he had lent me when I was in straits.

As far as debts are concerned, I can guarantee that I simply hated them. Better sell ancestors than run into debt.

This is a great thing in a young man, and I had it by nature and without any merit of my own. The first guarantee of a quiet, respected life is to be able to live on what you have, be it much or little. If, on the other hand, you start to live on what belongs to other people, farewell tranquillity and, unfortunately not rarely, farewell honour. Let young men ponder this, and let gentlemen remember that if Don Giovanni returned to the world today, he would no longer be able to show Monsieur Dimanche the door, mocking him. No one now laughs at the creditor, rather at the ruined debtor.

The excellent Bidone tried to calm my mother; he spoke well of me and gave her hope, so that she left him comforted. He himself had really laid siege to me, not with sermons and injunctions but intelligently, with knowledge of the world. He so organized it that I was attacked on all sides with the greatest efficacy, and without my being vexed.

Sometimes I fled from him—*monitoribus asper*—sometimes I was vanquished by his fine, serene intelligence, by the honest friendliness that beamed from his eyes that banished all doubts about the sincerity of his opinions and of his efforts on my behalf.

The ancient myth of the Choice of Hercules, the poetic image of a situation which everyone must, more or less, have experienced within himself, was re-enacted in full force in me. Sometimes, tempted by my gang of idle friends, I disappeared and Bidone waited for me in vain. Then, attracted by a fascination I could not resist, I knocked at my friend's door, almost despite myself. I used to enter his apartment, and I have never seen a house which so faithfully depicted its master; and notice how spick and span it was; how simple, severe, and as neat as a page of figures. He always received me placidly, benevolently, without fuss of any kind, as one who knows by what means the will can be conquered.

The alternatives of two opposed attractions lasted for some time. I recall now, with the most genuine and the tenderest gratitude, the great solicitude of that best of friends on my behalf so that I should turn out well. Although naturally studious and busy with the duties of his university chair, he found time to search me out, to waylay me, to make appointments, and to go for long walks with me in order to have oppor-

tunity to discuss things at length and to instil sound ideas into my head
in a hundred different ways. A whole volume would be insufficient to
contain them, although they all tended to one simple conclusion. That
man is of value in so far as he is virtuous and civilized, in so far as he
is of use to himself and others; therefore all things must be done that
lead to such a result, and all things avoided that lead to the opposite.
Everyone must so order his life in such a way as to maintain at full
efficiency his intellectual faculties and his will to do good. The first
material boon is health, without which great men are impossible; that
no price is too high to pay for this, that it is assured through temperance
in all things, etc., etc.

To support these truths by obvious examples, he used to point out,
on the seats outside cafés, those human wrecks from a disordered life;
those old men with rheumy, idiot eyes, with wasted limbs, to whom
age had brought no respect in fact or appearance, and who end up
useless, abandoned, despised by everyone. 'If you go on as at present,
that's what you'll be in fifty years time. Look in this mirror.' Sometimes he quoted some completely opposite type, some man or youth
who through strength and constancy, basing himself on quite humble
principles, had succeeded in achieving good and useful things. He did
not always blame me and often encouraged me with such words as:
'Providence has given you a good head; up with you and decide to
make use of it.'

I cannot recall those days and Bidone's friendship without remembering those affectionate verses of Dante when he meets Brunetto Latini;
verses that so well express what I feel:

> 'Were all my wish fulfill'd,' I straight replied,
> 'Thou from the confines of man's nature yet
> Had'st not been driven forth; for in my mind
> Is fix'd, and now strikes full upon my heart
> The dear, benign, paternal image, such
> As thine was, when so lately thou didst teach me
> The way for man to win eternity:
> And how I prized the lesson, it behoves
> That long as life endures, my tongue should speak.' [1]

I only wish I could honour worthily such a friend in my own language. But Brunetto Latini, who was much inferior, had Dante;
whereas Bidone, so much superior, had only me! Just think how fame,
lasting fame, just as oblivion, depends on such chances! Must we toil

---

[1] Dante, *Inferno*, XV, 79–87, trans. Henry Cary.

H

so for glory? And must we blindly accept as infallible the trumpet of fame?

For some time these ideas have prevailed with me, and as much as I would love—I do not deny it—to be mentioned with honour if the occasion arises, I can live marvellously well and happily if no one talks about me at all. As I go on, I've learnt that of all the approbation a man can get, the only, good, true one, the only one to strive for, the one that gives you a sweet taste in the mouth, and lets you sleep sound at night, is the approbation of that judge we all have in our hearts, when he says: 'You've done your duty.'

It has happened to me that I have been praised and applauded by all, while this judge told me that I did not deserve it. My mouth has then tasted bitter and my pillow has been of thorns, despite all the cheers.

At seventeen, however, I had had experience of absolutely nothing. The idea of glory, praise, fame made my pulses beat quicker. Bidone was aware of this and stimulated my *amour propre*, telling me I could do great things if I only wanted to. My mouth watered, I was all excited at the thought of—perhaps, who knows, one day—having my name in the newspapers! Amazing to think of now! I began to turn over in my mind all possible ways, forms, and means of achieving this delightful result. I began to question my inclinations, desires, tendencies; to try to guess at future possibilities. I finally made up my mind to do something, the only thing left to decide was what.

It was no use considering the exact sciences; poor Bidone was well aware of this, for in teaching me mathematics he had never got me to master the four basic operations of arithmetic. However, there was still all the rest of knowledge, and when I asked him 'What shall I do,' he replied with a smile, 'Do!'

'Learn an art, and put it apart' was a proverb that seems invented by him, as it was his maxim that every man should have the means of earning his bread, without rents or profession, etc., etc. He did not push this theory so far as to say that an educated person should be proficient as a carpenter, like Émile.

I increasingly felt drawn to art, for which I had always felt an inclination. It is certainly not the best way to avoid starving—my dear colleagues are well aware of that—but after all, the brush can be put to so many different uses that, provided you do not wish to cross the Sahara, in Christian country at the worst you can always earn your daily bread in some way or other.

So far there was nothing but good intentions, and apart from the rare moments when Bidone managed to discover me and snatch me

from my vices (exactly as Socrates did with Alcibiades, if you will excuse the audacious comparison), my idle life continued as before, in
the company of the scum who frequent cafés, billiard saloons, etc., etc.

But the blessed day did dawn when I made the great, firm, absolute,
lasting resolution. From one day to the next, a complete transformation! I abandoned all the previous company I had kept, all the cronies,
all the girl friends, cafés, billiard halls, theatres, inns, and the rest, of
which it is better not to speak. Habits changed, time-table, haunts, etc.,
all changed! The old man put off; put on the new! I began to get up
before daybreak and studied, read, and drew until lunchtime. After
lunch, more work and study until dinner, apart from an hour's walk.
After dinner, at it again! All this was entirely on my own, without
guidance, as hard as I could go, and without a word to my previous
associates. I vanished and that was that!

For a day, two days, no notice was taken. Then my companions
began to whisper. 'What has happened to Massimo? Have you seen
Massimo? What's the matter with Massimo?' Nobody knew anything.
I believe, though I don't rightly remember, that I had given orders that
I was out to callers. It wasn't necessary, for few, if any, of that crew
would have dared to venture near my father's abode, and in this they
showed a just sense of his, and their, standing.

Having, as I said, no one to guide me and wanting to study landscape
painting in oils, I had asked advice from one of our painters, Cavalier
Bagetti. He was a very talented man, a clever water-colourist, imaginative, bold, experienced in the world and society, much travelled.
Napoleon had carried him along with him to war so that he could
depict his fields of slaughter. I inquired from him how I was to start
painting. He advised me to copy two seascapes in the Marquis di
Cambiano's gallery. Fine pictures; I don't know or don't recall by
whom. I got leave from the Marquis and he had the two pictures
brought to a room on the mezzanine floor for greater convenience.
Before copying them in oils I made pencil sketches and worked on
them in the evening.

It was here that one of my old friends (enemies rather) found me out.
He entered smiling, but I could see he was sizing me up from head to
foot as though approaching a dangerous animal, but he seemed very
confident all the same.

'You're never to be seen—will you explain?—What have we done
to you?—what has happened?'

'You've done nothing; nothing's happened,' I replied, also smiling,
'except that I felt like studying painting and copying these pictures.'

Such a reply meant nothing, and my friend understood that. After a few more words he made off, and I heard, later, that after he had duly reported to the rest of them, and after the affair had been heard, weighed, and examined, they came to the unanimous conclusion that I was mad. When, rarely enough, anyone later asked after me, the invariable reply was: 'Off his rocker.'

13

I say this in all sincerity, that of all the things of those bygone days I am ashamed of and would like to forget, I am really rather proud of this. My dear reader, confess! Don't you agree that for a young man who has gone the pace for several years to change, all of a sudden, to a way of life almost like that of a Capuchin novice, demands a certain strength of will? That is not a very common occurrence. After having always run after one or other petticoat, the fact remains that, for four years and eight months, I abstained completely from such entanglements. It is true that sometimes I nearly burst, but I stuck it. I had said *no*, and if I am a man *no* it must be, and *no* it was.

Here is where the fruit of the example and education given me by my father and mother is apparent. Perhaps also what I had inherited from them counted, as, of course, the far-sighted, intelligent friendship of Bidone. The latter had also taught me a way of developing strength of will, by a kind of moral gymnastics, not unlike the physical gymnastics practised to strengthen the muscles and give elasticity to the constitution. He said: 'In everything you do, practice making sacrifices unknown to all others; without anyone realizing or appreciating your action or praising you; give up something you like, or acquiesce in something you dislike; starting with small things and gradually working up to bigger and more difficult things.'

I beg young men, I beg them in the name of all they hold most dear, in the name of our unhappy country, of our exhausted Latin race, which has such great need, indeed one need only, that of tempering itself, of acquiring character, strength, moral force; and, should it gain such qualities, would be the first nation in the world. I beg them, I repeat, to meditate on this precept of Bidone's and persuade themselves of its importance, and put it into practice, more assiduously and better than I did.

I do not mean that I did not follow it at all; in a way it was ingrained in my nature; it was a new application of an old theory inculcated by my father in my childhood, of which I had, thank God, sufficient good sense to understand the immense scope.

I therefore began to practise it in small things, for example, by giving up going to a party; persisting in some tiring task half an hour longer; getting up an hour earlier; postponing eating and drinking, although hungry and thirsty; all this without anyone else knowing, except myself. Don't laugh, reader, at trifles that seem childish; just think that, had I not determined to go to the trouble of writing a sound book of use to young people, a practical book in every particular, I should easily give up the toil involved. I should also reflect that only by analysis of everything does one reach a synthesis; that to become a good fencer one has to practise for hours against a wall; to become a ballerina one must practise millions of pirouettes; to temper one's spirit to the steely strength of my father's, and such I should wish to see all Italians, one must harden oneself and grow accustomed to suffer and sacrifice, first a little, then a lot; then, only then, can one be proud of belonging to a race of men destined to found, save, and resuscitate a nation. Before that, no!

I myself wanted to do the thing in one leap and begin with great sacrifices; I who changed from an active, energetic life to a sedentary one within doors, from the open air to the study; in one word from the kind of life that, excesses apart, makes dullards grow fat, to the other that makes men who are anxious to succeed, grow lean—(you must also add that I slept among paints, oils, and varnishes; smells enough to give a mule fits)—the result was that after six months of furious application I fell ill.

I didn't run a high temperature, or have to stay in bed; it was extreme nervous exhaustion. Previously I had a ruddy complexion, now I became of a waxlike pallor; I was thin as a rake; I was so short of breath that I couldn't fill my lungs properly as I wished; I had almost continual palpitations so that, especially after meals, I felt as if my heart was jumping out of my mouth.

You can just imagine the situation! Farewell work, farewell painting, reading, writing, everything! True, I was condemned to sit scratching myself all day long, with my mania to work as strong as ever. That period was indeed exasperating.

My parents who knew that, this time, my excesses were virtuous ones, did all they possibly could for me, and I had doctors and everything needed. The first decree was 'do nothing!' Oh, it was so boring!

Bidone brought me comfort and kept me company while I continued to treat myself, but with little success. In time, however, I got better and could once more start work, but I only rid myself of the palpitations and shortness of breath after very many years, and I still have signs of it, even now. I convinced myself I had some organic infirmity, and I was constantly feeling my pulse. None of this was very cheerful and I began to grow melancholy. So I made a peremptory decision based on the following reasoning: either I have a chronic complaint, in which case nobody can cure me, or I haven't, and it is folly to torture myself. In both eventualities it's better not to think about it; not to feel one's pulse, or listen to one's breathing; not to worry over all one's little indispositions. So I resolved; so I did; and so I've done ever afterwards; and I've always felt excellently well.

I didn't get better very quickly, however, despite a change of air and all the doctor's prescriptions. My love of art grew stronger and stronger. For some time I had frequented the studio of a certain Revelli, a mediocre artist, but as he had stayed in Rome for some time he had brought back a series of studies depicting that magnificent countryside. I began to long to go back to Rome and this became a positive mania. I remember today how I felt my eyes fill with tears while I was looking at a little picture by this Revelli, representing Monte Sant' Oreste. It was a poor enough thing, but at that time it seemed the acme of perfection, beyond anything I could ever do.

I began to speak of my longing for Rome with my mother and I got more and more enthusiastic about it. To cut a long story short, that beloved saintly woman, who would have done anything for me, spoke to my father about it and, partly to restore my health, partly in the hope that I should accomplish something, and perhaps also to obviate the risk of a moral relapse, they decided that I should go.

All preparations were made in a few days and we started off in a closed carriage, drawn by four post-horses: my mother, my brother Enrico, and I, with a maid and a man-servant.

My mother undertook the journey entirely for my sake. It is, otherwise, highly unlikely that she would have faced the discomforts, really a risk in her poor state of health. There was no one in the world able to support suffering so serenely as she could. Any slight precaution one took for her, any glance in her direction, was rewarded by a loving smile. There were no injunctions, no peevishness, no timidities, no complaints, but a constant serene tendency towards cheerfulness, only clouded sometimes by attacks of acute pain.

At our first stop (at Piacenza, I think) she caused us some anxiety, as she was very tired, worn out indeed, and seemed to doubt whether she could accomplish the journey. A night's rest restored her, however, and next morning she was another person. She said quite gaily: 'Things are going well. Let's be on our way.'

Monsignor Morozzo had found us lodgings and we went straight there. They were in Piazza Colonna, opposite the Chigi palace, on the first floor, in the house of an Abbé Natali. He was a high-ranking Monsignore, head of the weights and measures department, a very old man.

I soon had an example of the new environment I had come into, and how different it was from our own. One night there was a bit of a rumpus in the house. On getting up in the morning we made inquiries. 'Oh, they came to arrest Abbé Natali and they've taken him to the castle as a prisoner!' was what the neighbours told us. The devil they have! A priest too! A high official! An old man! It seemed impossible.

It was all true; we heard later that the unfortunate man had done something fraudulent in his office.

This fact made a great impression on me, 'High functionaries, venerable priests do this sort of thing at Rome and risk prison and I don't know what else, at eighty!' I said to myself, and wondered what lesser men were capable of.

Just as I was about to start my studies I fell ill with a gastric fever. It lasted a fortnight and that was the only real illness I have had up to the present day. I had no serious symptoms, only great lassitude and a tormenting hunger, which the doctor would not permit me to satisfy. I found myself then in the position of a poor man who cannot satisfy his hunger, though healthy.

The winter following our arrival in Rome I worked hard and constantly, but without good guidance. My life was more than regular. I went nowhere into society except to the Orengos, who were then living in the palazzo Falconieri at San Marcello; to Gherardo de' Rossi and a few others. I got up early and went straight to the studio. At first I had one at the Due Macelli, on the corner of the street that goes to Capo le Case; after that another quite near, next to the puppet theatre. I went to bed early, to the great astonishment of the Romans and their ladies, even when the weather was fine.

In Rome the time-table goes by sunset, as everyone knows. There are things that are done all the year round at the same time after the Angelus bell. One goes visiting, for example, at three o'clock of the night, as they call it. So in winter one goes at eight o'clock and in summer at eleven. There was always an argument. 'What,' they used to say to me, 'you are going to bed at half past two!' 'Not at all, I'm going to bed at half past ten, as I always do,' I would reply. 'But it's half past two, now'—'No, it's half past ten!' and so on and so on.

The regular life I was leading did a great deal to restore my health. Besides drawing, I was able to improve my knowledge of music, Italian literature, history, etc., and as I was just of the right age to fall into the sin of poetry, I fell like others, and, octave by octave, I manufactured a chivalrous epic. In fact, now I come to think of it, I had composed, at the age of fourteen, several cantos of another poem called *Rinier d'Aspromonte*—curious Garibaldian coincidence!

I have forgotten the title of this second poem. I know the scene was Saluzzo, at the Court of the Marquis, and that rather a humorous episode took place there. A damsel was to become the bride of the conqueror in a tournament. A wizard, hostile to the lady, wished to prevent the marriage. The joust begins, the defence being entrusted to the bravest paladins, who first beat all comers, but a knight appears (black horse, black armour, everything black, of course) and lays about him so that none can resist. More and more champions appear to take the lady's part, the joust goes on for so long that it lasts beyond a certain fated hour by which the decision should have been reached, after which there was to be no marriage, no bride; all over! On the striking of the hour, the black knight, who previously moved, fought, and spoke, suddenly stands stock still, both he and his horse. At first no attention is paid to this, but as he stays motionless they begin to take notice; then to marvel; then to speak and call to him; until finally someone gives him a push and the suit of armour falls apart, helmet here, cuirass and armlets there; there was no one in it. A ghost had ridden the joust to prevent the marriage, etc., etc., etc.

Wasn't that a pretty invention? I did not only write an epic poem, but a comedy, half a tragedy, odes and sonnets bursting with patriotic feeling for Italy.

The tragedy was called *Dido*. Act 1: Aeneas calls the chief of the Trojans to a council; he tells them Anchises has appeared to him and chided him for wasting time love-making instead of sailing on to Italy as Fate wills, and escaping Juno's wrath, etc., etc. They have to go then, but what about the Libyans and Hiarbas, and poor compromised Dido? But despite all, they decide to leave, so leave they do.

Naturally one couldn't have the complete tragedy in one act, so it was necessary to have a prolonged tug of war between Dido and Aeneas for another four, until the thing happened that all had foreseen, Aeneas departs and Dido kills herself. That was my plot, but half-way through

I had a flash of inspiration and I gave up the tragedy and wrote the following on my manuscript: 'A hero who says in the first act what he is going to do in the last, is a flop.' So I sent Aeneas, Dido, Anna, and the rest of the cast to the Devil.

Up to that time I had a decided tendency to think things out for myself instead of humbly taking ideas ready-made from others. At the time it was almost rebellion to treat Virgil's hero with such levity. But Virgil or no Virgil, I never could like Aeneas. His treatment of poor Dido as a mere globe-trotter's caprice, and especially his foolish sentimentality when he meets her soul in the mansions of the dead, as though he were looking for a snub, which, indeed, he got! Without speaking of the impossibility for us moderns of getting worked up over the scandals of ancient Olympus, the revenge of Venus, Juno, or Neptune. The reasoning which led me to abandon my tragedy contained an excellent principle which I have always tried to foster, the principle of looking for truth and professing it without respect for things or persons. Bidone was always proclaiming this and he applied his theory to every act and every moment of daily life. He always used to say to me: 'Look for truth and, when found, speak it openly and freely.' One must, of course, appreciate that there are considerations of respect and ways of doing it, even with the most complete sincerity. 'Above all,' he would add, 'never, out of timidity, measure your words to suit the audience, don't consider if your opinion pleases or displeases, etc., etc.'

I shall say nothing of a one-act comedy of mine with a plot based on an anecdote from the life of the Emperor Frederic II; a foolish thing without humour. And yet—it may be conceit—I have a notion I might have been able to produce something not too bad in this genre. But someone cut the ground from under me at one stroke. Guess who! The actor Vestri. It was like this. When I had written and made a fair copy of my comedy, I stuffed it into my pocket and, with Arcadian simplicity, went straight off to the Valle theatre where Vestri's company was performing. It was afternoon and they were rehearsing. I managed to get on to the stage, I called Vestri, who was busy with his actors, book in hand. In great trepidation I told him my mission and handed him the precious manuscript.

He gave me a glance which translated would mean, 'My poor babe, finish growing up before you start writing comedies.' He then turned his back on me with some producer's pretext or other, in order to dismiss me.

That's why I did not become an author of comedies.

However, the idea has often come knocking at my door. I've always sent it packing (as Vestri sent me) not with a pretext, but with the excellent reason that as in Italy there is no language, no actors, and no public, it is a waste of time to write comedies. Here one really ought to make a long explanation, but I put it off until a more opportune occasion.

The age in which one is prone to the sin of writing poetry is also when one is prone to the sin of politics and republican demagogy. Which of us has not been more or less a citizen of Athens, or Sparta, or at least of San Marino, in his student days? Which of us, between the age of fifteen and twenty, has not more or less killed a tyrant; only in theory of course. As far as I was concerned I would have given anything to have found a tyrant to kill, but I couldn't find one. I relieved my feelings by declaiming Alfieri's tragedies, which I learnt by heart. Locked in my room, foaming at the mouth, rolling my r's, I intoxicated myself with all that fury, but, on thinking it over in cold blood, and with all the love and respect I feel for Alfieri's memory, I really don't know what he's driving at, nor what purpose such works serve under modern conditions. Those goblets of poison, those daggers, come as a blessed deliverance after five long acts of fury, as they do at least put a stop to the play. Today it all seems stuff for the Assizes and God help us if that were not the case. I did not think like this then. We had formed a company to act these tragedies among ourselves. Every now and then we gave an evening performance for which we sent out invitations.

I remember one evening that Don Carlos, in drawing his sword, gave such a blow to a lamp that there was a torrent of oil over Filippo, Isabella, and Perez, not to speak of Don Carlos' sky-blue cloak embroidered with silver, most fitting garment for a lover.

However, if Alfieri had some very odd ideas in his writings, as he had in his life, it is no less true that he was the man who discovered Italy, and it is to him we owe the first breath of Italian nationalism. It is for this that we owe him the highest honour, and it is for Italians, while keeping his memory alive, to make true the prophesy he expressed in a sonnet:

> The day will dawn when warriors of our land
> Will face the French, armed with no foreign brand
>
> . . . .
>
> I hear them call to me, their prophet bard
> Who prophesies sublime and splendid days.

What if a voice had whispered in the poet's ear: 'The French Gauls will be the potent immediate cause of the triumph of Italian nationalism. They will be led by the nephew of the man who signed the treaty of Campoformio; and the Italian press of "those sublime times you prophesied" will express their loving gratitude by a string of insolences.'

I should be curious to know what the sincere, generous Alfieri would have replied to this counter-prophecy. I don't know what he would have said, but I do know what I should have been tempted to say to him, should I have had the honour to find myself in his presence as a grown man, as once I was as a little child: 'Respected Count, permit me to go to the limits of sincerity and say that you are in part to blame for this monstrous behaviour (all know the vicious attacks of the Italian press against Napoleon); just as much as that bizarre mixture of immoral pagan ideas, entirely inapplicable to our modern life, which has been the flavour, nay the very essence, of our education, and, I can add, of yours too.'

If only they taught us how to judge and understand the facts of ancient history. If only they had said, for example: nothing excuses assassination, because it is treachery, because it is an execution carried out by an incompetent tribunal, without trial. Nevertheless Alexander of Pherae, Nabis the Spartan, Agathocles, Phalaris, and Dionysius of Sicily, Nero, Commodus, etc., were such cruel brutes, so powerful, so well guarded, that one can admit extenuating circumstances in the case of someone who could, in one way or the other, rid the world of them. But there aren't any more such tyrants (I don't speak of the French terrorists who are exceptions); we don't now make brazen bulls, or sew living men up in sacks with corpses. Should a little modern tyrant arise, there are many other more efficient and more straightforward and honest ways of getting rid of him. We should have been told how fallacious and mistaken was the justice of the assassin and how badly he chose those who deserved to die, even should the procedure be legal. We should have been told of a modern age, full of a sense of the necessity for universal responsibility, eager for a law of *Habeas corpus* applied everywhere; inclined to clemency in all circumstances; against capital punishment, especially for political offences; most hostile to arbitrary judgements without trial, defence, confrontations, or witnesses. This was the sort of antidote with which they should have corrected the false ideas, which the study and reading of the pagan classics inevitably instilled in us. False ideas, if Count Alfieri will allow me, which his tragedies also instilled in us. What is the simple idea that emerges from his dramas? What is the act that achieves the acme of virtue, glory, and human fame? What is the remedy for the ills caused by wicked rulers and bad governments? What is the shortest way to lead a people to perfect happiness, liberty, prosperity, and so on? Hide behind a door and lie in wait for the tyrant; when he passes, *smack*, a good chop at his head and all is done, concluded, finished! Everybody's satisfied, independent, free, happy, virtuous, equal, brothers; in fact at one blow a country has become the land of Cockaigne! Do things really happen like this? Is this true and does it suggest what actually takes place?

Permit me to state—and I know it by experience—that it is Count Alfieri himself who is in part responsible for the politics that flourish in the universities, back-stage of theatres, in the billiard-saloons, cafés, barbers' shops, and in journalism in general; and with this list you have three-quarters of the population of Italy. Sharing responsibility with him is the old-fashioned classical education given us in the finishing school of the secret societies. If there is a touch of humour in my way of writing it is because I'm made like that, but it is only too damnably serious, the thing that sometimes smoulders and finally hatches out from certain brains without judgement or education belonging to limited people with romantic imaginations, immoderate desires, and unbridled ambition; all caused by ill-applied and misunderstood examples from antiquity, and from having seen glorified innumerable criminal insanities in histories, plays, and tragedies. And to think what immense interests, what incalculable consequences are left to the whims of madmen, rogues, and fanatics, who are rendered more dangerous, thanks to such perversions. When we Italians think . . . if Orsini had succeeded in assassinating Napoleon III!

But let us leave such thoughts, which make my hair stand on end! Let us thank God he did not succeed and let us see whether teachers, authors, poets, even pulpits, university chairs, the stage, could not once and for all persuade themselves that false ideas spoil minds, and spoilt minds are the ruin of society, and that therefore they should promulgate better ideas. Let them produce those which, when well stated and listened to without tedium, leave the individual better, and not worse, than he was before.

My mother, who was a cultured woman and had a refined literary taste and, above all, a supreme rectitude of heart and mind, could have been the model for such educators whom I invoke. She could have corrected so many of the false ideas abroad in the world. By my good fortune she was available to help me in every possible way. When I began to write I used to show her my productions as I composed them, and she found matter for intelligent criticism and adroit remarks. Both then and later, I could not reap the full benefit from what she said, nor could I be as grateful to her as I should have been.

14

HALF-WAY through the winter my brother Enrico, who was on short leave from the artillery, went off to Naples, as it was near, and so as not to miss the opportunity of seeing that interesting place.

After some weeks doing the usual sightseeing round, he fell ill. A few days later the Cavalieri di Germagnano, friends of ours from Piedmont, had to write to my mother to say that he was worse and that there were serious fears that things might turn out badly. It was a matter of urgency and my mother sent me to Naples immediately. I left in the evening in our usual carriage, driving post. It was the season for brigands and my mother, being worried, added to the expenses by providing money for an escort. However, I did a little reckoning too, and considered that the extra cash would be much better spent at Naples; so I decided to take a risk. The lottery came out well and no brigands were to be seen. When I got to Naples I had a nice heap of *écus* in hand. Alas! they all went to Barbaia's gaming house and slid down the broad way of the green roulette cloth! I only wish they had been the only ones!

I found Enrico better and he was soon up again. A young man from Macerata with whom we had become friendly came to visit him, so I got to know him too. He was the Marquis Domenico Ricci, who was studying music and drawing. We never met since that occasion at Naples and I heard nothing about him, until one day in 1852 when he came to ask me for the hand of my daughter Alessandrina for his son Matteo: a match that was happily arranged.

At Naples I found the Marquis of San Saturnino, my father's successor at Rome, who had been transferred there as minister. The legation secretary was a childhood friend, whom I was very glad to see again and with whom I spent my time. I drew from nature, studied, and visited the beauties of Naples (not those of the animal kingdom, please note!). He wrote poetry and composed tragedies which he used to read to me. This friend of mine, this tragic poet, was later for sixteen years Carlo Alberto's minister. He was Count Clemente Solaro della Margherita, with whom I used to wrangle. From that time on I could never agree with him. We discussed politics, religion, cosmogony, philosophy; something of everything, but without rancour.

That inner ferment which exploded in revolution in 1820 was beginning to move in the Kingdom of Naples. Everyone was aware of the organization and the training of the Carbonari Secret Societies and the great increase in the *vendite*, or lodges, of good cousins.

Neither he nor I, young as we were, were great admirers of secret societies; and it is a fact that for Italy to get up on her feet, she had to have recourse to a society, not secret at all—the society of big guns. In any case it was the legation's duty to keep its government informed about what was going on.

I still laugh at the memory of a poor devil of a Carbonaro, who eked out his meagre existence by acting as an informer about his lodge secrets to the Sardinian legation. When they pressed him too closely and inquired about the more jealously guarded secrets he used to squirm and wouldn't reply. 'Ah no, your excellency, that can't be told, it isn't possible.' As they continued to press him he exclaimed: 'But your excellency, you must understand I have sworn an oath not to tell . . . at least give me another *ducat*!'

I met another fellow-countryman with Count La Margherita, the Marquis Amat di San Filippo, an excellent, polished young man, who is now Cardinal Amat, one of the most distinguished members of the Sacred College.

If these pages come under the eyes of these two old friends, they should forget the very different paths we have taken in our careers, and remember the interesting excursions we made together in the mild evenings of that favoured climate; let them remember that excellent Federigo, our cultured, attentive guide, who piloted us safely through that vast labyrinth, and thanks to whom we could enjoy its beauties and rarities.

On the journey back to Rome I had an adventure, in which I could easily have broken my neck, had I not been destined to escape this accident, as others even worse, without a scratch.

The carriage had stopped at one of the post-houses on the long straight road over the Pontine marshes, and they were putting in the horses. The postilion of the previous stage had already received his money and uttered the usual oaths and curses to try to extract a larger tip. I had concluded that affair and was reading. The departure of a carriage and four from one of these post-houses is like the starting off of a company of devils and witches, such are the yells, leaps, bounds, and rearing of those six animals (counting the postilions); indeed of the eight or ten, counting the stable-lads, the little boys who push and crack whips and shout, the barking dogs, etc., etc. Finally—off one goes, usually along the main road, and by leaps and bounds, or at least at a steady pace, one arrives in God's good time, and providing nothing breaks, at the next post-house.

This time, however, was an exception. Instead of taking the high road, the whole equipage went into the canal, excavated by Pius VI to drain the marshes, which runs alongside the road for its whole length. Enrico and the servant, who were watching what was happening, had time to throw themselves out of the carriage. I, who was reading, only noticed later and got caught up in the step, so that I fell to the ground. I heard a pitying voice say: 'Poor Massimo' at the same time as I saw the back wheel just about to run over my spine. I thought: 'Good-bye to my back-bone.' In fact the wheel did pass over me, but was kind enough to break nothing. All I had was a bruise, to the wonder of all.

I got up jubilant, and gave a skip of joy. The carriage, horses, and postilions were stuck fast in the canal, while the post-master, fork in hand, was threatening murder. After being restrained and pacified, he finished the comedy by sacking the postilions, which only meant they had to take a turn behind the post-house and, after the parties concerned had left, come back and carry on as before.

The end of it all was that, that evening, our mother could welcome us both home once more safe and sound; with Enrico quite cured of his serious illness.

At the beginning of spring we rented a small house at Castel Gandolfo—the Pope's summer retreat—from some prosperous peasants called Albenzi.

My father came to visit us. He saw my paintings, and no doubt estimated them at their true worth, but, in order not to discourage me, he appeared well enough satisfied and was sparing of his criticisms. It must have seemed astounding to him that an idle scamp like me should be studying, even producing something, good or bad, instead of spending his time in cafés and billiard saloons as previously. It is a fact that, from that time to the present, I have always preferred the company of honest men and avoided rascals.

We saw interesting company at Castel Gandolfo; there was Monsieur de Blacas, his wife, and members of the legation, who resided at Villa Cybo; there was an English lady, Miss Knight, an old friend of my parents; sometimes the Torlonias came to their villa. Then there were constant visitors to one or other of these people, coming up from Rome.

Miss Knight had been governess to Princess Caroline,[1] daughter of the Prince Regent and wife of King Leopold of the Belgians. She had known all that splendid and rather improper generation. She had been in Italy during the concluding years of the previous century; she had known the Neapolitan Court, King Ferdinando and Queen Carolina; Acton; Nelson; Collingwood; Troubridge, captain of the *Centaur* who led the line at Aboukir as mark-ship for the following vessels, so that he had the bad luck to run aground and miss the battle. This excellent officer was to have married Miss Knight, but 'he was born unlucky', said she. His ship was ordered to the Indies and nothing more was heard of him. There was a rumour that she had gone to the bottom off Mozambique.

This good lady, already well on in years, taught me English and discussed literature, science, and art; there was nothing she didn't know. She told me about things she had seen; she adored Nelson and her perturbation was beyond all words in speaking of the fatal Emma Lyons; of the death of Gravina and of the faith broken after the capitulation of the defenders of the Castel dell'Ovo.

Through her I got to know, and became attached to, other English people; Lady Dawson, the Fairfaxes, Miss Mackenzie, who all showed real affection for me and loaded me with kindness. When with them, however, I experienced a very painful feeling of humiliation, so that I got more bitterness than pleasure from the association. I was ashamed of being an Italian!

I can't express the shame I felt at the political state of the Italy of that time. I seemed to be personally to blame, to have my own brow smirched; everything said seemed to allude to it, and they all seemed to stare at me. The cold English manner, the very natural indifference most of them showed to a callow youth like me; the tranquil assured pride written in their looks, seemed specially put on for me, to mortify me, to make me feel my inferiority, to make me appreciate that when a nation has for centuries been prey to all and sundry, when she permits anyone to come in from any quarter and batten on her, just as sportsmen go where the game is plentiful, then the citizen of such a nation may be tolerated by foreigners, never admitted as an equal.

I remember one day Miss Knight talked of Country. I replied with bitterness in my heart: 'And have Italians a Country?' She looked at me in surprise and my mother reproved me. I did not explain myself and made no reply. It was intolerable for me, too painful, to touch that chord. God knows what the good English lady thought of me, certainly

[1] An error for Princess Charlotte (tr.).

she was against all revolutionary excesses, but she was English, and therefore a lover of liberty and of her own country before all.

One's country is not merely the region where one was born; Italians have known that for some time.

This feeling of humiliation has been my sad companion for almost all my life; it has been part of the reason for my small inclination to travel abroad or to cultivate the society of foreigners. I recognize that in this I have been morbidly sensitive, and have exaggerated in resenting words and acts that probably meant something quite other than suggesting our inferiority (fortunate Gioberti who rejoiced in discovering the Italians to be superior to all others); but I was, and am, made like this and can't feel otherwise.

From 1849 to '59 this painful thought practically vanished. After '60 it has returned to my mind with renewed vigour. We are not the admiration of Europe, we must admit. I therefore live apart.

The Austrian Emperor came to visit Rome and you can imagine whether I left Castel Gandolfo to enjoy the festivities! I should rather have hidden myself in the dense undergrowth of Faiola, the vast forest that clothes the Appenine ridge from the lake of Albano for hundreds of miles. It is almost like one of the virgin forests such as they have in America.

The Pope and the Romans gave the Emperor a splendid welcome. The Romans were then very different from what they are today, and they could have quoted with real warmth to the Emperor Francesco the verse of Dante which only the Curia would wish to recite today, if it could:

Cesare mio, perchè non m'accompagne?[2]

It must be said, in justification, not only of the Romans, but of the whole world, that at that time the entire continent of Europe was sick and tired, after twenty years of massacre and ravage; republican plunder, imperial plunder, foreign plunder, Italian plunder; French, Austrian, Russian, Cossack, Kurdish, Tartar, and goodness knows how many more varieties of plunder. Europe wanted to see an end to it all; wanted to live, to live in peace; under King, Emperor, Pope, the devil himself, no matter if only she could breathe.

But all these troubles had occurred during my boyhood, and I had hardly been able to take them in. I did not feel this great need to relax and sit back. I had the seeds of the new era in my heart, and what it was to accomplish. There was no question of sitting back for me.

[2] Dante, *Purgatorio* VI, 114. 'Caesar mine, why do you not bear me company?'

While we were staying at Castel Gandolfo I used to go down to the plain below to shoot. But, instead of birds, I got the terrible marsh fever, ancient scourge of Latium. It was certainly prevalent in Horace's day for he complains of it, as everyone knows. I fail to understand how so many can believe that the ancient Latins were also troubled by it. How can one reconcile the large armies, that of the Rutuli for example, which Coriolanus led to the gates of Rome, with the existence of malaria? Anyone who has been to Ardea, their capital and the capital of fever too (I went there, thanks to the kind hospitality of my good friend Duke Sforza, owner of its ancient castle), has seen that their territory cannot have been larger than forty or fifty square miles, and will never believe you could raise an army of 40,000 men from it, had there been marsh fever at that time. Go today, if you feel like it, and find a thousand men fit to bear arms in the Pontine marshes!

When I got the fever, the decoction of quinine had not yet been discovered. One therefore had to drink large glass-fulls of pounded Peruvian bark. At the start of the attack, however, I had eight or ten bouts of high fever without respite, and the bark is not taken with a temperature. Thank God it didn't turn pernicious and I therefore did not succumb. Even after the fever had subsided, I continued with the bark and I must have taken seven or eight pounds of it in a few months. I suffered from these fevers for a year, but it left me with no ill effects, which is rare. There's a proverb in the Roman countryside which runs: 'With tertian fever, youth gets well; if old men get it, toll the bell.'

No one can have any idea of the iciness of the cold phase or the burning heat of the hot phase of these painful fevers. Quinine is certainly the most beneficial discovery for the Roman Campagna. They may have no steam, no newspapers nor other modern inventions, but at least they have quinine and that's worth all the rest put together.

Meanwhile my art studies progressed with the same assiduity in the studio of the painter Verstappen in Rome, and working from nature in the country.

Martin Verstappen of Antwerp was one of the best and most interesting artists of the period. He had no right hand from birth; in its place he only had two or three shapeless fingers which, nevertheless, served to hold a specially contrived palette. He painted with his left hand. He had the virtues and shortcomings of Flemish painters: colour, execution, but little sense of composition. Such was his passion for true realism, and not for ugly realism, but for *beautiful* realism, so assiduously did he study from nature in the country, despite all dangers and inconveniences, that he succeeded in producing pictures with the greatest of all virtues, that of having the sympathetic quality of making people like them. He was therefore able to live decently from his sales.

This worthy man was an excellent person, but he kept himself to himself, avoiding not only gay company, but everybody. He rose at daybreak and worked as long as there was light to see by. In the evening he walked for miles through Rome, always alone, with the sole object of stretching his legs and limbering himself up. His sturdy frame needed exercise, and so as not to lose daylight, he took his walks at night, even should it rain or pour. He was condemned to this hermit's life by a character diffident to a superlative degree. He had come to Italy with goodness knows what ideas about Italians. I don't say they are all angels! Far from it, and in Rome especially there were plenty of scoundrels of all kinds; and, rogues apart, there were those who, for their own advantage or amusement, would have been only too glad to interfere with or play tricks on a Teuton. *Ad un tufo tedesco, e farlo Martino,* is the technical phrase, and in dialect it means to make a fool of him!

Whether he was right or wrong, the fact remained that nobody saw him, he had no truck with a soul, not even with his pupils, only two in effect, a young Roman and myself. The former was the son of his landlord, the sculptor Cavalier Pacetti, only accepted owing to the virtual impossibility of refusing. I had been accepted for analogous reasons, but I think he saw us with the same pleasure that one's eyes welcome the smoke of green fire-wood.

The advantages we derived from his teaching were as follows. The apartment consisted of an ante-room with large studio windows, in which his finished pictures were displayed until sent to purchasers. There was another studio where he worked and through which one passed to regions unseen by mortals. The central keep of Hadrian's Mole is pretty well guarded, but it is nothing compared to the studio where our master worked. It was always bolted and barred and was only opened at irregular intervals of several days. At such time the good Martino issued forth with a face like a baked apple and two little pale round eyes like threepenny bits. We would be copying some detail of one of his pictures. He planted himself behind our chairs and stared for five minutes without drawing breath and we, who knew so little, who were ignorant of methods, rules, tricks of the trade—no one had taught us anything—waited for useful advice as though for the voice of some oracle.

'A little hard', came the profound judgement, and he passed to the next student. Five more minutes of contemplation and then: 'A little heavy', both remarks uttered in a gross Teutonic accent. Then he went off on his own business, for that, and not us, is what drew him forth and allowed him to view our daubs from time to time.

He understood the relationship between master and students rather as the old painters did—but without their affectionate attitude. If he took pupils he had the idea that they should kindly act as his servants.

I didn't really mind this. There was something patriarchal and friendly about it, that ruled out any question of humiliation. I know nothing, he knows a lot: I need his help, he doesn't need mine. My objective is not pecuniary advantage nor ambition, but art. . . . Then, I have to admit it, there is a dash of the Quixote in my nature. Just as the Spanish knight imagined he was the comrade of Tristan and Lancelot, I pretended I was one of the numerous pupils of one of the ancient schools of painting, who lived with the *maestro,* did everything for him, and looked on him as father and employer.

For two or three years, I will not say I swept floors and carried water, but I opened the house-door when anyone knocked, took and received messages, carried pictures, and, in fact, performed all those services which if they were a little above those expected of the lowest menials, could also be considered below the descendant of so many heroes; as indeed a future prime minister.

What do you think? Did I do well or ill, by agreeing to be a student in the ancient manner usual in the time of Giotto, Masaccio, etc., when painters kept shop, and employed assistants and errand boys like pork-butchers?

There is one thing to be said in my favour. If I acted as a servant for the love of art, I did not, thank heavens, do so to get a lift up the pagoda tree at the top of which, instead of sausages and capons, hang decorations, medals, ribbons, patents of nobility, and ministerial port-folios. And, in all conscience, I do not really think that I shall get into much trouble on the day of judgement, owing to the sin of servility.

To keep up artistic traditions we did from time to time take our little revenges against our uncouth master. If we had been kept waiting for his appearance for several days—sometimes he quite forgot we existed—we decided together that an example had to be made.

We piled up an erection of easels, chairs, and canvases in such a way that no damage could be done; then one push and down it all came as though the house were collapsing. Poor Martino saw all his pictures with holes through them, and I can tell you that he was out in a flash. Of course we had our explanation ready when he rushed anxiously into the room brandishing the chain of the door, calling out 'Vot is the matter?'

As you see, if my instinct for mischief was no longer predominant one couldn't say it had been quite banished! A touch adds charm to youth, and with me it was no more. My character began to give distinct signs of beginning to mature. I matured very slowly, however, and I didn't feel grown up, I didn't reach decided opinions, nor conceive precise fundamental ideas about the greater part of moral, social, and political matters, until very late in life. This late development is perhaps an inherent feature of my character; it may arise from the need I have always felt to know the truth, as far as that may be possible, about everything, without being able to be satisfied with probabilities, or resign myself to authority as a matter of faith. It takes time to satisfy oneself by reasoning about everything!

This long thorny process was hardly beginning at that period of my life, and let us say too that I was not at an age for reason, but rather for love and passion.

I was fated to experience many ardent passions of more than one kind, but then I was in a very curious state. I felt the full force of passionate love, but I had no object to give it body, soul, and life.

I often went for a walk early in the morning through the groves of Villa Borghese. I had with me all the materials for drawing or writing: paper, sketch-book, pencil. I used to sit solitary in the shade of some tree, but nothing came to be written or sketched. My heart and imagination were kindled by a confusion of aspirations, longings, hopes, dreams of love and glory, disasters, bold splendid deeds. It was a painful condition to be in, for there was no purpose in it and no outcome, but at the same time it filled me with an intimate joy by the full torrent of life that swept over me. Deep in my being, that mysterious flower burgeoned that marks the spring-time of our souls. This is a great treasure, the greatest of all for the man who knows how to use it, because it is the harbinger of the most potent force given by God to man. Unfortunately it is a treasure spent by most in sensual passion; the force is dissipated, and the loss is only recognized when it is too late. In how many things of this world is it only too true to say: 'He who knows has not; he who has, knows not.'

I had done as most others in my early youth; really only adolescence, for circumstances had expedited my development. I had trodden the first flowering of my soul and heart in the mire, but thanks to the examples and education that had been given to me, thanks to Bidone, that shameful madness finished early. The perversion was not complete, only the outer man had been damaged. Perhaps my nature had contributed to this, if so it had nothing to do with me, it was a gift from above. My nature is such that it tenaciously retains the generous impulses of early youth. In fact I did not grow old all of a piece. Youthfulness of soul lasted long with me, and it is not even yet extinguished, though my body has aged. Only from 1860 on do I begin to feel my heart grow old. Hope is the perfume that keeps one young, and the years, as the seasons pass, rob us of this more and more; it is their direst offence.

Just imagine what I was like in 1819 and 1820! I was searching for some way to realize the resplendent future that haunted my dreams. In painting, I imagined new methods, new conceptions; not pictures in the style of the eighteenth-century mannerists; not the close scrupulous imitation of nature of the painters of my day, for if that was all there was to it, you would give the prize to photography. I could not at that time take into account the scrupulous imitation of the *ugly*, as realism had not yet invaded the realm of landscape painters.

As I am on this subject, I must say that the realist school of landscape painting is an invention that really honours human ingenuity. Take a man without a spark of artistic sense; no feeling for colour; no wish to work. A noodle would have been as modest as can be and would have said: 'I've not got it in me to be a painter; no matter, I'll be a carpenter.' But the man of talent says something quite different: 'What is all this technique, composition, colouring, purity of tint, flash of truth? All conservative nonsense of by-gone art. This is the new art, the art of the future, etc., etc.' Anyone with eyes in his head can see what has been served up to us under this pretext. And the public swallows it!

But let's drop the subject now. There will be a more appropriate time to talk of art and artists—it will be a long story!

In art, then, I was building castles in the air and feeding on fantasy, but I did know that I had, first of all, to master the palette, to learn the technique, to acquire the ability of being natural. So, with great labour, I strove to lay these first foundations. I was also turning over in my mind the notion of writing, as well as painting. It only remained to decide on what subject, with what purpose, in what sort of language and style I was to do it. Mere trifles! I often discussed this with Bidone, when I was in Turin. He gave me his usual advice: 'Write!'—'But what about?'—'Write!'—'But the language, the style?'—'Write!' 'But,' I said at last, 'if there is really no Italian language and no readable prose, what do I do?' 'If there is none, invent one!'

Easily said! However, I chafed at not being able to reach a decision that satisfied me. I thought, and it was a good thought, 'Let's study meanwhile.' As long as I stayed in Rome, the problem of writing remained unsolved. I did not solve it, well or badly, until many years afterwards; at that time I shelved it, thinking to myself: 'To study nature and write at the same time is not possible', and I wasn't far wrong.

My poor brain kept beating its little wings, like those on Mercury's hat, striving beyond the fields of art and literature.

Blessed are those, who stay where they were born, smile at sky, earth, men, and beasts, swallow everything put into their mouths or their brains, and finally leave the world as they found it.

Alas for those poor others who, hardly out of the shell, utter their first cheep like a new-hatched chicken, have a preliminary look round, and give voice to that insatiable *why*!

They then begin to fidget, to move from one place to another, to weigh things up, to examine, compare, research, delve, and then? They too leave the world . . . but, God be praised, not always as they found it. For man is born to move, scrutinize, to know who he is (if he can), what he's doing, where he's going. If a man dies in the effort, he dies honourably, perhaps usefully to others. I therefore do not mean to complain that I have an inquiring mind. It always has been so and always will be.

Even at that period, quite apart from art and literature, I considered a hundred problems; political, philosophic, ethical, religious; things that sprang from within, not reminiscences of what I had read. But whatever could I have read, I, a soldier before I was sixteen?

My political ideas had undergone some modification; I no longer felt the urgent need to kill a tyrant. I think the exaggerations of Alfieri's work *Della tirannide* calmed me down. I was, however, increasingly filled with the idea that our country should be her own mistress, and I felt more and more the shame of our humiliation. The behaviour of foreigners in Rome, their treatment of all classes of Romans, at receptions, at public festivals above all, in the papal chapels, at the functions of Holy Week; their arrogant assurance in insisting on domineering, disobeying, and abusing the officers and soldiers charged with keeping order at those ceremonies; all this filled me with unspeakable anger. The English were the most overbearing of all; some even going so far as to lay hands on the Swiss guards in order to force their way through a closed door. It sometimes happened that these soldiers, armed and clothed as those of Giovanni delle Bande Nere, replied with thrusts with

the sharp corners of their armour and the stocks of their halberds, and
I blessed them and prayed God to keep them out of the hands of
Cardinal Consalvi.

As is well known, he was Pius VII's Secretary of State, and if in
some things he had more progressive ideas than the rest of the Sacred
College, in others he liked to copy Napoleonic methods of centralization, within the narrow limits of the little papal State. This idea completely broke away from the traditions and habits of the population.
When old agreements, precious for the government as documentary
proof of accepted sovereignty, were cancelled, it was, according to my
view, the real beginning of the end for the temporal power.

He tried to increase the public wealth, which had suffered so much
during the previous administration. He well understood that to make
the arid branches of the tree of riches sprout again is neither an easy
nor a short process. He therefore did his best to lure foreigners to stay
in Rome. Failing other industries, alas! Italy, from Florence down, has
for some time followed the trade of inn-keeper. Therefore every time
a poor Roman employé tried to stand up to the bullying of some
foreigner, the latter never failed to exclaim: 'I shall go to Consalvi.'
Unfortunately Consalvi generally sided with the insolent foreigner and
blamed the faithful employé. It was for this reason I prayed God to
save the Swiss Guards from his most eminent clutches.

But if my heart made me hate the foreign yoke, my intelligence
could point out no way to break it. Even at the age of twenty I understood that one couldn't send Austrian regiments back over the Alps
with the help of the Carbonari Lodges, and still less with their daggers.
It was a long, long time before a solution of this great problem seemed
feasible to me.

At that time the shady retreats of the Villa Borghese and many other
spots were the confidants of my gloomy speculations, of my tears sometimes, shed for our shame, which I judged eternal.

As though the arts, literature, and politics were not enough to set
my heart and mind in a whirl, there was also love!

If you had asked me: 'Are you in love?'—'Not on your life,' I
should have replied. This was my trouble, to be in love and not to know
with whom. When every autobiography reaches the author's twentieth
year there naturally arises the problem of love. It is not a subject
to be lightly dismissed. It must have its own chapter and this will be
Chapter 15.

15

ALL polytheistic religions make love a god. From one point of view, the Christian teaching makes God himself and his prime essence, love. But this love is the most inexplicable of mysteries. '*Vous m'aimez, vous êtes Roi et je pars!*' said Olimpia Mancini to Louis XIV, as she left the Court by wish of her uncle Cardinal Mazarin.

'You love me, you are God, and I suffer!' This, alas, says the poor human heart. What is the good? The key of this mystery is not on earth, let us hope to find it in heaven.

The intellect is a poor guide, of no use in such a labyrinth; it leaves us stranded in darkness. We should rather follow the heart. Who, with his intellect, could grasp, who could express in words, that primal love before which 'no created things were'. God can be felt, but not conceived nor explained; he is felt as infinite love, as the mover of the universe, as a defence, a refuge. One feels that he is good; that he is creator of an eternal future, for us inexplicable, hidden from mortal eyes, but happy, fortunate, just, and reasonable; worthy to have sprung from the mind of God. Let us have faith then, let us be pure of heart, and descend bravely into the gulf where so many generations have gone before us.

If you should tell me, 'I do not feel this God of yours', I should reply: 'I'm sorry but I do not know what I can do about it.'

This love, however, love of God for his creature and of the creature for his creator, although the first, is not the only love. Here difficulties multiply. What is this love in the human heart? Love of self, of others, of ideas, of things? Which is the noble, generous love and which the sinful and abominable, etc., etc., etc.? There could be thousands of such varieties of love. But all is confused, indefinite, illogical; all is conflict and contradiction in this great kingdom of love. Language itself reflects the perplexities of the subject.

What an inconceivable poverty and indecision of expression there is! In French, the language which I consider the most perfect instrument of inter-communication invented by man, the most exact, the clearest, the most logical of all (I speak few languages, but I think what I say is correct); in French there is but one word to express love: *J'aime Dieu, j'aime ma patrie, j'aime ma mère, j'aime ma maîtresse, j'aime la science, j'aime le vaudeville,* or *j'aime les épinards au jus;* forever *j'aime.*

It is a little better in Italian as in English; at least I can keep spinach in a separate category from my country and family and say *'mi piacciono gli spinaci'* as *'I like spinach'* and *'amo la patria'* as *'I love my country'*.

Is this poverty and lack of precision in language purely casual? Or is it a defect, inherent in the birth, growth, and refinement of language? Is it an inconsistency, a logical fault, or rather is it something that has arisen from a most delicate sense of values?

Should the latter hypothesis be true, a language should only have the noun *love* and the verb *to love,* for love is one and the same thing though its manifestations are numerous, however ill-understood and ill-defined. This is the cause of all the uncertainty and obscurity.

There is, however, one kind of love, understood, clearly defined, and known by all, for which our language has found, if not the verb, the appropriate substantive, indeed two—*l'amor proprio, l'egotismo.* Perhaps we can say that love for our good self can be called by the ignoble name of egotism, and love for anything beyond oneself should deserve exclusively the noble, beautiful word *love.*

Consequently the love that is true, generous, lovely, noble, and admirable is love for something outside us and distinct from us, for something we prefer to ourselves. Because of this preference we try to please and benefit it to our own cost, should the object of our love be an animate being. Should it be an abstraction, collective or material, we try to make it great, powerful, and glorious. My dear much-travelled reader, you must have imagined you have discovered many of these loves that prefer an object beyond self to the *ego* within. If you have discovered few or many, have you not almost begun to doubt whether this true, generous, lovely, noble, and admirable love really exists at all; or if it is not, with very few exceptions, rather a metaphysical sophistry of the literatures of civilized peoples? Consider the commonest kind of love, that between the sexes. Do you believe that between those persons who can't read, so have never read books, poems, novels, tales, etc., etc., there are many who experience love with all the anxieties, hallucinations and heroisms of the poets; with all the seductive phantasmagoria with which we have been plagued by those books which teach people to make love who knew nothing about it and didn't want it? Do you believe that among those who have never, really never, read a love-tale, there are many dozen who, for example, can be persuaded that there is only one woman in the world worthy to be loved? Who lose sleep and appetite on her account, who believe the greatest of all misfortunes is not to obtain her favour? Who die for her or throw themselves into the river?

Apart from eclogues and idylls, have you ever seen an enamoured peasant? Have you ever seen Hodge miss a day's work or forget to stir his porridge, for love? Should then this love be a disease of the gentry spread by books, does not one immediately consider whether there are more readers or non-readers in the world? And if it be probable that we discover that, over the whole mass of humanity, only one in a thousand can read, do we not conclude that love (in the sense of the novelette and not the mutual attraction of the sexes) is a very trifling reaction, a trivial pastime for ladies and gentlemen who have nothing better to do and find it difficult to while away the twenty-four hours of the day?

We live in a small country, in small Europe, in a small group of friends and acquaintances, and many think that is the world. But let us consider for a moment what happens elsewhere. What happens to this blessed love, that has upset so many (or did) in the west, among the analphabetic populations of the east, with their polygamy and their harems of slaves? Do you think that in all the region between Constantinople and the north-west coast of America you would be able to find many who sighed for years for an unkind beauty? They might sigh because they lacked the cash to buy her. Do you think in all Africa there are many Negroes who would rather die than offend some adored, dusky belle? Without labouring the point any longer, may I suggest you give a rapid glance over the world, and then tell me if you do not find that lovely, lofty, generous love, for which a man sacrifices his own good for another's, is very much rarer and more exceptional than what is commonly believed.

After all, what need is there to bring semi-barbarous nations into it? In Europe itself, literate Europe, the classes which had no need to work and who therefore read novels and made love, surely they do so less and less, for the simple reason that to 'play the gentleman' is no longer considered an occupation in itself, and now everybody more or less works.

The countries which were condemned by bad governments to idleness and who, to pass the time, made love *en masse*, have they not changed, directly the field of public life was opened to them? In Italy people don't make love one-third as much as they did in my time. Therefore a different practice now flourishes by which a man can be served according to his means, more or less as in his need for transport. He can take a cab by the hour or day, or reserve a carriage for an evening, month, or year. A busy man can therefore make his arrangements, but what can he do according to that other method by which, in pursuing an ideal, he has his ride for nothing, but must stick in the carriage at another's whim, while neglecting his own business?

This raises an important question. Is this progress or regression? Is it better to consider a woman as a goddess, or as a brougham to be hired by the month? Which method is more likely to lead to noble, useful consequences? For me I can reply immediately and absolutely. Better goddess than cab! It is not, however, a matter of better or worse. Our business is to find the truth and discover what actually happens and exists. And don't you seem to see that estimable love flies before us as we look for it and in its place, usurping its name, we find unworthy love?

Love found little place in classical literature. Briseis, the cause of the wrath of Achilles, we hardly get to know in the *Iliad*; Helen appears as the fifth wheel of the cart, and yet is the occasion for the whole poem. What part does love play in the *Odyssey*? In Greek drama, except for Alcestis, Phaedra, and a few others—and there is always the business of some God's revenge which shifts the centre of interest—what character do we see exemplifying on the stage, those grand exquisite passions such as we find in Rousseau's *Éloise*? As we go on, we do not find the Latins wasting much time on the metaphysics of love. With Horace's Lalage we reach the highest point without effort. In the middle ages with the Provençals there appears the northern tradition of the apotheosis of love and the metaphysical worship of beauty. As I am not lecturing on literature, I will not stay to expound names, dates, and systems; in any case all know about the flood of poetical love-making that swept over Europe in poems, romances, and amorous versifications of all kinds. It was a false, artificial literature that feigned frenzy and inspired it. But at least they were generous, splendid frenzies that uplifted the heart and could, though untrue themselves, lead to things that were true, lovely, and useful to society. But there are, alas, periods when the world, vexed by that false love masquerading as the true by which it has been deceived, throws itself off balance and wants to roll in the mire.

Europe owes much to France; and Italy, since the victory of Solferino, owes her great obligations. There is no question but that it was from France that that great ray of illumination shone forth which showed the world its deformity and shamed it into trying to reform. With her intelligence and through her writings France imposed a real and beneficent sway over the world, but I, a good friend, but no flatterer, must say to the French: 'You have made Europe pay dear for your bounty.' Never before has there been such a flood of books specially produced for the perversion of human nature, as those of French literature since the days of Louis Philippe.

The works of imagination, especially novels—I have seen some infamous specimens—have really infected the views of Europe with a morbid lymph. The one and only aim of authors—the exceptions are rare—was to make money, therefore to succeed, therefore to flatter the basest instincts of the mass of readers. As the surest way to influence people is not by promoting true democracy, that is to say, equality of all before the law, but rather that other democracy that derides all law when it can, and is the apotheosis of the foul and the ugly; authors who aim at getting on and winning a carriage for themselves have paid court to the mob and proclaimed the triumph of the obscene in their books.

For a long time now kept women (I'm not saying anything new), pimps, murderers, rogues of all kinds have been described as the only people capable of great deeds, whereas honest men have been shown as nincompoops and weaklings. The simple ideas which remain at the back of one's mind, after reading such books, were, and are, that any distinction between right and wrong is only a scarecrow to frighten fools; that violent passions are a mark of strength, whereas the contrary is the truth; that the infallible sign of moral superiority is in not feeling respect for anything, whereas the contrary is the truth; and as far as love is concerned, that never threadbare subject, the pivot on which all writings intended to please must revolve; tell me, respected reader, if you have ever found in French novels of this kind the figure of a modest, charming girl as, for example, Manzoni's Lucia, the figure of an admirable woman who is, at one and the same time, natural, attractive, and amiable?

The author sometimes, it is easy to see, would like to present something angelic, some innocent floweret, some being breathing purity and candour. But goodness me, what trouble he has, what constant effort, what lack of naturalness, true simplicity, easy manners, which should flow spontaneously from the narrative! It is very plain that the author, wishing to raise himself above his proper level, is walking on stilts.

But only look at a scene where kept women are described at supper! Observe their rich fare, wines, silver, lights, and low-necked dresses! Here there is a wealth of description, truth, sparkling imagination, inspired style in a torrent of eloquence. It is obvious that the author's mouth is watering, that he is in his element and is longing to get paid for his manuscript so that he too can join the party at table, or under it.

This literature is one of the causes of the notable lowering of the moral thermometer of the European reading public. From the society girl who reads secretly, down to the concierge's daughter who steals from the few hours of sleep allowed her by the dressmaker for whom she works, to devote the time to novels; what countless irregularities, what illusions, what irremediable demoralization! What is the reason for all this? In the last analysis, because Signor Blank wants to keep six horses in his stable, plus what goes with them. He knows that the public, the modern King, just as many Kings of the past, pays the man who flatters its basest instincts very handsomely, and the man who panders to them even better!

Now, after all this talk, my conclusion is that people make love very much less than is supposed.

More often than not, love is the outcome of idleness and leisure; it is the artificial product of literature, and French literature has turned it into an ignoble speculation.

These ideas are the fruit of my own observations, as usual. But because mine, I do not put them forward as infallible. What will the reader think of them? He'll probably say: 'That's all very well, but there are people in the world who can't read or write, who work like cart-horses, and yet fall in love.' I would reply that, in the first place, no two of these loves are alike and one has to make a scientific analysis of all, to assess the worth of any. Of course, in speaking of the rarity of love, I have limited the term to love that prefers the good of the person loved to one's own, otherwise it is but egotism. If we put all kinds of love to the chemical test, do you suppose that our alembic will distil a liquid as pure as spring water?

In the second place, apart from analyses and alembics, the question comes down to the fact that every rule has exceptions. I admit it. Even without looking farther afield, I can stand forth myself as exception and proof of the rule.

I certainly did not read love stories in my youth. I worked, worked to the point of falling ill more than once. Yet my nature was so impressionable, so passionate, that it would be impossible to describe the violence of the storms through which I have had to pass, for love.

'*Dieu merci, c'est fini!*' said Richelieu.

The appropriate moment seems to have come when I must begin to deal with my own love-affairs and describe them as they come along.

But I think I'd better not; and these are my reasons. First of all, such stories are all the same if you only change the names of the parties concerned. In the second place, when I read other people's autobiographies and find their conquests described, they always seem rather ridiculous to me. When they melt with tenderness in recounting the havoc they wrought in feminine hearts; when they notice a shop-girl gazing at them as they get measured for a pair of gloves and add her to their list of conquests; when finally they scatter flowers on the tomb of some little angel who died of love (or gastro-enteritis) for them; all these manifestations of an inconsolable heart, poured into the lap of the public, have always struck me as one of the most laughable exhibitions of human vanity. Very well then, to describe one's successes is ridiculous, to describe one's discomfitures. . . ! To speak frankly, my dear reader, don't you really think there are more amusing topics? Therefore the best thing is not to describe one's own love-affairs at all. So far the utilitarian reasons, now for the reasons based on good breeding and right feeling.

True, loyal, unconditional affection is a great treasure, the greatest there is. Should there have been a woman who gave all possible proofs of such a feeling for you, should you, in exchange, publicize her love? I know no names are mentioned, but when a man is well-known, can he so veil all the events at all periods of his life that names cannot easily be guessed?

I have always considered ingratitude as one of the depraved vices of the human heart. But ingratitude towards a woman who has loved you truly and loyally, even for a brief hour, has always struck me as the basest of all. What more could she have done, poor soul; what greater benefit or happiness could she have given than her love? What intimate moments of joy has she not shared indivisibly with you; what did she not risk; how greatly did she trust to your loyalty and honour! And now you would trample on the memory, betray her trust, give her name up to scandal-mongering, all for the stupidest of vanities, that of posing as a Don Juan?

It is rarely the case that a man, however unattractive, has not found love of some sort during his life, so that the best rule for all is not to talk about it, or at least not to write about it.

True it is that some good can be extracted from such accounts, some guiding compass for the poor barks setting sail for the first time, full of hopes and illusions, on that sea, that truly treacherous sea. To have the best of both worlds, I will, therefore, discuss the subject, but limit myself to generalities.

The worst feature of love, as it is often found in the *reading* classes, is the necessity for constantly telling lies. The man who makes love is rarely without the need for speaking, or acting, a lie. So feigning becomes a habit. One's character is vitiated and presently one becomes like those who lose their ear for music; lies, like false notes, cease to make any disagreeable impact.

Here I must exclaim a loud *mea culpa*! But when there's a husband, a father-in-law, a brother, etc., whose eyes must be kept bandaged, I guarantee there's nothing else to be done. That is to say, there is something else to be done, but who can do it with one's brain raging at 80° and one's heart at 100°! I never succeeded.

I never acted the lie—nay, worse than lie, perfidy—of making love deliberately for purely selfish motives. I have never told a woman, or tried to persuade a woman, that I loved her, unless it were true. There are men, and it is not so rare, who see a young woman, in accord with her husband, fond of her family, happy at home, without secrets or worries, with mind untroubled and heart serene; there are men, I repeat, who mark her down and strive to devastate this smiling garden and make those who live there miserable, in order to say afterwards, 'I succeeded!' There are those who do not feel love, are not moved by the smallest degree of passion, who undertake such an enterprise with continual feigning, and present themselves to the unfortunate victim as madly in love but a model of delicacy. Usually a woman is good, confiding, ignorant of human wickedness. She trusts, gives in, and the happiness, peace, and whole future of many persons are lost for ever. All houses are open to the perpetrators of such disasters, although the ruffian who assaults you in the street is hung. And they say, there's justice in the world!

I have no call for remorse here, whenever I had to utter that fatal phrase 'I love you', and say it seriously—not for fun, it was only too true.

In my salad days I lived like a scamp and my girl friends were scamps too, for whom the word love was not current coin. Later I passed through a bad phase, which only lasted for a short time, in which, more for craziness than anything else, I had several flames at once. Then came the day when I really fell in love properly, with indescribable violence. The affair lasted for many years. Meanwhile I was maturing, growing older and more experienced. I grew to hate feigning and falsehood more and more; I tried to limit my lies to what was essential, as is sometimes done with the house-keeping expenses. I was gradually led to lay down a rule for myself, not much followed by the young, that one must speak the truth and keep one's word to everyone . . . even to women!

I therefore believe that I have been one of the most faithful of men, principally because I could not have denied infidelity, if interrogated with my back against the wall. I should perhaps say I was truthful rather than faithful. In fact I used to say: 'In love constancy is a necessity, fidelity a luxury', and I said it partly as a joke, partly in earnest.

Actually it is quite possible to hate several people at the same time; why can't one do the same with love? Not in the same degree, of course, but differently? Constancy is the essence of every true heart-felt passion; but fidelity in minute particulars is like devotion to the ceremonial practices of religion, and should really be placed among the affectations of the literati.

Certain feminine readers known to me would scratch my eyes out, could they get me within range, for this lax doctrine of mine. Good gracious, how they would enjoy doing so! The curious thing is that despite such theories about infidelity, I have been quite different in practice. But I say again that this was due rather to my repugnance to lying.

For the same reason I have never pushed deceit so far as to make friends with a husband in order to lull his suspicions. This has always seemed to me to be unworthy. This is the evil of such loves; one's character takes on sorry propensities which persist after the affair is over.

Just as love has a beginning, so it has—unfortunately or fortunately according to circumstances—an end. This end is never reached on the same day and at the same hour by two lovers. While one of the parties says 'enough', the other says 'more', and this is a sad business for the latter of the two. Only once have I been the one to say 'enough', and I thought the quickest way out was to confess. This I did and saved a lot of lies, moanings, and useless reproofs. They do say that men have been raised from the dead, but I have never heard of the resurrection of a dead love-affair, certainly not by whining.

If once I was the one to say 'enough', twice I uttered the plaintive word 'more', and my suffering was the greater, because I would not descend to recriminations and laments, so that I nearly died. The method I adopted was to sheer off:

> *Le bruit est pour le fat*
> *La plainte est pour le sot,*
> *L'honnête homme trompé*
> *S'éloigne et ne dit mot.*[1]

---

[1] Protesting is for fools,
Complaint is quite absurd.
An honest man deceived,
Makes off without a word.

I could easily prolong this chapter as the subject is endless. I think, however, that what I have said is enough to illustrate my views about love. In writing about my life it had to find a place.

What the reader deduces from what I have written is his affair; he has a summary available of what can be brought against me. As for the observations to be made from the facts given, which could perhaps be of use to young men (as far as precepts and advice are of the slightest use where passion is concerned), these are what seem to me to be the most obvious.

Apart from all ideas of Christian ethics, illicit love-affairs are a source of trouble, annoyance, and sometimes misfortune, as society is at present organized. Therefore to steer clear of them is all gain. If you can't, there are two pieces of advice I can give: do as little harm as possible to others and to yourself. As far as you are concerned try to prevent yourself getting into a habit of systematic falsehood; as for others, yield to a genuine invincible passion, but never simulate it, and never sacrifice to your own vanity the peace, good, and happiness of those who have had the misfortune to find themselves in your path.

I do not put forward these ideas as the expression of a complete ethical theory, but I consider them practical and therefore useful.

To explain what I think of myself, I do not think, unless I am mistaken, I have been the cause of great harm to others, but I have brought much harm to myself. I have had to do a great deal to restore my character to the straightforward, sincere state which was how I had it from nature. I have suffered so much from the depth of sincerity of my sentiments that I have certainly frittered away a part of the vitality and health that I could much better employ in the service of my country. Thinking over the past, I seem to recognize that it was due to my very sincerity, and to my complete abandonment to love, that I may have become tedious. I have, alas! ended by suspecting that few women are capable of truly and steadfastly loving a man of integrity. Perhaps it is more his fault than theirs? ... Despite this, the impression I have, from what I have experienced and observed, is that generally women are worth more than men. If I have had to suffer much on their account, I did once find the compensation of an affection which never failed and persisted through all possible vicissitudes. Those who can say likewise should be satisfied. Not many can.

This is all I have to say on the subject *Love*, and I've probably said too much. I have no illusions about the conversions likely to be the fruit of my sage reflections. In everything, especially in love, people want to try for themselves.

All right, boys! Try then, and fifty years on you can preach a sermon to those who come after you, as I do to you ... perhaps ... with the same result. God forgive me!

16

IN the spring of the year 1820 my parents left Rome and I returned to Turin with them. We took the road through Umbria and Tuscany. From Florence we went to Modena, via Bologna. Here we stopped. My father had to pay his respects to the Duke, who had not then acquired the notoriety as a royal chief of police (and I could use a less civil phrase) which he afterwards earned. He was an Austrian Archduke who tried to win acceptance by his connexion with the house of Este, but who turned out to be one of the props of the evil brood who oppressed my country. As luck would have it I had no uniform with me—I have always done my best to forget it as the immediate cause of much trouble—so in this case I could successfully use this as an excuse with my father not to go to Court, and he was satisfied. The Duke, however, was not so kind and sent a message to tell me to come as I was. So I saw him and had to put up with an audience. Even though it was a nuisance for me, the Duke thought he was doing me a favour; so even though he is no less a person than the infamous Francesco IV, I had either to refuse his kindness or acknowledge it: this I do now.

From Modena, via Brescello, Mantua, Verona, and Padua, we reached Venice. There I saw a battery of two Austrian guns in position before the Doge's palace; I saw more in the arsenal, where *'bolle d'inverno la tenace pece'*[1] and where my blood boiled still more at the sight of that great covered area, and the deep docks constructed for the building of ancient galleys, thinking ... but I'm no longer a student and I must avoid rhetoric! So, my dear reader, if you are an Italian and have read history, you can well imagine what I thought at the age of twenty, loving Italy and hating the foreign yoke. How ashamed I felt to be an Italian! How I longed one day to have the chance of fighting the Austrians; to fight, even if to be beaten! But was it probable in May 1820? I therefore lived in a state of furious melancholy, relieving my feelings by writing sonnets and canzoni, awful stuff, enough to frighten away the Austrians if they had heard them declaimed.

---

[1] Dante, *Inferno*, XXI, 8. 'Where in winter the sticky tar boils.'

I derived comfort from the idea that Venice, Rome, and Carthage have all been great and strong, as powerful as Vienna; the day will come for Vienna as it came for them. Who would have said that my very eyes, before closing for ever, would have seen this happen!

We passed through Milan, and this time I was not escorted, *'cum fustibus et lanternis'*, to the police-station for lack of identity papers. I recall one trifling anecdote, which impressed me at the time. Many people came to call on us at the inn, among them a Monsignore, whose name I find it impossible to remember. Speaking of one thing and another, the conversation turned to the subject of education. After discussion, the Monsignore said by way of emphatic conclusion: 'I think ignorant populations are the easiest to govern.' I was not so surprised at the maxim, as to hear it frankly stated, and I thought to myself—I was fresh from Rome—'My dear Monsignore, if you continue to be so candid, you'll never get promotion.' I don't know if my prophecy has come true.

In Turin, society was in a state of feverish restlessness, such as invalids experience on the eve of a crisis. The revolution of the year 1821, or rather the famous Spanish Constitution, was just about to break upon us. I was a relation or acquaintance of many of the plotters, many of whom used to frequent my sister-in-law's house. I belonged to no coterie; I was neither a Carbonaro nor a freemason. Why masons are called freemasons, I do not know, unless it is because they have to obey two governments, instead of one. It must be admitted that my looks would not have inspired confidence in me as a conspirator, sectarian, or the like; never, never was I invited to join a secret society, and therefore I never did so. I am not so bold as to assert that I abstained through precocious good judgement, because when one is eighteen or twenty one acts more by chance than choice. The fact remains that I have had the enormous advantage of never having to fear that my name could be found on a list of plotters. Nor could anyone flourish such a paper in my face as evidence of betrayed comrades or broken faith. During the time when I was in public life, no one had any right to approach me and whisper in my ear, 'Signor Massimo, don't forget, we're bond brothers . . . , etc.' I should thus have had to fail in my sworn allegiance to the King as member of parliament, minister, senator, governor, and so on, or to break the oath sworn to the president of some Carbonaro lodge or other. A further and last advantage is that government, sect, party, etc., whether they wish me well or ill, can either leave me in peace or persecute me, even kill me if they feel like it; but I challenge them to call me a turncoat or traitor.

Finding myself then, as always, quite free and independent, I waited to see what the outcome of all the fuss was going to be.

The events of 1821 are well known; in fact they are now almost forgotten. The world has experienced much else since then. Nevertheless I shall make a few observations about them as they occur to me.

However much I esteem some of the leaders of that revolution and however much friendship I feel for them, I must say quite frankly that I cannot approve of it or the methods by which it was brought about.

A people cannot be moved except by something it knows or, at least, wants. Therefore, before starting to act, you must explain what you are doing, or, at any rate, rouse passions and desires.

The prodigal extravagance of Louis XIV and his successors, the barbarous privileges of clergy and nobility, the writings of the authors of the time, whose path was prepared for them by the stupidities of the old system, both political and religious, informed the people and roused a longing in them for better laws: the result was the French revolution. But in Italy in 1821, the memories of military insolence, of the continental blockade, of the violent annexations and divisions of provinces and kingdoms, which originated from the immediate ambitions of Napoleon, but had grown out of the ideas and events of the earlier revolution; such memories had not been cancelled by five or six years of the restored monarchy. In the opinion of the majority, by the law of nature always the least intelligent, the restoration was a return to life, to tranquillity, to happiness; a liberation from a hated tyranny.

Most people did not understand that in the Napoleonic era tyranny was an exception, while in the period of the restorations it was the rule. Rather than tyranny we should say absolutism. The mass was therefore very far from wanting change. The happiness which revolution had brought to Spain had not yet roused much envy! It all came down to an isolated effervescence, starting in the bosom of the secret societies, which did not, could not, spread to the rest of the nation, because their ideas were not properly understood and the changes they proclaimed were not wanted.

Here was another example of the good service rendered by the secret societies! They offered a phantasmagoria of a non-existent world and then precipitated us into an impossible situation. But do not let us forget that the secret societies were the fruit of the stupid, blind, retrograde absolutism of the restoration, so that the latter was the real cause of the revolution.

Cesare Balbo said that the revolutions in Turin and Naples set back our emancipation by many years, and he spoke truth.

There is another important point of view. The 1821 revolution was a military one and thus the worst, most corrupting, most harmful, in its bad example and interminable consequences. If I do not respect, and do not like a system, I do not serve it; if I agreed to serve it when I did like and respect it and then, rightly or wrongly, changed my mind, I cease to serve it; but break faith—never!

I hasten to add, however, that it would be unjust to apply an *a priori* argument to decide on the merits, or otherwise, of individual behaviour in a case of this kind.

The real sin is, knowingly, to go against conscience, and the sort of artificial conscience I attributed, as you may know, to the Roman Curia is not its monopoly; that is what they share with their opponents, the secret societies, or rather with the sectarians themselves, who supply the passion behind it.

Can any of us boast that he has not had this artificial conscience, even for a day?

If, then, I judge the military revolution severely, I am far from judging those who were guilty of it with equal severity.

Just as our physical senses can suffer from hallucinations, so can our moral, and this must be clearly kept in mind when pronouncing judgement.

One more consideration! Even for many years after '21 no better way to improve our conditions was found than that of secret societies and spasmodic little revolutions, which lasted a fortnight. Until '44 or '45 no one thought of winning over public opinion and founding reform on that. The authoritative voice of Napoleon III should have taught the plotters that the world is not influenced by secret, but rather by public societies. Now we see that his method succeeds. All the same the secret societies continue. You can't persuade an employee that it is an advantage for him to lose his job.

All I have said applies to revolutions brought about by violence. In general I have no sympathy for them. I have always admired the winning of some right denied, by means of passive resistance. Such victories are the real revolutions and they have always struck me as the most admirable, virile, and assured.

The spread of Christianity was certainly one of the greatest revolutions ever known. For the first time it obtained the recognition that a man had rights as a man, not only as a citizen. Before God, the lowest slave was the equal of the Emperor. This idea changed the world. How was such a revolution brought about? By knowing how to suffer and die.

At a lower level, but equally remarkable, was the conduct of the English Quakers at a time when the intolerance of the Anglican Church persecuted all dissenters. Rather than swear an oath they believed to be wrong—and if the gospel says *nolite jurare omnino,* as Christians they do not seem to have been much in the wrong—they preferred to emigrate or go to prison. At one time there were more than 15,000 of them incarcerated. They would rather suffer as Christ suffered and as the martyrs suffered, and just as these they remained victors in the field.

Passive resistance does not present the same splendid, moving scenes of passion as more aggressive revolutions. It will therefore never be favoured by the youthful section of society, especially among our southern races, because it demands an inflexible character and pre-supposes little, or no, imagination.

To speak candidly: which is more difficult, to charge a redoubt or barricade, in the midst of bullets and bayonets, shouts, smoke, and din, and find oneself either inside the objective or outside, unscathed or fallen; or to remain ten, five, two years, even a single year, in prison; there where the spirit grows faint in gloom, silence, solitude, and the sense of being forgotten; where the body sickens from lack of air, exercise, and its accustomed food; where the tedium is so great that a sparrow, a piece of grass, a spider can be an inestimable treasure to the unfortunate prisoner, and their removal an unheard-of act of barbarism?

Of this ability to withstand long suffering with fortitude, which I have said was rare among southerners, Italy has, nevertheless, provided noble examples. The solitary cells of the Spielberg fortress know that well enough, as do all those Italians capable of feeling who remember with gratitude, honour, and respect those who suffered there.

Everyone recognizes, however, the difference between a punishment suffered for having attacked a government, however illegal and tyrannical, and one inflicted when you theatened nobody, when your only crime was to refuse to give up your rights or to acquiesce in their violation.

In the first case there will always be some who will at least tax you with imprudence and impulsiveness. There is in the human heart a feeling that hesitates entirely to condemn a government, even an evil government, which defends itself when attacked: in the second case, the sympathy, pity, honour, and everything else are on the side of the victim; the hate, indignation, and infamy are all for the executioner.

What was it the old political wisdom of our fathers said? 'Don't make martyrs.' That is proof that the martyr harms a bad government more than a rebel.

Just rights are vindicated, not by active, but by passive force. One of the most singular and marvellous proofs of this truth is offered by the Jewish people. On the whole, the Jews today are accorded the recognition of their rights denied them since the days of Titus. For eighteen centuries, two or three hundred million Christians and about a hundred and sixty million Mohammedans were ranged against five million Jews. We all have an idea of the bitter persistence with which an attempt was made to exterminate them, to trample down and extinguish the last germ of that indomitable stock of Jacob. Who won in the end? The five million against the four hundred and sixty million!

Passive force was nobly practised by the Milanese and Lombards on several occasions. The poor Venetians are having to practise it today. Let them take comfort in remembering its invincible efficiency and let them be sure that they will win in the end. History will not rate their present patient firmness less than the splendid courage they showed in the siege of 1849. If their suffering is to be longer, their reward will be double.

Let us recapitulate. If in '21, instead of that blind gang of Carbonari, which only managed to stir up a brief civil war, soon extinguished by an Austrian army corps at Novara, there had been an attempt to win over public opinion through all possible channels of publicity then open, the change effected twenty-four years later, the unanimous impulse which started in 1845, and was only due to public opinion exercised in the light of day, might have produced a better, saner, and speedier result.

However, I halt before the endless terrain of the hypothetical. If it may be useful to establish certain principles, there is nothing vainer or more fallacious than trying to discover what might have happened had such and such things been done.

All great upheavals, all great social and political changes take place of necessity. They happen through a complex of causes, which no single mind can apprehend or control. While journalists and authors wear themselves out in offering advice and guidance, the unfortunate human race, like a sick man in convulsions, tosses and turns and gets into a thousand unlikely postures from which, unexpectedly, providence produces health, renewal, and tranquillity.

It is God, not we, who makes revolutions; and to be persuaded of this it is sufficient to think by what instruments he effects his purpose. One sees from ours, for example, that God has left us in no doubt whatever that it is being achieved without any assistance from us!

I spent the great part of the summer of '20 in the country, pursuing my studies from nature. I stayed, either at Saluzzo or at his Rivalta castle, with Count Benevello, who was as passionately fond of art as I was. I remember him as one of my best and most agreeable friends. He was highly imaginative, had an exquisite sense of colour, was full of new and sometimes very odd ideas, and had an insatiable curiosity of mind that led him to experiment in all branches of knowledge. This gave him a wide, rather than deep, culture. He was frank, simple, and easy to get on with in everyday affairs.

He drew and painted: figures; landscapes; night, cloud, and mist effects. I don't say he did very well, but at least he produced results. He was typical of most of our generation, in that we all tried our hand at something; we all felt a need for action, we all felt driven to try to distinguish ourselves in some way or other, owing to that powerful far-reaching electric shock, imparted to his age by the tireless activity of Napoleon. The outstanding men of that time in Piedmont, who all had brilliant careers, were Balbo, Peyron, Plana, Bidone, Sauli, Sclopis, Provana, Collegno, Vidua, and Santarosa. Owing to his artistic taste, his passion for learning and getting others to learn, for his assistance in promoting study, Benevello deserves a place among them.

His home was open to learned men in all branches of knowledge. The first picture exhibitions were held in a room he had had specially built in his house, which he lent free of charge. He allocated studios to artists on the top floor. It was unheard of that the owner of a house in Turin should arrange his attic so that there was light and room enough to paint a picture. Benevello took an interest in these tenants of his, as in all young men who started on the long, thorny, painful *via crucis* of art. He was one of the first people in Turin to draw a distinction between an artisan and an artist. He actually invited the unpolished followers of the Muses to his house. They were unpolished; but why? Because no one had ever deigned to admit them to an environment where polish is acquired and where men learn from others to broaden their horizons.

At that time Count Benevello initiated much that was of benefit to his country. Our society of the time was strictly organized according to rank, hostile to all innovations. People laughed at him, and indeed some of his ideas on art, architecture, and literature gave ample scope for mockery. The only man, however, who is safe from error and from being talked about and laughed at is he who does nothing at all. Those who laughed behind the back of this excellent friend of mine were in that category. He was a good citizen, a good head of a household, a careful, but generous, administrator of his property—qualities difficult to combine; he was courteous and hospitable and did not spend one hour of his life in that kind of idleness euphemistically described as 'acting the gentleman'.

At one and the same time—this was a defect of character—he would be working, for example, at an altar-piece; in the next room there was a chemical experiment under way; on a desk in the corner was the rough manuscript of a novel, a comedy, or the plans for a church; beyond, there was a machine devised to experiment with a method of propulsion he had invented, etc., etc. You will ask what was the outcome of all these attempts, experiments, and inventions?

I can reply at once. In regard to art and science, little or nothing. But in respect of civic life and civilized behaviour, he has left many useful examples, especially for the well-off and the gentry. He was a very rich man, but he lived with truly singular simplicity as far as his own way of life was concerned. He owned palaces, castles, villas, but if you went into his studio and asked him where his own room was, you would sometimes find that his bed was behind a curtain in a passage, or in a cubby-hole in the attics. He never felt the need for anything; ate what was brought to him; was indifferent to cold, heat, comfort, refinements; he dressed informally and slept little.

Such is the good example he has left, and it is to his lasting honour. Should he find imitators among the gentry, he will not have been less useful than if he had discovered some new salt or metal.

He had one son, who only survived him for a short time, so this is another line of men of integrity to be extinguished. Within the walls of his house, however, the tradition of his intelligent, kind hospitality has not been lost.

I too was forced to become aware at that time how difficult it was to live on terms with Turin society for one who dared to think, speak, and act in ways different from its usual procedures. God help one of us who wanted to think things out for himself, get an original idea and pursue it according to the rules of logic, deduce the consequences and act on them in his own affairs!

Just as in some countries they exhibit in public a specimen weight or measure, so that others can be verified as correct; so one would have said that God had supplied one brain only for the nobility of Turin, which was kept at Court in a showroom, so that all could go and get any ideas they needed.

But I had no intention of having recourse to such a social brain and wanted, as I said, to make use of my own.

When, thanks to Bidone, I had resolved to abandon my idle life and do something, my father and mother had naturally approved. Then came the trip to Rome and the stay in that city, during which I had in no way abandoned my project. I had studied, worked, and had nothing to do with doubtful company (it was the period when I had succeeded in completely controlling the most powerful inclinations of a young man of twenty); yet, all the same, my father did not wish to free me entirely from the bonds of my military career.

As is only natural, he always feared that these artistic enthusiasms of mine were a flash in the pan and that I should find myself one day with seniority lost, with no military rank and no equivalent compensation.

This was a moment for a definite decision; either take up the service again as a career, or break with it entirely, in order to follow that of study and free independent work on my own. I stuck to my decision. My parents were hesitant, thinking that to dispatch me alone, without guidance, at my age and with nothing to keep me in check, to a city such as Rome, to cultivate the very art that introduces youth into the oddest, maddest, gayest, most unruly company and, at the same time, the most perilous, was really to put me, my health, my morals, and my future, to the hazard: it was too much of a toss-up. I now feel the ungrateful injustice of my impatience. I now understand how natural were my father's and mother's doubts, they who knew my character and loved me so deeply.

She, who always sacrificed herself to her husband, children, and family, was inclined to let me try, and my father did not absolutely forbid it, until in late autumn the decision had to be made. It was affirmative.

The decision was a proof of firm character and good judgement in my parents. Nowadays it would only seem quite a natural step for me to take and something that goes without saying. But then the *Cavalier Massimo d'Azeglio who was retiring from the Piemonte Reale regiment and the Guards in order to go and be a painter in Rome!* ... These few words arranged in a single sentence meant for our society the return of the world to chaos and the abomination of desolation.

To give a proper notion of a time so far removed now from present ideas, the speediest and best would be to pretend we are at a party in the house of one of our old-fashioned nobility in the year 1820. The trouble is that the dialogue in Italian would miss the local colour and it would turn out rather insipid. I simply must do it in Piedmontese. Not all will understand? Very well! Those who would like to, must get it explained to them; those who don't, will have missed little. In fact I must warn the reader that if I amuse myself in painting this picture of a world I knew so well, it may not be very interesting to him. He has the remedy in his own hands, let him skip.

Of course I offer types, not individuals, and they have come straight out of my head. Well, here we are! I start by describing the scene and the background.

A palace in X street, seventeenth-century architecture. Carriage entrance, great gate, porch, courtyard from which one can enjoy the sight of the neighbouring houses; not less than twelve long balconies, tricked out with twelve, etc., etc., the only kind of public display permitted by the government. No porter, of course. We don't have porters now (and if we do, their only job is to close the great gate at eleven, so they live in the attics). Just imagine if there were any forty-three years ago! Contemporary stucco staircase. To finish this, there should have been, according to the style, a parapet with marble, or at least stucco, columns; but grandfather or great-grandfather had to go to the wars in the middle of things, and provide himself with horses, arms, and field equipment, so he ran short of money for the palace. The great staircase therefore had to be made provisionally usable by means of a banister or walnut hand-rail which, dating from the seventeenth century, now has a dark lustrous patina bestowed on it by the fingers of four or five generations. The said rail has never been changed because the successive masters of the house argued as follows: 'We've got upstairs like this hitherto, we can continue to do the same in the future.'

The drawing-room of a Turin palace in the year 1820 was still such a curious jumble that those who have never seen one can have no idea what it looked like. It is worth describing. I have in mind a wealthy house and a room with walls squared off into stucco panels of painted plaster-work, on which are oil paintings, dried up, peeling, broken things, with holes through them caused by the projectiles thrown by the young gentleman of the family. There is a big old seat locker which turns into a bed at night for the person who sleeps in the drawing-room. This is covered with a fringed green cloth spattered by oil stains. There is a brass olive-oil lamp (we are imagining the hour of an evening reception), whose wick has inches of exuding tinder fungus. On a nearby table are ranged the serried ranks of the household footwear; the cloth, or doeskin, shoes of the gouty old uncle, knight of Malta; an officer's Russian-style top-boots with spurs; clerical shoes with silver buckles; delicate little slippers for the ladies, and still smaller ones for the girls and children. Against the wall, stained to porphyry by shoe-cleaning operations, are brushes, bottles, and bowls of polish. Beyond is some man-servant or other, La Fleur or Alban by name, who hails from Viú, in the mountains to the north of Turin. He is dressed in the grey family livery, which was not cut to fit him, knee-breeches and far from spotless stockings. He is eating his supper at one end of a trestle table. He does not eat in the kitchen because he is on duty in the drawing-room. In a corner, quite visible to the naked eye, are brooms, a dust-pan, a wash-bowl on a tripod, and a copper bucket. On another table (none of the tables match) there are candle-sticks with stumps of tallow candles in them, little olive-oil lamps for the servants, etc.: in fact, all the confidential appliances for domestic use, exposed to public view.

Let us now leave the drawing-room—we say nothing of the two antechambers for the sake of brevity—and find the mistress of the house, the old Marchesa Irene d'Crsentin, where she is ready to receive the guests. She's rather poorly and we find her in her bedroom. Her face is the colour of wax, but she has delicate, aristocratic features with a sweet, fairly intelligent expression. She wears a cap, a compromise between the old and new styles, and a dark dress. She is sitting by a little antique inlaid table knitting coarse stockings for the poor. A shaded lamp lights her work, but all the rest of the room is in dark-ness, except for a circle above, which reveals the gilded stucco ceiling; and a circle below, where a small section of the polished wood floor is visible.

In the semi-darkness of the Rembrandtesque background loom a number of vague shapes. There is a great bed *à la duchesse* with em-broidered flowered silk hangings. At the head of the bed there is a Madonna by a good artist; beneath this, a whole host of little male and female saints, silver hearts, and *agnus dei*. Here you expect me to specify St. Philomena? But she still lurks in the minds of the most Reverend Fathers, who have yet to canonize her; so she cannot be hung here yet. At some little distance from the saints there are por-traits of friends and relations. There are grandfathers and fathers in pigeon-wing wigs; their successors in Directoire dress; others in Napoleonic uniform. In a ring round the lady of the house there are arm-chairs and other seats for her regular visitors, who have left their imprint on the cushions. These are General San Rouman, cousin of the Marchesa, who has never been able to explain to himself why Louis XVIII approved the *Charte,* while all he had to do was to reintroduce the system of the parliaments: Abbé Gerando, King's almoner, who sees Jansenists lurking everywhere, ready to pounce on a Jesuit father;

he dreams at night that Nicolle, Arnaud, and Quesnel have been made Court almoners, and that the bull *Unigenitus* has been withdrawn: Captain Marchese di Rubiera, her nephew, ex-captain of the French 18th Dragoons, who has lost a rank like all Napoleonic officers; but to lose a rank in Piedmont he had lost half a shoulder in Spain and two fingers by frostbite in Lithuania, and he never could understand why the last two losses should have, of necessity, brought about the first. Forty-three years after I don't understand it myself.

The captain is not up to much, but he is a man who has travelled, seen things, and had some experience. Conversation flags; only the General and the Abbé, seated next to each other, are talking in subdued tones.[2]

GENERAL: But don't you understand? I tell you it's a fact. There's going to be a Congress—they speak of Troppau—and they'll decide something to do.

ABBÉ: But I want them to get down to it at once. You see what's happening in Spain; now Naples is blowing up . . . God help us.

GENERAL: My dear abbé, you seem to see them already in the middle of Turin, don't you?

ABBÉ: God save us! we're not at Naples here. Nobody wants such things in Piedmont; nobody dreams of it.

MARCHESA: My dear abbé, for goodness sake, haven't you had enough of revolutions? I'm old and I've seen the whole magic lantern show . . . you must remember that we are in the year 1820; in 1789 they started, thirty-one years ago . . . and you imagine the thing's not over yet?

CAPTAIN: You see, aunt, the trouble is that people change . . . if they were always the same persons, I'm sure the troubles would be over. Just you see, if anybody starts anything, they'll get their fingers burnt.

MARCHESA: Well! you all know more than I do. I'm only a poor woman and I've never studied politics . . . nowadays everyone grumbles . . . it may be—but what I can tell you is this, that before 1789, I thought everyone was very well off, much better than now—everybody was as happy as a King.

CAPTAIN: Excuse me, aunty—you mean we, the gentry, were contented; but what about the others?

MARCHESA: But no, my dear Eduardo, you know you have served under that wretch and been so many years with Jacobins—I'm sure they never told you people were better off before; but I was there, I've seen

---

[2] As there is no point in translating this amusing dialogue into an English dialect, I have tried to give it a period flavour (tr.).

what I tell you—everybody, the people, the bourgeois, the peasants.... Oh, I well remember, when poor Crescentino was alive, we often had the lawyer Silverani to dine, he was the treasurer at St. Pauls; poor Doctor Araldi used to come too; then in the country, at Bernasca where we used to go, we had all the local gentlemen.... I never heard anyone grumble. No, no, you must believe an old lady ... the truth is that after Voltaire and his friends began to upset people, everybody started to complain and grumble and protest....

CAPTAIN: You mean, aunty, that they grew lean from over-eating?

MARCHESA: Oh very well, rascal, poke fun at your old aunt!

SERVANT: The Signora Contessa Datis.

MARCHESA: Good evening, Gina!

CONTESSA: Good evening, mother! General! Abbé! Oh, good evening, Eduardo! I thought you were on duty at the palace.

CAPTAIN: No, it's Collegno's turn.

CONTESSA: Abbé ... excuse me, behind you, look, on the seat—that little basket—well done, that's it. Now, do tell me your news.

MARCHESA: Eh! I've not been too grand since last evening. During the night I began to feel my usual pain, rather worse.... I've felt poorly the whole day.

CONTESSA: But is it really true, my dear mother, that you were at the triduum service at San Filippo's this morning?

MARCHESA: Certainly I was!

CONTESSA: My dear mama, I simply must scold you—Abbé— General—back me up!

MARCHESA: But, dearest daughter, don't you wish me to attend Mass for that poor Montanera woman? How is she this evening? I ordered the coachman to go and inquire ... Eduardo, ring the bell, please. Is Giovanni back?

ALBANO: No, my lady.

MARCHESA: What a tortoise that man is. Do you happen to know anything about her, Gina?

CONTESSA: They told me she was just the same. They had her bled for the eleventh time yesterday; they called in Tarella as a consultant. I heard from Madame d'Azeglio who sat up with her in the night.

MARCHESA: Father Mellini, her confessor, spoke to me about her yesterday and I thought he seemed rather ambiguous.

GENERAL: She is certainly a very good soul. Every morning, rain or snow, she was always at the seven o'clock Mass ... and you know Gabriella's no chicken.

GIOVANNI: I have been to the Signora Contessa di Montanera and she returns her compliments and thanks. She says the doctor has found her better this evening and I heard that they sent someone to tell the Marchesa Azeglio that there was no need for her to come to sit up with her.

MARCHESA: Excellent! God grant her a good recovery.

CONTESSA: They've really looked after her wonderfully; that good Costanza never left her side.

GENERAL: Yes, she's really an angel.

ABBÉ: A very virtuous soul.

GENERAL: Speaking of the Azeglios—do you know what they tell me? The youngest, Massimo, is leaving the army.

MARCHESA: The youngest? He must be about twenty or twenty-one. Why? Is he ill?

GENERAL: He must be ill indeed. . . . Oh yes . . . in our time we never had these whims of leaving the service at twenty . . . unless infirm or crippled. Quinto, his colonel in the cavalry, told me that he simply didn't want to do anything.

CONTESSA: From what they say, however, he is popular with his comrades: giddy as a goat, that I have always heard, but quite a good lad.

GENERAL: Always under arrest.

CAPTAIN: Excuse me, General . . . it is true that he was often under arrest, but never for service misdemeanours. Certainly after duty no one could restrain him. He'd be on a horse, without a saddle as likely as not, hop–la, a furious gallop and here he was at Turin. I know all about it as I was on garrison duty and four of us played old Harry all night long.

MARCHESA: These are fine things to tell!

CAPTAIN: Well, aunt, soldiers, you know! We can't be expected to be seminarists. Towards morning, another gallop, and at four o'clock there he was on the square at the Veneria, ready for duty.

GENERAL: All very well, my dear Marchese, but horses and men . . . the night is meant for sleeping—we aren't bats . . . they wear out themselves and their horses like that; I don't know how far you can call them good officers. Then he retired from Piemonte Reale and joined the Territorial Guards. He went round Turin in that white cap and loose bow tie; always in bad company; painters, singers, and so on; one day didn't he take the notion of singing in opera at the Paesana? Revel called him up and gave him a good dressing down! Dear, oh dear!

CAPTAIN: There was no end to his pranks! One day he rode at full gallop, bare-back, across the main avenue at the Veneria ... dressed as an angel.

MARCHESA: Oh fie! Don't talk such nonsense!

GENERAL: Dear oh dear! Oh dear! Taparelli, Taparelli! They're all the same!

MARCHESA: But what does his father say about his leaving the service?

CONTESSA: Let me tell the story as I know all about it; Costanza told me everything. He is not leaving the service for the sake of leaving the service; he is leaving in order to go to Rome to be a painter.

ABBÉ, GENERAL, MARCHESA: Oh! (*incredulity*)

CAPTAIN: What the devil is he up to?

CONTESSA: After all, everyone can choose whatever career he wishes.

GENERAL: A fine career!

MARCHESA: Yes, yes, certainly, I agree, but just wait a moment! That's not all. I must say even an unprejudiced person such as myself can scarcely believe it ... the fact is that he wants to go to Rome to be a *professional* painter.

GENERAL: The devil he does! Wants to go to Rome to take a job as a house-painter?

CONTESSA: No, not a house-painter, but he wants to be a painter and sell pictures—I know all about it. . . .

GENERAL: It seems to me that the Taparellis want to surpass themselves in this generation. But, 'pon my word, this is beyond everything. First he wanted to be an actor and now a professional painter. If I were the King I should pack him off to paint the view from Fenestrelle prison, just to make him see reason.

MARCHESA: My dears, I'm an old woman and I can't understand your modern ideas. Do explain! Massimo really wants to take up the profession of that hobbledehoy Vacca who painted Gina's miniature? Look, General, it's there behind you.

GENERAL: I don't know.

CONTESSA: No, it's not a question of the choice of one career rather than another—as far as that goes—everyone—after all there was an Alfieri who was an architect; there's Breme, the one at Milan, who paints; there's Canelli—but they do it as gentlemen. I remember at the time of the French, when we were at Florence like the Azeglios, Perrones, and Balbos—I heard Count Alfieri repeat a thousand times that he never made a *sou* out of his tragedies ... he had spent a lot in getting them published certainly, but never, never did he make any profit.

L

CAPTAIN: However—not that I wish to gainsay you—but it is a fact that in England all the gentry and lords write for the reviews and publish books and insist on payment, good payment too.

GENERAL: Well done, Marchese. You've found a splendid argument. What don't they sell in England, even their women.

CAPTAIN: (*sotto voce to the General*) I prefer Italy where you get them for nothing.

GENERAL: (*sotto voce*) You'll get into trouble if your aunt hears you.

CONTESSA: If I were in the position of his father, do you know what I'd say to him? I'd say 'My dear boy, be a painter, if you like, but for your own pleasure, like a gentleman.' Then I would say that all his family had served the King and the Country; that he had no lack of means, that all roads were open to him, that he could become something useful in the world, make a name for himself in some way better than painting; but that needn't prevent him amusing himself by painting pictures if he wanted to, etc., etc.

That is enough of this comedy, which, unless I deceive myself, gives a pretty fair picture of the ideas, manners, and speech of our society in 1820. I appeal to those who frequented it and can remember.

Up to the present we have been laughing at the upper class of Turin and their strange ideas. But the proverb says 'He laughs best who laughs last.' Let us hear the other side. Before hearing it, however, listen to an observation I should like to make at once. After having mocked my own class, I think I have the right to add that types like General San Rouman, who preferred the old régime to the new, were quite ready to lay down their lives for the new (like Passalacqua and others at the battle of Novara) when it became their duty to defend it.

17

PLUTARCH, in the introduction to his life of Pericles, says as follows: 'Antisthenes, hearing that Ismenias was an excellent flute player, rightly said—"He is however a bad man, otherwise he would not be such a good player." ' When Philip's son sang in dashing style at a banquet, the father said: 'Aren't you ashamed to sing so well?'

So much for musicians! Now for painters and sculptors. . . . 'Certainly no well-born youth who saw the Jove at Pisa or the Juno in

Argos would have ever wished to be a Phidias or a Polyclitus.' Forward the poets!—'Nor would anyone have desired to be Anacreon or Philemon, however much he had enjoyed their poetry, etc., etc.'

These quotations prove that the Marchesa d'Crsentin, General San Rouman, Countess Gina Datis, and the Abbé Gerando, Court almoner, thought in 1820 what Plutarch had already thought in the year A.D. 60 or 80. Such a coincidence reveals another, not at all to my liking. Plutarch's expression, 'Certainly no well-born youth', is a sure sign that everyone of his time agreed with him. No author today would dare to write: 'No well-born youth would wish to be a Rossini, a De La Roche, a Thorwaldsen, or a Manzoni', because he would be laughed at if he did.

However, while Plutarch and all sensible people thought like that, at the same period we find that Nero made his celebrated journey to Greece so that he could compete as a private person in the poetry and music contest, where, as could have been guessed, he gained an ample harvest of palms, and a galaxy of crowns.

You can appreciate that my *amour propre* is not at all flattered at finding myself ranged with Nero, rather than Plutarch, the Marchesa d'Crsentin, General San Rouman, and the rest of that party.

The thing deserves closer attention. So as not to lose our way among metaphysical subtleties, let us go straight to the practical issues.

On the day a State is menaced by a foreign army, is it better to have at your disposal a mediocre general or Rossini? When a State has lost all reputation, to win back the world's esteem would you rather have Thorwaldsen or a politician of average good sense and experience? When a State is about to go bankrupt, which is better, an ordinary accountant, or De La Roche?

Finally, go and ask Manzoni if it would be more sensible to choose him, or a mediocre senior civil servant, grown old in office, in order to set about the reform of the navy, the law courts, or the civil service.

For society, a general, an economist, an administrator, etc., however mediocre, are much more useful than a first-class painter, musician, or poet. Consequently those who, owing to circumstances or their own inclination, cannot become proficient in a more useful art or science, in order not to do nothing, let them cultivate the less useful ones. In those families in which the difficulty of launching their sons on useful careers is reduced by half, owing to their situation, their influential connexions, or their wealth, it will be advantageous to the State that they try to turn them into good accountants, administrators, soldiers, and economists; rather than violinists, poets, and painters.

If the links in my chain of reasoning are sound, we end up by finding that the Marchesa d'Crsentin and Plutarch have hit the mark, rather than Nero and I, when he wanted to be musician rather than emperor, and I painter rather than soldier.

How often have I not proved, in the various vicissitudes of my life, the profound truth of that conclusion! How often have I not thought, 'How much more useful would it have been had I studied and knew well, for example, military field tactics, rather than knowing how to draw an oak tree from nature! To know the law, to have some knowledge of administration, to understand the mechanism of finance and credit, rather than being able to paint a sky or a distance; or perhaps to write fictional nonsense to draw tears down some lovely young cheek!'

This accusation I bring against myself is not, however, without defence. I invoke extenuating circumstances.

Among the ancient Romans, as among the Greeks, the only worthy occupation for a free man, especially if well-off, was politics. The same idea is prevalent among the English. Why is this so? Because all these peoples lived in countries, not always free, but always struggling for freedom; because the citizens had rights, laws to protect them, a political arena, supporters, opponents, with a useful, great, and glorious objective for which they had to fight.

But what could a despotic government offer me, with the ideas and feelings I had? However full of right and honest intentions it might be, as I believe it was, its representatives and arbiters were four old chamberlains, four old ladies-in-waiting, with a swarm of friars, monks, priests, and Jesuits! What future was there for me in diplomacy, administration, or the army? A future in which I must always know where a minister, general, or lady-in-waiting goes to Mass and makes confession; in order to run up with the holy water as they go into church, and to get into good odour with their spiritual father. If one does that one can make spanking progress in one's career; if one doesn't, one gets shelved and, after thirty years of the office stool, one passes to the bench where the pensioners forgather at the Caffè Fiorio.

At that time, as you know, I professed a loathing for aristocracy and I was living under the ambiguous circumstances of the time, that is to say when democracy was not considered to be the acquisition of common rights for those who had been kept down, but, rather, a reprisal against those hitherto privileged. Furthermore, one could not see beyond the present—what human mind could foresee 1848 in 1820? —and how could I possibly become a humble neophyte of that witless, mistaken, hypocritical system? How could I embark on a more useful career, against all my inclinations?

My demagogic infection was certainly no longer at fever heat. I no longer felt obliged to avenge the turbulence of the barons of long ago or the insulting behaviour of the Court nobility, by frequenting taverns with rascally street boys and cracking up, as far as I could, all that was base and polluted in society. This behaviour, fruit of the ambiguity just mentioned, was no longer mine; or rather, it had been reformed, since I had turned over a new leaf, so that my environment was healthier and my reasoning sounder. I was, however, amused at the idea of annoying relations and certain people of my own class who had peeved me in various ways, by making them uncles, cousins, or at least friends, of a member of the nobility who asked money for his brushwork.

If they pay me, I said, for bumping my buttocks on a saddle, why shouldn't they pay me for painting a picture? If it isn't shameful to buy, why should it be shameful to sell? An act carried out by two persons at the same time surely can't be shameful for one and honourable for the other? These were my arguments, and they have now become commonly accepted. At that time, however, there was some merit in discovering them and accepting the consequences. As I tell all the bad about myself, you must not find it odd that, when possible, I give myself some little credit.

I call to mind a certain little water-colour of mine, in which I depicted myself, dressed as an artist in shirt sleeves, in the act of sketching before the d'Azeglio castle; meanwhile ghosts of my ancestors, as paladins, were giving me a scolding, which I received with a modest air, as though excusing myself and asking them to forgive me.

Now, after reflection and experience, I think I have arranged my ideas better.

Just as chamberlains, ladies-in-waiting, and lordlings had cured me of aristocracy, so tribunes of the people, Jacobin club heroes, and Italian-eaters have cured me of that sort of democracy which I have described as retaliation.

It is important nowadays to have clear, precise ideas about everything, especially on this matter. The feeling of respect for what deserves respect (we've talked about that) is diminishing in the world today, and the fault is not all on one side. It is essential for society to try to revive it: it is therefore important to classify the differing degrees of what deserves respect for the general benefit of the public.

Let me tell how I see it: then you must judge for yourself.

First of all I should like the man of integrity respected. Then I should like the majority of people to stop admiring and applauding those, great or small, who oppress and swindle their neighbours, to their own advantage. The sort of men who are considered geniuses and are admired precisely for their great talents in oppressing and swindling others. I prefer to see the admiration go to those most useful to mankind. Today, for example, I very much admire and respect M. de Lesseps and prefer his great work of making the Suez canal to a hundred conquered cities and a hundred battles won. I respect Napoleon III (beyond esteem there is gratitude) because he snatched Italy from the hands of Austria, because he saved the French consumers from the claws of the producers and the Mexicans from several gangs of thieves, etc., etc. I respect the Emperor Alexander of Russia, not when he has poor Poles hung and shot, in order to preserve the fruit of the great rapine of the 1773 Partition, but when he liberates the royal serfs and gets liberated all those who have hitherto groaned in slavery in Russia. Today, more than ever, it is important to learn impartiality and apply it to everybody, everywhere.

I should therefore give pride of place to an economist, an administrator, an educationalist, a professor, a school-teacher, an engineer, an author of books which, after perusal, leave the reader better rather than worse; and here we can admit men of letters, novelists, and poets.

Finally, and in the second rank, I should place the artists, among whom I modestly include myself, instrumentalists, and singers. I make this reservation in regard to the latter, however, in that though their art belongs to the second class, as individuals they can, provided they so desire, qualify for the top class of all, that of the men of integrity.

There follows from this, that when we pay a tenor or a ballet-dancer ten times more than a good administrator or a good general, no injustice is done and the latter have no right to grumble. Let us remember what the singer Brigida Banti said to Catherine II: *'Qu'elle fasse chanter ses feldmaréchaux.'* The reason is plain. If a single individual is capable of producing an effect which can be enjoyed by two thousand at the same time, and if these are happy to pay a pound apiece, I should like to know where there is any injustice if a fortunate mortal can earn two thousand pounds.

But when people take out the horses from a ballet-dancer's carriage and substitute two-legged animals for four-legged, when honours and distinctions are awarded only for trills and capers, then the generals, administrators, and economists of the country have the right to complain; for that is where there is injustice.

Please don't think I despise the arts of singing and dancing, nor those who follow them honourably. Not at all! But here is an example of the propriety of having an exact, universally accepted scale of what is estimable.

The professions of general, administrator, etc., are more estimable than those of ballerina, tenor, etc. Why is this? In the first place, because they are more useful; in the second, because to take up a very difficult, poorly paid occupation, in order to serve the true, essential interests of one's own country, is a finer, more virtuous act than to amuse the public and to subject oneself to receiving mortifications and insults in public, without any possibility of winning respect; and all this simply to earn a lot of money.

One of the surest signs of a people's decadence is an exaggerated appreciation of those who entertain and amuse them, and the fashionable infatuation for stage performers. If the sensual instincts become sated and depraved, the result is cruelty and scandal.

The corruption of the Imperial Court led to Hippia running away with the gladiator Sergius, who was neither young nor handsome, who had a wen on his brow, was half crippled by wounds, *sed gladiator erat!*

Who among us has not had to marvel sometimes at seeing a Hippia of the highest rank, at the feet of some actor or other, neither young nor handsome: *sed gladiator erat!* Who has not seen actresses, miracles of vulgar ugliness, kindle loves which, rather than blinded by a mere bandage, appear to have had a blanket over their heads? *Sed ludia erat!*

When from the Italian stage I have heard discordant bawling by singers who couldn't control or modulate their voices, I have thought to myself: Italy is improving.

Rages for actors and actresses, triumphs, torches, paens of praise, adoration for ballerinas are, as a matter of fact, more common elsewhere than in Italy. There is some progress here! Nevertheless it is not without use to point out, in Italy too, how important it is to have a scale of what is to be respected. There are theatres, stages, actors, and *soi-disant* actresses, producers, and especially 'engineers', who have nothing whatever to do with real theatres, such as San Carlo, the Pergola, or the Scala. To judge them, it is well to have handy, not the Scala, but the scale of values we have been discussing. Very often they trip over the 'Scala', or step, and the audience couldn't care less.

To revert to my history, my parents agreed to my wishes; the question of selling pictures remaining for the time being in abeyance. In fact, before selling pictures, one must paint them and find a buyer. My father called me to him one day and told me he would fall in with my proposal, that I was free to leave for Rome whenever I wished, but he had decided to give me nothing. I raised my eyes modestly to his face and inquired, in some surprise, if he really meant nothing, for nothing seemed not very much. He went on to explain that by 'nothing' he meant nothing more than the allowance for clothes I had while living at home : I think it was 130 or 150 *francs* a month.

It certainly wasn't very much, especially as living in Rome was much dearer than in Turin. But I would have gone with nothing; so that I was all the more determined to accept what he had fixed.

This minute income certainly impressed me. I thought to myself at the time that he might have been a little less miserly towards me. Now, after experience, I am convinced that my father was absolutely right. The practice of spoon-feeding the young produces men without stamina, enterprise, or ability to resist the rubs of the world outside. I bless him every day that he adopted a different method with me. He was not in any way excessive in what he did.

If all young men starting their careers had 135 *francs* a month to spend, the world would be better off.

For me, however, it was a notable descent. From having two or three horses, a valet, and, when with the regiment, a batman, I now found myself without horses and servants and with my board and lodging very much worse. But, I repeat, I should have gone under all circumstances; and I went.

For my mother particularly it was a grievous wrench. But her brave heart, that beat only for others, enabled her to make the sacrifice without protest. She accompanied me to the top of the staircase and descended a step or two in order to catch the last glimpse of me. After forty-three years, I see the look she gave me as though it were today.

At that time the Giovio road did not exist. I went by the Bocchetta pass and reached Genoa. There I met Cesare Balbo, a major in the Casale regiment; also Alberto la Marmora, in the service too. They talked nothing but politics together and discussed the events of Naples and what was going to happen in Piedmont.

I was not then intimate with Cesare Balbo, as I became later. I was then merely his cousin. I told him about my plans and my intentions to arrange my life rather differently from that of the usual young nobleman of Turin. He loved everything that smacked of independence and youthful audacity. He took to me, wished me well, and applauded. He encouraged me and did not speak to me of politics. As I have said, I had remained outside, and he, as I also said before, was little in favour of what was in preparation and did not willingly discuss it. We made up for it later.

There was an English brig leaving for Leghorn. In those days one had to take one's own victuals with one and didn't know for how long. Sailors tell you that you can go a hundred miles to the loaf, or that a hundred loaves are insufficient for a mile. I took a passage in this ship and arrived loaded with provisions. We left in the evening, I was sick all night, and at eight o'clock next morning we were at Leghorn. The seamen inherited all my untouched chickens and bottles of wine.

I shall say nothing of the journey from Leghorn to Florence and Rome. Every mile cost me much patience as I dragged along by the usual mule transport. I shall only mention an English doctor with us. On several occasions at our stops I noticed that when they gave him change, they only gave him half what was due. I protested on his behalf and went so far as to start a quarrel. Gravely and coolly he told me not to get excited as *l'homme est le même partout*.

I've never forgotten this axiom and it has been of great service to me in that it has saved me from getting angry on hundreds of occasions, or at least calmed me down.

I arrived in Rome. My father had made arrangements for me to live with the family friends already mentioned, the Orengos. I was received like a son and soon began to organize things so that I could begin work.

The first thing was to make sure not to aim above my means. My total wealth was not more than twenty-five Roman *scudi*. Fifteen went for board, lodging, washing, etc. The rent of a studio swallowed another six; there were two or three left for paints, models, clothes, footwear, theatres, entertainments, and petty expenses.

Having discovered the real state of my finances, I did what the Chancellor of our Exchequer should do with our national budget, I cut relentlessly. It is true I did not have to reckon, as he must, with people who, having made Italy, want to gobble it up. I only had to deal with myself and my *amour propre*.

When I came to Rome before, it was with my father, a minister. I wore a fine, elegant uniform; I rode or went in a carriage; I lived on equal terms with all the Roman gentry and nobility, with ministers and ambassadors, etc. Now, with my three *scudi* for clothes, footwear, theatre, entertainment, and petty expenses, there was little enough with which to play the prince.

I must change my environment, I thought. *Coelum novum et terram novam*. I must descend the social ladder until I find myself on a level with those who will consider my three *scudi*, not only a sufficient income, but an enviable one.

At this point I display a pride like Lucifer's, and with no thought of the existence of the word modesty, I say to the rising generation : try to imitate me!

Everyone ought to be able to live on what he's got; those who run into debt are, more or less, living at the expense of others. I had—still have—a horror of debt. Therefore, having little, instead of borrowing, I learnt to live on what I'd got. Thus I have always done, and still do. In this, as in other matters, what ruins us is vanity, what saves us is pride. Vanity humbles itself before a creditor simply in order to be able to show off. Pride goes modestly and is thankful that he has to bow and scrape to nobody and has no obligations anywhere.

I was very careful not to pay visits or drop cards on all my old aristocratic acquaintances. My uncle, Cardinal Morozzo, had gone to reside in his diocese of Novara. Cardinal De Gregorio, a close friend of my father, was the only fashionable connexion I maintained.

I found a studio in a small house in the Monte d'Oro square and, with a little money I had brought with me for initial expenses, I fitted myself up with everything necessary and at once started on my new plan of life.

As it was winter and one couldn't study out of doors, I occupied myself as follows : I rose a couple of hours before daylight and visited a master who taught, by candlelight, several pupils who had other duties by day. His name was Garello, a Genoese, a man of great intelligence, who had found useful new applications of mnemonics to the study of history and English. Lessons stopped at sunrise and we all went about our business. I had made friends with the Rospigliosi riding-master and, for a few *soldi*, I could get an hour's trot and gallop in the courtyard of the Monte Cavallo palace.

Without undue boasting, I knew more about equitation than he and all his school. In Rome at that time, I don't know about today, their methods can be reduced to one word : the whip. If the horse won't trot—the whip; if the horse goes too fast—the whip; if he won't turn—the whip; if he turns too far—the whip, and so on.

It makes one's heart bleed to see those poor colts, who live free in the Campagna until they are three years old, lassoed and, just to start them off, greeted by a rain of blows. Then they trot round on a rope held by a boy, who deserves nearly as much sympathy as they do, running panting round in a smaller circle with a long stick in his hand with which he beats the horse whenever he gets the chance.

It is incredible how they jump and rear, what desperate contortions the poor animals go through. Often they end by maiming themselves, or breaking their necks, and sometimes the neck of the first rider who mounts them, after all the suffering they have had to endure. There are stories to be told about this, but should I tell you all I should never have done. I find it impossible not to repeat the following. Just imagine, those riding-masters always made the horses gallop right-handed without ever changing feet. I asked why and they replied: 'Really, don't you know? Because horses won't gallop anti-clockwise!'

I used to help them train the horses; and while I was having this conversation, I was mounted on a carriage horse, probably to teach him to carry a rider; for some reason I had no saddle and only a single rein. I laughed at this strange theory and said: 'I bet that, mounted as I am, I can get this clumsy old animal to change feet at the gallop.' There was nothing in it. Anyone who knows horses knows that they must start off with the foot you offer them first. When I had got on to the track, I tugged on the rein and made him turn his ugly head to the right, and having made him shift his crupper with a good dig with my heels, I guarantee that he simply had to gallop to the left. By this difficult operation my fame as a great rider rose sky-high.

After horse exercise I went to the studio and worked until dinner-time, drawing and painting from the model. I studied human and equine anatomy, beginning with osteology, first drawing the outlines of the skeleton, bone by bone, then diligently clothing them with muscles. After my meal, I went to the nude academy, kept by the model Antonio, well known to all artists, except the very young. He was not handsome in face, but he had a most beautiful body, real type of that ancient race of men to be seen in the bas-reliefs of Trajan's Column. Antonio was an excellent person; he was interested in art and in the young students who lacked means. He gave them credit, sometimes helping them out of his own pocket. I remember, one day, he sold some knives and forks, his sole treasure, to help a stony-broke little painter. Who knows if he ever saw the colour of his money again! True it is, that Sor Antonio, in a *momento di vivacità,* had killed his brother. One can't be perfect in all things.

Studies from the nude finished at nine o'clock in the evening, the hour for bed for those who rise early. This is what is called work, and it was certainly work with a will. I was under an obligation and I had to honour it and quickly. After having had my way against everybody, after having been the first to go against the family traditions, I couldn't dally in giving some proof to all those eagerly waiting to attack me should I fail in my project. I recognized that I simply had to produce a picture and send it as a proof of my progress, and as earnest of progress to come.

I racked my brain to find a subject, a choice that would not demand too much skill. Basing myself on some of my few sketches, I put together a picture with a castle in shade to the right, and, in the background to the left, the mountain Soracte. It was stuff of little artistic merit; but it had colour and a certain specious effect that together might please those who understood little of art.

Amour propre was not the only incentive I had to work; this was supported by the other incentive of need, from which I had good hopes of escaping, could I demonstrate without delay that I had not gone to Rome to have a good time. It really was impossible for me to buy clothes and many other necessities, so that I had recourse to strange expedients.

The landlady who rented me the studio was the widow of an architect, whose name I do not know, but whom she always called 'poor Mr. Basili'. She was an old ballerina from Milan, an ugly but excellent woman. Having been left on her own, without means, she had to get in money how she could. She was now selling the contents of her husband's wardrobe and, as a tenant, I was given the preference of a first pick. As the late departed was as tall as I was, I was able, with small expense, to add to my outfit from his leavings. But as he was much bigger, his boots were three times too large for me. My friends roared with laughter when they saw me walking round in these boots. For many years, when they wanted to remind me of my first attempts in art, they always used the phrase 'at the period of Mr. Basilio's boots'.

I had a workaday coat made from that stuff they call *borgonzone* at Rome, warm and shaggy, made to last and not for show. I wore it then and for years afterwards.

There was sacrifice in all this; for many it might have been a painful sacrifice, but I do not wish to deceive the reader in order to get credit. The truth is that this descent into relative indigence gave me not a moment's regret. First of all, I was twenty, in good health, completely independent; I challenge anyone to grumble under such circumstances. In the second place there is a touch of the Quixote in my character, as I think I have stated already. When Don Quixote slept in the bush, with an empty stomach, and, if that were not enough, with ribs aching from some beating or other, he thoroughly enjoyed it, because he pretended to be a genuine knight-errant. I too thought of myself as a real serious artist when I found myself broke. It cannot be denied that this was one of the distinguishing features of the artists of those days, I mean, Italian artists.

So, constantly studying, always solitary or with some fledgling painter such as myself, away from society, from theatres, from all possible small amusements—why I don't know—I lived through the winter, and when the season began to change, I found I had completed my picture and sent it to Turin.

I then began to look for a possible place where I could establish myself for a longer stay, without too much expense, so that I could continue my studies from nature.

Although I no longer lived with Verstappen, I had not given him up. Whenever I could penetrate to him I tried to keep on friendly terms. He had married, as I said, the daughter of the sculptor Pacetti. As I knew her, her brother, mother, uncle, and aunt, I could freely visit the house. I thus learnt that he had the intention of going in May to establish himself at Castel Sant' Elia between Nepi and Civita Castellana. Although he was an experienced artist and a man of about fifty he used to spend three or four months every summer studying from nature like a beginner. I really was a beginner, so the advantage of being near him, of getting a little advice, of possibly seeing him work, decided me, and I resolved to set up my tent at Castel Sant' Elia.

18

VERSTAPPEN's brother-in-law, in whose studio I had worked on several occasions, chose the same country retreat, for the same reasons as I did. We were both apprentice landscape-painters, both young, and both short of cash. There was every reason, therefore, for us to keep company. We agreed to wait until Martino had made his arrangements and taken a house, before we descended on him unawares. A visit from us certainly did not enter into his plans, and without our informants on the spot it would have been very difficult to trace him, once he had left the gates of Rome. We wished to let him settle in, before we appeared on the scene, in fear that with warning he might slide off without permitting us to track him down.

At last the day of his departure came, and, directly we were sure he was ensconced, we left too.

Having left Rome early in the morning, we slept at Nepi. The host of the inn was called Veleno and he is the original of the innkeeper I introduced in *Ettore Fieramosca*. His inn was no better kept than the one at Barletta in the novel; you can judge what it was like from the following incident. We had been in bed and asleep for some time in a miserable little room on the top floor, when we were woken by a din of horses, harness bells, and shouts, from which we gathered that new guests had arrived. While we were trying to go to sleep again, the maid-servant knocked at the door and shouted through the keyhole: 'The master says he needs your mattresses for the new-comers.' I fear our reply lacked the respect always due to the fair sex, but I have really forgotten what we said; I do remember there was protracted argument about the mattresses, only broken off when it became evident that we would have defended ourselves to the utmost before giving in. Such were the customs of Veleno's inn.

On one of the warmest and finest days of May we made our entrance into the village of Castel Sant' Elia.

One of the most beautiful and picturesque parts of the Roman Campagna is that which begins at Nepi and, in width, stretches as far as the Tiber; in length, it reaches Otricoli and even Narni. It is un-known to foreign tourists even today; it was still less known in 1821. I have always enormously enjoyed those parts of Italy untrod by foreign feet. Whether it be rich or poor land, it is our own virgin soil as God made it, spoilt by no one.

Seen from afar, it appears to be a slightly undulating plain. Go farther, and you will find yourself, all of a sudden, on the brink of a wide ravine cutting across the land, at the bottom of which runs a small torrent. These streams rise in the hills of Sutri, Vico, and Viterbo and, at first, run almost on the surface of the earth. Little by little they excavate their channels and wind along in the middle of deep mile-wide gulches. It is not easy to conceive how these little streams have been able to dig out such deep, extensive beds for themselves. On the other hand, what powerful force other than water could have made them? The walls of these gorges are, for the most part, impressive perpendicular slabs of rock, sometimes grassy slopes covered with scrub. The bottoms are fresh and green. There are great trees and dense shadow, running water-courses, little tributary streams, and marsh where pools, when not hidden by the lush undergrowth, reflect the green of the Campagna or the blue of the sky above. I have never seen a richer treasure of natural beauty for the study of landscape.

One of these ravines begins at Nepi, and two miles farther, on the left-hand brow, is Castel Sant' Elia, a hamlet of five hundred souls.

The inhabitants live in old houses or hovels over which time, the sea breeze, and malaria have spread the same kind of patina, which gives such a vivid colour to the rocks on which they are built and from which it is not easy to distinguish them.

Coming from Nepi, one enters a broad street flanked by two rows of desolate-looking houses. Those on the right-hand side are on the very edge of the ravine and their windows open on to a sheer drop of some hundred metres. Continuing along the street a hundred paces, one comes to level ground where there are traces of a ditch and a wall surrounding the ancient keep, which once stood on an isolated crag formed by an abrupt elbow in the cliff. This castle was a fief of the Panimolli family, now represented by a last, and extremely odd, member. He deserves a mention.

This fine specimen, a society man *par excellence*, lived in Rome. There was no house, no hostess he did not know and, for the most part, visit. He was to be seen at all receptions, balls, and festivities; he went to dinner parties, especially those given by the great Roman families, but also to those of foreign visitors and diplomats. He was popular, and welcome everywhere, because no one had anything to reproach him with; on the contrary all had something to thank him for. He was a serviceable person, useful in an emergency. He knew all about everybody's business, secrets, news, gossip, marriages, love-affairs, anecdotes, etc. He never changed his appearance nor his humour. He always dressed in black, rather the worse for wear, but never less than decent. After the parties, theatres, and suppers were over, Panimolli, no longer able to continue his social day, proceeded to the Specchi Café on the corner of Piazza Colonna, where he found his servant standing waiting for him. He collected any letters, messages, or requests there might be for him, he gave his orders for the morrow and then good-bye. He simply disappeared and no one knew where he went. As far as I know, nothing was extracted from this servant, whose only communication with his master was once in the twenty-four hours, at three or four o'clock in the morning, at the corner by the Caffè degli Specchi.

Well, as I said, we entered the territory of this charming oddity one afternoon of a lovely day in May. I was on foot and Michele, my associate, mounted on a donkey he owned and I envied. He had come all the thirty-two miles from Rome on this animal at a leisurely pace.

Our first visit was, naturally, to Verstappen, who, believing his country retreat at Castel Sant' Elia unknown to all in Rome, was relaxing in a state of blessed tranquillity.

When our smiling, but respectful, appearance roused him from torpor, he did not have the strength of mind of the civilized races which enables them to feel annoyed and show pleasure, for his little round mother-of-pearl eyes glared at us with the undisguised distaste caused by our arrival. We asked him in vain how we could get settled in lodgings or an inn. He knew nothing at all and no doubt prayed to some God or other that we should find nobody to take us in. His prayer would have been answered if it had been a case of more particular persons, for there was no inn nor tavern in the village, nor a sign of houses, lodgings, or rooms to be let. What was worse, there was no butcher nor grocer; merely a baker, if I remember.

At the conclusion of our visit, which was not long, we started to search for rooms, knocking at doors and proposing ourselves as tenants and being sent about our business at most of them. 'But is there no hole, no attic, no cellar we could have in this charming (I hope I said 'charming') village?'

The peasants did tell us there was a tumble-down house perched on the edge of the precipice, without doors, shutters, or glass in the windows, which had been vacant and abandoned since the days of the French-made Roman republic of 1798. It had then been sacked by the soldiery with whom Italy, without knowing it, had made a commercial treaty, not invented by us, by which they imported the 'principles of '89' and exported all they could find in our pockets. But neither the soldiers nor the Italians suspected the final outcome of what was happening. However, as always, men thought they could change the world; instead it was changed by God.

As there was no choice and we didn't want to leave, we accepted the sacked house. We looked for the owner and, for a small sum, were invested with the property, which we received without the important ceremony of handing over the keys, for the simple reason that the French had carried them off in 1798.

With the courage of lions we went to take possession. We kicked open a lop-sided gate and entered a little courtyard overgrown with moss and mould. Here we left the donkey in his element and better off than we were. We then explored the rooms. The only piece of furniture left was a prie-dieu, which luckily had a drawer with key, and a big old leather arm-chair. As for beds and all else—nothing at all!

But there's a cure for everything, except death. We hired two large corn-sacks and bought enough straw to stuff them. We had brought a pair of sheets with us and, when we had laid the sacks on the floor, and covered them with white sheets, the bedroom looked quite decent.

So as not to eat on the floor, we got a table. I don't know how we got it so I don't say, as I don't want to tell fibs even in trifles. For the first evening, then, we reckoned we were well enough provided with the first necessities.

There was still the outstanding problem of putting the ass in a safe enclosure for the night, Castel Sant' Elia not only being inhabited by honest men; in fact, to judge by the looks of some of the villagers, one might suspect the opposite. We found a remedy for this too. I took the donkey by the bridle, his master pushing and goading from the tail end, and we got him up the twenty steps to the first floor. We tied him up as best we could, left him a bundle of grass, wished him good night, and retired to the next room ourselves, to our straw sacks. The door of the room was closed with a cross-bar and a twisted rope which hung down from the hole where the lock had once been. We slept the sleep of exhaustion and youth, which is even sounder than that of innocence. But all of a sudden a roar made us leap from our sacks, a resounding burst that, half asleep as we were, seemed like the last trump. We had forgotten we had a donkey in the next room. His early morning bray about dawn, what with the stillness and the empty rooms, really seemed to herald the day of judgement.

The next day we stretched paper across what was left of the window frames, so that we did not have to sleep under the night dew. We then set about organizing the important kitchen department.

The room where you came in had a wide fire-place with a protruding hood in the ancient fashion. This was therefore to be our kitchen. We made a trip to Nepi and returned with the necessary equipment: two or three saucepans, frying-pans, ladles, and some provisions. The second day we were all three established, we two in the house and the donkey in a stall, now made so that it could be secured, with all comforts and luxuries one could reasonably desire.

But the rations seemed on the thin side, even to me, which is enough said. We took it in turns to go to Nepi with the faithful ass for provisions, every other day. This kept us in bread, a little soup, etc. There was no question of vegetables, herbs, fruit, sausages, milk, butter, or the like.

In order to vary our diet, every now and then we bought a live kid from the shepherds; but we had to begin by killing it, swelling it, skinning it, cleaning it, and so on. To serve a fry, or a joint with gravy, was the eleventh or twelfth of the operations, none of which had been very pleasant. The worst was to see the little white face with pink nose and great, stupid, innocent eyes, looking at one in supplication,

M

and to have to give it a blow on the head and cut its artery. Hunger is an evil persuader!

Another change of diet was frogs. When resting from work we speared them in certain pools, sometimes returning with a rich bag. We took it in turns to cook.

Such was our household economy, perfectly suited to our poverty. Setting up house took barely a day, so that the second day after our arrival we could start out to work at sunrise. I had no donkey, my means did not allow it; I therefore hired a lad of about sixteen who, aiming at a clerical career, served the curate, acted as sacristan, and dressed as a priest. Let me make myself clear, however; in those parts in the great heat, everybody goes about in shirt-sleeves, so his only distinguishing marks were black trousers and stockings. This little priestling carried my equipment and washed my brushes and was an excellent youth. Who knows what's become of him? Perhaps he's a canon or a monsignore? Quite possible; for the ecclesiastical career is open to the humble as well as to the great, according to the system of the Roman Church.

It seems to me that this is a good place to say something about my art. If you are not a painter and are not interested, you have the usual remedy: skip!

During the eighteenth century, social manners had reached the ultimate of the artificial, the affected, the contorted, the extravagant, the illogical, etc., etc. One could apply this remark to higher and more important spheres than manners, but enough has already been said on the subject. I will restrict myself to saying that the aberrations of taste, in matters concerned with aesthetics, were almost incredible. As to fashion in dress, there were those piles of powdered hair with a little straw hat or a wreath of roses a-top, that we see in the portraits of the women; as to art there are those water-colours, landscapes for example, of one colour only. And what colours? Red lacquer or pure vermilion! Young people who haven't seen them will not credit me; but I saw them all right and my vision was not distorted.

In art, however, there was a strong movement towards realism. In historical painting Graeco-Roman ideas, which served, or were made to serve, the politics of the time, filled canvases with figures of Achilles, Ajax, Miltiades, Horatius, the Curiatii, the Gracchi, etc., etc. Confronted by the monotonous stylization of ancient figures, artists tried to find the nude under the dress; they painted the human form as though the dress were wet and clinging. The mania got so far that for a classical sculptor the navel was visible under a medieval cuirass, and a painter, having to paint Napoleon on foot, depicted his knee-caps under his top boots.

Landscape painting was free of political influences and followed a more reasonable line. From chiaroscuros of lacquer or vermilion, from mannerist painting (examples of which remain over the doors of noble houses of the period), artists turned to precise, minute imitation of nature, without introducing a trace of imagination in regard to subject, design, or effect.

Jacob Hackert was one of the first to apply that theory, apparently so simple, but in fact so often denied, namely that art is the portrait of nature, and as you can't paint a portrait without knowing the original, you must study nature and, as far as possible, keep it in your mind.

He died in 1807. The Countess of Albany had one of his landscapes. It was very large, showing a wood of lofty trees with a distant view and a few stags in the foreground. I remember it in a confused sort of way, and I recall that I used to gaze at it at length with admiration. His talent, the success of the new style, his fame, and the riches he amassed attracted, as is always the way, many imitators. His school flourished in Rome for over twenty years. Woogd, Therlink, Dutchmen; Verstappen, a Fleming; Denis and Chauvin, French; Bassi, a Bolognese; these were the leaders of one of the most fortunate artistic schools ever known. These men were experienced artists in the prime of life in 1814, when Europe was sick of the smell of gunpowder and the sight of blood and longed to revive its spirit with the blessings of peace. The English, chiefly, who had been kept in quarantine on their island for so long, poured into the continent like a stream of lava. Although they knew little about it, they adored Italian art. The painters we have mentioned were not enough to satisfy the demand they created. Every painter had the subject in which he was rated most successful. I remember that Bassi's subject was the waterfall of Velino. I believe he produced more than sixty in a few years. To speak frankly, they gave the impression of being turned out by a rubber stamp.

I followed most scrupulously the precepts of this school, and I think them the best. I painted from nature on fairly large canvases, trying to finish a nature study on the site, without adding a brush-stroke at home. I studied detached details, in smaller dimensions, always attempting to finish as much as I could. This was the work of the morning. In the afternoon, I continued to draw from nature, finishing off with great care and paying great attention to detail. By this method, the stay of a couple of months at Castel Sant' Elia resulted in my first real progress and got me beyond the material difficulties of a beginner.

Finishing at the site, as one would finish a picture in the studio, helps one to scrutinize and fill in the background by simple natural means, not with the forced contrasts of mannered art. One must always remember, however, that our means are very limited, whereas those of nature are infinite. On her palette is the light; on ours only white paint. We must make use of artifice and hence the word 'art'. It is easy enough to produce a background of pale blue, misty distance, if one places a great dark tree in front like the mannerists. It is not so easy to obtain a similar effect by the use of Nature's infinite means, where, often enough, there is a light-coloured foreground and it is dark in the distance. It is not only difficult but impossible to approach such an effect, unless one alters the perspective in some degree, unless one avoids stressing the background and touches up the foreground rather more than in nature. Even such an artifice must be kept within bounds. How are these bounds to be fixed? By talent and taste. The first, the real mainspring of art, derives from these. Inspiration is the bright ray that alone can make it germinate. In landscape painting one can suggest rules, ideas, etc., but it is all of no avail, if inspiration be lacking. Great landscape painters are, therefore, rarer than great painters in other branches of the art.

The method I have indicated has been followed by me for very many years. I spend the whole summer in the country. Now people study less from nature and differently. Which is the better method? Perhaps a compromise.

A man's fruitful years of work are limited. It is well to apportion them. First of all the landscape painter must learn to copy from nature, afterwards to make pictures.

Perhaps I gave too much time to the first phase and too little to the second, whereas if one wants to do well, one must allot the proper time to each.

Nowadays people give too little to the first. But art is quite different from what it was thirty years ago; it derives from different impulses, exists in a different atmosphere, and it is constrained by other requirements. That cursed phrase that has deceived so many and caused them to perish or live in penury—'protect the fine arts'—a phrase that people thought they could best dispose of by founding academies of fine art, that phrase now produces the results we all see.

By turning out artists as from a factory, art has had to become an industry. As the supply is much greater than the demand, it has been necessary to think how to provide for the mass of workers out of a job. To do this, the good people of many towns have started societies, real benevolent institutions. Governments help with contributions, and use the funds collected for buying pictures which save the mass of artists from dying of hunger, those who according to the laws of economics would be unemployed. I too, when a minister, did the same, and may God and the contributors forgive me.

But really one does not always appreciate what noodles men can be! The best of it is that today all talk about economic laws, free trade, real values, demand and supply, etc. Let us make an hypothesis. Assume a town of 50,000 souls: 25,000 males, of whom 15,000 are adults, so 15,000 men need hats. There are hatters to supply them; if the work grows they employ more hands; if trade declines they dismiss them and these have to look for work elsewhere. In this way all manage and no one has to be concerned about them. But a great man comes along who becomes a minister and persuades himself that the hat-trade needs protection. He founds an academy, appoints the best-known hatters, pays them well, and they teach even better, so that every year there are more and more new hatters for whom there is no need, because there is no increase in the number of heads wanting hats. The new hatters, starving, make strident complaint and distress the public. Thereupon worthy persons found a society to buy extra hats so that the extra hatters can get a living. The minister presents the Chamber with an application for funds to meet the expense involved. But would it not have been better to spare the first expense and not have a factory to turn out hatters for whom there is no work?

This form of protection, known as 'Promotion Societies', has further disadvantages. In the first place, that of wearying one's neighbours by waving these blessed fine arts under their noses. If you want to make a thing attractive, stimulate desire. Now there is no place safe from some ramification of that blessed 'protection'. However, the idea of standing exhibitions was not an Italian invention; whoever was to blame, it was a bad idea.

Another disadvantage is that the exhibitor, with very few exceptions, wants to sell, indeed is under the necessity of selling, and his creditors more than he. If some little picture gets sold, the tailor, bootmaker, and colourmen have their bills settled, or get enough on account to extend credit for another year. The consequence is that godfathers, god-mothers, protectors, and friends get busy and supplicate, in every way and to all lengths, ministers, officials, and gallery attendants; not for-getting those secret threads of influence emanating from the feminine sex, which give hidden impulse to the social mechanism. Consequently characters are abased and warped and the famous 'protection of the fine arts' is changed into a charitable operation or an ignoble piece of corruption.

If only the taste of artists and public were improved by this, but the contrary is the case! The need to sell leads logically to the need to attract notice and to be different from others; thence to be fashionable and to follow, not one's conscience, as valuable in art as in everything else, but the whim of the day. Therefore the artist must be on the alert, in order to discover from which quarter the wind blows, so that he can reproduce, not the truth and beauty all artists feel in themselves, but the particular genre and style that, here or elsewhere, has caught the fancy of the public and especially of purchasers.

Therefore one no longer tries to produce one's own genuine art, but to copy this or that painter in vogue in Paris or London, so that art becomes a more or less successful counterfeit.

There is a curious contradiction between this and many ideas now generally accepted. We love independence and nationalism, we love Italy; further, the landscape painters all chant together 'Rome or death', but when they take up their brushes, the only thing they don't paint is Italy. The magnificent Italian landscape, the glorious light, the rich hues of the sky over our heads and the earth we tread; no one considers these things worthy of being painted. Go to exhibitions and what do we see? A scene from the north of France, imitation of so and so; a seascape at Étretat or Honfleur, imitation of someone else; a heath in Flanders, a wood at Fontainebleau, copied from God knows whom! All this with washed-out skies, the pale light of those latitudes, and with such drab colours that it looks as though a dusty veil had been stretched before them. If they sometimes choose subjects from our own country, they seem to fear to give us light and reality; they are afraid of the blue of the sky, the green of the trees, and they produce an invalid Italy suffering from the gusts of a wind from the north. They were born in the true home of all natural beauty, under the strong, limpid sunlight that paints seas, plains, mountains, trees, and buildings with such a marvellous variety of colour; yet they prefer a servile art which looks to Paris or London for models and inspiration, newly imported with the other novelties of the season. They prefer a nature without a soul, without character, weak and tempered like a muted violin. For this they renounce Italy, her sky and the beauty which once brought so many enemies into our land, but which today, thank God, brings only friends who never tire of acclaiming it.

The woods, the oak and chestnut thickets which clothe the long ridge of the Appenines, are they not to be compared to the forest of Fontainebleau? Are the coasts of Albenga, Sestri, Port' Ercole, Sorrento, Amalfi less splendid than those of Étretat or Trouville? The yellow waves of the ocean are to be preferred to the blue waters of the Tyrrhenian or Ionian seas?

It is no good having independence in one's mouth if it is not in one's heart and in all one does; art too. We are a nation, we're Italians, we are ourselves once and for all, in every shape and form. Very well, if we are not prepared to do more, let us make less noise about it!

The landscape painters of 1814 I have previously mentioned were all foreigners, except Bassi. They all found Italy worthy of being painted, and the whole of Europe was of their opinion. I can still see the sea-shores of Naples and Baia by Denis; the Caudine Forks by Chauvin; the wide views of the Roman Campagna by Woogd; the thickets along the banks of the Nar by Verstappen; and Bassi's Marmore waterfalls. In Naples, painters like Vianelli, Gigante, Smargiasso, Carelli, and many others felt no need to leave their favoured climate to win fame and wealth; and God knows what times those were in regard to politics. And now when everything should breathe independence, spontaneous action, free original initiative, my poor landscape art has to be servile, plagiarist, a copy of a copy of a nature not her own and miles away.

After having said what I think about academies and societies for the promotion of originality and artistic independence, I am the first to recognize that it would be an error to consider such things as isolated facts. They are the result of conditions in the modern world, and no amount of talk will change them. We shall continue for a very long time to protect the fine arts, as the bear in the fable protected the man against flies. We shall continue to copy artists in fashion, indeed, to counterfeit them, just as we do with medals, armour, and interesting antiquities. We shall continue to obey the public in its whims and bad taste, instead of reforming it and leading it to what is beautiful, true, and good. We shall continue to generate superfluous artists and keep them alive by Promotion Societies. I shall go on paying my share to keep them flourishing, and in the last analysis I shall suffer the fate of all those who set out to preach.

In this case the obstacle does not consist in any lack of understanding; anybody with any sense and with a knowledge of the subject thinks as I do. It is inertia that prevents reform. Habit is half the ruler of the world: 'my father did it' is always one of the great forces that guide our actions, even in this revolutionary era. Perhaps it is a good thing; otherwise our planet might spin too fast.

I return to Castel Sant' Elia. We had gone there to observe Verstappen work from nature, but (would you believe it?) we never had enough nerve to see him put a stroke on canvas, hardly even to see him in the flesh. We went to his house in the evenings, but he was almost always already in bed. Being young we made a great deal of noise, we used to play the guitar and the lute to accompany the Saltarello, which is the Roman version of the Tarantella. Just imagine how poor Martino must have wished us to the devil. His house, however, was not our only retreat. After the early days, the villagers had accepted us as harmless folk with something to spend. The door of the chief house of the place was opened to us. It belonged to a family called Saetta. There was the master of the house, a married man, and a priest, who first vouchsafed us a wave of his hand, then a wave and a touch of his hat, then, with that, a smile; finally, words and an invitation to the house. I offered to play the organ on Sundays, so that I became acquainted with the curate whom I accompanied at sung Mass. This excellent old gentleman had undergone an unusual experience, that of having been shot by the French, twenty years before, on the day he had witnessed the massacre of those in the house we now inhabited. He told us that he had been taken, escorted to the Nepi road, made to kneel with several others; then came a volley and off the soldiers went without looking back. He had not been hit, but threw himself down and stayed silent and motionless among the dead and dying, until nightfall. Then he peeped up, saw the coast was clear, and sneaked off along the hedges, until next morning he found himself once more in his own parsonage.

At home I had had a bird's-eye view of the world and society, now I saw it as a tortoise, or any other creature humbly restricted to flat earth. I was enthralled by the study of mankind from this new vantage-point; I was much amused by the lofty, patronizing attitude of Abbé Saetta and his brother; I compared their condescension with what I had been able to observe in other classes and my ideas became clearer on the subject. I recognized that the English traveller was right when he told me that *l'homme est le même partout*. I now saw that effrontery and conceit are simply one characteristic of human nature, not peculiar to the nobility, as I had supposed. So I acquired new ideas about men and their follies; not from books, but working from nature, as it were, from models of flesh and blood. This is the way to form your own lasting opinions.

I most jealously used to hide my origins, but there was always, to my great chagrin, some unforeseen circumstance which revealed who I was. This is precisely what happened at Castel Sant' Elia. It is necessary to know that in central and southern Italy sons, however many there may be, are given their father's title. My father was a Marchese, so I was a Marchese too. One day I had written to the Orengos' house for some clothes, and they came in a parcel addressed to the 'Marchese M. d'Azeglio, Nepi'. In the meantime they had written to tell me, so that I should know where to collect it. I went in person and presented myself to some carrier or other who undertook commissions to and from Rome. I hadn't tidied up and was dressed as usual, shirt-sleeves, waistcoat flung over my shoulder, and no stockings on account of the heat. In I go and say, 'There should be a parcel for Azeglio.'—'There is, but it's for the Marchese.'—'All right, I'm here to collect it. How much to pay?' 'Wait a moment, I can't let you have it, the Marchese himself must sign the receipt.' 'But I am the Marchese,' I said at last, annoyed at having to reveal my identity. 'You are the Marchese?' I still laugh when I recall the look of incredulity and scorn my questioner gave me at hearing such enormous presumption from this bare-legged fellow. I don't now remember what guarantees I had to give or if I ended by convincing him. I know there was a terrific wrangle before I could carry my clothes back with me. When the great news of my title got abroad there happened to me in Castel Sant' Elia exactly what happened to Almaviva in the last act of *The Barber of Seville*. 'I am Almaviva, not Lindoro!' Luckily I was in the last act of my summer stay. It was July, the malarial season was about to start, and it was necessary to move.

My unhappy passion for adventure decided me to leave for Rome, in the evening, on horse-back, alone, with my gun slung round me. There were thirty-two miles of the most desolate part of the Campagna to cross. I left under a splendid sky full of stars. I made my way over the undulating plain towards Rome, through a region where, at night, honest folk never travel unless in groups. Except for a caravan of mule carts in bivouac, with the animals grazing near and the drivers snoring in the carts, I never met a soul and had no shadow of an adventure. That is why I called my passion for adventure unhappy. For years I have travelled alone, more by night than by day, in countries with an evil reputation, and nothing has ever happened of sufficient importance to gain me a reputation by the tales I could tell.

It was day when I reached la Storta, at the inn of Fosso, famous for the landlady who could sit down at table with twenty-two children, all strong and healthy. Before midday I entered Rome.

PART II

1

LET us retrace our steps.

In March of that same year the revolution in Piedmont had broken out. It was finished and over within a month. It left grievous wounds behind, and still more grievous seeds of future harm, both in society and in the country at large.

Although I was away and, on the whole, had little hope, I still felt my blood run quicker as the news spread through Italy. We heard accounts about it, even in Rome.

My friend Bidone wrote to tell me to come at once, so that I could play my part in these innovations. On the other hand my father sent me several letters written at the same time in case I had already started, one to Rome, another to Florence, a third to Genoa. He ordered me not to come under any pretext and I obeyed him. Afterwards my obedience was considered a great virtue, but I deserved little praise for it. Even at twenty-two I already understood that, with the Holy Alliance at the height of its power, to proclaim the Spanish constitution, without warning, in an Italian State without military power or allies, was nothing more than to provide victims for the gallows. Why, too, choose the Spanish constitution? Just as though Spain and Piedmont were twins, who could exchange clothes cut to the same measure. There was, however, a reason. It was easier to stir up the mob with such a constitution. Always the same story!

While the invasion of the Kingdom of Naples, decided at Laibach, was in preparation, I had written to Cavalier Micheroux, the Neapolitan minister at the Papal Court, offering to serve in that army. He replied coldly and evasively in the sense, if I recall, that it was not the intention of his government to recruit foreigners. As I had not taken this step with any enthusiasm—believing little in the Piedmontese revolution I believed still less in the Neapolitan—I did not pursue the matter. It was lucky! I was spared being involved in the defeat at Antrodoco!

The public turmoil had sad consequences in my family, as in many others. My father was considered a supporter of absolutism, although in fact he wasn't. He had too much intelligence not to recognize the harm it does and the impossibility of its continuation. He was, however, the enemy of revolutions, which merely change rulers for the worse. I guarantee nobody could think otherwise, who had followed the French revolution from start to finish, had seen Mirabeau change to Robespierre; Robespierre change to Napoleon; and Napoleon change to Louis XVIII with Cossacks camped in the Place de la Concorde.

When, on March 10th, the first move was made outside Porta Nuova at Turin and the revolution began, my father, as soon as he learnt of it, donned his uniform and ran to place himself by the side of the King, who was in the palace, hesitating between opposite courses of action. Many other gentlemen had done the same. Most of them were elderly retired officers. Among the others, I was told, was the Marchese di Rodi, an old officer I knew and who was fond of me, a most honourable, energetic man. They were all old and out of practice, more willing than able.

The King was at the cross-roads. Was he to go out, place himself at the head of the few troops available, and fight the insurgents, or yield to their demands? Opinions differed. Many of the old gentlemen had horses saddled in the courtyard. Fearing, if it were decided to go out, that they would find it difficult to mount in a hurry, they left the Council before a decision was reached, went downstairs, and got helped up into their saddles, so that they would be all ready if they had to ride.

However, good King Vittorio, true and honest, but abrupt, decided otherwise. He was loath to spill blood and equally to give in. He therefore took a third course : he abdicated.

Those excellent old gentlemen had to dismount as they'd got up. My father took leave of the King, whom he had first served as Duke of Aosta, and whom he now left with gloomy forebodings for the House of Savoy and the Country. Fortunately the future was not to confirm them. I was told later that, on reaching home, he came into the hall, unbuckled his sword, and threw it scornfully on the floor; he then locked himself into his suite.

My mother was in bed ill and had been for many months. I quote the words I find written in her manuscript as I find them.

. . . I go back to say something about the fateful year 1821, a very sad time for all faithful subjects of the King, among the first of whom was Don Cesare, equally owing to the sacred duty imposed by his religion as to the gladly given oath he had sworn to the House of Savoy and the love he felt for it. . . . Cesare passed those first agonizing three days in the King's antechamber as a Court official, together with other gentlemen, seventy, eighty, and more years old, who were awaiting orders from the King to follow him and, if necessary, die in his defence. The King's abdication and departure settled all doubts. I cannot fail to say that, before leaving to do his duty, Cesare embraced his beloved companion, who had been tied to her bed for six months, and tenderly, but firmly, said to her: 'Our sentiments have always been alike and you are not likely to change now. I am going; I shall remain at my post to the last; perhaps I shall not return. God be with you!' God was with me, because I had enough strength to reply: 'Go! Stay there! If it must be so, die! I should be too unworthy of you to speak otherwise!' He then went.

Oh Italians, men and women alike, take this for an example, and be sure that when you are like these two, Italy will truly be a nation!

By 'like them' I do not mean you to think like them or share their opinions. I mean that, first of all, you must have opinions; then they must be your own and founded on reason and justice and held as true and certain; finally you must be able to sustain them under all circumstances, even to laying down your life for them.

My brother Roberto, although not among the chief instigators of the revolution, had been sufficiently compromised for it to be prudent for him to remove himself from the reach of the first reprisals of Carlo Felice's government. At that time, as always, there were zealots, who acquire merit by attacking others and further their own affairs to the detriment of even their own friends. It cannot be said, however, that the government was excessively severe, although the King was called 'Carlo Feroce'. Only one capital sentence was carried out, that of Captain Garelli. Even this was too much. One must, however, realize that the maxim commonly held today, that there should be no death penalty in political cases, was not prevalent. The others condemned, Collegno, Caraglio, La Cisterna, etc., were hung in effigy, having fled the country. But not even in 1821 could a government stain a man's reputation, and the hangman who affixed the honoured names of those young men to the gallows left them unsullied. The public was already aware that it is the crime, not the punishment, that brings infamy on the condemned. If there had been a crime in violating their military oath of allegiance, the intentions and the characters of the guilty, not to speak of the circumstances of the case, save them from all imputation of dishonour.

They were no great hands at politics; that was their crime! They had not known how to make beforehand the indispensable calculations as to the resistance to be met, without which you can't get even a grindstone to work. How much more difficult is it to make sweeping changes and get a people to follow new laws and governments!

They had so wrongly gauged the situation that, most of them being nobles and therefore of the privileged class, and taking risks with the sole object of stripping themselves of their privileges, they never even found valid support among the great throng of the under-privileged, for whom they were making the revolution.

The gift of liberty is like the gift of a fine, strong, high-spirited horse. In many, it stimulates the desire to ride; in many others, it confirms their preference for walking.

My brother, meanwhile, had retired with his wife to Switzerland, where they stayed for some time. My other brother, Enrico, did not wish to get mixed up in this affair. He remained with the colours and did well to do so.

It may be that on some future day, when standing armies will all be disbanded and even their existence, and the traditions, the cult, the very idea of the ancient profession of arms, forgotten, a flag will be reduced to a mere curiosity, a museum piece, a rag fastened to a pole. It may be, as some would like, that States will have no other forces than citizens armed as the occasion arises; rather like the English special constables. When that happens, those then alive will have to make the arrangements.

This future is still far distant, and arms, big guns, and battle-ships proliferate more than ever in the fair pleasance of Christian civilization. It will therefore be well that the new generation has firmly impressed on its mind the respect, religion, idolatry, superstition if you like to call it so, of their own flag.

If such a sentiment be not much developed in certain Italian provinces, it is not to be wondered at nor imputed a fault. Whoever could thrill at the sight of the banner of Francis IV of Este, or that of the Bourbon Dukeling of Parma, or that of the Papal keys, etc.?

But now, thank God, there is an Italian flag and it should be the business of all—young and old, great and small—to give reality to and spread the cult of the colours. Let everybody share the feeling that the flag represents Italy, Country, liberty, independence, justice, dignity, the honour of twenty-two millions of fellow-citizens. This is the reason why it must never be lowered, or stained, or deserted; one must die rather.

Youth must impress this on their minds so that it becomes second nature.

The military revolution of 1821 was something unique in our army, as far as I am aware, and could have proved a fatal example. Fortunately it was a sole occurrence and remains as a grievous memory of an exceptional aberration. Piedmont, and now the whole of Italy, will therefore escape the unhappy fate of some countries, which have been enslaved and rent by military risings, then torn to bits to become the prey of ambitious vulgarians. God preserve us always from such things.

I am happy that neither of my brothers committed the sin of breaking faith to the flag. Roberto was not in the army and Enrico, who was, remained loyal.

That did not satisfy my father. To think that his name had perhaps to figure in the history of a rebellion against the King; 'to think', as he said to me gloomily, many years later, 'that my name could have been affixed to the gallows as the name of a rebel...!' This memory remained stuck in his heart like the barbed point of an arrow, that once in never comes out.

His was the true portrait of those severe, historic figures, rare even in history, who could never change, never alter their opinions, intentions, looks, language, or words, any more than a fish can leave water and perch in the tree-tops. When I created the character of Niccolò de' Lapi, anything found true and good in him was due to the fact that I based all his best qualities on those of my father. His love for his son, my mother's pacifying words, his strict religious feeling, all induced him to forgive, and he did forgive, but to forget and not to grieve was beyond his strength.

My brother Roberto, on his side, felt he had the right to follow whatever political opinions he thought best. Was he wrong? Certainly not; and the respect I owe to my father's memory must not prevent me from saying that he, perhaps, did not sufficiently appreciate that right, failing which Christians would still be pagans, governments would be—you can just imagine what, and the great machine of the world would have been stopped for centuries like a watch whose mainspring had snapped.

This notwithstanding, his inflexibility was to be respected. Poor old man! To see him in his resigned, but invincible, silent sadness went to one's heart.

The relations between father, son, and daughter-in-law could not be pleasant for a long time. The intimacy of a common domestic life gave too much scope for clashes between two characters, little disposed to give way. It was therefore arranged that Roberto and his wife should go to Paris. The Marchese Alfieri, his father-in-law, who was the Sardinian minister there, took him to live with him and this arrangement lasted for several years. Alas! This was too short a period to dissipate the impressions of 1821, and the previous harmony never returned.

Our father, who had treated us with inexorable severity as children, had changed his ways with us when we had grown up, and treated us with scrupulous consideration.

If, sometimes, in everyday matters, he interested himself in our affairs and offered advice, he adopted the cautious attitude of a friend with an equal. Things went smoothly, therefore, even well, when my brother came home again. From then on, he devoted himself to the education of his children (Emanuele, now minister in London, and Melania, who married the Marchese Villamarina and died young); he took up art and art-history, in which he became profoundly learned, and started on the course of assisting and educating the children of the poor, which he later continued and which did so much good to the humblest class of citizens of Turin.

As far as Piedmont was concerned, after everything had been quietened down by Bubna's Uhlans, poor Garelli hanged, those compromised exiled—the usual last scene in tragi-comedies of this kind—the population found itself somewhat more humbled and compromised than previously; Italy took note of yet another foreign intervention; the ultras and the Jesuits raised their heads higher than ever, and Turin, which now seems to me the city in Italy where there is most liberty (if by liberty one understands respect for the rights of others and not the right, for example, of breaking the windows of those who don't illuminate their houses during patriotic celebrations): Turin became the dullest, most insupportable city in the whole of Italy. I couldn't stand it, as you can well understand, and remained in Rome.

The opinions I have expressed about the revolution of '21 are not, perhaps, shared by many in Piedmont and Italy today; but they are my opinions. My programme obliges me to say what I really think, and not what might be agreeable or popular. I write to be useful to others, if I can, and to keep my reputation as a trustworthy person—so I speak clearly.

After leaving Castel Sant' Elia I did not stay long in Rome. In July my one thought was to get to the mountains; elsewhere there is fever. I therefore selected Rocca di Papa and at once set about finding a house. This I did through my art-student friend who owned a little villa on the slopes of the mountain where the village lies.

Today the Roman Campagna is beginning to be opened up by the railway. In my youth such luxuries did not exist, so that one evening, just as the sun was setting, I arrived in the square outside the Frascati gate with my legs tucked under one of the six seats of one of the usual little carts.

Here I hired a donkey on which I loaded my luggage, and, driving him before me, set off on foot up the mountain along the tracks which lead to Rocca.

This place is situated in one of the most beautiful sites of the Roman countryside. If you do not know Rome, I must tell you that, if you look south-east from the St. John Lateran gate, you can see, through the heat haze in fine weather, over about fourteen miles of gently undulating plain, where there are tombs and broken aqueducts (but never an inn), a line of splendid blue mountains. They stretch from the Sabine country to the plain not far from the sea, rising with various graceful contours to Monte Cavi, the highest point of all, from whence they slope gently down in a long chain to sea-level.

Near the summit of Monte Cavi, where once they held the *feriae Latinae* at the Temple of Jupiter Latiaris and now there is a Passionist convent, there is an isolated crag shaped like a sugar-loaf. Alexander VI found the place suitable as a mews for his hawk-like *bravi*, so that they could keep their claws on the Colonna adherents at Marino. The crag was, therefore, soon crowned with fortified walls.

All know that in those centuries there was a choice between two ways of getting murdered open to the poor and the weak; you had, perforce, to choose between vagrant robbers who happened to come your way, or the permanent robbers established in the castles. Preference was generally given to the latter; so that all round castles a timid clientele of peasant huts and cabins arose, which later developed into villages, towns, and cities. This preference is much to the credit of those poor medieval barons who are so often calumniated!

Such was the origin of the place I had chosen for my residence and where, late at night, I arrived at the house I had luckily been able to rent, to find its door open to receive me. Let me now give an idea of Rocca di Papa.

Above, there is the crag with the ruins of the old castle. On the crag itself huddle the oldest cottages, clinging to the irregularities in the cliff face as in a wasp's nest. Where the crag partly merges with the crest of the mountain and the slope becomes easier, the more modern houses start and form the sides of one long steep street. This descends to a small level space beyond the village, where there is a convent of Franciscans of the reformed rule.

Above another little square, where the crag ends and the mountain

N

terrain starts, there is the church, the fountain, a little café, and the best of the dwellings.

My house was the end one at the bottom of the descent on the left-hand side. Between it and the convent below there were some two hundred yards.

Here there was no question of a sacked house as at Castel Sant' Elia. I had two clean rooms on the first floor. One faced the street, the other the open country, as the house was at the end of the village. I rented the place from a middle-aged widow who belonged to that class of peasant, villeins as they call them in those parts, who are peculiar to various districts of Italy, especially round Rome, but quite unknown in Piedmont.

If the female villeins of all Italy had been like these, the name would never have got changed to villains. Their special characteristics are as follows. In Piedmont and several other districts, the peasant woman is no more nor less than the wife, or rather the female, of the peasant, just as the hen is the female of the cock; she shares everything with her man: way of life, food, customs, everything except her sex. In some places, this equality is altered to the detriment of the unfortunate female. On Lake Maggiore, where I am at the moment, if things have to be carried from one of the little villages half-way up the mountain down to the shore, for example a bundle of fire-wood and some chickens, the task is distributed among the family as follows: the wife carries the wood weighing half a hundredweight; the husband, the chickens weighing a few pounds. This is the usual practice in the mountains. Which only goes to show that gallantry towards the fair sex is an entirely human institution, apart from poultry and pigeons.

But the peasant woman from the mountains near Rome is usually the wife of a peasant who owns the house in which he lives and a strip of field or vineyard, more or less distant from the village. The climate makes field-work so hard that it is beyond women. Besides that, as the inhabitants are concentrated in the castle villages and there are no houses scattered through the countryside, it is not a good thing for women to be out in the fields at all hours; especially if, as more often than not, they are singularly beautiful.

Consequently it is the custom for the husband to leave the village with his spade and his gun (inseparable) on his shoulder to work in the fields. In summer he leaves home at midnight. The wife hardly ever leaves the house, but attends to the family and her household. The man, therefore, is burnt brown by the sun and is as shaggy and black as a goat. His hands are horny, so that they look like an eagle's claws;

his muscles protrude from continual exercise; while his wife, who has been sheltered from the extremes of the weather, has a complexion of a golden transparency such as one sees in Venetian pictures. Her hands are shapely, clean-cut, showing no signs of strain; she is neat in her attire and in the white cloth she wears on her head. Every village has its own distinctive head-dress, so that you can easily know where a woman hails from.

Intellectually there is little difference between persons of the two sexes. Ignorance, prejudices, susceptibilities are about equal. Although, as always, the women are rather better than the men. They do not drink too much wine, or swear, or come to blows with knives; they are chaste (or were so) except for rare exceptions. They also have a quite spontaneous gentility; they speak a language adorned with charming expressions, such as *figlio mio, core mio, bello mio,* pronounced with an attractive timbre, which makes the most agreeable music. Their costume is picturesque and suits them well. They have a certain natural intelligence; they are quick in repartee, so quick that they miss nothing. All this puts them in a very different category from the Piedmontese peasant women, who are shapeless from toil, dirty and dishevelled, and who stare at you open-mouthed if you have to say a word to them.

I don't, of course, mean the Roman peasant women are all angels of sweetness and peace. Sometimes their passions are like whirlwinds. The silver pin with which they fasten their tresses is not called a 'dirk' for nothing. This charming weapon has sometimes been the instrument of feminine vengeance or the dangerous means of settling an argument. I never saw it gleaming in a fair hand; but I remember one year of drought at Genzano, when the water of the fountain was fought for, even with these 'dirks'.

My widow, now no longer young, is likely perhaps to have made use of such a weapon on special occasions. One day she came into my room with her eyes starting out of her head, saying abruptly 'Sor Massimo, give me the gun.' And without pressing, she confessed she wanted to point it at someone who had annoyed her. As may be imagined, I gave her nothing and sent her away in peace.

Such is the general character of those peasant women, which I think I have fairly faithfully portrayed. If, my dear reader, your lips are curled in a smile, and if you think that I must have been on close terms with them to have described them so well, I can tell you that you are mistaken.

On my honour I never had the slightest shadow of an affaire with any of them. I went to the country to work, not to play. What is more, if a certain other person had questioned me about my goings-on, I did not wish to find myself at a cross-roads where I should either have to confess or tell a lie.

2

DURING my life I have seen many beautiful great expanses of landscape in mountainous country or plain, with views of sea or lakes, etc., but I have never, anywhere, met such a view as I had from my balcony at Rocca di Papa, or indeed that anywhere approached it for what it presented to the imagination; its associations with past grandeur; its artistic scope and its poetry.

At that time, apart from my study of painting, I was continuing other studies in which my education, as I said, had been sadly deficient. I had brought with me books on history, which has always seemed to me to be the most profitable of studies. I tried to learn what had happened on earth and to our race after the Romans, Greeks, Egyptians, Medes, Assyrians, etc. As you see I had a big gap to fill.

Not having money, I couldn't buy the necessary books. I was content to get what I could. The first book I read was Pignotti's history, which I bought for a few pence from a barrow. Today it would be considered old-fashioned, so great has been the progress in method, research into original documents, and the philosophy of history. But then, especially for me, it was a treasure. I had also been able to get hold of Plutarch's *Lives*, so that I could alternate between ancient and medieval history.

The enthusiasm of Alfieri's heroes had gone, and I no longer felt the need to slay a King. The little knowledge I had gleaned about the periods of history nearer to our own, had opened new horizons, and the modern attracted me as much as the ancient, and more. However, I had not yet been able to strip off the classico-scholastic prestige those old societies of men enjoyed in my mind and I still considered them superior in every way to the modern.

I had not yet formulated the criterion which is the only true one; the only one on which to base a right judgement of things in this world; by which to consider philosophic systems at their proper value, be they political or religious; to judge historical events; the acts of nations, governments, parties, and sects; the productions of genius, literature and art; everything, in a word, done by man as an individual, or by mankind in general.

This criterion is the simplest thing possible, and at the same time the least adopted, it is merely *the good of mankind*. This is the yardstick with which to measure everything. Ask yourself: was that a good or an evil for humanity? According to the answer to this question, accept or reject, and you cannot be wrong. We must suppose that we agree on what is good and on the varieties of good, and that we say that, first of all, it is good for men to be honest, then healthy, then sensible and intelligent, then free, then educated, then with sufficient means, strong, active, comely, etc., etc.

If one weighed things on these scales, how much coin, currently accepted as valuable, would be found faulty and be thrown on the rubbish heap! How many peoples, rulers, governments, heroes, resounding names, hitherto admired by all, would topple from their eminence into the evil category of public calamities!

The true, substantial difference between civilization and barbarism consists, not in the possession or lack of knowledge and its consequences, but in the acceptance or refusal of the above criterion when men and their works have to be weighed and judged. For anyone who considers the matter, this is the sole criterion by which to recognize the true progress of a people and an age.

In the first part of this book I have already expressed the opinion that Christian civilization is advancing steadily on this path, and I gave examples to point the difference between their times and ours. I repeat it here, and add that it is the duty of governments and their leaders, as it is the duty of all those in any way concerned with publicity, that great mover of men, to co-operate in urging the world to adopt a better criterion.

Let Princes and potentates by example, ministers and parliamentarians by their words, writers with their pens, proclaim from the rooftops, towers, and mountains that the first law of all is to work for *the good of mankind*. What leads to their happiness, that is great, honourable, and glorious; what makes them less happy than they were before, that is bad, mean, and shameful.

If such were the universal opinion, violence would vanish from the world. It would appear, then, that this should be the creed of the weak and inconspicuous, that is to say 99 per cent. of all men. However, what does the human race admire most? Violence! By dint of being knocked about, let us hope that, one fine day, our species will have its eyes opened and award honours to those who protect it, and scourging to those who afflict it.

As we are now on my balcony at Rocca di Papa, from which one can command a view of the whole of Latium, where on the far horizon rises the dome of St. Peter's, an isolated shape in the desert, whereas the highest edifices of Rome, shrouded in mist, are merged with the plain, it seems a suitable place to bring together the numerous ideas about the history of this region that have been germinating in my mind.

I was of an age when one is dominated by a need to explore, to orient oneself about everything, to see if the world corresponds with what schoolmasters taught us. It is a great moment in one's life when one dares to ask the reason for systems and principles, hitherto beyond dispute. I marvelled at myself when one day I said: What, after all, is this Rome? Can the religion of love be true, seeing that Christians worship the triumphs of force? In fact, if we study the history of Rome, from the point of view of the happiness of mankind, how different it seems from what they taught us at school.

For one thing, it seems to me that, to form a right judgement, it would be no exaggeration to demand a faithful account, not only of the battles, the victories by land and sea, the triumphs, the conquests, and all the Roman grandeur; but also a no less faithful account of all the killing, blood, tears, sorrow, suffering, exterminations, and desolation, which was the price the mass of humanity had to pay for the pleasure of having presented to their eyes and ears for centuries this great Roman phantasmagoria of victories and triumphs.

If the fundamental principle of modern society be just and true, that is to say, that the legality of a government depends on the will of the governed, I should very much like to know whether, if the human race had been consulted in Roman times, it would have voted for the Roman Empire. And if, according to ideas we believe to be true, and among them that one man is equal to another man, and that therefore the basest of the Germans killed in the circus for the amusement of the greatest of the Romans had equal rights; if, I say, that is so, why do we always kneel down with closed eyes before that immense monument of human arrogance called ancient Rome?

As you may well believe, it is not that I do not see what was unique and admirable in the virtues and talents of individuals, and also sometimes in the lofty, generous sentiments of the whole people; it is not that I underrate the fortitude of Regulus, the serenity of Cato, the generosity of Curius Dentatus, the great sacrifice of the Fabii, and so on. In fact among all the States of antiquity it is Rome I admire most: up to the period of the Gracchi, of course! I admire the time when law was supreme, when the fiercest passions roused by the most vital interests sought no other weapons, no other victory, than a vote in the assembly; when the whole plebs, worn out in the wars, covered with scars, and, nevertheless, throttled by the usury of the great (Rome, as all know, was the paradise of usurers), instead of crying 'Down with the rich', or *'La propriété c'est le vol'*, instead of stoning their creditors, or worse, limited themselves to leaving the city and demanding Tribunes.

I doff my hat to such a people. But the people who take as an article of faith that they are the masters of the liberty, the goods, and the life of the universe: to whose children the master teaches *tu regere imperio populos, Romane, memento*; and when these children grow up they consider it a right to reduce all nations to slavery, by violence, subterfuge, or fraud, as may be convenient; when in this age-long arrogance they see a divine mission, a destiny of greater glory than that of all other peoples; so that the most unbridled, implacable cupidity, the sweets of an idle life, fed by state bounties, is presented to the world as the fulfilment of the will of the gods: then I consider this people and its long existence as perhaps the most colossal fact of all history; but the blind adoration shown by many towards this fact, I consider as the most colossal nonsense ever demonstrated by mankind.

When (and I am never tired of repeating it) the human race stops burning incense before those who trample on it, or have trampled on it, there will be fewer oppressors to trample. But aren't the works of Tribonianus, the Codex, the Decisions, the Digest, the *Novellae* of Justinian, the whole *Corpus juris*, the most wonderful monument of human wisdom? Is this not the everlasting monument of law, a Roman monument?

After Rome had been ruled by Odoacer, Theodoric, Theodatus, Totila, Theia, etc.; when Romans had torn themselves to pieces in the Circus at Constantinople for the pleasure of different factions of spectators; when the Emperors passed their time discussing obscure points of dogma; it is rather late in the day to speak of Rome!

The genuine old Roman law gave the head of the household power of life or death over his wife and children; consigned insolvent debtors to their creditors with the right, laid down in the XII tables, of cutting them to pieces and sharing the bits; it was inexorable with slaves. On the other hand it was a man of Slavonic origin, Justinian, who brought light into the chaos of Roman legislation. He created a homogeneous corpus of law and followed up the work of Constantine, making every effort to introduce into that pagan jurisprudence, which only recognized fellow-citizens as human, the new Christian principle of equality of rights among men.

The real legacy of ancient Rome is not the feeling for what is upright and just, but what has remained more or less latent in the consciousness of mankind for fourteen centuries, the consecrated glorification of force against right; a sad legacy indeed! 'Ρώμη meant force and it was well named. All the leaders of the first barbarian invasions begged the title of patrician from the weak emperors. Why ask for a despicable title from despised rulers? Because in the public conscience the notion existed that Rome had received the right to oppress from the gods, and that the title of patrician procured some part of this right, something so favourable for the happiness of mankind!

Without now giving a history lesson, haven't we ourselves lately heard the last echo of Rome in the Germanic Holy Roman Empire? If so many emperors and rulers jealously preserved this Caesarian title, and only renounced it when forced, was not their only motive their belief that it was the strongest of the chains with which they bound the peoples they wished to oppress?

The last fruit of this ancient error is to be seen in Italy's present excitement at the idea that first dominated the ancients, then the barbarians, then the Germanic Emperors—that Rome is the firm foundation of civil power. Do they think that once established in Rome, the Italian Government will reform, and become strong, wise, and beloved?

As you see I make an effort to express the opinions I believe to be true, without fear or favour. But alas! if the Constitution can declare men to be free, it cannot give them either understanding, or that lofty feeling for liberty, which alone makes men independent.

Previously we were frightened of Austria and the police; now we're frightened of the revolutionaries, and of their old men of the mountain. The only difference is that the object of our fear has changed. I see very few individuals who feel free and independent and so act and speak. This is the favourite phrase of the majority: 'Yes it's true—but they are things one can't mention.' There's a long way to go before we become a free people! But don't let's despair! One can't wipe out in three years a century-old corrupting oppression. Italy has risen once more; the Italian character will rise too.

I should not like you to think that what I have been saying about Rome, the conquerors, and the heroes who harried the world, arises from a spirit of contradiction, a desire to be different from other people, or from the petty glory of running down great things and famous names.

Not at all! I never let slip an opportunity of speaking like this, because I am struck by the way true and sane views towards authority, its aims, the reason for its existence, its duties, value, honour, and glory, are distorted; and because I think it important that the public be set on guard from all sides against old misrepresentations.

For a couple of centuries there has been no lack of free thinkers and writers, searchers after truth and justice. They were men, without thought of peril or gain, who spoke out what they believed to be the truth. There have been most progressive schools of philosophic, political, legal, economic thought. It is certainly not the respect for antiquity nor for immemorial usage, nor the yoke of ancient scholasticism that has imprisoned thought and shackled the judgement of the world.

What, then, is the feeling that one finds in the very deepest part of the public consciousness? It is the cult of physical force.

Does one perhaps admire authority for the happiness it brings to men? Does one above all admire the authority which, with equal fairness to every individual, makes them better educated, freer, richer, etc.? What is respect for authority? Is it for its justice, beneficence, moderation, reasonableness? It is the old pagan idea of subjection, constraint, compulsion, dominion that brings authority respect, however much one chatters about rights, independence, and liberty. Let us look at this respect for authority that appears to pretend to be similar to respect for private persons. Here's an example. I, as a private individual, have landed property on which live a great number of peasant tenants. I know that the peasants once owned the land, but that my father or grandfather, taking advantage of a period of anarchy, occupied it by force, or got it by means of fraud. So these people have been changed from masters to servants, from a state of happiness to unhappiness. They now come to me and, politely or not, claim their rights and protest at the usurpation.

What do I do as an honourable man? I recognize that they are absolutely right; I give them back the land. I compensate them for the damage they have suffered; they are happy, and my reputation as an honest man is increased.

But if the Poles say: 'You've pillaged and murdered us, give us back what belongs to us!' If the people of Venetia say: 'You bargained and bought us from Napoleon by the treaty of Campoformio; were we your property? Give us back to ourselves.' Goodness gracious me! They begin talking about honour! It is a question of honour! The statesmen of St. Petersburg and Vienna are irked that you think them capable of dishonouring themselves to such an extent! And the public conscience, but with many exceptions, finds at bottom they are not wrong.

Now, the public conscience, which is a synonym for public opinion, is sure to win in the end. If previously, when its mouth was sealed, it could blame authority for all its ills; now, when it can speak freely and it has changed its role from that of servant to master, it must blame itself and its own stupidity, if authority brings yet greater unhappiness upon it.

Very well then! We, as public opinion, as the mass of people, as the governed; we who are most concerned, let us try not to admire that authority, which is the cause of our unhappiness; let us, on the contrary, admire the authority that makes us contented. Let us try to set a new fashion. Let us speak out with our voice, now so potent, and say to authority that honour does not consist in staining oneself with murder and theft and, if one is stained, one should cleanse rather than excuse oneself. Let us try to tell them that their function is to lighten the lot of each most obscure individual of the governed. It is for this that God has chosen them and men have elected them. Ask them if a Russian peasant in Orenburg is much happier when Warsaw is governed by some corporal or other, rather than by laws voted by the Poles themselves.

In practice, let us give a good reputation to those who do us good, and a bad one to those who do us harm.

As for me, I should consider the reputation accorded to ancient Rome as undeserved and one which leads men's minds astray and away from what is healthy, true, and just. As a test to see whether my idea be right, although unusual, just tell me if you would desire the world to repeat that complex thing called the Roman Empire. I don't think you or anyone else would, for a moment. So I'm right.

As I said, I had not yet worked all this out when I lived at Rocca di Papa : but such ideas were sprouting in my mind, as I was striving to form my own judgements, and not just take them at second-hand like other people's old clothes.

But despite these thoughts, I was only twenty-two years old, with a lively imagination, so that I could hardly help feeling a glow of enthusiasm, on seeing stretched at my feet, like a great map, the very regions where the events took place, which have been more extensively and more eloquently described than any others in the history of mankind. The events, in fact, which made the inhabitants of Italy masters of the most cultivated and civilized part of the western world. . . . So you see, my dear reader, your humble servant is caught in the act, for he must have tucked away in a corner of his heart an altar to the Goddess Violence, whom he has just renounced! True it is that our devotion to that Saint is in our blood; it is the most obvious legacy we have from our forebears.

The beauty of the scene, especially on those evenings when there was a new moon, when its sickle, which it is inevitable to call 'silvery', was still above the horizon a couple of hours after sunset, has made an impression on me I shall never forget. The panorama seen from my windows began, on the left, from the mountain crag, covered with dense masses of chestnuts and walnuts, rather like a painted scene in the wings of a stage. This mantle of green leaves covered the whole village and then descended steeply in waves to the plain below. Have you ever had the feeling you would like to plunge into and immerse yourself in a sea of leaves as in water, when you see the fresh soft contours of a forest below you? I always do, and I had the feeling as I stood at my window then. Half-way across the farthest horizon there was the blue strip of the Tyrrhenian Sea; the rest was filled by the distant Viterbo mountains, and by the mountains of Umbria and Sabina; in front of the latter stood the ancient height of Socrate (now Sant' Oreste) which was only a few miles from me when I lived at Castel Sant' Elia. From Sabina, still passing from left to right, I could see Monte Gennaro; the mountains of Tivoli; then, only a few miles away, the arid heights of Tusculum, with, beneath them, the villas and gardens of Frascati and the towers of Grottaferrata; and still farther the roofs of the ancient fief of the Colonna family, Marino.

The stretch of country between the distant horizon and the slopes of Monte Albano, where I lived, was the Roman Campagna, called by Vittorio Alfieri 'that vast, unhealthy region'. There is no doubt that, feeling peeved, you could find it merely a fever-stricken desert; but it must be confessed—despite the philosophy of history, logic, morality, and a love of independence and hatred of conquests—that it is quite impossible to escape a sense of respectful wonder, induced by the sight of that huge tomb, in which the arrogant sovereignty of ancient Rome lies buried.

It must also be admitted that the eternal city, however much we smile at such a title, seems chosen by Fate to deserve the name. There was a Rome before Romulus. Was it Siculan, Oscan, Tyrrhenian, Pelasgic, Etruscan, or Sabine? God knows; but it existed. It must have had a history. God knows what virtues, glories, grandeur are entombed with those ancient peoples, now forgotten. How many heroes who thought themselves immortal, and were believed to be so, have left no vestige on earth, not even a name!

Shall we not suffer the same fate? Ten thousand years hence, who will know that Paris and London existed? Who Napoleon and Washington were? Who knows? Perhaps after ten thousand years the earth's surface will be quite changed from what it is now; perhaps the earth on which we stand will be engulfed by some cataclysm. Perhaps miners of the future will discover traces of our modern civilization underground, fragments of our art mingled with those of ancient art—perhaps Canova's huge statue of Napoleon, carrying globe and baton, now at Milan, compared with fragments of the colossi of Castor and Pollux of the Quirinal, will be thought to be of the same age. If they find the bronze ball that now crowns the dome of St. Peter's, what they think it was for?

After the unknown Rome of Saturn, Evander, and Pallas comes the little-known Rome of Romulus and the Kings. That huge cyclopean underground cavern, the sole surviving evidence of that age still intact, which has collected the waste water from the city to discharge it into the Tiber, speaks to us and says: 'If this was the drain, whatever can the Palace, the Temple, the Law Courts have been?' But do we know the history and the way of life of those who inhabited and defended the place? Livy says we do; Niebuhr doubts it. Which is right? But the Cloaca Maxima tells no lies; there was a Rome, and a powerful city it must have been.

Republican Rome up to the time of the Gracchi, as I have indicated, is for me the great, admirable, truly glorious Rome. Human achievement can go no farther. Then comes the atrocious Rome of civil strife, the cruel Rome of Courts and Caesars and Emperors, the Rome which fell into the power of the Heruli and Goths. Then we arrive at Christian Rome. Let us stop here and give a glance back at the past.

The star of Rome which rose amid the mists of an uncertain origin never sets; and how many other stars did she not see decline and fall? The stars of Etruria, Magna Graecia, Sicily, Carthage, Athens, Sparta, Pontus, Judea, Egypt, all fell from the sky. The star of Byzantium appeared and Constantinople arose and emulated Rome, the city which seemed doomed to flicker and disappear in the massacres of Alaric. At the time of Claudius there were five million inhabitants of Rome, but after Alaric only some five thousand, who had escaped from fire, famine, and the sword, and wandered like ghosts amid the ruins and the corpses. 'Rome is no more', is the cry of all, barbarians, Romans, Christians, pagans alike. But St. Augustine has discovered a new Rome. The world hears his voice, which proclaims that Rome is the *Civitas Dei*, the city of God, of the apostles, of the martyrs; that it lives in the hearts of the faithful rather than in basilicas, porticos, and palaces.

Christendom finds another Rome; hope is renewed; the eternal city takes courage; people flock in, repopulate the place. From that moment one can say that Christian Rome truly begins, as it is the Cross of Christ that has called it back to new life from death. The ancient power of the sword was broken; Rome perished, but found a new strength, a power that will grow to be no less inexorable, rapacious, and arrogant than the old. This new power too will make the nations tremble with its frown and their sceptres fall from the hands of distant Kings.

Compared to Christian Rome, how long did her rival Constantinople last? The ages pass: the Empire of Goths in Italy, Visigoths in Spain, Burgundians, Franks: the Carolingians arise, Charlemagne dominates the nations by sword and the authority of his name: he, his sons, his dominions, his palaces, the pomps of Aix-la-Chapelle; all fall, all die, all have disappeared; the Frankish Empire gives way to a Germanic; the Franconian and Swabian dynasties rise and fall.

All fades and only Rome remains.

Nations, new States, are constituted from the remains of ancient kingdoms. Cities grow from the now abandoned feudal castles. Great, illustrious capitals are born. In Italy, Venice, Verona, Milan, Bologna, Florence, and Naples arise. Vindobona becomes Vienna; Lutetia, Paris; the old Roman fortress on the Thames becomes the Tower of London, the centre of a city of three million inhabitants.

But in the heart of nations, excited by the dawn of nascent civilization, there appears a new, stronger, more inexorable foe. Over the new kingdoms and cities a wind is blowing that will soon become a gale. There is loosed upon the world the phenomenon of free, unshackled thought.

Papal Rome had tried the patience of the world too far; she had tried to buy the life to come with gold, rather than virtue. Luther cried 'Enough' and a great multitude repeated it after him. The Reformation seemed destined to supplant Rome: yet Rome remains and, after its first conquests, the Reformation, little by little, loses ground and fails to find its *Credo* among a thousand different alternatives.

Dynasties follow revolutions; revolutions, dynasties. In the old palaces of Europe, today there is a Prince of ancient blood, tomorrow an obscure representative of the people. But the age-long dynasty of St. Peter has been established in Rome for two thousand years and has ruled over Christendom from the dark recesses of the Catacombs or from the splendours of the Vatican, and still it rules. The first French Republic plucks the proud old Pontiff from his seat and sends him to die at Valence of grief and hardship, while on his tumbled throne they raise up a Republic. Napoleon harries his successor from one prison to another. The second French Republic, unlike the first, puts an inglorious end to its sister Republic in Rome, and sets itself to guard a re-established Pope.

Are these soldiers, Princes, Republics burning with faith and zeal? Faith? They believe in nothing! What do they want, then? What fate impels them? What has the world wanted for centuries, as it hurled itself furiously on Rome to tear her to pieces, or fell at her feet, terrified by its daring, and offering her its blood and treasure.

Who can explain this unique historical fact? I certainly cannot; I merely repeat that Rome really deserves to be called the Eternal City. Rome, whether you are a believer or not, has existed and still exists, fascinating the hearts and imaginations of mankind.

Should Florence, Naples, or Milan fall, the world scarcely looks round and continues on its way; should Rome fall, all mankind is perturbed. This is an undeniable historic fact, never denied by one who has studied the past.

This rapid review, with the train of reasoning that has guided me, will not be useless when I have to describe, not only the events of my life, but the origins of my thoughts and the formation of the opinions I later held. If it be not too presumptuous, I have in mind that it may serve another purpose. To raise doubts, that is to say, in the minds of those politicians who speak with such assurance about the Roman question, which, in truth, they seem to have studied less than they should.

If they had concerned themselves more with the subject, they would have considered the Temporal Power as what it really is: an anachronism, harmful and fatal for Italy; an immediate cause for sin to the Church; a continual danger to the Faith; a solvent of religious feeling; a denial of evangelical doctrine to Christendom at large. They would have been able, by comparing past and present, to speculate about the future, and draw the conclusion that the time had come to put a stop to that long series of events; now good, now bad, now atrocious, now holy and beneficial; but always grand, always an object of love and hate and worship of the world, on which the Papal power was founded. But they should have understood as well, that such venerated remains, the cult of so many ages, could not be satisfied with any ordinary tomb, and that the whole of modern civilization was concerned and should be invited to the funeral.

They should have understood that though Rome is an Italian city and its inhabitants are citizens of this kingdom as we are, with the same duties, rights, aspirations, and wishes, they were, nevertheless, born within the walls on which the weight of a unique, mysterious destiny bears, accepted and feared by all from the dawn of history: that a secret bond exists between Rome and the world, a bond first guarded by the terror of the sword and then by the terror of the wrath of Heaven. This bond, whether we like it or not, is a fact and all wise politics are founded on fact rather than fancy. Although our national right to Rome is entire and absolute for us, another fact, two thousand years old, does not, certainly, destroy it; but it does invite every thinking man to take it into consideration, to respect it, and to judge the question of form, time, and opportunity as of the utmost importance. In one word, they would have taken more account of it, and not offended and scorned the ideas of the civilized world; they would above all have shown themselves to be juster, fairer, worthier, and more deserving of respect than the men of Rome. In that case the fears and suspicions of public opinion would be over and the Roman question would be nearer to solution than it is now.

The Christian world would perhaps have admitted an Italian Rome, free, living under the common law, and at the same time the religious capital of Christendom. They would perhaps have understood a Pope, defended by his title and prerogatives as an independent religious head, not by his authority of a Prince.

But by the way things are now conducted, modern civilization cannot yet accept the idea of seeing the Papacy come out of the wide-open doors of the Vatican, while in through another door stream the courtiers, male and female, of the revolution.

This is why I have penned these pages, but I have a further motive. No one can say that I have shown a lack of respect towards the great memories of Rome, or that I laugh at the superstitions of those who believe in Rome. I think I have expressed myself in a way to satisfy the most exacting, and lauded her destinies and glories above all other cities. I have done so that the conclusion I wish to draw may have greater value and importance.

All the grandeur of Rome, all the grandeurs in the world, do not make up for a single act of injustice or violence, and if their price were misery and grief to men, they were too dear. Let us learn, therefore, not to let ourselves be dazzled by ability, glory, and false splendour. Let us praise and admire those who make men happy. Let us always condemn and scorn those who make them miserable and unfortunate.

3

THE manner of my entry into Rocca di Papa, alone, on foot, driving an ass before me laden with my scanty possessions, had not betrayed my incognito. Usually the sight of painting paraphernalia—mahlsticks, easels, white umbrella, paint box—inspired the village boys with the hope that the Punch and Judy show had arrived. Sometimes I was greeted with the joyful cry: 'The puppets, here come the puppets!' On this occasion, however, I had arrived after sunset, so I did not obtain even this modest ovation. I started my life of work. I got to know several of the villagers, who took me for a poor artist (they had hit the mark in regard to the poverty) and a humble descendant of father Adam (here of course they obviously did me less than justice!).

On the little square, at the top of the rise, there was a small café, kept by a young man called Carluccio Castri and his wife Carolina, who was one of the beauties of the village. All the principal inhabitants forgathered there after the sun had gone down and stayed till one o'clock in the morning. Just as sparrows do, before tucking their heads under their wings, they indulged in a good deal of chatter.

I went there too and sometimes sang tarantelle or little songs to the guitar, which soon made me the favourite of the village. My popularity increased after I had put together some sort of a triumphal arch for the village festival, for the procession to pass under. I painted a Madonna on it, not, I'm afraid, quite immaculate from the point of view of art. The people accepted her, however, just as she was.

I made friends with Carluccio, the café proprietor. He was one of those I really liked. Poor Carluccio, my coming was a misfortune for him as I shall presently relate. But who can read the future?

He foresaw nothing, and we soon became friends. We were always together; at festivals, at the fairs in the neighbouring towns or mountain villages, one never went without the other. Carolina too, without either of us taking much notice of it, showed me much kindness and was quite at her ease with me. As I had a fair complexion and wore a blond beard as Christ is often depicted, she used to say: '*Sor Massimo, tu pari el cor di Gesù.*'[1]

The Madonna del Tufo is a little sanctuary, a small chapel about a mile from Rocca, approached by a level, shady road which was the favourite walk for the village.

[1] Signor Massimo, you are the living image of Jesus.

For one of the first sketches I did at Rocca, I planted myself down by the side of this road. The first day I worked there I saw Carolina coming along, dressed in the charming village costume: red bodice, a white cloth on her head, and a large silver pin in her hair with its knob in the shape of the traditional emblem of a hand with its thumb clasped between index and middle finger, last memory of who knows what forgotten cult of long ago.

Carolina had what the French call *un port de reine,* the gait of a queen; she stopped for a moment to see what I was doing, and then continued on her way towards the Sanctuary. The next day she did the same thing and, as long as I continued to work in that spot, she made a regular visit to the Madonna del Tufo.

The village, whatever the truth of the matter might be, had little difficulty in coming to the conclusion that she had a decided fondness for me.

One day, when the sun was high and the heat great, she appeared in my house, saying that the village was gossiping, and she didn't like it, and God help us if Carluccio got to hear of it, etc., etc. I never even posed the question which any young man would have done in similar circumstances, much less answered it in the affirmative and acted accordingly. I wanted to study, to work, not make love. Then Carluccio was a friend, I liked him; further, in the moral ferment that was working within me, feelings for justice and loyalty were gradually getting the upper hand; I therefore didn't utter a word or do anything that was not irreproachable, and Carolina left as she had come.

Up to this point there was nothing that could lead to catastrophes, just as there was never anything later between the excellent Carolina and me. But in certain cases it is not enough to be guiltless. Unfortunately just as there are vipers in the real world, which it is sometimes impossible to avoid, however prudent one is; so in the moral world there are souls who seem to have the charge of poisoning and fouling everything lovely and happy and honest around them.

A Roman lady had come for her summer holiday to Rocca; she lived alone with a baby she was suckling. I had met her in Rome at the period when politics were at a standstill and the whole population, men and women alike, from sixteen to sixty, thought of nothing else but making love. Signora Erminia, a woman of over thirty, could not be justly blamed for having wasted her time in this respect or put it to bad use!

The successful suitor at the moment was a friend of mine. He was a

o

nice young man, half painter, half singer; he had also been on the stage, but had left it for a modest, but less precarious job. This kept him tied to Rome and therefore now far away from Signora Erminia.

Thanks to the easy manners which are the distinguishing feature of Italian society anywhere south of Florence, I was always in her house, without it once crossing my mind that there could be anything between the lady and myself. I remember that almost every day I ate a second dinner there, thanks to the excellent digestion proper to my age and to artists in general. My discretion with her was not really very meritorious. I should rather have sought the favours of Carolina than of a woman ten years older than me, and who, at a period when the Roman ladies were not too particular in regard to personal cleanliness, used to appear in the picturesque and scented deshabille of a wet-nurse on the job.

There is nothing to boast about in having received a favouring glance from this lady. She belonged to the category of females for whom to spend a month without making love, in some form or other, either at close quarters or at a distance, is absolutely impossible.

To speak the truth, I think I can argue quite frankly, from certain intimate confessions about her own attractions, that, *faute de mieux*, I had been privately destined to fill the gap in her busy career caused by this country holiday. But for the usual reasons (plus the most cogent of all—my indifference towards her), I would have nothing to do with it. Without going so far as to leave a piece of my garments in her hand, I nevertheless caused the same thing to happen as my prototype Joseph when he fled from Potiphar's wife. I aroused in the lady such poisonous spite that it led, alas, to tragic consequences.

After a few weeks her titular lover put in an appearance: 'titular' meaning one who is about the house from morning to night, on whom the husband relies, who takes the children to school, and who even boxes their ears. Despite all this he does not accompany the lady when she goes to a party, but arrives a quarter of an hour before, or a quarter of an hour later, so as not to 'strike the eye'—a technical phrase.

He had a few days' leave which, however, did him little good. The happiness he exhibited on arrival, at being free from his stool and in pure country air and in the bosom of his 'family', soon changed to looks of gloom. He became bitter and sarcastic, full of allusions, of phrases such as 'I know', 'I'm not blind'. He would burst out against feminine impositions and tyranny.

I, who was as innocent as a lamb, had no wish to apply these vague expostulations to myself, the legal axiom being *qui s'excuse, s'accuse*.

The lady herself did not seem in the least put out by the suppressed scorn and tirades of her friend. I saw by the expression of her face and by her malicious little smiles that she seemed pleased rather than not. Her satisfaction, however, was of the kind felt by witches when they paralyse babies in their cradles, if the legends be true.

The devil only knew what all this meant. What had she said, or caused to be said, or allowed to be supposed, or insinuated? Whatever it was, if her plan was to make bad blood between my friend and me, it failed to come off. After a few days he went off about his business and I was still less inclined to admire the physical and moral qualities of the Signora Erminia.

Meanwhile I went on with my work assiduously. From time to time I received letters from Rome bringing news of the happenings in the gay world of my contemporaries. I do not deny that a certain longing for that richly spiced fare did arise in my heart. When one is twenty-three one is not a hermit; but good intentions conquered in the end, and continued to conquer. I was less influenced by any abstract love for virtue than by a feeling, that gave me profound satisfaction, of having won a major victory, and being in a position to believe that I was worth more than lots of others.

At that time there were gangs in existence, which four centuries earlier would have been called companies of soldiers of fortune, and their captains would have been Count Lando, Fra Moriale, or Duke Guarnieri, 'enemy of God and of mercy'. Now they were led by Barbone, Spadolino, De Cesari, and later Gasperone: they were called 'brigands' and had the police and the magistrates at their heels. How much less romantic the world has become!

The Papal government had made efforts to rid the country of these gangs: but if, for example, every rope you pull in a sailing ship comes loose, I should like to know how the ship is to sail and the crew steer.

The government of the Pope was, is, and will always be in an identical situation. All its efforts to suppress brigands were vain, because the instruments it used were rotten. It therefore achieved nothing up to the day when it made a treaty with them, as between equals; a treaty which the brigands observed, but the government violated by capturing Gasparone and all his gang by treachery at the castle of Riccia.

But these things occurred several years after the period of which I am writing. In my day, they tried one expedient after the other. The expedient of the moment was to form bands of brigands who had retired, or been converted, or were merely sick of the life. They were given the same arms, the same clothing, and the same organization as

the real brigands. As far as their feelings and inclinations there was no
need to worry; there was nothing to choose between them and brigands
proper.

One day I was in the middle of the scrub, beneath the so-called Fields
of Hannibal, those which were put up to auction by the Senate while
they were occupied by the Carthaginian army, and found purchasers.

So they have progressed from refusing to treat with Hannibal to
coming to terms with Gasperone! A far cry, a distance of 2,000 years!

While I was drawing certain fine young tree trunks, I suddenly
heard the report of four guns behind my back. I turned round and saw
men dressed as brigands. Were they real or copies? My situation was
precisely as found in the tenth satire of Juvenal, *cantabat vacuus*, so I
had no reason to take it too much to heart. I got up and approached
them. Luckily they were the sham brigands—an advantage! I asked
them whom they were shooting at and they told me they were practis-
ing at a mark to keep their hand in. Would you like to know how they
do it and what their target is?

They fix a sheet of paper to the rough bark of a tree trunk, then they
start to run away with their guns loaded (they call them cherubim, and
not carbines); after some hundred yards, they spin round at a command, fire, and run on. Everything has to be instantaneous. I went
to see where the bullets had gone. They were all in the tree with barely
four fingers between them. It would have been all up with a chest or a
head that happened to be there. In that war, he who shoots straight
wins.

The group was composed of rough, uneducated men, but their leader
was a tall young man, slender, handsome, and well-mannered; he
seemed to be a well-bred person dressed as a brigand.

I accompanied the band and had a talk with this exceptional person,
to whom I felt drawn. I thought I would try to sketch him and thus
make friends, but ten days later he was treacherously killed in a tavern
by a hunchbacked dwarf in the midst of his men; and the hunchback
got away. I met the band one day, and they told me about it. They
were enraged and swore to look for the hunchback until they found
him and then they would nail him to the tavern door like vermin.
They were types to do such a thing.

Such happenings are not rare in those villages. The brigandage of
past centuries, which has entirely vanished elsewhere, still persists round
Rome. The most peaceable, temperate people are more or less involved
in it. Apropos of this I will tell the story of a man I knew, one Jacobelli,

in whom filial piety and conjugal love took on a colour more in keeping with ancient than modern ways.

Jacobelli was a small landed proprietor, about fifty, with a modest, unassuming air, a member of the Church Council, a Guild brother, everything that was normal and respectable. He had a young wife, quite pretty but pale and always melancholy. What was wrong with this young woman? An old husband, I thought to myself. Afterwards I found that my supposition, though not wrong, was very far from the whole truth.

Before this wife, Jacobelli had had another, of whom he was passionately fond. The poor woman died and was carried to church and buried, according to the practice of the village. The next day, the widower disappeared and, while they were fearing some rash act, he returned home after an absence of two days. If not consoled, he seemed resigned, and no one worried about his affairs again. Where had he been so suddenly? To Rome! Without seeking advice from anybody, he had bought large bags of various spices which, in his ignorance, he believed good as disinfectants: pepper, cinnamon, camphor, salt, and so on. After returning to Rocca with his purchases he succeeded in bribing the sacristan-gravedigger and with his help went by night and brought home his much beloved better half. He then set to and prepared her. God knows by what strange methods! The fact was that, stuffed and wrapped with spices, he shut her up in a box which he kept in his house and often gazed at and wept over.

But as everything comes to an end in this world, his posthumous fidelity to his loved one finished too. He fell in love with another, married her, and the box containing his old flame was nailed up and put on one side. I was told it was used as a dining table!

One day the feminine curiosity of the new bride led her to wonder what was in the closed box. She unscrewed the lid, opened it, and you can imagine what she saw! As you can also imagine the amazement, the investigations, the revelations, and finally the confession of the unfortunate husband, who was first made to bundle up the dear departed and take her back whence he took her. They tried to hush up the matter but via gossip it reached the ear of the Assistant Governor, and the end of the matter was that one fine day Jacobelli found himself in prison, accused of violation of sepulchres. He only got out after a period, which may have seemed long to his wife, but certainly seemed much longer to her husband; he old, jealous, and locked up; she young, pretty, and free.

This was not the only event of the kind in Jacobelli's life. When his father died, he insisted on sitting up with the corpse. 'Shall I never see you again?' he repeated with sighs and sobs.

As he couldn't stand such a complete separation, he hit on a brilliant idea; he unscrewed the coffin and cut off his father's head. He made all ship-shape and kept his memento. I don't know how it ended, but it hardly matters.

This then illustrates Signor Jacobelli's tender heart and the way he expressed his affection.

4

THE Romans follow the sensible custom of staying in Rome during the very hot weather in their cool spacious houses, coming out only at night; whereas, if they were in the country, they couldn't leave home by day, and at night there would be nowhere for them to go. So as the cool season had come, the neighbouring Castle villages filled up with holiday-makers, who had come into the country as usual.

I was in the house one day when I heard a chorus of voices in all keys, high and low, calling for me. When I looked out, I saw a cavalcade of donkeys, on each of which rode a lady or gentleman. I recognized Princess * * * with her daughters, her daughters' swains, her own swains, the children, friends, supporters, and hangers-on; in fact the entire personnel of a Roman holiday of the period, a caravan of some twenty people.

'Come on out,' they shouted, suiting their style to the degree of intimacy proper in addressing me. I caught sight of the rose-bud mouth, the simper, and the magnetic little screwed-up eyes of the young lady who was supposed to be in love with me, but who was really in love with a scoundrel who had a wife and children and who was later discovered to be a downright thief. This predilection on the part of a young Princess seems odd; but the refrain of the period was 'The heart is unconstrained', and it is quite incredible what scope this axiom permitted to youthful fancy.

The temptation was too great, and there I was setting off with the party to climb Monte Cavi and afterwards to spend the evening at their villa, which I do not specify by name, to allow myself more freedom in describing the life of the time.

My dear reader, I now offer you a study of manners, which shows how quickly the world is improving, if you compare what went on then with the present. Here it is!

The Princess was a woman of over forty, once very attractive, even beautiful, but now faded, owing to having neglected the *ne quid nimis* (don't overdo it!). She had once been adored by an almost sovereign Prince. Now she had to aim lower. A young man of twenty, with an athlete's body and strength, boorish and ill-educated, the son of an inn-keeper, was now her lord and master and behaved in such a way that the fact was plain to all. The young ladies had various fathers; one was the daughter of a postilion and knew it. The children were under a priest, a contemptible creature, who shared their revelries in some distant quarter of the palace. Then there was an old foreign music-master, who gave himself airs and was treated by the Princess with respect. No one knows why, but it was conjectured that he knew some unsavoury secret. Finally there were several of those types who, by performing some useful service, by acting as buffoons, by accepting all that comes their way, putting up with everything, and flattering those above them without mercy or measure, manage to get what is equivalent to an income, and live abjectly, but fat, greasy, and gay, without doing a stroke of work. Among the latter was the fellow with the wife and children, who, as I have mentioned, shared half a certain young lady's heart, the rest apparently belonging to me!

This was the elegant party with whom I climbed the slope leading to Monte Cavi, after having left my solitary abode.

The Princess invited me to spend a few days at the villa she rented. and I accepted. The good lady's finances had been ruined through carelessness: her own, her family's, and several other people's as well. I simply don't know how she kept going. It is true, however, and I know it for a fact myself, that the Pope granted her permission not to pay the host of creditors she had at her heels. I remember hearing her say on the way back from driving in the Corso: 'What do you think! In front of the Caffè Ruspoli there was that A. (a poor devil who had lent her several thousand *écus* without hope of repayment); he glared at me with such an air...!' She meant: 'Did you ever hear of such insolence!'

But the enviable permission not to pay her debts was not enough to make her comfortable. She had to have diversions; she therefore treated her guests without ceremony. In the little villa, of which she rented one floor, there was a living-room at the top of the staircase. At meal-times, this was completely filled by a large table, lengthened when required by boards on trestles. This filled the whole space, so there was no possibility for servants to go round. Nothing was handed; plates were not changed and everybody grabbed what they could. The Princess with her daughters slept in an apartment on one side of the living-room; on the opposite side was the dormitory for the family friends, where the athletic inn-keeper's bed had pride of place, as was only right. There were a number of mattresses and sacks on the floor on which the various guests and visitors could choose their place of repose when night came. All this was considered the most natural thing in the world and did not in any way mar the gaiety of the party.

To fill in this picture of manners, I will add a few anecdotes.

Among the numerous passions which inflamed the heart of the Princess was one for her coachman. It was certainly a great convenience to have a lover in the house, without causing scandal. Even in Rome, people do not easily take things as true without obvious proof. In this case the evidence was only too plain.

The Princess used to drive in the Corso. She had the habit of stopping in the Piazza del Popolo, where the young men used to gather round the carriages to chat with the ladies. If some admirer of whom the coachman did not approve stopped by the Princess's carriage, he whipped up the horses on his own initiative and away they went. If his rival was leaning against the carriage, as is usual, with his feet in the way of the wheels—worse for him!

One day, when the Princess was in a low-hung, open two-seater vehicle, and therefore within reach of her beloved, he turned and gave her a resounding slap, despite all the people and carriages round. It was either through jealousy or for some other unknown cause.

Some people have such depraved natures that they do not relish things unless there is scandal, shame, and baseness as an appetizer.

This sort of thing, if not common, was far from rare in Rome before the revolution. A lady who had lived there a long time said to me: 'There were few ladies who, besides a regular upper-class lover, did not also have a coachman, a soldier, a nobody, etc., etc.'

Such was the state of society, now upset by those dangerous fellows, the liberals!

This coachman I have mentioned was the father of one of the young Princesses. She was slender and gay, a sweet little love of a girl. She married and—as blood is thicker than water—she fell in love with *her* coachman too. Her husband discovered her love letters and showed them round as a *curiosity*, and eventually handed them on to one of his lovelies, whom I knew. I therefore read them and I recall a note which ran as follows: 'My own Joe, I am desperate: T. (her husband) does not wish to take you (on a trip to the country), he says you'll have to harness Cencio and the estate horses, etc., etc.' This was scribbled in pencil on the morning when they were leaving for the country.

This little madcap, when her love affairs went awry, sought the help of no less a person than the Prince of Darkness himself, through the agency of an old witch who enlisted his frightful aid. As I laughed at her, she said one day: 'You may laugh, but just listen to this. When I was in love with R., who left me, I was in despair. I went to my usual witch-woman and told her about it. "Ah Madam," says she, "the thing is possible, but I must warn you that I can bring him back to you, but mind, I can't ever rid you of him afterwards." I was quite demented, so I accepted.'

She then gave me details of the incantation and added: 'I went home and the witch had told me not to fret as I should see him within two days. He had been away for months and months. That very evening at sunset I was standing at the window looking down at the street. The noise of carriages did not allow me to hear anything within the house. Suddenly someone said "Angelina!" I turned round and there he was. Well, I can promise you if you had tapped me then you would have found no drop of blood in my body!'

So you really must believe in magic, you see!

This unfortunate creature lived very poorly after she and her husband had frittered away all they had. She went down all the rungs of the social scale in her love affairs, and finally she was seen embracing soldiers for a few shillings in a dark alley near the barracks. I believe she followed a soldier to the '48 war. I saw her in Bologna and then in Venetia, and I had to enforce General Durando's regulations; he stopped many tender souls from trekking round the world after us. I was sorry to see her fallen in that mire. I had known her when she was a child, at the threshold of life, which might have been a tranquil, honoured life. But there was no going back for her. I heard a short time afterwards that she had died; where I do not know, nor from what cause, but probably from want, or from disease picked up in her sordid career.

The rest of the family did not end so badly, though not well; on the whole, its members have left little good to remember them by.

An active aristocracy has achieved some good. The French, Piedmontese, Austrian, and others in war, the English in government, have produced real men and much that has been useful and great; but an aristocracy of *non far niente* such as the Roman, daughter and servant of the Papacy for the most part, what can one expect from that?

The clergy, who enriched it, suspected it and grudged it any power. They excluded it from all political activity; they extinguished every virtue by luxury and enforced idleness. Thence sloth, abasement, and ruin! But we shall come back to this question later.

Such vice is not specially a feature of aristocracy. You can produce it in any class by privileges, which save it from having to have real merit, and a worthy aim in life. The Roman plebs, who led a privileged existence without labour owing to the regular bounty and shows of the Emperors, became the most colossal mass of canaille known to history.

Unfortunately the old practices of largesse and indulgence payments of Papal Rome have continued the bad tradition, still alive and powerful in the people today. Its Eldorado is *to make money without earning it*.

Therefore for ceremonial they use Romans, for real work non-Romans. The repugnance for work shown by the citizens of Rome is very curious; it is due to pride rather than laziness; in fact one is faced once more with the *tu regere imperio*. For all heavy work in the countryside, gangs come from away. To dig and cut ditches men come from the Marches; to harvest, from Aquila; to tend the olives, from Lucca, etc., while the Roman citizen, wrapped in his cloak, looks on.

If the Romans want to make Rome a healthy capital city, which will give a strong, energetic impulse to an Italian Government, they must give up the traditions of the Imperial plebs and become a modern people that reckons work honourable, not idleness. Let them consider this, and consider too that something done is worth a hundred words.

After a few days I returned to Rocca and, as the season was getting on, I got ready to leave. I have sad memories of the place.

My friendship with Carluccio had continued on an even keel. No suspicions had disturbed his mind. They would have been unjust suspicions for I had no single word to reproach myself for on Carolina's account.

But Erminia put her spoke in and Carluccio learnt that there had been gossip in the village.

The day of my departure came and he wished to bear me company down to the plain. We mounted our horses, or rather, we led them by the bridle to make the steep mile-long descent, through thick woods, to the Marino vineyards. When we reached the densest part of the wood, he began to speak of Erminia and, gradually warming up, he said things about her she really deserved, indeed more so. He ended by planting himself firmly before me, stared into my face, and out came: 'Do you know what she wanted me to know—that you have been carrying on with my wife.'

Anywhere in the world, such a statement in similar circumstances could be the immediate forerunner of something serious; but more particularly in those villages it would be accompanied by knife thrusts; I therefore kept my eyes on his hands. Anyone will appreciate, in a case like this, how difficult it is to know how to reply, as it is to find an expression, a look, a tone of voice that will be natural and carry conviction.

In the end, thank God: 'My strength was as the strength of ten, because my heart was pure.'[1] A clear conscience is worth something in one's dealings with other men: 'My dear Carluccio,' I said quietly, 'Signora Erminia can say what she likes, but I swear to you as a man of honour, that I have said no word to your wife nor done any single thing of which you have any reason to complain.'

This excellent young man, who wanted to lift a weight off his heart and have it out with me, rather than do me any harm, recognized that I had spoken the truth. He had not read novels; he therefore did not shake me by the hand, he uttered none of those phrases such as one picks up from novelettes. He looked at me, wagging his head and raising his shoulders, and said 'I believe you without any swearing! . . it is that Erminia's slanderous tongue, etc., etc.'

There is no point in handing down to posterity the string of imprecations he let loose to the honour and glory of that lady. However little imagination the reader may have, he can easily invent them for himself.

We continued on our way, talking of one thing and another, and it seemed that his mind, so agitated but a short time before, had not preserved a very deep impression of his earlier words. We parted at length as the best of friends and with many mutual promises for the future. I spurred off for Rome, while he turned his horse's head back towards Rocca.

I never learnt exactly what happened that night between him, Erminia, Carolina, and perhaps others. A long time afterwards I was only informed of the following: late that night he met Erminia, who, knowing he was just back from having accompanied me, burst out laughing and said scornfully: 'So you even see him off! Ha, ha, ha! You even see him off!'

Blind with rage, poor Carluccio went home. The next morning they found him dead.

[1] Dante's *'usbergo del sentirsi puro'* (Inferno, XXVIII, 117). I have taken the liberty of translating Dante by Tennyson (tr.).

Men are punished for the blows they strike with sword and dagger; but the law takes no heed of wounds caused by the tongue.

Various suppositions were made, all more or less unlikely. I never got to the bottom of the sad story. I have always cherished the memory of this obscure, but straightforward, honourable peasant, who gave me frequent undoubted proofs of friendship. At the same time I still feel deep regret—I cannot call it remorse—for having been the indirect cause of his death and of the misfortune of his whole family.

On my return to Rome from Rocca I carried with me a tolerable crop of studies, the result of my summer labours. There were three or four large studies, completed from life, some twenty small ones, and a great many drawings. I considered I was due for a month's rest and relaxation, so I went off to spend October at Albano.

I think I can give some advice to young men who work seriously; I have found it excellent from practical experience.

Everyone's powers of creative work, intellectual or physical, are limited. It is good to use them to the utmost; in this way rapid progress can be made. But it is a bad thing, which leads to relapse, rather than progress, if you try to force yourself beyond your limits. It is a bad business to strain yourself by too much effort, and a sensible man avoids it as much as dissipation of effort. Distraction can be good or bad; you can be intelligent and sensible about it. There is, however, a more important rule for hard-working young men. Nature can put up with a single distraction; never with two at the same time. Therefore, young men, if you haven't got the strength to abstain altogether, one distraction at a time! By following this rule, I have been able to do a very great deal of work, although not robust, but healthy enough.

The company I mixed with in Rome was spending the summer holidays at Albano. They were of the upper middle class, but their conditions of life were peculiar to Rome. Land round Rome belongs to the gentry, the churches, or the charitable institutions. It is divided into those *latifundia quae Italiam perdidere*, those large estates which have been the ruin of Italy, as Pliny said, but which now ruin only a small part of the country. For the middle class's livelihood there are the paid posts, only a few being available to laymen; commerce and industry; tenant farming; and finally, besides the liberal professions, several nameless, more or less anomalous, occupations as, for example, that of expediting affairs pigeon-holed in the Papal committees and secretariats. For this, one has to know everything and everybody; all the intrigues, the way up the back-stairs, secret embarrassments, influences, love-affairs, antipathies, and jealousies of the place;

and know how to put them to work at the right time to forward the interests one wishes to see brought to a favourable conclusion.

Enough of these anomalous occupations! Even the regular (or nearly regular) are uncertain and, more often than not, insufficient. The father of a family must often have recourse to expedients to be able to make do by the end of the year. The tendency, indeed the insistence, of all on enjoying themselves not squaring with either incomes or the desire to work, they have to have recourse to expedients. For example, an employee with a family, besides the hundred *écus* he gets from his government post, will find almost as much by playing *monte* or *toppa* in the evening, these being card games in which he always has good luck. Another will have made something by buying and re-selling a consignment of oil. Certain boxes of French hats that came in under the customs counter at Ripa will have helped the yearly balance. In such ways a man who apparently earns no more than a hundred *écus* a month, with a wife, sons, and marriageable daughters, who should live on a third floor in Via Giulia or the Campo de' Fiori—and the rest in proportion—has, on the contrary, a fine first-floor apartment on the Campo Marzo or near the Gesù church, a carriage, shares a box at the Tordinona theatre, goes to the country in October, with all the sundries of the *toilette* which are a bottomless well for families without judgement. As by Roman standards one is reckoned rich if one spends one's whole income without getting into debt, but without putting aside a *sou*, dowries for daughters can be computed as nil. They hardly get a trousseau. When the day comes and the father of the family dies, everything collapses like a house of cards; from luxury they pass, without any transitional stage, to great straits and quite often to abject poverty.

This is the happy state to which the middle class is reduced by the laws and exclusions of clerical politics.

The influence of such conditions on their characters is no less unhappy. Even men of integrity learn to stretch a point in regard to speculation and business; rectitude and delicacy of feeling become blunted. Want, uncertainty about the future, the pliability of laws and law-courts according to persons and circumstances, arbitrary action, and insolent abuse of power destroy independence and dignity of character. Servility and duplicity become the means to *savoir vivre*; living from hand to mouth and compromises are the sad conditions to which a numerous and respectable section of society is condemned. They are oppressed by the two privileged classes alike, the clergy and the aristocracy.

It is not only the middle class which finds itself in peculiar circumstances; those of the nobility are no less singular and uncommon. Most Roman families inscribed in the Golden Book owe their existence to nepotism. While in Piedmont the nobility, as I said before, earned its titles on the battlefield, the Roman nobles earned theirs at Court. In regard to their wealth, I do not think I libel their origins too much by saying that if we could evoke the shades of all the Cardinal nephews, and they could be made to produce their ledgers, some very queer things would come to light!

This is the reason why the temperament, if so we can call it, of this aristocracy is without energy and without great distinction or fine feeling. It lives in a complete nothingness, between the hammer and the anvil of the dominating clerical caste and the populace beneath. The worst is that they don't seem to be aware of their unenviable lot; they don't try to escape from it and appear to be perfectly contented.

I never could get on with this class or live in their milieu. I hasten to add that I did meet many worthy exceptions and I received much politeness from members of the aristocracy. But as like turns to like, the intellectual level of the Roman parties is generally below what is tolerable. They are dominated by gossip, intrigue, and, to a large extent, the parasitical element. You frequently meet there those types which are also to be found in many of the rich families of Milan and Naples. Amphibious beings who enjoy a treatment half-way between that of servants and friends. People who call the Prince or Duke 'Your Excellency' and get the *voi* back. Such a custom seems incredible to those who don't know Rome, but it is the usual thing in the relations between nobility and bourgeoisie.

As I was not looking for invitations to dinner and as I had no reason to consider close terms with a family inscribed in the Golden Book as a step up, it was natural that such people were little to my taste. With few exceptions, therefore, I kept aloof.

As we are depicting classes and manners I repeat a couple of anecdotes I consider significant.

One evening at Prince A's house I noticed a Flemish tapestry in one of his rooms, which showed armed men scaling the battlemented tower of a fortress. It was done in that spurious Roman style adopted by the Flemish manufacturers in the seventeenth century. I asked the Prince what feat of arms was portrayed. 'It must be the battle of Lepanto,'[2] he told me!!!

[2] A sea battle (tr.).

I glanced at him to see if he was being funny, but he was perfectly serious, so that was the end of that!

On a very different occasion and much later in my life, I was on a semi-official visit to Rome. One day I set out to pay some duty calls. I stopped my carriage at the gate of Palazzo X and told my man to inquire if the Prince were 'at home'. After some time a servant came down to my carriage door and said: 'His Excellency says, will you come back at 11 o'clock tomorrow', bowed, and went back into the palace. I laughed so much that I had no time to send the ambassador back with the observation that I had asked if the Prince was 'at home', not that he should grant me an audience.

My October at Albano passed happily enough, though I did not approve, and never have, the Roman way of spending a country holiday. One goes to the country, unless I am mistaken, to enjoy rusticity in the open air, and this is to be done by day rather than by moonlight. But when one spends the evening playing cards, sups at two a.m., and goes to bed at four, logically one must get up at midday. Therefore for the Albano vacationists the rural element of their stay merely consisted in a late stroll through the woods of Villa Doria.

Such was the custom then; it may be otherwise today but I doubt it.

However, such as it was, I conformed, inspired by the beginnings of an uncontrollable passion, which later caused me infinite sorrow and bitter delusions.

As I have said before, I have no intention of describing love-affairs. I only mention this so that, as I proceed, facts, otherwise inexplicable, can be understood.

On my return to Rome I rented a studio towards St. Isidore's, up above Piazza Barberini, in the house of two old ladies who were terribly kind to me. I buckled to enthusiastically to produce a presentable work from the studies I had made and after the experience gained from my long season's work. I put a picture together of a crag and a cavern studied at Castel Sant' Elia and it was quite effective and had a flash of truth in it. It was the first result of the six months in which I had continually viewed and studied nature.

That winter, a Piedmontese gentleman, a friend of mine, came to Rome with his wife and only daughter, who later married Count Camillo Cavour's brother, the Marchese Gustavo, who recently died. He was the Marchese Lascaris of Ventimiglia, one of the ancient family of Lascaris from the east, who had come to Italy in the fifteenth century, after the fall of Constantinople.

My friendship with him now grew warmer; he was a real gentleman, honest, cultivated, affectionate, vivacious, and amusing; a most original person. He had a passion for art and the art world and I acted as a guide to him in my spare time. He saw the picture I had finished, liked it, or what is more likely, wanted to show me a kindness, and gave me the welcome information that he was going to buy it.

So the great problem discussed at the house of the Marchesa d'Crsentin was about to be resolved.

It was not settled, however, without my feeling in my heart a sentiment hard to define, but which was not at all unlike a decided repugnance. So difficult it is for reason to expel one's early prejudices! All the more important is it to impress on the minds of young children from the start true, sane ideas rather than prejudices.

I did not, however, refuse the sale, as you can guess; in fact I insisted, as a form of self-discipline, that I should receive payment directly and personally, looking the purchaser in the eye while I did so. I thus avoided all the little hypocrisies, common in certain professions at the moment of payment, as though the reality of the fact could be glossed over or altered.

I reasoned as follows: if an act be shameful, it should be avoided under all circumstances. If it be not, it is humiliating to do it as though one were ashamed of it. It is as though one said: I know I am doing something for which I should blush, but I do it all the same because it is in my interest to do so.

Very well then, I made no bones about it and took the cash. I am not quite sure that I carried out my intention to the dot, and that I did not lower my eyes at the critical moment.

The fact remains that for an artist, as for an author, it is a moment of great emotion, the first time he sees a little pile of gold coins before him and can say: I have earned this with my brain or my hands. It is one of the least reprehensible satisfactions experienced by one's *amour propre*. Those who praise your work may do so in order to deceive; but not those who pay for it! Where can you find sincerer admiration?

There is another worthier satisfaction: that of feeling more independent, of realizing that, at need, one can make a living without the necessity of yielding to another's wishes. The richest man in the world who loses his wealth, unless he knows how to do something, is poorer than the man proficient in some art or trade. Therefore the Italian proverb (before Rousseau) told us to 'Learn an art and put it apart'. From youth up, this has been my own maxim, and, at a difficult time many years later, I thanked God for it. When I resigned from the government for certain reasons, I found myself without a penny, and for three or four years I lived entirely by my painting. It was well worth while having learnt a trade.

It is first necessary to have the feeling of being independent one-self: the necessary consequence will be the independence of the country.

When I started to earn money, my occupation was decided and, indeed, it was what I had longed for. To my great regret, I had for some time had to walk. I could not afford a horse and I couldn't save up for one, seeing that my pension terms had risen to forty *écus* a month. The animal I now bought was local-bred and was of the age of discretion. He was a good beast, however apt to shy, but he served me well on my sketching tours, and in the meantime I was able to ride in Rome to my great satisfaction. My passion for horses has been a source of real tribulation. Every now and then fortune allowed me to keep them and indeed to be obliged to do so, only to have to sell them again after I had grown fond of them. As soldier, minister, and governor, I had lovely horses; but directly I was out of office, good-bye to my stable. I had to sell.

This has been one of the most painful lesser vexations of my life. How I understood Alfieri's love for horses, and how I envied him! But I have always sacrificed everything rather than run into debt, which often means living on other people's money, rather than on one's own.

Had I remained in Rome I should have ended up by selling the horse to have money to buy his fodder; but the winter was ending and I was making preparations to continue my laborious search after artistic truth. The cost of keeping a horse in the country was supportable, even for my purse.

When spring came, which drives foreigners in flocks back north like ducks from the marshes, I lost the friendly company of the Lascaris family.

I have spoken of him, but I don't want to separate his memory from that of his wife. She was a little woman of delicate health, certainly not beautiful, but sweet and good, with a character firm as rock. She gave more than one proof of this during her life; I will mention only one.

She succeeded in doing what the whole of Europe for long failed to do: stand up to Napoleon. 'I was a lady-in-waiting to Marie Louise,' she told me one day, 'and we were staying at Saint-Cloud. One afternoon we went out driving with the Emperor and Empress. The weather was cold and damp and I, as usual, was far from well. I was in a closed landau. The Emperor sent word that the carriages should have their hoods down. I wouldn't have mine down. There was a wrangle with

P

the equerry on duty, then a parley, and then . . . the landau stayed closed, so before the Duke of Wellington did so, I beat Napoleon.'

Meanwhile April came. As I wanted to go somewhere different in order to study a different landscape, I decided on Genzano, a place about eighteen miles from Rome on the road to Naples. Perched on the brow of a hill, it dominates the open plain and the sea, from the uplands of Cervetri to Monte Circello on the one hand: on the other, it looks down between cliffs and crags, as on a mirror, to the depths of one of the ancient craters of Monte Albano, now called the Lake of Nemi.

We were almost at the period of the *infiorata*. There could not be a better moment for an exploratory expedition. So when the day of the festival dawned, I set off early, on horseback, for Genzano. What is the *infiorata*? It is the name given to the Ascension Day procession through the streets of Genzano, which passes over a carpet of flowers strewn over the whole ascent from the Piazza to the church. Some days before the festival, the women and girls of the place visit meadows, woods, and gardens and strip them of their flowers, which they carry home in bunches. Then they pick off the petals and heap them up according to colour, so that in the end they have a kind of painter's palette charged with different colours. Every house facing the street takes responsibility for covering the space in front of it, and makes its own pattern. Some make a formal pattern; some a frieze; some the coat-of-arms of Duke Sforza, ancient lord of the town; some their own, if they have one; some that of the Bishop or the Pope and so on. It is all linked by an old, frayed, and therefore flexible rope which is laid along the ground according to a previously agreed design and then filled up with flowers of different colours. The whole effect is most brilliant. Seen from the bottom of the slope it looks like a magnificent carpet, which one is sorry to see spoilt under the feet of the procession.

I arrived at Genzano, where I knew no one except a small landowner whom I had only met once before, where I don't know. It was hardly wise to put up my horse at the inn, with all the confusion there was in the place that day. I went to my acquaintance, whose name was Raffaele Attenni, and he allowed me to shut my mount in a little stable of his, where I left the animal happy enough with a couple of bundles of hay. I saw the festival, the crowd, the really stunning beauties of the place, the troops of Roman visitors, the holiday-makers from the neighbouring castle villages; and then I set out to explore the surroundings, so that I could get some idea of how suitable they were for my purpose.

I was delighted with the Sforza castle. It stands on a mountain ridge, a short way beyond the built-up area. It enjoys an immense view towards the sea and hills, the grim-looking Monte Cavi, Nemi, the Fajola woods, and the gulf in which the deep waters of the lake lie sleeping. If possible, I should like to stay here, I thought. I found the caretaker in the village; I got him to open up and inspected the interior of the place. It was uninhabited, ruined, one could say; not so completely as the house at Castel Sant' Elia, but little less so. But such as it was, I liked it.

While I was occupied in this way, night had fallen and it was necessary to find shelter, unless one wanted to sleep under the stars. I had seen an empty tub in the horse's stable. There was straw to hand, so I was better off than Diogenes. After having attended to the horse I retired late, curled up in my tub, and closed my eyes. But the master of the house, who had learnt that his guest had found his bed so modestly and discreetly (I say this myself!), came down with a lamp, and there was nothing for it but to get up and go up to the family apartments, where I found the daughters and a son, who scolded me for not having come to them for a proper bed with sheets, instead of kennelling up in a corner like a dog.

After all these years I still remember with pleasure the loving kindness of these dear new friends who, not even knowing who I was, showed me a really patriarchal hospitality. Thirty-two years later I returned to Genzano, as guest of my excellent friend Don Lorenzo, the present Duke. I saw the Attenni family once more. They couldn't make up their minds to recognize the guest of the tub of long ago in the celebrated minister, a guest in the palace of their master the Duke.

It was not difficult for me to get permission from the then Duke, Don Salvatore, brother of Don Lorenzo, to inhabit his ruined castle as long as I pleased. Not many days after, I presented myself one morning at the door of the caretaker's house in the village, to hand him the title of temporary investiture I had received from the Duke. He read it and came out with a great bunch of keys, which he gave to a peasant woman he employed. She and I, leading the horse behind, started off to climb up to the castle.

We had first to open the great gate with a key, which could easily have been the 'blunt instrument' of a murder trial. Then came the main staircase; then an antechamber with a rack for lances; then a room with an eighteenth-century theatre, all falling to bits; then more rooms, in one of which was a series of Sforza portraits. From Giacomo Attendolo, grim, dark, shaggy, and smoke-blackened, one passed to one of the latest Dukes of the Pompadour period, all pink and white, powdered, pretty, and graceful, in blue knee-breeches, dove-coloured coat embroidered in silver, and starched waistcoat.

The progressive change in those faces was the faithful portrait of the transformation in the great Italian families. They rose by activity and energy; they declined in sloth and ineptitude.

These rooms I have mentioned were all in a row at the front of the building. There were others behind, in one of which were the remains of a couple of beds. So much for the first floor. I climbed to the second, always followed by the peasant under-caretaker. Here the rooms were as below, but divided by partitions and almost entirely unfurnished. I came down again and deposited the bundles I had unloaded from the horse, in the room with the beds, and I began to make preparations for my lodgings.

The girl watched me, without knowing anything of my intentions. When she finally guessed what I was meaning to do, she said with an indescribable expression of amazement: 'And you are going to sleep here, all by yourself?'

'If God and the Madonna please,' I replied.

'But don't you know there are ghosts here!'

'Ah well . . . it is as God and the Madonna please.' There was nothing to say to this edifying reply. She shrugged her shoulders, gave me a last pitying glance, accepted gratefully the tip I gave her in proportion to my means (probably a couple of *sous*), and departed, after leaving me the whole arsenal of keys.

When I found myself alone and sole possessor of this tumbledown castle (things belong to the user, not the owner), its keeper and garrison, my heart was flooded with the joy of being independent and free. I spent five minutes dancing a solo to celebrate my complete emancipation. But before thinking of himself, every knight must think of his steed.

Mine was tied to a grill near the main gate, swishing his tail to keep the flies at bay.

Wherever shall I put this poor creature, I thought. The old ducal stables, in the first place, were too far away; in the second, inconvenient for a master who was also the groom. I searched high and low, under the great gate where there was a Madonna, and found no suitable place for a stable. I therefore took the bunch of keys in order to discover what was on the other side of a door I saw in a dark corner.

The key was on the bunch. I opened up and, from its worm-eaten furniture, I recognized that I was in the old pantry, where they used to make sweets and pastries. Under my reign this would certainly not be needed, so I therefore turned it into the stable.

I got help, and with a pound or two of nails and by pulling apart the tables and fittings, which were piled up in confusion, I made a kind of manger in one corner. I sent for straw and four bundles of hay, a day's ration costing almost nothing, and introduced the poor horse to his new home. After I had given him a good grooming, I left him contentedly munching his hay.

To finish the job, I had meanwhile sent off a lad to cut me a bundle of elm branches. In a few minutes the pair of us had fitted up a leafy trellis-work over the window so as to darken the stable.

If you ever go to Genzano, observe the low iron grill immediately to the left of the main door and, if the information interests you, you must know that that was my stable.

Now, I thought, I have the right at last to attend to myself. The luggage and painting equipment I couldn't carry I had had brought from Rome by the Genzano carrier. I fetched them and had them brought up to the castle. I now began to get straight.

Out of the remains of the two beds I made one, which gave me many nights of the untroubled sleep of the innocent. I chose as my bedroom the apartment at the back, next to the stage. Its doors shut badly, but those of the other rooms even worse. There had been leather tapestry on the walls, decorated with arabesques. Only half remained, coming away in many places and hanging in strips and tatters against the wall. There was an old cupboard with drawers for linen. In the great picture-gallery I deposited my painting things, a dozen books (the usual Pignotti and Plutarch), material for writing; in fact it was my work-room or study.

So my house was ready and all was perfectly organized before noon. At that time, and for many years after, noon was my hour for dinner. There was an inn at Genzano, kept by a Milanese, situated in one of the last houses on the right as you leave the village for Velletri. I made it my first revictualling station and, not being too particular, I found it excellent and went there daily.

It is incredible how, in general, everybody has become so much more exacting than they were then.

In this much-praised inn there was one big ground-floor room, once a granary, one end of which was occupied by the fire-place, a couple of stoves, and the host's desk.

At midday one was always sure of finding, cooked and ready, a *minestra* and a choice of two or three dishes: good home cooking. The *menu* was soon studied. The meal was laid on long, narrow tables, with a cloth at each place, half a metre broad, a napkin to wipe your mouth, iron knives and forks, half a litre of wine, and two rolls.

After dinner, a local peasant boy who acted as waiter appeared, pulled off the cloth, leant his left elbow on the table, and, with a piece of chalk in his right hand, wrote out the customer's bill on the dark, polished surface of the table. When the account was settled, he rubbed out the figures with his shirt-sleeve, and so this ready-money book-keeping gave rise to no misunderstandings.

My fellow-diners were not usually from the village, where everyone ate at home, but employees or people passing through. These mess-mates, each of whom ate on his own on his separate cloth, soon became acquaintances and finally, some of them, friends.

There was the police sergeant—the bigwig of the company—a fair young Neapolitan, a good devil and good company; there was also a friend of his, who was a strange case. This man had had a long, serious illness, and had recovered by a real miracle. He was staying at Genzano for his convalescence. Before falling ill, he had been in business, a bold, active fellow who, by the age of forty, had tried all sorts of things. After his illness, God knows what had happened to his constitution, but he had become as timid as a two-year-old baby. He was afraid of the dark, afraid to be alone; any little incident or noise upset him. One day towards evening, I recall, we went together to Albano. I had some business or other to transact and I said to him: 'If you don't object, wait for me here in the café. As you see, it's full of people and at this hour it will certainly not be left empty.' He said he was quite agreeable and I told him that I should finish my business immediately and be with him in a quarter of an hour.

I got back after ten minutes and I saw from a distance that there was a knot of people at the café door. 'Well! this is it,' I said. True enough it was he who had fainted on his seat and they were all round him trying to bring him to.

On another occasion, five or six of us went together to the festival at Cisterna in the Pontine Marshes. We slept at Velletri, all in the same room with the light on, on account of his fears. During the night the light went out. He began to rave and, none of us wanting to get up, we told him in a chorus to keep quiet and not disturb us. In a moment he was up, had opened the window, and, had not the nearest of us been quick enough to hurl himself on him and catch him as he fell, it would have been all over, and we should have had to retrieve him from the pavement below. He and a couple of nondescripts were the regulars. The wine-carters, the most respectable class of men, and most respected by the Roman populace, were the occasionals. I'm not joking. As everybody knows, Rome has been the refuge of sinners of the entire world and, if one didn't know it for other reasons, one could judge from the variety of surnames. These names are of all languages and nations, without those who bear them appearing to be foreigners. But this occurs in the middle class and, to some extent, among the nobility. But there is nothing of the kind among the working class, especially in the quarters of Trastevere, Regola, and in the hill districts. Even among this population itself one recognizes a kind of oligarchy, more jealously intent than others on keeping the Roman blood pure. This oligarchy is principally to be found in the two trades of the paviours and wine-carters. They hardly ever contract marriages out of their class, and there is no congregation of German canonesses more convinced of the superiority of their birth than the members of these humble, though not low, professions.

By physiological law, marriages restricted within a limited circle are harmful to the species. In this case, however, the physiological law is wrong. Or perhaps decadence only strikes idle, weak classes and not the strong and active. One glance will show the difference between them and the rest of the population. Their square frames; the size and modelling of their muscles; the fine articulation of their limbs; the spare anatomy without surplus fat, without paunch, whereas both sexes of the other Roman classes tend to be fat and flabby: all this proves them to be true descendants of those legionaries who carried on the march, not only their arms and victuals, but also stakes, so that before resting they could fortify their camp with ditch and bastion. We can see from the marble bas-reliefs how these ancient men of iron were made, and the wine-carters of today are just the same flesh and blood.

It is true they are rude, ignorant people, but in their looks, in the way they stand and walk and bear themselves, there is a lofty expression, a proud assurance that I have never come across in any other people in the world. It is impossible not to remain struck by the characteristic of superiority in this stratum of the population. In their features and expression, in their way of life; even in the materials and tools of their trade, they reveal something grandiose special to themselves, a majesty, an attitude of being masters, which you will look for in vain in classes above them.

In Rome, indeed, one has the surprising impression that the servants have expelled the masters from their palaces and chased them into the street.

Neither is this section of the people without fine qualities. They have a certain generosity of feeling; they do not generally give way to excessive indulgence (in the carter's trade you must keep sober). They are, it is true, accused of tapping the barrels they carry. I should not wish to maintain that their stops at country fountains are only for the sake of watering their horses. But who in the world does not sometimes put a little water in his wine? If you treat them as equals, they treat you well, but if you look down on them, they remember that they are the true Romans.

They use carts of splendid shape, as I previously indicated, and at the same time of an antique simplicity. Two long, strong timbers rest, at one end, on a pair of high wheels; at the other, in a straight line, on the horse's back. The horses themselves are tall animals, almost always dark black in colour, with necks and heads and general appearance that remind one of the horses depicted in ancient art. The cart has no side rails. The timbers are joined below by simple cross-pieces on which rest eight barrels. When evening comes, the carters leave Genzano and travel all through the night sitting dozing on the barrel nearest the horse's quarters. They lean up against the so-called *forcina*, the bough of a tree stuck in the cart which, ramifying like the fingers of a hand, forms a kind of niche which they line with sheepskin. They usually travel several together, one of whom keeps awake (a prudent arrangement in the Roman Campagna), and in this way a single linen-faced lantern hanging under a cart serves the whole cavalcade.

I was usually entertained at midday by having seven or eight of these fellows at table in front of me. To watch them, listen to their talk, and study them was a real treat for an artist. They were fine, strong figures of men; they always posed well and were always dignified. I challenge anybody to surprise one of them in a commonplace attitude. There was one who was called Pizzetta. I remember one day when it was very hot, one of them after his meal had stretched out, face downwards, on the same table where four or five of his companions were still seated. He rested his head on his two strong sun-burnt arms and he was snoring. All of a sudden his friends gave a shout all together, for some reason or other, and it woke him. I see him yet as he raised his sleepy head and looked at them blinking, saying: 'The devil take you!' Then he went to sleep again. I repeat this trifle to show how extraordinarily artistic their figures must have been, to have so impressed themselves on my mind that I still see them vividly after forty years, as though they were alive before me. Yet even poor Pizzetta was useful to me. In the description of the Sack of Rome in my novel *Niccolò de'*

Lapi I described him as one of those who looted San Giovanni de' Fiorentini.

The evening of my first day I supped at this same inn. Late at night I made my way up to the castle, along the elm-lined path that leads to it. In one hand I carried the bunch of keys, in the other a stable lantern I had bought as an essential piece of furniture.

I have already admitted to having a dash of the Don Quixote in my character. He saw an adventure in every event, in every most common-place occurrence. I too, without taking things quite so seriously as he did, nevertheless allowed my fancy full play as I approached my solitary, dramatic abode in darkness and silence.

When I got to the front door, I chose the great key I knew already, and opened and shut the door behind me. I climbed the stairs, which echoed under my steps, crossed the rooms that by day had seemed so huge and mysterious, and reached the chamber in which I had already made my bed.

Considering that I had no enemies in the place; that the accoutrement, with which I had appeared, did not suggest I was bringing strings of pearls or sums of money large enough even to tempt a peasant; that apparitions, witches, and gnomes did not, alas! enter into my beliefs (I say 'alas', because the world would be so much more amusing if they *did* exist); I thought I could safely reckon on a quiet night, without special precautions. But as, in this world, bailiffs are not always pleased to see the ghosts in their master's house treated with scant respect; as in this world there are, to say the least, those who enjoy practical jokes, although now fairly discreet in what they do; and as the old proverb says 'Watch out and stay whole', I took the precautions I always do in unsafe places and which I recommend to be as excellent as they are simple.

There were some big leather arm-chairs with enormous backs in the room. I placed one of them, slightly tilted, against the door, so that it was balanced in such a way that the slightest push would cause it to fall over. It was, I can assure you, an alarm like a cannon shot. On my bed, instead of a wife, I laid my loaded gun. Having snuffed out the tallow stump of the lantern, I was asleep in five minutes. My sleep, however, was brief. The profound stillness of the night, as everyone knows, makes all noises seem louder. When I came to my senses, the castle seemed to be full of people in all the rooms on all the floors. There was a general running to and fro and there seemed to be a play being acted on the stage of the theatre. There was something twisting and turning to and fro in the air close to my face. A bread roll I had brought with me for the morrow's breakfast moved and fell from the table where I had put it. It then continued its journey across the floor.

I sat up in bed and listened. I said to myself, 'What the devil's happening!' I thought that anyone prone to believe in ghosts and apparitions would easily have imagined, with all that scurrying, that the spirits of all the Sforzas, from Giacomo Attendolo to Ludovico il Moro, were there at his side.

Meanwhile the roll happily continued its journey, and I confess that I did not immediately find the physical explanation of the phenomenon. But, to use a modern expression, light dawned. It must have been a mouse, who, as a good husband and father, was trying to supply his family with bread, and who would only gnaw it on the spot if he were obliged to. When it got to the stage door the roll came to a stop, although one could judge from the thumps and thuds that it was doing its best to proceed. These attempts lasted for half a minute and then I heard the crackle of a crust being eaten, evidently by teeth in first-class order. So the mystery was explained. I fell back on the pillow and continued my interrupted sleep. 'We'll attend to this tomorrow,' I said to myself.

In order to conclude this instructive episode for the benefit of anyone who goes studying art from nature under similar circumstances, I will tell you what I did.

The next morning I found a slab of stone, half a door-step, and, with some difficulty, carried it into my room. With three little sticks I propped it up as a trap. The next night I had the satisfaction of hearing it fall and the squeak of farewell of a big fat mouse underneath. I was barbarian enough to jump from my bed in my shirt and dance on his tombstone so that he should be well and truly squashed.

I could find no way of ridding myself of the bats which fanned my face. They came out from behind the leathern arras from cracks, too many to be repaired. But they are the most harmless creatures in the world and gave me no further trouble.

Now began one of the most laborious study expeditions I have ever made in my life. The beauty of Genzano is at the lakeside. You reached it (I don't know about today) by a rough, steep path. Every morning I went down with all my gear round my neck. Going down was nothing, *facilis descensus Averni*; coming up in the burning heat of the day, *revocare gradus*, was something, I can tell you! But the will was there and, to back that up, a little *amour propre* and something of a sense of duty which began to develop in me.

On the shore of the lake, not far from the cottage of a man who followed the trade of steeping linen—the so-called *macerare*—is the famous plane tree of Lake Nemi. It no longer has the mottled, variegated bark of young planes, but has grown a great, knotty, wrinkled trunk like that of an old chestnut. I studied it at my leisure during the whole season. Directly I finished one sketch, I started another and was able to collect a good number. I combined painting with reading and re-reading my few books. More important still was the ferment of thought which filled the long, solitary, delightful hours I passed, surrounded by the inexhaustible treasures of a lovely landscape.

The linen man was an old policeman and told me about his experiences. He had always to be in the water and I was sorry to see how the leeches attacked his legs. He plucked them off directly he felt a bite.

5

AFTER some time solitude began to pall, as always happens with people of lively imaginations. The return to the castle at night with lantern and bunch of keys; those resounding echoes up the staircase and under the arches; the old Sforza portraits—magistrates in their robes, captains, cardinals with moustaches (they were unusual in those days), all those stern faces which seemed to look me up and down with distaste—had finished by plaguing me and making me melancholy. I was also upset at the time by a sad incident. A woman who had shown me real affection, and whom I had left *in extremis* on my departure from Rome, had shortly afterwards died. There was a suspicion of poison, administered by a certain person whose only motive seems to have been that his advances had been rejected. I shall not go into details, as it is not my intention to write about such matters.

This news reached me when I was living in isolation. Her last words to me—I had not given them the importance they afterwards inevitably assumed—were: 'Farewell, I leave this world with only one regret. . . .' These words now continually echoed in my ears; and although, as far as I know, I had nothing for which to blame myself, they seemed like a reproach.

How terrible are such reproaches! The dead are impassible; oblivious to repentance, deaf to explanations and excuses; they never tire, never change, and are never pacified. How easy it is for a sensitive soul to think he has been remiss in his behaviour towards them! I, who was not to blame in this case, almost grew to believe myself so and passed days and nights of real, bitter sadness.

Then, as happens to the young, and indeed, by the law of self-preservation, to everyone, impressions faded, and little by little I got my usual spirits back.

This inevitable return to one's normal peace of mind has always seemed to me an ugly feature of our nature; but I am far from thinking it could be otherwise.

Alas for the dead! Why weep for you today, and in some months, a year, laugh and joke? You have not changed; the love you bore us, the good you did us in your lifetime, is still a reality: why have we to change?

For this reason the cult of the dead has always seemed to me to be a sign of sensibility. I understand and honour the Chinese. I praise the Jesuits (not an everyday occurrence), who never would consider the sweetest, justest sentiments of the heart as sin; for the same reason I blame their opponents the Dominicans, who through their fanaticism simply succeed in banishing such feelings and all others of the kind.

However, how could one expect any sympathy for the departed from people who, for five hundred years, have burnt men at the stake for an article of the Creed?

I like the common hopes and interests between the living and the dead implied in the idea of Purgatory and prayers for the departed. This is one of those cases where the heart will have it so, even if reason doubts and scrutinizes.

Unfortunately the sentimental, sacred aspect of this dogma has, in practice, an ugly side. There are, alas! those who are on the watch to exploit the carelessness which always accompanies great sorrow. There is an industry that speculates on filial piety, conjugal love, and the affections; on the most intimate, sacred instincts of the human heart. I myself have had bitter experience of it, and I have seen similar circumstances repeated with others. In saying this, I do not accuse the generality of clergy; indeed I am glad to give recognition to many cultivated, honest, able priests who are spreading quite the opposite principle. Many of them now appreciate the true basis of their moral authority, but there are still too many of the followers of the old practices. Those clergy who complain that religion is neglected and diminished, would do something more valuable and more intelligent if they would examine the actions and personal behaviour of the priesthood in general, and try to verify if religious decadence can all be blamed on philosophy and a desire to avoid restrictions.

Religion and the clergy today are paying the arrears of century-old accounts. It's time Rome appreciated the fact. It is time to recognize that present effects come from ancient causes. Her friends would serve the cause of religion well if they advised her to do away with the causes rather than trying to rejuvenate them. However, this is wasted breath, so I will return to Genzano.

A friend of mine came to put an end to my solitude and share my house and artistic activities. It was with him I made the excursion to the Pontine Marshes, which I spoke of when I told the story about my convalescent fellow-diner. I'll say something more about that trip.

From Velletri, which is situated on the lower spurs of Mount Artemisio, the Appian Way descends to the plain and, after a coach stage, reaches Cisterna. This is an old fief of the Gaetani family, later of the Braschi; a district of buffaloes, fever, swamps, and highwaymen. At the mid-August festival of the Assumption, in the very middle of the worst malaria period, the village holds its annual celebration. There are only a handful of houses built round a large unpaved square, with the old feudal castle in one corner.

We slept at Velletri, where our companion tried to jump out of the window, and arrived at Cisterna at midday when sung Mass was just starting. Mass over, the procession came out and took an hour to go round the square. I still seem to see the priest who carried the relics or something. He came at the tail of the procession, surrounded by candles; he was quite bald, so that the terrific sun of the marshes struck directly on the polished skin of his cranium, from which it was reflected as it might be from a yellow ivory billiard ball. By his tight-shut eyes and wrinkled cheeks one could see what a wonderful time this semi-martyr was having!

However, a more unexpected sight soon made me forget the priest. I heard a whisper spreading from mouth to mouth, a murmur communicated from one to another, and I heard people near me clearly saying: 'The brigands, here are the brigands!'

I turned round, raised myself on tiptoe (although with my height it was hardly necessary), and saw, not far off, in the middle of the crowd, a number of conical hats wreathed with fluttering ribbons, the emblem of this respectable corporation.

It was they! Although used to the customs of the place, I should never have imagined that Italian 'live and let live' would have gone to such lengths.

The fact was, nevertheless, that these worthy assassins strolled through the fair, some arm-in-arm with respectable citizens, wearing their uniform, covered with froggings, medals (or rather coins), chains, and gold ornaments of all sorts. I saw no guns, blunderbusses, or other arms visible. They were clean and tidy; their linen puttees were newly washed; their faces were serene and kindly, as though to say: 'Enjoy yourselves, good people, we are no wolves or bears, we want to enjoy ourselves too!'

The policemen on duty were always at the corner of the square diagonally opposite to where the bandits were—it seemed destined that they shouldn't meet. In fact, order at Cisterna was better kept than in many other places I know: so there was no need to worry.

You must know, my dear reader, that the bad air seduces its victims with its balmy quality in order to overcome and kill them, just as the sirens of old. It could be that the myth of those marine beauties originates in some region which, lovely and full of attractions, welcomes incautious travellers with pestilential vapours. It follows that the real defence against the sirens was not Ulysses' wax, but sulphate of quinine.

However this may be, the air of the Marshes induces a not unpleasant lethargy, which is accompanied by an invincible tendency to fall asleep. If you sleep for an hour, it is all up with you.

Having seen the festival, the brigands, the fair, and all the pretty girls who had come in from Velletri, Cori, Sezze, Piperno, Sermoneta, and the neighbouring castle villages, I felt the moment approaching when, fever or no fever, I should have to find some corner and fall asleep. I gave myself a shake, found my mare, and saddled her. Having mounted, I set off for home, as the sun had already sunk low on the western horizon. I managed somehow or other to keep awake until I had passed Velletri; then finding I had reached the high region of pure air, and being at the end of my tether, I settled myself with my right leg over the pommel, in the way ladies ride, and fell fast asleep without a thought that my mount was apt to shy at night. She soon reminded me of the fact. I don't know what happened, except that I woke up in the dust of the road, as white as a miller. Luckily I did myself no harm as usual. In a whole series of tumbles, experienced at various times, I have always escaped whole. Towards midnight I got back to my castle, safe and sound.

In my description of the place, I forgot to include in the inventory a number of candelabra in the shape of cornucopias, attached to mirror plaques fixed to the walls for the illumination of the portrait gallery.

The sight of them suggested a brilliant idea—no pun intended—which was based also on the notion that I owed something to my neighbours. During my stay at Genzano I had received much kindness from the inhabitants. Up to a certain point, I think I can modestly claim that we deserved it. I was no nuisance to anyone and, when possible and the occasion arose, I laid myself out to be helpful. What is more, my friend played the flute and (the confession is hard to make) I played the guitar; only a few chords of course, but enough to accompany me when I sang *L'alba è ridente in cielo*, or the *Tarantella degli Dei,* or to get people to dance the Saltarello. One evening after supper at the inn we gave a specimen of our skill and soon had a large audience clustered round of lads and lasses attracted by our harmonious, or rather gratuitous, performance. Soon we were receiving timid petitions and blushing requests to play serenades under the balcony of some adored one. We always complied and became extremely popular.

Even though we were on the credit side with favours given and received, we thought it better to be generous, so with the incentive of the cornucopias all ready for use, we decided, before we left Genzano, to give a ball.

I'm sure the reader has a boundless faith in my sincerity; I do not wish to try him too far by asserting that all our candles were of wax. No! we stocked up with bundles of tallow candles and filled the candelabra one by one. We brought up from the inn to the castle several large jars of wine; our girl friends (*honi soit*, etc.) prepared a basket of cakes; invitations were sent out; and one evening just before dark the youth and fashion of Genzano began to arrive. People there didn't wait until one o'clock in the morning before they danced, as is the custom in some cities, inhabited by lazybones who sleep all day.

The hosts and the orchestra were one and the same, and as they were busy playing they couldn't receive the guests, not being able to be in two places at once like St. Anthony. Anyone could come in and there was a crowd as thick as at the routs of the London season.

As an act of prudence the wine had been watered by us, and what with that, and the water the landlord usually put in it, it turned out a most innocuous drink, powerless to inflame the brains of the dancers. After two baptisms it was really innocent! In fact the party was gay and friendly. All varieties of the Saltarello were danced, even, when enthusiasm had reached its height, the one when both partners throw away their shoes and dance barefoot. All passed off well and there was no disorder and the guests went away with the impression that '*Messieurs NN. avaient fait les honneurs d'une manière charmante*'.

Meanwhile the time came for me to return to Rome. After I had settled all bills, I found that my high style of living had reduced my wealth to not more than eight *paoli* in ready cash, that is to say to less than one Roman *écu*. I simply had to stay a further week at Genzano, in order not to leave a last study half finished.

The situation became gloomier still. One morning what do I hear but carriage bells at my door. Down I go and find a Roman lady with her son of about twenty-five whom I hardly knew. They were at Genzano on business and asked me for hospitality. That meant at least lunch. And I only had eight *paoli*!

No matter! A guest is a gift from God, says the law of the Patriarchs, the Bedouins, and the Red Indians. Avanti! Don't spare the expense! Lunch in the castle; steaks and café au lait. We'll think how to pay later.

Luckily it was only a short visit; God took back his gifts, fortunately, before dinner. That was of first importance! But my eight *paoli* had not sufficed to pay for the modest fare I had provided, so that I was five or six *paoli* on the wrong side of that zero figure which permits one to sleep peacefully.

I have always loathed debts; but even the Romans, who hated despotic power, had more dictators than I had ever had creditors from the day I was born.

But this time I simply had to borrow. I gave a mental glance round all those I knew of my own age, without discovering one who could help me. Luckily in Rome as minister at the time was Count Barbaroux, one of the most learned, honest, and best of our officials, to whom I had been recommended by my father. I wrote to him and, by return of post, or more precisely by the next carrier, I had the sum requested: ten or twelve *écus*, if I remember rightly, which indicates that my extravagances had not been immoderate.

So, laden with sketches, not to speak of the blessings of my creditors and of the youths and maidens of the entire village, I took my leave of Genzano and, at the beginning of October, returned to Rome.

As in previous year, I considered I had earned a month's relaxation, so having put the work I had done in order, I went off to Albano, where several of the people, both male and female, I usually consorted with had gone for their holiday.

My circle of friends included excellent people, as far as the place and the time permitted, but they did more harm than good to a young man, as indeed did the greater part of Roman society of the period. When one is twenty-three or four, what one needs is surroundings that will guide, elevate, and inspire one. If one is also in love, it is a thousand times more important to come across a noble soul, capable and desirous of moral beauty.

I grant to the theologians that illicit love is always a social wrong, but it remains undeniable that a worthy, generous love can instigate useful actions and noble sacrifices; while the sad mistake of allowing oneself to be taken by beauty alone, associated with a soul—if not perverse—weak and trivial, leads to incalculable consequences, torment, and hurt for the whole of one's life.

I found myself precisely at the age when those capable of ardent passion must run the hazard of this dangerous tempest, which is to the moral side what smallpox is to the physical side of man.

Both these illnesses take a long time coming and then suddenly attack one, and both sometimes leave the patient badly scarred. It was in that October that I gradually approached a crisis, which then became most violent, so much so that I marvel that I came out alive.

I met a woman who, despite some good qualities, had no shadow of superiority of mind. She had been brought up, as was the custom in Roman families of the period, without the guidance of anyone with the slightest knowledge of how to educate character and sentiment. As for intellectual powers, one can say she had none, so much so that she hardly knew how to write without spelling mistakes. But her looks were remarkable, even in a country where perfect feminine beauty is common. For an artistic, impressionable temperament such as mine, beauty dazzles like the sun and one can see nothing beyond.

From that October, not for months, but for years and years, I wore myself out in an obstinate struggle between duty and inclination. My duty was to work, to do my utmost to become a man and a gentleman useful to my country and to others, if only I could. My heart concentrated all my longings, all my aspirations, on one single object. Yet I made an effort of will and my will triumphed, but it was a sad and, for some time, a sterile triumph. I could indeed force myself to remain in my studio, or at my books, for the same number of hours as before; but I couldn't command my poor mind to understand and learn. I could get on my horse, leave Rome, establish myself in a hamlet to study from nature all the summer, but I could not re-awaken in my heart the spark that takes fire before the beauties of the creation : the skies, the distant views, the forests, the waters were lifeless deserts. What gave them life, their inner soul, was only one thing for me—and that was elsewhere.

All these years afterwards, I still shudder at the thought of the torments I endured at that unlucky period.

Q

Now I examine my behaviour in this episode, I find I had one merit, a merit of which experience has shown me the value: namely, to have recognized that duty must take precedence over love, and, however inadequately defended, it is rarely overcome.

Do you wish to know the outcome? After seven years during which I had not given a thought elsewhere, I was shown the door to make way for a broken-down noble, who some years after was reputed to be a usurer, and then a thief! . . .

That's the way things go in this world. Luckily I recalled the jingle:

> Protesting is for fools,
> Complaint is quite absurd.
> An honest man deceived
> Makes off without a word.

I did just that. Following what I have laid down, I shall not give further details about this romance, other than the indications indispensable for the understanding of what follows.

I worked all that winter and did a picture depicting the Three Hundred at Thermopylae; for me it was relatively not too bad. There was an idea in it and quite decent colour. In the state I was in it was miraculous that I could do as much.

Owing to my new circumstances I soon modified my habits. The regular ways of the first two years gradually changed. I began to go into society in the evenings. I simply had to be where she went. I was well known in several houses, I knew a lot of people and I began to familiarize myself with modern Rome and form clear ideas about it. Previously, as a semi-diplomat, mixing with Princes and Ministers, or as an art student, living on my own or with a handful of people without roots, I had not been in a position to form an overall view of Rome—rulers and ruled.

As I think it hardly necessary to relate the long series of foolishnesses which, as a dutiful lover, occupied my existence that winter—and it was not the only winter—I will relate a few details that may give some idea of a world so very different from ours, but which to some extent explains ours, and what has happened since.

You are aware, dear reader, that I follow the rule of not expressing likes or dislikes: I look for truth, and when I think I've found it I speak out without minding who complains. As far as sincerity goes, you need have no qualms.

It was 1823, the last year of Pius VII and Consalvi. The latter was a man of distinguished intelligence, who had played a large part in the

Congress of Vienna, as is well known, in getting the Papal Legations restored. At the time, it seemed to be a great windfall obtained by great ability. Now, considering the implacable rebellions on the one hand, and the implacable repression on the other; daggers and secret societies versus tribunals and gallows; Carbonari assassins ranged against Cardinals' henchmen; all this on account of Consalvi's great ability; can a sensible man really consider it a great windfall?

Acting justly in just matters, that is the way to advance without trouble and succeed: and one does make progress; something I am never tired of repeating for the hundredth time.

But justice is too simple a concept to be adopted by the ignorant. Much knowledge and much intelligence is required to understand elementary truths. Consalvi, despite the distinguished intelligence I granted him, was not one of those great brains who can embrace, in one glance, past and present, and know how to harmonize the future with them.

He could neither maintain what was good in the old semi-federal, semi-anarchical-popular Roman state; nor accept the benefits of the modern, revolutionary centralization.

In fact, the Roman Government, after 1815, was worse than either of these systems, and went from disaster to disaster, until it has reached the point where its inefficiency is plain to all.

Pius VII was a good, simple man, but not very astute; he therefore let himself be led. His sense of duty, his firmness in the face of persecution, of which he gave noble proof, were sufficient for him when the path he should take was plain; but in the pacific exercise of sovereignty to distinguish between what is good and what is wrong, to support the former and repress the latter, under conditions where the system of government stifled all public expression of opinion, would only be feasible to a ruler with a hard head, strong character, knowledge, warm heart, youth, good health, etc., etc. The poor old gentleman did not have these qualities; he saw everything through Consalvi's eyes and let things slide. He was loved by those of his household for his simplicity, but he was reputed to be incredibly apathetic. In fact, he died old with his hair still black and hardly bald at all, despite the fact that he had lived through experiences any one of which would have been enough to turn his hair white.

I once visited Castel Gandolfo with my father and had the honour of playing a game of billiards with him. I well remember his long black hair under the biretta, making a strong contrast with his white robe.

I have already pointed out that Consalvi favoured foreigners in order to attract them (or rather their money) to Rome, and always sided with them, should the natives protest against their insolence. In general he favoured the upper class, the rich and the powerful. Owing to my personal circumstances, I was in a position to know the full details of a really incredible episode, which I will briefly relate, as it is very much to the point.

It is quite a good thing to have accurate ideas about that era, which some good souls would like to compare with the present.

In Via Gregoriana on the Pincio, not far from the church of the Trinità de' Monti, there are, or were, several small houses containing artists' studios. They belonged to the Pacetti family and went as far as the Via Sistina. The Pacetti are a family of artists, and the grandfather of the present generation was a certain Cavalier Pacetti, a fairly well-known sculptor, very proficient in his art.

At the period of the Roman Republic, I refer to the one established by the French (in 1798) and not the one overthrown by them (in 1849), the gentry and wealthy of Rome were hit by a heavy tax, which, given the hard times, even the rich found difficult to pay. Everyone tried as hard as they could to scrape up money, and they sold off furniture, jewellery, *objets d'art,* etc. The Barberini family displayed several antiques in a room of their palace in the Via Quattro Fontane, among which was a male torso, a Greek Pentelican marble of the best period.

Cavalier Pacetti went to the sale and, for seven or eight hundred *écus,* was able to bring the fragment home. It had no legs and hardly any arms and I'm not sure if it had a head.

Having put it in his studio in the Via Sistina, he decided on a complete restoration. He modelled the missing parts in plaster, and produced the sleeping figure, stretched out so realistically, which is known in art-circles as the Barberini Faun.

Apart from his labour, before he could proceed to carving, he had difficulty in finding marble of precisely the same grain. To obtain this he had to destroy another Greek statue of lesser merit.

So with much toil and great expense (the statue is over life-size) he finished the work, which was praised by Canova and the best judges of the time as a restoration in which the ancient and the modern were in perfect harmony, and, if not of equal merit, at least perfectly matched.

Meanwhile Napoleon had gone, the French occupation had come to an end, the Pope had returned. Now was the time of loving charity, justice, happiness, abundance, and all the charming features of the restoration and priestly rule!

Foreigners flocked to Rome from all quarters. To one or other of these—representative of a German court I think—Pacetti sold his Faun for many thousands of *écus.*

As the statue was on the point of being packed and dispatched, along comes an order to halt. The Faun must not be exported. And why? Because the agents of the Barberini family, whose head will have known nothing of the matter, or who will have been told the story in distorted form, had applied for a *motu proprio.* This ordered the Cavalier Pacetti to give back the statue, as it was entailed property. He was offered the seven or eight hundred *écus* which he had originally paid, plus the value of his restoration, to be fixed by expert arbitrators.

The poor man nearly fell backwards at being threatened by this dastardly stroke. He was, however, a man of great energy; he didn't give up and appealed.

Had he not, he claimed, attended the auction attracted by the advertisements, bid against others, obtained the fragment, paid for it in ready money at a difficult period when money was scarce? No one had warned him then of any family entail; he was therefore the rightful owner of the torso he had bought. He and his assistants had worked hard on it for a long time and used up the marble of another Greek statue, in order to obtain the perfect result now to be seen. He could be the sole judge of what work he had done, and equally of any estimate to be made, and he recognized the right of no one else to price it as he fancied. The statue was therefore his and anybody who wanted it must agree with him as to the conditions of sale; they could not be imposed on him by others, etc., etc.

'All fiddlesticks', as they used to say.

Sic volo, sic jubeo, stat pro ratione voluntas. What I say, goes. Such was the reply of Authority. But Pacetti did not give up. Some days passed and, as it was clear he was not knuckling under, lo and behold, a court bailiff armed with a document, stating that the seven or eight hundred *écus* were deposited at the bank, plus I don't know how much more for the work of restoration, and that for every day he failed to collect them there would be a fine of a gold doubloon. Still Pacetti held out.

After a certain time, there arrived one week up the Via Sistina forty porters and policemen *cum fustibus et lanternis.* They stopped at Pacetti's studio door and, finding it shut, broke it down. They went in, hoisted up the statue, put it on a cart, and disappeared.

The poor sculptor, so vilely treated, took to his bed with a bilious attack. He was nearly laid out, but he partly recovered, dragged on a little longer, and then finally departed for the next world.

There was a case in the Papal Court between Pacetti's heirs and the Barberini. It was now won, now lost, now won again, until finally it was won outright. All fiddlesticks! The Faun remained in the possession of those who had taken it and, if I'm not mistaken, it was sold to the King of Bavaria. I think it's now in Munich.

Should I really be right and the matter be as I have described, what had happened to the entail?

The Pacetti family ended by accepting a compromise, the terms of which I do not know. Such was the government under a person of integrity such as Pius VII and an enlightened man such as Cardinal Consalvi, which everyone now thinks it a good thing to preserve for the support, honour, and glory of Christendom, religion, and evangelical belief. Then they complain that people are losing their faith!

Anyone familiar with other countries finds it hard to understand how, when one has obtained—not one, but ten, favourable judgements—having gone through all the steps of judicial procedure that exist, one still gets no satisfaction. Yet I have repeatedly seen such a thing: after numerous judgements, nothing has happened if it were a case of the weak against the powerful. The carrying out of the terms of the judgement in such cases is impeded by some invisible force; it is always promised, but never takes place.

This decadence of the magistracy has been long deplored by honest men most attached to the Pope. As long ago as 1820, I remember having heard Cardinal De Gregorio bitterly deplore the small 'respectability' (a word only coined thirty years later) of the Roman Courts. The Cardinal was an excellent person, a great friend of my father's, who would now be called a reactionary.

'Once upon a time,' he said, 'all the most famous cases were brought before the Papal *Wota* (he couldn't pronounce his Rs), the whole of *Euwope wespected* its findings; but in those days there were *weal* men. Now one finds a little *Monsignowe*, only a boy, standing up with a poor little attendant behind him hired for the occasion—whoever's that? Oh, he's a judge of the *Wota*, etc.'

These junior judges, boys or at any rate men not up to their task, had an expert clerk who studied cases and wrote out the findings.

A very strange practice was to be seen, a clear proof of what opinion the public had of the dignity of judges and the respect due to them. In all countries of the world, to go and commend a case to a magistrate would lead to one's unceremonious expulsion from his chambers, or at least to a severe rebuke. In Rome, on the contrary, on the day before a trial before the Rota or any other tribunal, lawyers would go round commending cases to the judges, sometimes accompanied by their clients, and this was called going for the 'Informazione' or instruction.

For this reason one found included in Counsel's fee to his client the hire of a carriage for the day; and there were certain second-hand carriages, painted red, remnants of ecclesiastical legacies, which could always be seen in all the streets of Rome on Thursdays.

The 'Informazione' only lasted a few hours. The carriages, however, had been hired for the whole day and, in order not to waste them, they were to be seen driving about full, not of lawyers and abbés, but of women and children. This was quite in order; because the lawyers, although they dressed in clerical garb, were actually laymen, often married, with wives and children and everything that goes with them.

I have noticed one very odd thing. The Roman people don't show undue disapproval of abuses. Sometimes one hears a person declaiming against some powerful oppressor, but behind his anger one has the impression of an underlying semi-acceptance of the situation, as though the evil he was execrating were natural and inevitable.

After all, the Roman is right, because at all times and under all systems of governments, past, present, and future, the big fish nearly always eats the little fish. But, nevertheless, I seem to recognize in this attitude of mind, as in several other characteristics of modern Roman society, evident traces of their past history.

From antiquity up to the present, the powerful have always oppressed the populace in Rome: the story of the Consul Menenius Agrippa proves it. How is it that it has never occurred to the people that this evil can be remedied?

Apropos of this, I remember the ideas of a sportsman I met at Marino, the mountain village where I spent two seasons painting, as I shall presently relate.

When I knew him, he was an old man, and he spoke of pre-revolution times. He told me about a certain famous gun-dog of his, the best of the whole district, which had surpassed all rivals, and had achieved many great feats in the field.

'Ah well!' he said, 'one day he disappeared—I loved him like a brother—I was distracted. I took my gun and searched the whole countryside; all the hamlets, cattle sheds, holdings ... if I'd found the thief I would certainly have killed him. I came to Pantano di Borghese; the owners were away. Directly I got to the gate of the courtyard, there he was! I could see him behind the gamekeeper's legs and the poor beast recognized me and gave a great leap towards me, but they held him. I turned about and went home to Marino.'

'But surely,' I replied, 'you complained to the Prince or the Authorities?'

'What do you mean, complain! (and he shook his head as though to say, where have you come from, you fool?). A Borghese wanted him—the thing was over—you know how it is!'

That 'you know', or rather 'if only you knew', means much in the mouth of a Roman. It can signify fate or the inevitable; propriety, custom, or even justice.

This is how I understood it on this occasion: 'Prince Borghese has taken my dog, it is useless for me to oppose him.' If you had asked this peasant: 'Would you rather get your dog back, under the condition that the Borghesi did not exist?' he would have replied, 'After all, I can get on without my dog, but who can imagine a world without the Borghese family?'

This is why the antipathy which, for example, once blazed up between nobles and bourgeois in Piedmont does not exist in Rome, although there would be much more cause for it.

That winter I worked, but the result was merely an effect of will and cost me incredible efforts. I felt no pleasure in anything I did: I thought of nothing, desired nothing, but that ill-starred love. Fortunately I still preserved in the bottom of my heart a sense of duty, and this was my salvation. Although distracted, listless, vacillating, I never entirely gave up. I was supported, as well as by the idea of duty, also by the shame of being so unworthily upset by a pretty face and an attractive appearance.

However, my previous peaceful life of study had gone; and I found myself living another, full of restlessness, anxieties, rages, hopes, and fears, which proves the truth of the Italian folk proverb: *Cicisbei e damerini, vita da facchini.* (It's a dog's life, squiring dames.)

The occupation of 'ladies' man' has almost disappeared. The result of idleness, it was killed by the need for energetic action. In other words it was born of despotism and shrivelled under the sun of liberty. How could making love be the exclusive occupation of your whole life, nowadays?

Previously you could so make it, you almost had to; except in the rare cases of those who dedicated themselves to some branch of learning or art, as I did.

This Venus Isle had its statutes and laws, its wars and revolutions. The whole thing was sufficiently curious to warrant a page of description.

First of all, those people only approved a genuine love, true, scrupulously faithful, and free of all idea of any pecuniary advantage.

The *roué* was considered as the most abominable of heretics. The sort of lover who pretended, who courted several at the same time, who was fickle, inconstant, indifferent, tepid, all these were heretics of different classes, but all deserving of greater or lesser penalties in the Tartarus of that religion.

Public opinion pronounced judgement. As you see, universal suffrage had been invented long before Napoleon III proclaimed it in 1852. At parties, in groups of friends, love-affairs were discussed; evidence was brought forward, matters were weighed, disputed, and, finally, sentence was pronounced. The suffrage, known as universal, was in fact also in this case the opinion of a few leaders who imposed their views.

What is odd was the kind of morality, probity, and honesty professed by the faithful of this cult.

The common opinion holds that everyone is free to do what he likes, but at bottom everyone will agree that deceit is not honourable, and that *even a husband* should be protected by this formulation of public morality. But to deceive a lover! God help us! But a husband—'well, you know how it is!'

The general opinion proclaims that, if a deceived husband pretends to notice nothing and goes on as best he may whatever happens, it is his business and nobody has any right to interfere. Nevertheless, a shade of ridicule, sometimes worse, pursues him and it is difficult for him to escape scot-free.

But Heaven protect us, if we make a joke, or utter a word of mockery at the expense of such an interesting, useful person. The women, specially the middle-aged women, raise a chorus of protest: 'Oh he's such a gentleman, an excellent man, so discreet!' etc., etc., etc.

Should a husband, not so discreet, do what would be found most natural in any country in the world; should he rid himself in one way or another of the company of the gentleman who had proposed himself as a partner in the home; or should he merely fail to welcome him with the same warmth as his wife, there was a general outburst of indignation throughout the whole of Venusburg.

I well remember the case of a young man, the son of a lady who kept open house, frequented by everybody in Rome. He fell in love with a girl, the wife of an officer, also young, a handsome man of excellent character, who had the strange idea that his better half should be satisfied with himself alone.

But his better half was not at all satisfied. Finally, one day, the officer had the hardihood to say in good round terms to the pair of them, that he had no intention of wearing horns; and he added words usual on such occasions, when the speaker has had as much as he can stand.

The same evening I was at the usual reception. I joined a group in which was the hostess (the mother of the lover) and saw her looking very cross. I overheard her grumbling and uttering a crescendo of cutting remarks about someone and I well remember she called him a 'vile object'.

I whispered to a friend: 'Who's being railed against by Cintiola?' The officer's name was given me. 'But why?' 'Because he's made a scene with his wife and that chap. . . . He's gone for them. . . . I know all about it.'

I soon had the story confirmed; it was quite correct. I remember with satisfaction that I was not so corrupted by their way of thinking that I did not marvel at the strange expression used on this occasion prompted by our hostess's maternal love.

La Signora P. did not put in her usual appearance that evening. The son of the house kept away and an air of melancholy hung over the company, alarmed by this novel and unfortunate example and considering with terror all the possible consequences.

But it was all a false alarm. Things went on as usual, and poor P.—far from keeping clear of horns—soon had to forget their existence or lose them among all those of his many successors.

This goes to prove that the profession of husband in Rome of those days was not a bed of roses. But things became really desperate at Carnival time. Only the final week is properly so called. The great bell of the Capitol tower tolls at one o'clock. This signifies that it is permitted to go about Rome masked up to sunset.

Everyone has often read descriptions of the Corso with its confetti and tapers. In any case these delights are importations; everybody knows it and enjoys them the more.

I shall rather describe lesser-known traditions.

From ancient days the unfortunate Jews have provided entertainment for Christians. Previously, it is said, one of them was rolled down the Capitol hill in a barrel. Later, the Synagogue managed to get this changed to a foot-race (or sack-race?) between a number of Jews. Later still, two-legged runners gave way to four-legged and the Ghetto had to pay for the prizes: eight lengths of parti-coloured fine velvet for the eight Carnival days.

On the first day a ceremony takes place on the Capitol which is worth describing. The Senate in the person of a single Senator is seated on a throne (a reduction from six hundred of the ancient Senate to one, in the way maps are reduced to small compass). The Rabbi and a deputation from the Ghetto kneels before him bearing an address of humble and devoted subservience to the People and Senate of Rome. After reading the address, the Senator makes a gesture of kicking the Rabbi with his foot, while the latter retires full of gratitude, as is only natural.[1]

The Carnival merry-making is well-known to everyone, as I said; but the guide-books leave out the best part. I shall try to make good the deficiency.

The December Saturnalian revels of the ancients (which have been moved to February by the moderns) are the climax of all the desires, projects, and conspiracies hatched during the rest of the year.

Let me explain myself.

Anyone who wants to discover a secret, conclude or start an intrigue, ask for an explanation, make a declaration of love, etc., and cannot find time or opportunity under normal conditions, reckons on Carnival time.

At that period custom permits to the sex, hypocritically called *weak*, absolute liberty and independence. I can tell you, if you are in Rome at the time, you can just see how *weak* they are!

Women friends get together and have no need of helpers or guardians. I don't have to mention husbands; but not even lovers.

The former just give up. I have seen some of them retire to bed and spend the Corso hours fast asleep. For the latter, however, the moment has come to keep very much awake and keep a sharp look-out. But the little-used sub-title of the *Barber of Seville*[2] must not be forgotten. The more precautions are necessary, the more unavailing they are.

Seeing how masquerades are arranged ('systematized' in journalese) it is almost impossible to know what's going on.

One generally has the idea that when a woman puts on a disguise she does not, therefore, forget to make herself as smart as possible. It is not necessary to have a hump back or a swaddled foot in order not to be recognized. They think otherwise in Rome at Carnival time! A

---

[1] *Author's Note.* In the Middle Ages at Carnival time the mob ill-treated Jews and sacked the Ghetto. These unfortunates had recourse to the city authority and ransomed themselves with money, declaring they were the subjects and slaves of the Roman people. This is the origin of the ceremony I have described above, and the declaration of citizenship on the condition of safety of life and goods. The kick was administered up to 1830. Previously, instead of the kick, the Senator placed his foot on the Rabbi's neck. Then they accuse Jews of having spoilt their own characters!

[2] 'L'inutile precauzione' (The Unavailing Precaution) (tr.).

woman transforms herself into a bundle, a mere clothes-horse, and she
has to renounce human form when she goes (or used to go) to take her
seat on the steps of Palazzo Ruspoli during the procession.

These steps, now vanished, formed the pavement in front of the
Caffè Nuovo, a couple of feet above street level. There was a row of
straw seats there, where the ladies, disguised with masks, ensconced
themselves. Those who walked along the pavement, in front of the
raised step, found the arrangement most convenient for conducting
more or less intimate and secret conversations, as appropriate to the
participants.

It is obvious that one obstacle had to be surmounted, for anyone who
wanted to have a talk with a lady not available during the rest of the
year—to recognize her on the 'step'!

Apropos of this, I remember one occasion when I brought off a real
tour de force of diplomacy. I wanted very badly to talk at my ease with
a lady to whom I had not been introduced. I succeeded in learning that
on Carnival Thursday she intended to go to the famous steps, and that
she was looking for a man's cloak, sleeveless, and cut on the round, as
was then worn. I so arranged that I got her to pick mine, without her
knowing whose it was. It was therefore simple for me to find her.

The 'step' is the neutral ground where the innumerable interests of
love-making meet, get tangled or smoothed out.

To conclude my exposition, I must add that lovers cannot always
enjoy the delights of the 'step' or any other of the Carnival entertainments.

If the goddess be forced to stay at home, on account of lying in,
indisposition, or any other reason, the faithful swain must not enjoy
himself either. While the fun is at its height all down the Corso, he
may go for a walk in the Forum, St. Peter's, or Villa Borghese. If at an
evening party it is discovered that X, whose beloved is in bed with a
slight cold, has been seen during the carnival hours, alone, on horseback outside Porta Angelica, let us say, the women say: 'What a sweet
young man that X is! He really is a faithful friend!' If their own young
man be present, whose conscience may not be quite so clear, he gets a
look, by way of reprisal, which signifies: 'Take note.'

Another rule is that if any misfortune should happen in *her* family
or in her husband's family, *he* must sacrifice everything, his life if
necessary, to remedy it.

All of this seems, and is, very odd, and far removed from present-
day practice, but no one, I think, will prefer the world of today to that
of the previous age.

Love which in seeking satisfaction accepts sacrifices, which supports indescribable anguish for a moment's ineffable happiness, is fine and noble. It contains, I can almost say, something virtuous, as all pain voluntarily and bravely borne.

Love, from which all thorns have been removed, what is it? An ignoble moral decadence, and a more ignoble animal instinct. The last extreme and the most convenient expression of this instinct is the 'kept woman'.

To speak of 'kept women', at that time, was to speak of an absurdity, something quite incredible. Those few foreigners who arrived in Rome with such companions, or whom one knew were on the look-out for such arrangements with actresses, seemed to us too stupid for words and we never ceased laughing at them and mocking them.

If one could lift the veil that covered the mysteries of the 'step', very odd things would transpire. Here and there one got a glimpse.

I recall a youth (I was present) who had stayed with two of these bundles during the whole time of the procession down the Corso. When evening came he was invited to see them home. They went by San Lorenzo. As they passed through the Fiano palace, right in the middle of the courtyard, one of the two began to rain blows on the young man and followed him with slaps and punches all the way to the Piazza di Pietra.

He must have put his foot in it badly!

The Carnival laxness did not much amuse me. I was bored with it at the age of twenty-three or four, and when the crazy period came along I fled to the opposite quarter of Rome. In the early days I did play my part in masquerades, and particularly in one I should like to remember.

Paganini and Rossini were both in Rome: La Liparini was singing at the Tordinona theatre, and I often went there in the evening with them and other madcaps of my own age. Carnival was coming and one evening we said: Let's arrange a masquerade.

What should we do, or not do? In the end we decided to dress up as blind beggars and sing, asking for alms. We hatched up some verses which ran :

> Blind men are we;
> Of your charity,
> Give alms, give alms.
> On this day of mirth,
> Remember us in dearth;
> Give alms, give alms.

Rossini set them to music there and then, rehearsed us again and again, and finally we decided to appear on the Thursday. Our dresses were decided upon: very smart below, but covered with patched rags. In fact, poverty over elegance. Rossini and Paganini were the orchestra, dressed as women and strumming guitars. Rossini filled up his already plump contours with rolls of tow and looked like something out of this world. Paganini, as thin as a rake and with that face of his like a fiddle handle, dressed as a woman, looked twice as lean and nobbly as usual.

I must say we were an enormous success; first in one or two houses where we went to sing; then on the Corso; then at night at the ball.

But in entertainments I always held 'Enough is as good as a feast', and I spent the ball in bed.

6

SPRING was coming. All the winter that cursed passion had given me no peace. It was not that I had worked little; it was that I had worked unprofitably. I could make the effort to stop in the studio for so many hours; but no effort could put those hours to good use.

However, I give myself credit for not having allowed myself to drift completely, and to have always tried to breast the current. Now, however, I was faced by a terrible decision. In previous years I had left Rome in May and stayed away until All Saints Day. In the state I was now in, what was I to do? God alone knows the tortures I suffered.

I had bought a very suitable horse for the country, with harness such as cowherds use; a cowboy saddle with high pommels, a leathern bridle a span broad, and all the rest in keeping; satchels, a cloak of dark cloth lined with green silk, and a whip or goad. My outfit was to match, all velveteen corduroy such as country people wear.

The day came when I had to make up my mind. One morning I left by the Porta San Giovanni, alone, on horseback, with my gun across the saddle bow. My poor heart, so full of pretensions, so unbalanced, so careless of the trouble it was causing its owner, had a strange sensation which can only be described by a yet stranger simile. I felt as though one end of me had remained behind in Rome, attached to the street and house of that certain lady. It was the thread of life; and as I went farther and farther away it unwound and left me empty, worn-out, spiritless, incapable of anything; with nothing to show I was a man, except my stubborn, inexorable resolution.

I reached Marino and put up at the inn situated at the top of the village, at the crossing, where one road leads to the church, the other to Frascati, Castello, and Albano.

The inn was owned by a good, kindly old couple, Sor Cesare and Sora Marta. They had let the place to a young man, a romantic chatterbox, a great player of *morra,* but a good fellow withal. I settled into one of the rooms with all my pictorial baggage. The bed was clean; and as for board, the landlord's wife cooked simply and cleanly; the village had all one needed; there was a café and the surroundings were lovely. I should have lacked nothing, had it not been for ... you know!

A contented heart lacks for nothing in this world, but there is nothing that can satisfy a discontented one. It is only too true, and it should be satisfactory to those who are always complaining about the unequal distribution of wealth. If we could see inside people, we should find that Providence is less partial than it seems at first sight. Metastasio says it better than I can. In its justice, Providence lays down that it is not enough to be rolling in money and loaded with honours, to be happy: she says that on the top of all this one must have a contented heart and she alone has the key to that.

I certainly did not have one at that time, and I cannot tell you how bitter and deep was the sadness I fed on every minute of every hour.

I got up, prepared my paraphernalia, and set to work drawing. I could not do well because I felt troubled, filled with one thought, one image, which never faded, however tired and downcast I myself grew. She never left my horizon, I saw her in the sky, the waters, the gloom of the gorges, the heart of the woods. Knowing that she was in the power of another, my tormenting imagination conjured up with inexhaustible fatality all possible happenings that would be most bitter for me. Sometimes the pangs of certain desperate jealousies seemed like actual knife wounds, so much that I recoiled physically.

I returned home miserable; my food seemed bitter and disagreeable. I was surrounded by quarrelsome boors, whose rough voices became deafening as they shouted out the numbers at the game of *morra.* I can't tell you how greatly I was offended by the contrast between my inner thoughts and the images that came to me, and that rude, sorry company. I seemed all the more alone and desolate.

I dragged out a week, working badly and little, but usually lying prone on my bed, or aimlessly wandering round the countryside. When

Saturday came, as it was not the custom for even painters to work on Sundays in those parts, I mounted my horse in the evening and set off for Rome.

The ball of thread I described wound in as I got nearer, and life began to return to my veins. With what anxious mounting joy did I not pass all the stages of the Appian Way. I knew them by heart, and each one meant so many fewer miles to go! Tor di Mezza Via, Roma Vecchia, the Tavolato, then, with the innkeeper Camillo seated at his door with his leg bandaged, propped up on a stool (I quite forgot to ask what ailed him); after that the Casa degli Spiriti. Finally, the great straight road, at the end of which could be seen the looming, majestic mass of St. John Lateran, standing out against the last orange streak of the sunset, which thereabouts hardly fades before the sky above one's head is twinkling with stars.

I went through the gateway arch, where there is the skull of a celebrated highwayman, bleached by the sun and rains, preserved in an iron cage. Even those sunken eye-sockets seemed friendly to me in my homecoming mood! Then, counting the steps and the minutes, reckoning the distance, I reached home. I brushed off the dust, I put on clean clothes, I hastened *there*. But if I may properly describe my state of mind at that time, I have no intention of writing of love, as I have repeatedly said; so I draw a veil over the *there* and will raise it only on leaving.

My departure came in the night between Sunday and Monday. According to Roman custom I went round visiting until one o'clock or one thirty (5 or 5½ hours after sundown), then I supped at the Armellino or Monte Citorio tavern. My horse was brought to me there and, having shed my yellow gloves and once more a cowboy, I took the sad, sad road to Marino. I knew that the sorrow of a new departure would be so much loss; that, in any case, I should do no good at my work; and that it would really be as well to stay in Rome. But if I had allowed myself to be conquered (and I had the sweetest, dearest opponent begging me to remain), I should have felt ashamed of myself: that is the worthiest and most useful way to feel shame. As long as one only feels ashamed on account of what others think, it is only a matter of being able to get away with it.

Everybody told me that the constant going to and fro between the mountain air and the air of Rome would seriously threaten me with malaria. Luckily I was spared; and, after the early fevers I contracted in the country near the sea, I had no further trouble all the time I was in Rome and its neighbourhood.

The opinion of experienced doctors of the place is that though prepared quinine is a quicker and more reliable cure, the Peruvian bark was more lasting in its effects. I was a proof of this theory. Journeying by night, I have got off my horse to rest him, and fallen asleep in the heart of malarial country. Once I spent a night at Baccano, where Alfieri wrote his well-known sonnet, '*Vasta insalubre region*', a place where, I think, even the toads catch fever; but I never came to harm.

I only wish I had caught the worst quartan fever, with the possibility of cure, rather than the much worse fever from which I was suffering.

When I got back to my remote inn on Monday morning, and thought that I must stay there for an eternity of six long days, it seemed as though I should not live to get to the end of them.

Spending the summer at Marino were the Marchese Venuti, and the Conte Roberti and his wife from Bassano in Venetia. Both were artists, although the former, being very rich, hardly worked at all; the latter, who painted groups of houses for which he was much admired, was poorly off and worked hard. They were all excellent people and the best of company.

Propinquity and loneliness soon brought us together and it wasn't long before we dropped all formality and became intimate.

They lived in the last house on the right on the way out of the village to Frascati. It was a pension called Casa Maldura, and was quieter than an inn. Virginio Maldura was the titular master of the house, but the real master was Signor Checco Tozzi, his father-in-law, one of the principal men of the village. Here it will be suitable to say a few words by way of introduction.

Years ago, my friend Cavalier Torelli published a little periodical called *Il Cronista,* in which several of my sketches appeared under the title of *Stories, Legends, etc., etc.,* in which I described my stay in Sor Checco Tozzi's house.

These sketches, as much else in the periodical, were read and were not considered too bad (all hypocrisy, in order to feign modesty, because I know they were extremely popular), but nevertheless it would be too much to assume that everyone had read them.

As I do not wish to presume too much, I shall tell the story of my stay with Sor Checco as though it had not been told before. I shall, however, for the sake of those who may have read the *Cronista,* try not to repeat myself too much and find something new to say. I haven't yet exhausted my material and I didn't describe everything in my *Racconti.* That said, let us go on!

R

Sor Checco was, as the Spaniards say, *hijo de sus obras*, a self-made man. His beginnings were obscure and undiscoverable (just like the world of the pantheists); but as he was owner of houses, vineyards, and cane-brakes; an influential member of a religious confraternity; a well-considered anti-revolutionary; and, at fifty-five years old, tall, active, upstanding, and all muscle; no one cared to inquire about them from the only person who knew, that is to say from Sor Checco himself.

He was feared and respected in the village, but rather left alone. He cared little for cordiality and didn't bother about that. As long as they fear me, they can dislike me, was his motto. Although he was rich he never missed going to work every morning in his travertine quarry, whenever he had no need to attend to his vines. It was an outlet for his energetic nature and thirst—if not for gold—at least for silver. Five *paoli* earned by the grace of God are good for body and soul, he used to say.

At the period of the Republic, when Championnet passed through on his way to Naples, it was whispered that Checco had obtained what amounted to a *lettre de marque,* but in this case it gave him the right to pillage the rich aristocrats, rather than enemy shipping.

In fact Sor Checco disappeared for a long time. After this total eclipse the inhabitants of Marino, one fine day, saw him among them once again, without knowing where he'd come from. As he was a stone-cutter by trade, he went back to the quarries; a day labourer as before, with the same behaviour, the same look, the same temperament, and the same clothes. The only thing was that during the next two or three years he became the owner of lands, houses, and wine-cellars. True it is that he had married a widow older than himself who, it was said, had a nest-egg.

However that may be, Checco the stone-cutter had become Sor Checco; and who could complain?

Sora Maria, his wife, was a good old soul, somewhat lame. The story was that this was due to a lively moment between her and her husband, rather as when Nero killed his wife Poppaea by a kick in the belly. She had one peculiarity—in two years she was never seen to laugh.

The sole fruit of this, not always comfortable, bed was a daughter called Sora Nina. Her complexion was like boiled potatoes, she had two pale eyes like the bubbles that form on pap made with oil; in fact she was the most repulsive object ever seen.

Love for this snail in feminine form was the sole, great passion of Sor Checco's life. His ardent longing was to be able to see Nina led one day to the altar as his rightful wife by a gentleman, in the sense of someone not a peasant.

A few years before my appearance on the Marino horizon, Sor Checco had moved heaven and earth, and had finally discovered in Rome a man who would do: a broken-down country squire.

I must confess I have forgotten his name, though I well remember the following incident.

Everything was made ready for the wedding, which was to take place at the Marino church. Kitchen, house, bridal-bed, all was ready; even Sor Fumasoni's Muse was on tiptoe. He was a notary and village poet, another original type who appears later.

Came the day of the happy event. Sora Nina's outfit was beyond description, and her parents in their brand-new clothes matched her splendour.

The bridegroom was expected from Rome during the morning, so that the ceremony would permit the banquet to take place at the usual hour of twelve o'clock.

Half the morning, all the morning, the afternoon till the Angelus bell, went by: they were still waiting for the bridegroom! Only one's imagination—no pen—can do justice to Sor Checco's wrath; the disappointment of his wife; and the perfect composure of Sora Nina. She retired to take off her finery; at dinner, which was two hours late, she ate heartily, and that night slept as usual a good nine hours without waking once.

The village laughed and, following the well-known, innate kindliness of humankind, on the whole felt profound satisfaction in seeing the arms of the great house of Tozzi deprived of the quarterings of a Roman fop.

'Serve him right,' they said, 'he wants to go with the gentry ... it's a very good thing!'

At this point they quoted that great proverb about the pride of a jumped-up peasant, which has a rhyme and a vulgar word, which didn't frighten Dante, but as I am no Dante I haven't the effrontery to pronounce it here.

Naturally enough it never again entered the bridegroom's head that he would care to visit Marino, or even to come within six miles of the place. The anger, as the amusement, faded under the daily beating of Time's wings; nothing happened, and things returned to normal.

Sor Checco, *tenax propositi vir*, a tenacious fellow, went on looking for a gentleman, but this time he meant to take all necessary precautions to prevent the repetition of another scandal in his household.

He made inquiries; he took advice; he followed the maxim: lots of measurements and one saw-cut. Finally he discovered a second bridegroom, and he was a reliable one and went through with it.

His name was Signor Virginio Maldura, a lean little man, ashen-coloured, short, and rather delicate. He was the real type of a bullied son-in-law: an important feature, this. He came from a decent family of artists; he was not devoid of culture, had good manners and an easy compliant character. He wore a suit of cornflower blue with yellow buttons, certain evidence of his high standing and qualities, as indeed of the high destiny prepared for Signora Nina.

This time the wedding happily did take place. Sor Virginio became a son of the house, with the sole function of eating, drinking, and going for walks, so that it was plain to all that Sor Checco's daughter had not married a peasant.

Italians today seem to be coming to the conclusion that acting the 'gentleman' is neither a profession nor a job, and that it is not so, even for a man with ten thousand a year. But Signor Virginio had not been corrupted by modern ideas, and found it the prince of occupations.

Besides those I have mentioned, there was an old maid called Aunty Annie, a sister of Sora Maria's, who lived in Casa Tozzi. She had made over some property to her nephew for an annuity; a free gift, with the proviso that she should have board and lodging as long as she lived. This ingenious arrangement for assuring a carefree old age had led to the result, inevitable in all such cases, of her having to lie on a bed of thorns.

To prove the great goodness of the human species, listen to this! Sor Checco, who exercised the absolute power of a despot, when he saw peace and good order established in his happy domain, felt the need, like all tyrants, to survey benevolently his faithful subjects and reward their blind obedience with a smile and a joke.

The pleasantry at table was to give torture by water to poor Aunt Annie.

'Do have a drink', and pretending to reach for the wine jug, he took the water bottle and filled her glass from that.

The poor old thing, who would dearly have loved some wine, would protest: 'No thank you, no thank you, I've drunk enough!' It was no good! I've seen her eyes fill with tears that begged for compassion. But the jest led to economy and that was Aunt Annie's undoing. I, however, used to fill up her glass with wine, on the quiet, and I can therefore boast that I was her last and (probably) her most passionate love.

I have still to speak of one more personage, Signor Mario, younger brother of Signor Virginio's.

He was an ill-conditioned youth of seventeen who, somehow or other, had managed to introduce himself into the household. However he had done it, the fact remained that he had become a naturalized inhabitant, and, to judge by appearances and the complete idleness in which he lived, I can only conclude that his desire to live for nothing without working had reached a point of high genius and that, thanks to this rare quality, he had, in some way, bewitched or conquered Sor Checco, who had finally accepted him as a subject and maintained him.

Otia si tollas, periere Cupidinis artes, said Ovid: no love without leisure. As Sor Mario had never run the risk of disturbing the latter, Dan Cupid had occupied the field, and tied him to the apron-strings of a fair wench who did not entirely reject his ardours. Unfortunately her barbarous papa, Master Titta, rejected them out of hand. He was a well-to-do owner of vineyards and, as they say at Marino, a bit of bad meat. He had a very rude name for poor skinny Mario.

'Tell him to come here and just let me catch him!'

He uttered this generic, and therefore all the more terrible, threat from time to time. The apprentice lover was terrified and hardly dared raise his eyes to the cracked saucepan which served as a vase for carnations on the window-sill of his adored Nanna. However, one festival day, the devil tempted him to lead the band, which had blasted away all day in the village square, to soothe the slumbers of his beloved, after night had fallen.

They had hardly played for five minutes when the window opened, and Mario, who thought he was about to see a pair of sparkling eyes (think of Ariosto's Ruggero with Alcina), only saw stars, as a musket was let off which peppered him, the band, and everyone else present.

Off ran Mario, off ran the band, off ran the onlookers; helter-skelter down the darkest alleys they could find. At last they reach the square, cursing and lamenting, one crying: 'It was Titta; it was Tom; it was Dick; it was Harry.' They draw breath when they get clear; look at each other; feel themselves all over. Here a groan, there a groan, everywhere a groan. As a matter of fact only two or three of them could show blood from scratches of no importance, otherwise there was no damage, although the shot could easily have killed more than one of them. God looks after fools!

The *carabinieri* went to Master Titta's house and found his musket still warm and the touch-hole foul; so they locked him up.

But it is the custom in those parts, so long as the offended parties are satisfied, not to proceed with the action; the State does not prosecute. It would have its hands full if it did!

So when the wounds were healed and everybody pacified, compensated in all likelihood with a barrel of wine—a matter of a couple of days—Titta saw his home once more and all went on as usual, except that Sor Mario's love had perished on the field of honour.

I believe, as a matter of fact, that its ashes were respected so far that he never loved again. A complete cure, or rather conversion!

In our Piedmontese villages a musket shot fired at a group of twenty or thirty persons, by way of a simple warning, would have a certain effect. At Marino, however, it seemed the most logical and natural thing in the world. But you must remember the temperament of the people of Marino is nothing like ours or anyone else's.

In the album in which I made lightning sketches of men and animals from nature, I amused myself by noting down every time there was bloodshed in the village. In two months I counted eighteen dead or wounded.

But I would be far from suggesting that the population of Marino was wicked or corrupt. Quite the contrary! Family, marriage, parenthood are deeply respected. With regard to regular habits, and modesty among the women, I never saw anything to complain about.

True it is, and I can't deny it, that the argument used by Master Titta with regard to a difference of opinion about music can easily be adopted, if necessary, in conjugal matters. But I do not impugn the virtue of the people of Marino for this.

I never heard any complaints about thefts. I found an admirable readiness to give mutual help, and to please anyone who was polite and did not put on airs. On several occasions, when I was in some little difficulty, I found all eager to come forward to help. One young man, a poor day labourer called Venanzio, was so fond of me that he was always badgering me to let him know if I had an enemy.

'If there's anyone who is a nuisance to you,' he frequently repeated, 'one word to Venanzio . . . !'

Luckily I had no enemies then, nor, thank God, have I ever had any up to the present. Such a friend was not therefore needed.

The source of evil in those villages is not any inborn wickedness, but hot blood, which from time to time is exacerbated by wine and the climate. Besides this there are evil traditions and evil examples, and education is, you can say, non-existent.

I shall first tell you about some local episodes and customs; then the conclusions I draw from them.

This prattle of mine, I say again, is not aimed at telling the reader about the trifling events of my life. I shouldn't waste time or ink on such a thing. But as opportunity offers, my book will examine and discuss matters from which may spring the improvement of the new generation and the moral progress of our people.

It is a lofty aim and perhaps I am presumptuous in attempting it. But to build this edifice, those who can't supply a stone must bring a grain of sand. Provided all work, the building will be completed.

Let us remember, too, that constitutions, political systems, and laws are useless, as long as the men who put them into effect are not better.

Europe, society, peoples, governments and heads of States, all now achieve nothing. And why? Because individual by individual they are worth little. If the hemp is rotten, you'll never make a good rope. If the gold is of poor assay, you'll never have good coin. If the individual is worth little, ignorant, and bad, you'll never make a sound nation and you'll never succeed in producing anything solid, ordered, or great.

7

A PIEDMONTESE friar whom I met many years later at St. Benedict's grotto at Subiaco said to me, in speaking of the peasants of those parts: 'You have no idea what good souls they are, both men and women, in their natural state; but if they get excited by wine or in some other way, they start swearing and out comes the knife.'

You can say the same about the population of the whole region, including Marino. In hot blood they'll go for each other with knives or anything else handy. I witnessed a fight in which one of the combatants used a large cellar key, the other a heavy lantern, and they split each other's skulls.

When they have committed a crime they rush to the threshold of church or chapel and find asylum. Their relations bring them food and there they spend their time, doing nothing, or some little job within the bounds of their place of refuge.

I remember that the notary Signor Fumasoni, who had made a fine crucifix of painted wood, life-size, for the chapel half-way down from Marino to the Parco Colonna gate, where the fountain is, asked me to paint the wall behind it, which he disliked leaving white, and he asked me what he would have to pay me. I discussed the matter with my friends, Venuti and another. I agreed to accept the commission and fixed the fee as a picnic out of doors for the whole company.

I began work early, with the intention of finishing by noon. I brought my paints and paint pots, large and small, and found unexpected assistants to grind my colours and for other jobs, in the persons of three bandits who had sought asylum in the chapel. They were not very advanced in art, but they were wonderfully useful. The job was done and approved by noon, and we all sat down in a meadow to enjoy Sor Fumasoni's hospitality.

As may be imagined, these fugitives, spending months and months in idleness or playing cards, sometimes quarrel—they are safe from prison—and go from bad to worse. Their situation as semi-bandits rouses no aversion against them.

History and popular traditions fully explain the present condition of that society. I have noticed that the inhabitants of the ancient fiefs of the great Roman families are more prone to arrogance and law-breaking than other people. Breaking the law is considered as a mark of superiority. It is only natural. Has this not been the distinctive feature of the upper classes for centuries? One must add that the arrogance of the great has persisted in Rome up to the present, and I was about to add—still persists. Or shall we say it could persist if those in a position to exercise power were not held in check by public opinion.

Popular traditions form the pabulum of rude, ignorant, naturally fierce men, who cannot admire the great heroes of past ages, of whose very names they are ignorant. They admire, therefore, and choose as their heroes and models, famous bandits, whose deeds they constantly hear extolled by the professional story-tellers at fairs and village festivals.

Fra Diavolo, Spadolino, Peppe Mastrilli, and the like indicate to wild young men the highest rank they can attain in this world, if only they knew how.

But this 'knowing how' demands a variety of rare qualities: iron constitution, strength and agility of a leopard, eyesight of a lynx, a sure eye and a sure hand on gun and knife; courage, cold blood, audacity fit for all trials. All this goes without saying and on the top you must have ability. Certainly! However much the first foolish fellow who goes along the road would like to, he cannot make himself a brigand.

As a counterweight to the influence of traditions and popular ballads, what have we invented? Nothing! We let things drift, as usual. Certainly the catechism would provide the best of antidotes: do not steal;

do not kill; charity, meekness, etc., are its bases. But the way it is
taught, the quality and the example of those who teach it, rob it of all
efficacy. Peppe Mastrilli, who, according to the ballad:

> . . . with a single shot
> Killed four guards; a horse; the lot . . .

offers a much more attractive picture. One cannot, it is true, make him
out a saint; one must admit that his life was full of sin not all con-
fessors would absolve; but tradition usually allots its heroes an exemplary end. According to legends, it seems that things are so arranged,
almost miraculously, that the hero goes straight to Paradise. And his
secret? His devotion to the Madonna of Loreto, or degli Angeli, or
some other place; his always having round his neck the amulet of some
confraternity; his paying for masses to be sung or candles to be lighted.
After such precautions he simply can't come to a bad end.

Such is the gist of doctrines, not promulgated by Catholic dogma,
but by an ignorant clergy with ulterior motives; and such are the
results.

The influence of civilization and of better educated regions on these
men is non-existent. As there are neither persons nor books to modify
the ancient customs, they pass their lives as though still in the Middle
Ages. Anyone conversant with the chronicles, tales, and way of life
of the fourteenth and fifteenth centuries will find identical conditions
here. The so-called *beffe* (practical jokes), once considered humorous,
such as one finds in the tales by Boccaccio, Franco Sacchetti, Lasca, etc.,
still flourish in the little villages like Marino, just as in Florence of the
time of Calandrino and the buffoon Gonnella. Jokes fit to give an unfortunate man an epileptic fit through fright, or leave him crippled for
life. I remember how at a convivial party they tied, with double lash-
ings, a large cracker to the braces of a certain bumpkin. When it
exploded it was a miracle his backbone wasn't broken, as he and his
chair rose into the air.

Another fellow was induced to hide in a chest, I have forgotten
whether on the pretext of a love adventure, and he was shut in for so
long that he nearly died of asphyxiation.

The most barbarous trick (from the point of view of morality)
was that invented by Sor Checco in one of his lighter moments, and
played on a lad who groomed his horses and did odd jobs about the
house.

This simpleton, called Stefanino, slept in the open in an old sarcophagus without a lid which stood in the courtyard. He once fell sick

and lay there during the whole course of his illness, just as though he had been in a comfortable bed in a well-kept room, As the sarcophagus was six foot up off the ground, I remember that the doctor who attended him had to climb up a ladder that normally served to get into the hayloft.

This poor youth lived on what he earned from Sor Checco, while he really longed to be independent, an ambition for which everyone laughed at him.

One day, his unfeeling employer had the notion of getting him to believe he had suddenly become rich. He began to give him numbers for the lottery, numbers certain to win. Stefanino scraped together a few shillings he had reserved for a rainy day and made up his mind to play it big. Two days passed in fear, hope, and palpitation; then, on the day of the draw, his very five numbers were displayed printed on the door of the lottery office. When he saw them he nearly swooned away.

He rushed home demented, leaped at Sor Checco, Sora Maria, everyone in the house; shouting, roaring with laughter, stamping his feet, weeping, embracing and kissing anyone whom he could grab; until finally, when he had got his breath, he announced that he had won, was rich, and meant to be the 'best-dressed man in Marino', etc., etc. Sor Checco said: 'Then you don't want to stay with me?' To which he replied: 'My dear Checco, I promise nothing.' So he continued building castles in the air for his future existence.

The reader will have guessed already that Sor Checco had conspired with the keeper of the lottery office and that the village knew all about the joke and was implicated in it. He will also have imagined the last scene of the comedy. True enough; the next morning a delighted Stefanino, dressed in a new suit (he had already borrowed money), mounted on a mare lent him by Sor Checco, who said it was not fitting for millionaires to walk, went off as fast as he could go to Albano, the centre where winnings were paid. Instead of the prize, however, he was welcomed by the lottery manager, at first with laughter, and then by abuse and shoves which put him out of the door. He was sure that they wanted to murder him and set up a hullabaloo, weeping and protesting. That he found the way back to Marino was thanks to the mare, for he was completely distraught. Add to this that he not only couldn't get his own back on Sor Checco, but had to continue in his service, and thank him for overlooking that he meant to leave him.

Such were the practical jokes of the village, obviously worthy to figure among the tales told by Lasca, Sacchetti, and the like. Now for other stories, rather less diverting, and equally suitable for medieval chronicles.

I have already mentioned Sor Fumasoni, notary and poet. We'll begin with him.

He was a big, heavy man, a real Hercules for strength, health, digestion, and lung-power. He had some learning and was a semi-literate and extemporary poet. It is curious to note how common the gift of improvisation is among these villages. Poor stuff! you will say. Very true, or at any rate common-places and clichés. Yet I do not know if many highly gifted men would be capable of doing what I have seen Sor Fumasoni do, without stuttering or stammering for a moment. I have seen him at dinner parties of twenty or thirty persons held to celebrate the village festival, or the passing through of some Monsignore. After having eaten and drunk like an ox, when dessert came, he would stand up and dedicate a terzet or a quatrain to each one of the company. I will admit they weren't sublime poetry or sublime ideas, but they did express a compliment, or a joke, or even a satire suitable to the person addressed, with good sense, rhyme, and often grace.

Do you, who are reading my words, feel up to doing likewise. No? Then don't despise Sor Fumasoni.

He had, however, a more precious gift than that of extemporizing; he had strength and courage comparable to those of Mucius Scaevola.

One evening, on his way home, a gun was fired at him from behind—he didn't know, or wouldn't tell by whom—and the bullet entered his kidneys and came out in front. Many, under such circumstances, would have fallen to the ground and started to shout. Sor Fumasoni, however, stood still and then quietly went home as best he could. In order not to frighten his wife he said to her: 'Tuta, go and fetch the doctor, I've got a bad pain and am going to bed.' Luckily the wound was not mortal and Sor Fumasoni lived to tell the tale. I only hope it was appreciated.

I knew another man who received a knife wound at a fair two miles off and came home on foot with half his inside in place and the other half in his hat.

This goes to prove that here we have a strong, courageous race, who would make excellent citizens and soldiers, should they escape from the clutches of Papal rule.

It is not even true that they are only fit for wounding and killing by treachery, and then running away, as is generally believed, both abroad and in Italy. I do not say that doesn't occur sometimes: but doesn't it occur in all countries?

For the most part, it is a case of pre-arranged fights between two men. For example, they practise a singularly ferocious duel with knives.

Two men have words. One says to the other: 'Have you got your knife?' 'No.' 'Go and get it and come to such and such a cane-brake in half an hour.' 'Very good!'

The cane-brakes are extensive, but not so thick that you cannot pass between the canes. When each of the combatants arrives at opposite sides it is impossible to know exactly where his opponent is. He must be sought almost blindly, as one can't see far enough through the dense foliage. You can imagine the numerous possibilities of such a fight; usually, almost inevitably, both men are killed.

Sometimes groups challenge other groups. I once saw a fight in a vineyard: three against three, with knives and guns. They beat each other up very thoroughly, but no one was killed. They are tough, those fellows!

Sometimes quarrels flare up spontaneously in the village. I'll tell this one last anecdote.

Towards evening, one day, we heard a noise down in the square: shouts, shots, a hullabaloo. We were having supper. Virginio and I got up and seized our guns (one never went out unarmed in those parts) and were just about to run to the scene of the conflict to see what was happening, when Sor Checco, as head of the house and experienced, pitched into us saying: 'Look out! Don't interfere in other people's business. It's those who intervene who get hurt most.' As he saw we did not heed him he hurled this paternal blessing after us: 'I hope you'll get well and truly beaten up.' With this good augury in our ears we ran out.

It was a quarrel that had started between a certain Natale Raparelli and another, Peppe Rosso if I remember aright—and by degrees it had spread to a brawl between about eighty people. Natale was one of the village bigwigs. Peppe had recently been proclaimed bandit, because one day after vespers, when people were standing about in the square in knots, he had the notion of drawing his knife, tracing a line in the dust, and saying: 'I'll stab the first who crosses this line.' And that is exactly what he did.

The battle ended without many notable casualties and we returned to our supper, proud of having avoided Sor Checco's kind prognostications.

The morrow brought the best part of the story. I had to go to Rome and I hired a conveyance in which I left during the hottest part of the day. As we reached the end of the vineyards, out pops someone from the hedge and jumps nimbly on to the box next to the driver. It was Peppe Rosso. 'What's the latest news, Master Peppe?' 'Eh,' he replied half laughing, with a sly look, 'it's a good thing to have a change of air for a few days.' 'All right,' I said, and my eyelids began to droop and I dozed off.

Peppe's retreat was prudent, probably imposed by his family; not so much because Natale was one of the first swashbucklers of the village, but because the Raparellis were powerful and the Rossos had need of them.

We went on, for I don't know how far, at the bored trot peculiar to horses during those hours when the very air seems to burn. All of a sudden Peppe threw his legs into the carriage, hurled himself down, and crept round behind me, so that I acted as a shield. 'What the devil's up?' I cried, waking up with a start. Not a word; but the coachman clasped his head in both hands and exclaimed: 'Whatever shall we do now?'

'For goodness sake tell me what's wrong with you?'

The driver pointed miserably across the fields and I saw a man on a horse coming at full speed to cut us off. 'It's Natale,' they said.

Innocent words, but words which were synonymous in Peppe's ears for being killed without mercy, unless he succeeded in killing the other man. But what with? He was unarmed and I only had a sword-stick. It was certain that Natale wasn't coming to the party without fire-arms.

I passed some extremely unpleasant moments, because the custom of the place in such cases was to say to anyone near: 'Get out of the way.' If the bystander doesn't or can't, the assailant fires into the brown, as had recently happened at Rocca di Papa.

In the meantime the horseman drew nearer and the driver recognized the white flash and nose of a horse belonging to Natale: 'Madonna, it's himself.'

But, no, sir, it wasn't himself! The happiest at this discovery was Peppe, who released me from his loving embrace and returned to the box seat. I certainly felt better, I can tell you! So did the driver! Feeling much relieved and in the best of spirits we continued on our way.

However, as we neared Rome, it looked as though the Curia was coming up the road. It was Galante's squadron, the chief of the rural police, making its rounds. Another bad fright for friend Peppe, who turned to me and said that he hoped they would not be so bold as to touch him in my company! This was a hope based on the ancient tradition of baronial immunity. Fortunately we had misjudged the situation and I had no need to put my influence to a test that probably it would not have survived.

From the general picture I have given, you will have been able to get an idea of the stuff of which the population of this area is made. With small variations it is typical of the whole of Southern Italy.

All they lack is a good government and good education. I don't mean only reading, writing, and arithmetic, but the much more important education which teaches respect for the law, be it moral, civil, or political. I am never tired of repeating that laws will be respected and obeyed by the people when rulers, heads of States, administrators, and all persons in higher classes provide a good example.

Liberty and independence must be sought and won as the essential conditions in the life of all nations; but one must not forget that if the individuals concerned have no moral standard of their own, all the rest is valueless. Either you do not get liberty and independence, or it is corrupted or lost.

Yet in Italy, where the individual, by long servitude under foreign or bad governments, is worth little, the last thing one considers is education.

I have forgotten to say, but the reader will have guessed it, that I had moved from the inn to the pension where Sor Checco ruled so benevolently! Here I had a good room; I had brought my books; I had my own place at table for dinner and supper: all at a far from extravagant price.

At the time I was facing the hardest trials of my whole life; but through sheer obstinacy I ended by even conquering that cursed passion of love, which enabled me to work with advantage.

Youth is a wonderful time! It is the age of faith, audacity, trust in oneself, in one's own strength, in the future: it is the time when one trusts and loves others; when one believes in what is good, lovely, and honest—I do not mean, thank God, that I have lost that belief; but now I have to convince myself; then it was spontaneous. A big difference, this!

At that time I was always striving to acquire strength of will and control over myself. My friend Bidone was always hammering away at this idea; he was right and I was convinced of it. Without strong will, one never succeeds in doing anything worth while.

Staying at Marino was the principal and most difficult of my victories; but I was always struggling to win lesser ones to keep myself in practice. On the first page of my sketch-book I had copied the following octave of Tasso's:

Not underneath sweet shades and fountains shrill;
Among the nymphs, the fairies, leaves, and flow'rs;
But on the steep, the rough and craggy hill
Of virtue, stand this bliss, this good of ours;
By toil and travail, not by sitting still
In pleasure's lap, we come to honour's bow'rs. . . . [1]

On my return from work under the merciless rays of the sun, as I toiled up the 'steep, rough and craggy hill' at the top of which was (if not virtue) Casa Tozzi, these verses came into my mind and I faced heat, sweat, and fatigue with greater determination. On other occasions, when I came back famished, and was served, for example, with a mixed grill which, under the circumstances, filled the air with captivating fragrance, I held back and waited for some time before I touched it.

These youthful enthusiasms seem, and partly are, puerile. They have, however, their useful and serious side and I consider them a sign of good tendencies and a capacity for moral improvement. Experiments in self-control of this kind, which anyone can vary as he likes, are not wasted effort. I advise young men to think them over.

Even though I think it useful to reveal the methods I adopted to strengthen my character, I do not mean to boast that I succeeded as much as I should and could, then or afterwards. I simply intend to make my methods known, the practical steps I took to help towards self-control.

The worthiest activity, indeed the object of living, is surely that of controlling, purifying, and elevating one's own nature.

This work must begin as soon as one can reason and it lasts all one's life. Most young men never hear such ideas from parents or schoolmasters, who do not themselves hold or practise them. Let parents and educators think about it.

Although grumbling against the young is the privilege of advanced years, I do not wish to be unjust. Great political upheavals are not brought about without much social disorder. Luckily the latter are transitory, and it is up to a people to shorten their continuance. But as long as they do last; farewell education; farewell teaching! It always was and always will be so. The fault, therefore, is not all to be imputed to modern youth, but it well may be to their credit that they will be able to abandon the disorders inseparable from periods of transition without delay.

[1] Trans. Edward Fairfax (*Ger.*, Lib. XVII, 61).

8

THE news of Enrico's death reached me at Marino during the second year of my stay in Sor Checco's house. I pass rapidly over the intervening winter, during which I continued to lead an existence of moral destitution, little happiness, and much angry frustration: the sad harvest of a lover's life.

I did put together a picture representing Leonidas at Thermopylae. I sent it to Turin, and my father offered it to King Carlo Felice, who on his side presented me with a box with some diamonds on it.

As is usually done, I sold it as soon as possible, in his memory.

I believe the picture still exists, tucked away in some corner of the royal palace.

Casa Maldura, during my second stay there, was more than usually full of holiday-makers, attracted by the climate, the freedom, and the cheap living. As the proverb rightly says: 'When the crowd comes in, peace flies.'

I knew a young man in Rome, a member of the Noble Guard, Don Luigi de' Principi Spada, who had resigned from the service on account of his irresponsibility. He was an honourable, well-meaning youth, extremely vivacious, and he was not without talent and education. But such a madcap! God preserve anyone wanting peace and quiet for study from such friends! There was one thing in his favour; his mother had died demented!

He had got embroiled in the secret societies, and carried a dagger marked with the number 3. One supposed that numbers 1 and 2 were allotted satisfactorily, not to speak of all the subsequent numbers. I don't know about the feats of the others, but I would put my hand in the fire if number 3 ever belonged to an assassin. Luigi Spada was not a rogue, he merely had a screw loose.

When least I expected it, here he was at Marino! He introduced himself, and following him came a sinister trunk, proof of a long stay.

He was a handsome young man, tall, slim, lithe, well-built, and pale, with an ash-blond mane of hair which stood up from his brow as though starched. He had two pale grey eyes, always goggling, which did not always give the impression of lucidity of mind.

After the first greetings he announced that he was so placed—on account of some love-affair, he said—that his life was in danger. It was threatened in Rome by rivals, offended relations, or somebody or other.

He added that one night, as he was going down some dark steps, he had been surrounded by enemies he couldn't see. They made lunges at him with their daggers, but they only succeeded in chipping the plaster off the wall, and he got away unhurt. It could be, or not! I couldn't answer for that; but there must have been something in it, from what I heard later.

At that time (1824), the political opposition was entirely restricted to a few secret societies of the lowest sort. As I said, nine years of complete peace had not yet cancelled the memory of the Napoleonic era, and Europe still felt no desire to start another epic. The totally suppressed revolutions in Naples and Turin had left the impression in the masses that politics was a trade for madmen and rogues, not for honest men of good sense. On considering the many changes through which we have had to pass to reach the point where we now find ourselves, one cannot help admiring the way nature produces its effects, both physical and moral. When we see in what corrupt and muddy swamps the first germs of some great and useful change appear, we recognize the extent of our ignorance of the first laws of the world we inhabit.

Who, in the whole of Rome, then gave a thought to Italy, its independence and regeneration? A few exceptions apart, only the scum of the *canaille*, who met in Carbonari lodges and taverns, etc.

Good corn springs up from dung; and from corruption the spark of life is born. Can this be a general rule? Let us hope, if so, that it only works in the material world. In both worlds, however, it is undeniable that evil has a mission . . . but we mustn't get into metaphysics!

I knew many who belonged to these societies. In the art world one mixes with all sorts. Luckily, I didn't have the look of a conspirator. Nobody ever suggested that I should get implicated in their nonsense. I say 'luckily', because despite my natural aversion to simulation, falsehood, and a life of hidden mysteries, it could have happened that, at that age of little judgement, had I been invited, I might have accepted. However, I hardly think I should.

I remember very well that even then, this binding oneself slave in the name of liberty (not like a soldier under a brave, loyal, intelligent, and known superior; but slave of a hidden anonymous power whose methods and objects one knows nothing about) seemed to me, I say, a contradiction and swindle. At that time it was an instinct rather than a rational belief. Later it was both these things. It led to the happy result that I have always been free from secret oaths and obligations, and never frightened that anyone could justly remind me of them.

s

The habit of constant feigning, necessarily learnt in the long practice of secret societies, has, according to my way of thinking, been one of the principal causes of the decadence of the Italian character.

Whose fault is that? Of the Italians? In part, yes; but much more of the governments, who made the expedient of the secret societies meritorious, seeing what men are like.

Natural forces are never destroyed. If normal channels are blocked, they find abnormal ones. When society is so organized that lies, hypocrisy, flattery, cowardice are the best protection, and the easiest way to fortune, it is not surprising that moral ideas become confused and obscured, and that the problem of life is reduced to trying to be stronger and more astute than others. All kinds of depravity spring from this situation; among them the fatal doctrine of political assassination; the mad enthusiasms of otherwise estimable people for well-known murderers; the restlessness of the public, who, groping in the dark, seeks a cure for its ills, like a sick man, grown intolerant by much suffering, who abandons himself to empirical treatment.

Nevertheless, it is rash to assert that love of country, independence, liberty, equality of legal rights among all citizens, the cult, in fact, of the noblest concepts of the human race, had found their only refuge in a secret society, which in Rome was recruited in great part from real criminals.

The highest ideas and the holiest affections have served with men of all periods as a mask for crime. This is a truth as well known and old as the world itself. The members of these mysterious societies were, for the most part, steeped in vice, incapable of any honourable effort to gain a position in the world such as their vanity longed for, and as would satisfy their thirst for the graces and splendours of life. To become apostles of a secret society, by dint of all the tricks of the trade— seduction or threats as required—and dominating others with equal ambitions, but less cunning and energetic than they were, this would assure them a respected position of influence among themselves—a pale image, it is true, of what they would have liked outside, but one which had the great merit of not needing real work and not being without material advantage.

What altar, what idol, be it religious, political, social, scientific, etc., does not provide a living for its priest?

I think this brief analysis of secret societies is quite true, but there is one reservation. There are certain passionate, well-intentioned souls who lack the safe guidance of a lucid, balanced intelligence. These unhappy mortals are incited, on the one hand, by the love of an indefinite, beautiful ideal; on the other, however, they lack a sure criterion with which to distinguish between the real and the apparent, between good and bad. They rush in pursuit of phantasms and tragic illusions, victims of the greatest and most perilous of all, that of considering as acts of sublime and virtuous heroism what in reality are nothing but execrable crimes. Among all the abysses of corruption this is the most horrifying.

I have known several such men, one of whom is worth describing. He was the panel doctor of Rocca di Papa, a certain Montanari from Romagna. I had known him before and I used to meet him sometimes at village festivals, fairs, etc. I liked him, as I usually do like Romagnoles. I think that Romagna is the Italian province where men are born most complete; physically and morally.

'What?' you will say. 'What about all those stabbings, murders, sects, and rivalries?' Quite true! But tell me, if you saw a man taken unjustly to the gallows, do you think that, should you say: 'Rogue, you've deserved what you've got', you would have cleared the matter up satisfactorily? One of the most complex problems that exist is that of culpability. And nature, character, education, example, temptation, illusions—where do they come in?

It would make a long digression to insert here an ethnographical-historical study of the Romagnole race. I shall restrict myself to saying that I believe in the difference of breeds among men, as among dogs and horses (I do not agree, of course, with the theory that man is a perfect animal—at the most he is sometimes a perfect beast), and I maintain that the Romagnole breed is one of the finest I know. It has red blood in its veins and not vanilla cream like some others I do not name. Where there's blood there's something good.

Montanari was a good specimen of the breed. He was dark-complexioned, tall, well developed, strong, with a bold, passionate nature.

One day I happened to go into his house and found him reading. 'What's your book?' I said. He showed it to me and he was reading a chapter on conspiracies by Machiavelli. He read it, poor young man, but it did him little good, as I shall presently relate.

While I was living with Sor Checco, we were just going to bed one evening, when we heard the distant sound of a carriage and carriage-bells approaching. It stopped at our door. Out got a party of young men, half tipsy, of whom I knew only two, one of whom was Montanari. They said they had come to sup with me! I had to be patient—a host must put up with much that is tiresome—prepare the table, and provide a plate of ham and omelettes and large measures of wine, God knows with what difficulty. After an hour, thank goodness, they left.

A certain Targhini was among them, whom I then saw for the first time in my life. A year later, almost to the very day, I saw him again in the Piazza del Popolo, where his head rolled into the basket of the guillotine on the top of that of Montanari, who had preceded him.

Targhini was the son of the Pope's cook. I cannot imagine that there can have existed a more perverse character than his. He was the evil genius of most of those companions of his and led them to the gallows, prison, or exile. Poor Montanari was his lamented victim. He really had the stuff of a good man in him, but died the death of an assassin. One Pontini had betrayed, or was thought to have betrayed, the secret society to which they all belonged. He was condemned to death by the society and Montanari drew the lot which chose him as executioner. He then treacherously stabbed him between the shoulder-blades in such a way that the blade came right through the chest.

It so happened by chance that at that second he had breathed out and the lungs were empty so that the blade passed between them. It turned out to be a slight wound from which the man recovered perfectly.

It was only just that Montanari was condemned to death. But I cannot help being struck by the barbarous inconsistency to which the religious authority is driven owing to its temporal authority.

Neither of the two condemned men would confess. They reached the square at noon and were placed in an improvised chapel in the house next to the gate, which later served as a picture gallery. Until evening they were surrounded by priests, even, I think, by monsignori and cardinals, all trying to induce them to take the sacraments. All to no purpose. The order came to execute them and the sentence was carried out. They died. According to the Catholic faith what consequences should follow such an end? And, on the other hand, even if their hearts were shut against the sentiment of religion on that day, who knows if they would not open the day after? God would have allowed them time; it would not have been his intention to tumble those souls down to the place where Catholic dogma declares there to be no hope of pardon. It was the Pope who improved on divine clemency, by hurling them inexorably into the abyss of the damned.

If anything can make an impression on men of that party, such cases should be noted. They should awaken in those concerned at least the doubt that there is something that needs modification in the complicated procedure of the Roman Church. But the denial of established truth has always been one of the weapons most familiar to egotism, and it is not to be expected that it should be discarded to please us. Let us go on.

Prince Spada, perhaps compromised by the revelations that came out during the trial of these sectarians, took himself off, or he was sent, to Paris. I saw him there again in 1836 and once more at General Head-quarters at Bologna when we were just about to cross the Po in April 1848. He was still straightforward, but more deranged than ever. He disappeared without bidding me farewell and some years later he died in Paris.

I do not want to leave Marino and Sor Checco (this time it must be for good) without telling a little story which seemed to me, and still seems, very typical of the place, which you can say has taken a long time to reach civilization.

Among the favourite tales told by Sor Checco was one about a journey he took to the Madonna of Loreto, many years previously and, I think, shortly after that famous mystery expedition of his 'at the time of the Republic'. I should not be surprised if this trip, in regard to its inspiration, had much in common with the longer and more peri-lous journeys undertaken by our ancestors to the Holy Land. In both cases perhaps the resolution to go stemmed from the desire to put the book of conscience that we all carry in our hearts into credit balance. I must say I should be very curious to examine for five minutes the debit side of Sor Checco's account: a curiosity no one now will be able to satisfy, so we must have patience. However matters stood, this is what he told us.

'I had a fancy for some time to visit the Holy House at Loreto. One evening I ups and says to my mate Matteo: "Let's go to the Madonna di Loreto." He says he's all for that. We get together a party of five and take a carriage, four inside and one on the box. One of them—dead now—was mad. We took him along to see if the Madonna would show him grace and cure him. Off we go, and all the way he kicks up a fuss, there were howls and blows with his fist. Either he threw himself at us or wanted to throw himself out of the window. I was the only one he was afraid of. I ordered him: "Now repeat the *Miserere* four times", and that done: "Now say twenty-four *pater nosters*." One way or the other that kept him quiet. After Foligno, near the church of Santa Maria degli Angeli, all of a sudden he jumps out of the carriage and runs off. Down we scramble and run after him as hard as we can. But could we catch him? It was like running after a hare. Then he takes to the open country and gets into a field of maize and that was that; no hope of spotting him. A party of farm labourers was passing, on their way home from a Pardon at Assisi. I says: "Come on lads, help us catch him and there's a drink in it for you." An old chap of about seventy comes up to me and says: "Gimme a *scudo* and I'll cotch 'im", and there he stood. "I'll give you the *scudo*, blast you. We'll see!" The old man goes to the end of the furrow where the loony had disappeared and I see he's mumbling some sort of a prayer! Before a quarter of an hour goes by, here comes our friend as though nothing had happened! He gets into the carriage as mild as a lamb.'

'And how was it done?' I asked. 'Ah,' replied Sor Checco, shaking his head with a strange little laugh, 'It was done. He did it. That's what happened! Those chaps know a thing or two—but it's better not to discuss such things—It cost me a *scudo*.'

I omit the rest of the pilgrimage as of little interest.

One must not infer from this that there is much superstition among the population of the towns and countryside of those parts. One of them, an old one, is that the inhabitants of the Appenine Chain are inclined to necromancy.

Benvenuto Cellini tells of a certain priest-magician who wanted to take him with him to consecrate a magic book in the Norcia mountains, and who assured him that the peasants there would be able to help them, as they understood such things.

But I never heard a word from a soul about this mountain magic, except on this one occasion from Sor Checco. As for apparitions, gnomes, witchcraft, etc., and all the fantastic spectres who haunt northern countries—not a trace! Such inventions are creatures born of the long nights and northern mists; they do not show themselves under the calm starry heaven of our clime. It is always the same, both in the material and spiritual worlds; darkness leads to error; light to truth.

I left Marino and broke my connexion with Sor Checco, the two old women, and the youths, and, apart from Sora Nina, I was never to see them again. After twenty-one years I was passing through Marino and knocked at the door of my old dwelling-place. While I waited for them to answer, I saw a middle-aged woman on the other side of the street shutting up the entrance to a cellar, from which she was coming with a decanter of wine.

It was Sora Nina! I accosted her and thought I saw she didn't recognize me.

'Sora Nina, don't you know me?'

'You are Sor Massimo.'

'And Sor Checco?'

'Dead.'

'And Sora Maria?'

'Dead.'

I went through the whole household and she said in her calm voice that they were all dead, men and women alike. I looked at her; she looked at me. We said nothing. I became aware that our meeting after all these years was not going to produce the emotions usual in novels.

'Sora Nina, I wish you luck.'

'I wish you luck, Sor Massimo.'

Such was the close of our twenty-five-year-old relationship; and as I went I exclaimed 'damned potato face', by way of an amen.

Meanwhile, in Rome, Pope Pius VII had died and Leo XII had been elected.

Whenever a Pope dies the whole population of Rome is filled with indescribable joy. Not always because they hate the dead man; but at the delightful prospect of the imminent extraction in a grand lottery, in which everyone has a ticket, and which is abounding with prizes of all values. The richest can only be won by a Cardinal; but every Cardinal has an endless tail, which all taken together embrace the whole city and even the State. Each individual pins his hopes on his special Cardinal and feeds on illusions without end.

How could one not be happy in similar circumstances? The happiest moments in a man's life are founded on hopes and illusions. As far as I am concerned, I have always believed they are the only real blessings. This at first seems paradoxical, but if you think it over you will find it to be true.

On this occasion happiness was double in the high spheres of the clerical hierarchy, for the important reason that it was not only the rule of a Pope that had come to an end, but another more tangible and more impatiently endured, that of the Secretary of State, Cardinal Consalvi.

This man, distinguished for his personal qualities, his character, and the important services he had rendered to the Holy See in grave times, was on this account the more disliked by the majority of his colleagues. His superiority, which he took no pains to hide, weighed on them all the more. Whoever had felt put down, now allowed his *amour propre* and long-stifled envy free rein, as though a longed-for emancipation had at last arrived.

As is always the case, those who had no more to fear and no further need of the ex-minister did not forgo the pleasure of making him aware of it. Everyone knows that every Secretary of State relinquishes office at the death of the Pope who appointed him. On this occasion nobody could suppose that the new Pope would wish to change the established custom.

Consalvi and Della Genga could not, by common consent, be friends. Many anecdotes were told about them, one of which I give as current at the time, but which I certainly do not vouch for as true.

It is said that, wishing to relieve Della Genga of some office or other, he said to him drily: 'Monsignore, from this moment your functions cease', without any attempt to sweeten the pill.

Whether this be true or not, the yoke of Cardinal Consalvi was neither gentle nor light; likewise the reaction against him, immediately apparent on the death of Pius VII, was violent.

If one considers impartially this man's life and character, one cannot ignore the qualities of firmness, honesty, and prudence which adorned him. His errors were more of his age than his own; they were due to his upbringing and especially to the atmosphere in which he had always lived.

In judging men of all periods, one too often neglects these important elements in their evolution. Seeing how high party feelings run, one especially forgets them in judging members of the Roman Curia.

Consalvi, like many others, failed to understand even the nature of the modern movement. This was his great mistake. He only saw the Terror of '93 in the French Revolution: in the Congress of Vienna he only saw an act of divine mercy, intent on healing the wounds of Europe. Like the majority of governments of the time, he saw the remedy in the renewal of the very causes that brought about the disease.

If some intuition, a flash of common sense, had warned him, it is not to be supposed that such a profound change of ideas, things, and men could have taken place without leaving a trace worthy of being taken into consideration. He did not, however, have such elevation of mind (this is where the fruits of his environment are obvious), nor sufficient independence of thought to be able to judge his time rightly.

He could not discern the really lasting effects of the Revolution.

He did imitate the centralization, which was essential for the revolutionary and Napoleonic despotic rule, but which could not be the pivot for a new society. He reduced all the vitality of the provinces, in order to concentrate things in Rome. If it was his hope that, during the reign of subsequent Popes, Rome was supposed to have strength, ability, and energy enough to govern the provinces, the history of the last twenty-six years in the Papal State has sadly deluded his hopes.

Despite all this, when one considers where he was born and brought up and where he passed his life, one must number him among the most remarkable men of our time.

9

I HAVE always had a tendency towards the study of mankind, their passions, vices, and virtues, as well as an inclination to see new things. So, on the death of Pius VII, I came to Rome to observe, at first hand, the great Roman hurly-burly. There was another reason which prompted me. My great-uncle, Cardinal Morozzo, Bishop of Novara, had come to Rome to attend the Conclave, and it was proper for me to pay him my respects.

I found him lodged in the house of Cardinal De Gregorio, his old and close friend. The latter was a man of unshakeable firmness of character, who had accepted imprisonment at the hands of Napoleon, but not his false promises; still less had he trembled at his wrath. His political opinions would have made the present Monsignor De Merode look like a Jacobin. His nature and his manners were those of a perfect gentleman, and he did not fail to show me every kindness all the years I spent in Rome. I dined with him once every week; he invited me to Casal de' Pazzi, an ugly house of his a few miles beyond Porta Pia. I shall always preserve a feeling of lively gratitude for all his kindness. Gratitude has nothing to do with politics; although sometimes politics is a good excuse for ingratitude.

If only that excellent old gentleman had been able to know that sitting at his table was the future author of the *Ultimi Casi di Romagna!*

My uncle, who had moreover baptized me, showed me kindness which, considering his undemonstrative nature, was all the more to be valued. He even offered to help me financially, were I in difficulties. But, even though my finances were low indeed, I thanked him and refused.

My friends declared I was an idiot. 'That man is an idiot', I replied, 'who when he can get some advantage honestly, does not do so. But it all depends on what you mean by advantage. There is moral advantage and material advantage and therefore two kinds of satisfaction. If my satisfaction consists in having a good reputation, in being modest and sensitive, rather than having a few more coins to jingle in my pocket, would you contribute anything to help me attain it?'

A magnificent argument, which still further confirmed my idiocy in their eyes.

My friends got to know three important facts: (1) my uncle was fond of me; (2) my uncle was a Cardinal; (3) I could therefore act as a link to serve their ends for introductions and testimonials.

The first time I was approached in this way was by a lady who had a relative on the threshold of an ecclesiastical career. She took me aside one evening at her house, where I often visited, and spoke to me about it.

Here I must insert an explanation. There are no kitchens in the Conclave, but as one must eat, every Cardinal has food for himself and his few attendants (a secretary and one or two servants, if I am not mistaken) prepared at home. His dinner is then carried from his house to the Conclave by two waiters in full livery, in a box covered with a purple cloth on a kind of stretcher. Four or five more servants in livery go first, and behind come two empty carriages. To lead this gastronomic procession there is some sort of an apprentice priestling who in this way tries to win the favour of a Cardinal. You can understand that the office is much sought after. His only function is to escort the victuals, so that he is known as the *dapifero* (*dapes*—victuals; *ferre*—to carry).

I was unaware of all this, not having been to a Conclave before, when the lady recommended her favourite priestling: and you can imagine my astonishment on hearing her say: 'You, Azeglio, who have an uncle here, do see what you can do to get Francesco appointed a *piffero* (piper).'

I looked at her and asked with a laugh what I was supposed to do.

'What? Surely you know all Cardinals have one to carry their dinner to the Conclave.'

'This is news to me! And they have it carried by a piper?'

'But, no! Whatever are you thinking about? I know the Latin name for it, it's *dapifero*.'

Then she called someone else who knew more than we did and all was clear. I got the much-desired honour for the little abbé. This was one of the very few times in my life when my influence did not end in a fiasco.

In Rome the fair sex specially, not having studied Latin or Greek, make the oddest blunders. The same lady asked me one day about the great *Paramano* she had heard so much about, just arrived from 'Paree'. She meant Panorama. Pretty well the same!

The funeral of a Pope has the somewhat theatrical artistic character special to all Catholic ceremony. It takes nine days, called *novendiali*. For three of them the corpse is displayed on an inclined plane in the Chapel of the Holy Sacrament, garbed in pontifical robes, with face bare and the feet against the railing that separates it from the church.

The people, out of curiosity or devotion, kiss the feet as they file past. Every day there is a funeral service. In the middle of the nave is a huge catafalque towering up to the cornice.

Directly the nine days are over, the Conclave immediately begins and, after that, the ceremonies for the exaltation of the new Pope.

The circumstances that accompany a Pope's death are worth describing shortly. Everywhere, except at the Papal Court, the semi-barbarous usages, customs, abuses, and traditions of the Middle Ages have disappeared. It is only natural that Rome fears the present, and is attached to the past by an instinct of self-preservation.

When a Pope reaches his last hours, and it is evidently impossible that he should pick up again, all ties that bound him to his most intimate associates are snapped. Private interests are unchained. There is no time to lose. It is only a question of hours, perhaps less. It is necessary to put them to good use. Therefore everyone seizes and tucks away anything that belongs to him, and even what doesn't belong to him. Private papers, jewels, money, property; it's a case of a general *sauve qui peut* and often the unhappy old man dies unattended.

This is what happened to Gregory XVI. I quote the words of a friend of mine whom I believe to be trustworthy:

A poor man who worked in the Belvedere garden was devoted to the Pope, who in his walks had often stopped to talk to him and had given him small tips, had got to hear that his end was approaching. This poor man felt he would like to see him once more. He found the private stair open, went up and knocked at the study door. No reply! He went on hesitantly. Found another door and went in. No one there! He opened a third door and found he was in the Pope's bedroom. He saw him there with a pile of pillows at the head of the bed; but perhaps in trying to prevent himself suffocating, he had bent over to one side and there he was with his head hanging down. The poor gardener rushed to help, and got him properly back on the bed. He called to him, felt him, and found him cold. He threw himself on his knees, weeping, and recited a *De Profundis* for the dead Pope. At that point one of the household came in, who must have returned from tucking things away. He was amazed, scolded the man, threatened him should he ever tell, and drove him away.

But the gardener did tell!

What is really more extraordinary is the fact that while such atrocious things can happen in the inner household of the Pope, the antechambers of the palace swarm with Noble Guards, Swiss, sentries, monsignori, ushers, servants, etc., etc. The Rome you see and the real

Rome always remain the great mystery for anyone who has not had a great deal of experience, and for many, many years. Not being able to draw this distinction is the origin of all the errors of those now debating the Roman question.

When the Pope is dead, the Cardinal Deputy is informed and arrives with other dignitaries. He calls the Pope by name three times. Getting no reply, he is handed a silver hammer with an ebony handle, on a tray; with this he taps three times on the forehead of the corpse. Thereupon the death of the Pope is held to be proved and the fact is announced to the Roman Senator, who is called in from the antechamber where he has been waiting. The *annulus piscatoris*, the fisherman's ring, is broken. He then declares, 'I therefore take command of Rome'; but, in reality, he does no such thing and is satisfied, on returning to the Capitol, to order the great bell of the tower to be tolled. All the bells of the city echo the chime.

After a lapse of twenty-four hours, the corpse is carried into a bare room with its floor covered a foot deep in sawdust, and laid out on a table of planks. The body is opened and the heart and entrails are removed, placed in a vessel, and deposited in the church of Sant' Anastasia. Then the body is embalmed, dressed in pontifical robes, and carried with great pomp downstairs into St. Peter's, where it is deposited in the chapel of the Holy Sacrament.

When Leo XII died there were sinister rumours about his end. I was never able to clarify the matter sufficiently for me to comment on it as true, or very likely. Nothing of the sort was said in regard to the deaths of Pius VII and Pius VIII.

The kind of looting I mentioned, that goes on when the Pope is dying, is to some extent conformable to medieval and Roman traditions. I say this to be fair, not to justify the practice. For example, when a Cardinal was elected Pope his house was sacked. A last shred of this custom is still to be seen today. The Swiss Guard seize the carriage of the elected Cardinal. The coachman breaks his whip in two and climbs down from the box. Nowadays the new Pope buys back everything for two hundred *écus*.

Everything now takes on a festive air. The Cardinals and their suites; the bishops; monsignori; all members of ecclesiastical households, according to their degree, change from black and purple to red and white, with rich gold and embroidery. The most splendid hangings appear on the walls of the churches and all those officiating wear vestments reserved for the occasion. Even if he had not had the symbolic tow burnt under his nose, with the reminder *sic transit gloria mundi,* the new Pope would have a sufficiently severe lesson before his very eyes. He can be quite sure that the same joy will break out when he comes to die. I should be curious to know if such a sobering thought comes into the minds of many Popes at such a time.

There was a moment of great interest in the events I am describing. I very much wanted to be present, and by dint of pushing through the crowd I managed to get where I could see everything.

In one of the ceremonies the Pope is seated on a throne at the end of the church. The great chair is supported by four colossal bronze bishops.

The Cardinal officiating at the altar near the Confession had to carry to the Pope something or other, covered with a silver cloth. On this occasion the Cardinal was Consalvi. There was a long way to go; on both sides were ranged the members of the Sacred College, all staring (benevolently?) at him, closely watching his face, his mien, and the steadiness of his gait. It was running the gauntlet, indeed.

He came out well and honourably, but I seemed to recognize in his pale, impassive face (if it is not mere fancy) the signs of an immense effort. I said to myself: 'He'll be lucky not to fall dead before he gets there.'

I should not be at all surprised if he had, during that journey down the church, received the mortal stroke that carried him off a few months later.

Anyone who knows the degree of intensity certain passions can attain in the hearts of priests, precisely because they have to bottle them up within themselves; anyone who knows with what a veil of serene calmness they have to keep hidden the most burning ambitions, the most persistent anger, and the most longed for revenge, perhaps will not be far from sharing my opinion.

A few months later I was passing the church of San Marcello and I saw there was an important funeral taking place. I went in and saw the corpse of Cardinal Consalvi stretched on his last bed.

It seems that it would have been better for him to have died a year earlier. But who can fathom these mysteries!

I spent the winter of 1825 working with all my might. I had now a fair capital of work to my credit and of sketches done from nature, and it seemed to me that I could tackle major difficulties without too much presumption. I got the idea that I would like to undertake something big (big in dimensions, I mean) and in a new style. The Flemish–Dutch school which reigned in Rome peopled its pictures with nothing but flocks, herds, and shepherds. I brought to my aid a whole host of paladins, knights, and maidens errant. It was no new thing in literature; but it was new in landscape painting.

I chose a subject from Madame Cottin's *Malek Adhel*, the *Death of Montmorency*. I began to think of it all day and dream of it all night. I started to make sketches, studies, trial after trial, until a first attempt took shape which I found acceptable. I bought a large canvas and set to work with such furious ardour that I almost forgot that cursed love.

I built many castles in the air about this picture; it was my *pot au lait*.

One of the very first notions of Pope Leo had been to proclaim the great universal jubilee of the year 1825. This meant that for twelve months Rome was transformed into a great factory of spiritual observances. No theatres, festivals, balls, parties; not even Punch and Judy shows in the square! Instead there were sermons, missions, processions, ceremonies, etc.

Not that I was keen on those boring things society calls amusements, then or subsequently. But I must say that gloom and, what was worse, general hypocrisy was a pastime with no appeal to me. You should have heard the young men, the military, the employees, having to decide between losing their jobs or singing *miserere*. What a lot of candles they lit to ward it off. It certainly gave one an idea of how they would behave if they had to go through with it.

In fact it was a tragi-comedy and, not wishing to take part in it, I decided to pay a visit to my parents in Turin and take them a specimen of what I had learnt.

When my picture was finished I put it on show (privately in my studio, however) and it had real success. Up to a point it deserved it. There was a good deal of originality, bold composition, colour, and it was effective. The young men came to see it and several established painters, and on the whole they liked it. I had it packed up and sent it to Turin, via Genoa. I started for Florence in the company of a certain Monsignore, half dotty and half an original, but extremely intelligent. He had a love-affair in the same family where my affections lay, so that we had formed a sort of friendly alliance to guard our interests.

If I meant to tell all the heroi-comic and semi-tragic devilries which resulted from our foursome, I should never have done. But not a word about these loves; I leave that for others to tell.

However, I will tell this. While we were travelling post towards Florence one morning towards dawn, I saw my priest huddled in his corner, who seemed to be holding up a little book in front of his eyes.

'What the devil are you doing? Reading your missal?'

I leant over and saw it was not a book, but a case containing a portrait of his lady-love.

I found my relations at Turin, who welcomed me with open arms, as may be imagined. In God's good time the picture also arrived. I set it up in a room with fair light. My people and several friends looked at it, and if it had met with favour in Rome, in Turin it seemed marvellous. My father was convinced that my picture was worth more than all the diamonds of Golconda.

He soon had the idea of presenting it to the reigning King Carlo Felice, and arranged for me to have the use of one of the rooms of Palazzo Madama, where I placed my picture with all the advantage of dark background hangings, in such a way that the painting made the maximum effect.

Crowds began to come and it was admired more and more. I was happy, not so much on my own account, but for the profound satisfaction it caused my father and mother. Besides this, I was able to demonstrate, beyond all likelihood, to all my clan that in the end one could, by one's own labour, succeed in making one's way, without the necessity of being a Chamberlain or Equerry.

Nevertheless, it was not possible to escape scot-free from the atmosphere of the place and of my class. My father shared the accepted ideas, though not to an excessive degree. Anxious for my future, he thought he could assist me by attaching me to the Court in some way or the other. To see how many nowadays try to join the Court, it was not surprising that he thought it opportune at that date.

One day, in fact, he proposed that he should seek to get me a post as *gentiluomo di bocca*, whose office is concerned in some way with menus and victuals. My heart dropped into my boots! To think of myself at Court, and what is more a gentleman *di bocca*, seemed so desolating that I simply couldn't get used to the idea. On the other hand, I was not brave enough to refuse and give pain to my father; so I agreed. But I must have shown so great a repugnance to the project that it fell flat, was soon forgotten, and was never mentioned again.

When I went to Court it was in quite a different way and for other reasons, twenty-one years afterwards.

What I could not avoid was going to Court with my picture, in order to present it to the King.

What with picture and frame it was a fair weight, but as a knowledge of fine art was somewhat deficient in Court circles, no one had had the outlandish idea of preparing an easel on which to place the picture.

When the two servants, dressed in black, had been admitted to the royal presence, bearing the picture with some difficulty, they had to stand holding it while the King received my father and me with a few polite words. Then, in his own good time, he turned his eyes to the picture, drawing nearer in order to study it better.

One of the two porters was my Roman servant, who was a plump individual of little stamina. As no ruler in the world, however well-meaning, has bothered to consider the limits of endurance of human muscles (horses, certainly!), the King, on this occasion, gave no thought to it. He therefore looked at the picture in a leisurely way, while I observed that my poor Roman, red and swollen like a balloon, with sweat pouring down his face, was tottering. I thought to myself—here goes the picture on the royal head, and the King will come right through it like an acrobat through a paper hoop. In fact, it was within an ace of happening just like that, and I had to come to the help of tired arms, until the porters were dismissed and, shortly afterwards, I was dismissed too.

When summer came, my good father, who was very pleased with what I had done, sent me off to get some fresh air. I made a trip from Courmayeur over the St. Bernard Pass, through part of Switzerland. But it rained continuously and it was cold. I was used to the hot sun of Rome, where I was in my element, and now felt like Ulysses in the country of the Cimmerians. One fine day I was so vexed with the rains, fogs, and mountains of Switzerland, where I was charged for even every breath I took, that I most heartily sent them to the devil. Back through the Simplon Pass I went, and never stopped until I felt the good Italian sun blazing down on my topknot.

When I got back to Turin, I stayed there for some time. After all, I had left Rome to be with my people and not to post about the country.

My brother Enrico's death, which had happened the year before, still spread a veil of sadness over the family. The internal struggle between his desire for a coveted perfection and the frailty of a highly-strung, impressionable nature, incapable of firm decisions, had brought him gradually to the grave. My father, who had been the confidant of his anxieties, his efforts, and his discouragements, had had to watch their destructive action, without being able to save him.

I found in my father a deep-seated melancholy and a reserve of manner, hitherto absent. My elder brother, after spending some years in Paris, in order that the impression of what happened in 1821 should have time to fade, had come home again. His two sons, now grown, were charming boys. Their father busied himself in teaching and educating them, with the constancy and devotion inspired by his sense of duty. As you see, things at home went quietly enough; but alas! though time, reflection, and morality prompt opposite characters to agree, if they seem to do so by outward appearances, it is not enough to create what is called 'good blood' in the family. Without this, it is possible to continue to live together; it may be a virtuous, worthy, and useful arrangement, but it can never be a happy one.

My character was always a quietly happy one and I recognized that it was a useful thing in the family for me to be there in the midst of these antipathies in order to neutralize their effects.

Beyond the family circle, too, my father received undeserved wounds. His fixed, irremovable opinions were not, for him, mere speculations. He tried to make them prevail by his action, his writings, and all other means acceptable to an honest man. As we have seen, he sacrificed his peace, his property, and risked his life for them. In speaking of such a man, it is ridiculous to add that he had never tried to obtain honours or advantages of any kind.

After the 1815 restoration, many professed his opinions because they were fashionable, or because they saw advantage in them. After the events of 1821, there had been a recrudescence of zeal. I found Turin full of Catholic societies. The entrance fee was trifling, but they served to attract the crowd and to tighten the Jesuit hold. I used to laugh when I saw some of our ladies subscribe their mite with such a goody-goody air in public; whereas I had opportunity to watch them at other times with an expression in their eyes and on their faces not at all mystical. So wags the world!

My father's upright character was such that he found it impossible to suspect duplicity in others. This noble defect was one of the few one could find in him.

He had founded a society among his friends and acquaintances who professed his opinions. They held meetings, discussed the interests of their party, made resolutions, etc. Most of these zealots considered themselves lucky to be able to hide their little games under the shelter of my father's unquestionable probity. Whether these people went too far, or for some other reason, the fact was that the government got suspicious of the society and, without more ado, dissolved it.

Such an order, and the harsh terms in which it was couched, profoundly wounded my father. His character and his services certainly deserved more consideration; but as in all succeeding Italian Governments, courtesy was not something in which they shone.

T

A yet more bitter disillusionment awaited him: that of being left alone, isolated, and cold-shouldered by his friends; who as soon as they realized that what they thought was a means of climbing had become a precipice, disowned him with all the zeal normally shown by time-servers under such circumstances.

I could name some of them, especially one, made famous by better men than he. But what's the good? I should not, by so doing, extirpate this brood of vipers.

This event was one made to show my father at his best. He uttered no complaint about the decision, nor the form it took. Feeling blame-less, he did not stoop to seek for absolution or a return to favour. He obeyed and held his tongue. What he felt towards his miserable com-panions, no one knows; but he must have been terribly moved by his youthful hot blood and by that spirit of his, so scornful of all meanness. It is good to think that every virtuous action is recorded in God's eternal registry.

The government (I think I have said so before) did not hold my father in high esteem: or, to be more precise, it held him in too great esteem for the ministers and other bigwigs to like having him too close. All governments, monarchical, republican, or coalitions, are alike in this. They want people to be honest, but ... *ne quid nimis*, not unduly so.

At the summit of modern bureaucracies there is a very special kind of masonry, which watches over the common interest and is full of guile. Their ability is particularly marked in cases when it is a question of blocking all roads and shutting all doors against someone whose only sin is being too honest. Foolish people marvel. 'It seems impossible that X, such a good, honourable man, is not given a place!' It's all very cunning.

It was only natural that this secret conspiracy should have condemned my father *latae sententiae*. The two Kings Vittorio Emanuele I and Carlo Felice (as all Kings, especially absolute ones), ignorant of the great science of knowing men, were surrounded by incompetent, mediocre, or hostile people, who kept their real friends away. My father, who would have given his life, and his children's lives, for the House of Savoy, was neglected and lived apart.

In a letter to my brother Roberto, after a brief beginning he con-tinued like this:

The information that there is a movement to constitutionalize the whole of Europe including Italy, may be true. It will probably happen. Time will prove. Should it come to pass (after our time) it will be seen if it is for the advantage or otherwise of those then alive. That has nothing to do with what I wrote before. What would happen if Piedmont became a constitutional state? Through a rebellion? I don't know through what vicissitudes we should pass. I do know what my attitude would be. I should certainly oppose the rebels with all I had of mind, strength, and influence, but I should probably not be there to see the end of a revolution carried out without the King's approval.

Should it happen with royal assent, whether obtained by persuasion or through fear of worse evil, I should conform to the royal command. Once the new constitution were established I should be its tenacious supporter. To obey the ruler is a duty with but few exceptions. Had the King agreed to any other form of monarchy, mixed or constitutional as might be, there would be no limitation to this duty.

Then, after a few lines without significance for the understanding of the general purport, he continues:

Long before getting your hint, I had taken up the special study of administration, precisely because, should this change come about, I did not wish to be entirely ignorant in such matters. Should it occur peaceably, it is probable I might have a place in one or other of the Chambers; and *the interests of the State should not be argued like blind men with sticks and blows* [open your ears, Senators and Members of Parliament!]; or as doctors usually do, try something blindly and if they guess right, the patient recovers; if not he succumbs.

From this one sees that, had he been alive at the period of political change and taking a part in public affairs, he would have been seated with those loyalists who proclaim themselves ready to obey absolute Kings and Popes; provided that the Pope and the absolute King obey them.

10

TOWARDS October I left my family and went back to Rome. I shall never forget the marks of boundless affection obvious in my parents at the moment of parting. My mother accompanied me downstairs as I left and today, forty years after, I still see and feel the look she gave me.

My father went with me to the mail-coach, full of attentions, anxious to see I had everything I could want in the way of little comforts for my journey. He showed an almost feminine solicitude, which went to my heart, knowing the stern resolute nature of the man.

And to think that I was going of my own free will, that I was simply longing—it hurts me to admit it—to be off, all on account of that most damnable love.

Luckily my father and mother couldn't read my heart; and God, who can, is merciful towards those who have lost their reason. But as is only fair, I was in the end paid in the coin I deserved, as will be seen later.

I reached Rome very flush in money, thanks to my people's goodness. In order not to lose the opportunity I bought a horse. This was an invariable mark of prosperity. When the wind blew from the opposite quarter, which at the end of the year was the prevailing wind, the first indication of the change in the weather was the disappearance of the noble steed.

This option has accompanied me throughout my career. When I left the ministry, and when I gave up the governorship of Milan, I became a pedestrian and this will be my permanent condition from now on.

I can boast in regard to my expenditure that I have always cut my coat according to my cloth, and I stick to it.

I spent the autumn at Tivoli where my friends had forgathered. As the description of my occupations during that country visit has little interest, I will omit it. Nor does the following winter deserve any special mention. I worked and studied as far as those fetters of foolish love allowed me, fetters with which I had fairly tied my hands. I achieved little in my studies and still less in moral improvement. The disease took its course.

I did not really notice that the Jubilee had made any sensible improvement in Roman morals. My contemporaries who, owing to position or job, had had to undergo all the vicissitudes inherent in the situation had their bellyful of ill-digested sermons, processions, and ceremonies, all forced on them, and were raging against priests and their system, more than ever. You can imagine what real religious or moral profit came of it.

When spring came I prepared to go off as usual to work from nature. I chose La Riccia, Horace's first stage on his way to Brindisi with the learned Heliodorus.

Although the modern inns of the villages round Rome are not brilliant in regard to cleanliness and conveniences, Signor Martorelli's tavern on the square at La Riccia certainly outdid all the others mentioned by the Poet Laureate of the Imperial Court.

I have always been amazed at the contrast between the excessive luxury of the society of ancient Rome and the miserable state of their means of transport and of the roadside inns. It would, I think, be an interesting subject for research, to discover which of the many known civilizations has best been able to make progress in all branches of its activity.

I have no intention of undertaking such a study: I only observe in passing that our big guns and battle-ships give a lofty idea of our state of civilization in regard to our knowledge of tools; but in regard to justice and well-being I think we must feel less self satisfied ...; but let's get back to Sor Martorelli.

He had taken the place of Sor Checco Tozzi for me. But what a difference! Sor Checco had something artistic and dramatic about him: his life was a poem, an epitome of the history of mankind. There were virtues, vices, passions, tragedies, and comedies: had he been a contemporary of Shakespeare, God knows what a subject he would have provided for that great artificer of ebullitions, emotions, tears, laughter, terror, joy, sadness, and mirth!

Sor Martorelli was simply an ordinary inn-keeper.

His wife stood at the coffee counter and counted out the change to the customers. They had a fifteen-year-old daughter who led them by the nose and ruled them with a rod of iron; she was passing ugly and ill-mannered. It is true she told me one day (a Roman phrase this) that I was as long and gaunt as calamity. It could be therefore that her opinion of me makes me unjust in my opinion of her attractions.

In the year 1826 Martorelli's inn, full from top to bottom, could have been called the 'Inn of the Four Nations', except that there were many more nationals than that in residence.

One long table took us all at mealtimes. I got to know several at table who, young then, were starting their careers in art. Many of them were French and I got on well with them—really charming people.

Every morning we each went off with our paraphernalia to find places to paint from nature. At dinner-time we all deposited our work in the common room, which thus served as a permanent exhibition. This was most useful as it encouraged competition.

(Had not modesty restrained me I was about to add that my studies were considered the best. But modesty has just arrived in time.)

That period was most profitable for me and I had never succeeded in doing so much from nature.

A German painter said that such study is divided into four parts; first, one goes slowly and badly; second, slowly and well; third, quickly and badly; fourth, quickly and well. I think I can say I had reached the last stage, as far as my potentialities went.

Among my companions who worked with me then, some later became celebrities, and I have seen their names mentioned with praise, mostly in articles about the exhibitions in Paris. I reserve some doubts, however, on their having been transformed into distinguished painters. At that time they hadn't the first idea. But I have always noticed that if one believed the judgements of French literary art-critics, one would be subject to very odd illusions.

Anyone who accepts their judgements runs the risk of forming opinions of French art which will have to undergo considerable modification when he sees what it is like with his own eyes. This was my experience when I visited the Salon for the first time in 1836. I found some good things; but what I had read about them was very much better. No one more than the French has improved upon the art of advertising.

My life at Riccia was harder than at Marino. There I had a humble donkey. Donkeys understand the difficult art of showing a decent appearance to the world with few means. Whoever uses a curry-comb on a donkey? Every hundred years one gives him a rough brush down; yet it is rare that a donkey appears other than neat and tidy. Just try to forget to groom a horse for three days! He looks rough and dirty—a filthy sight! At Riccia I had a horse; as I have always liked cleanliness, I had to spend about an hour every day in curry-combing, washing, brushing, making up his bedding, carting dung, etc., etc. Let us say, several hours in the open, painting in the heat, pestered by flies of all sorts; then, into the bargain, the operations mentioned above. You will appreciate I was dog-tired when evening came.

If this had not been enough, some ill-begotten messenger arrived from the parish council to warn me that I was infringing a by-law because, to save trouble, I had been piling manure outside the stable and only shifted it periodically. I had to resign myself, obey the powers that be, and add a further nuisance to my toil. To such straits was reduced a future prime minister, governor of Milan, etc., etc., etc.!

The company at Riccia was, however, more respectable than that at Marino. One did find people with whom one could exchange a word or two, and discuss things in general. There was some sort of spinet, or inferior piano, which was used in the evenings to accompany ballads, songs, and reminiscences of operas, etc. Here I would like to insert the story of a poor villager, which still moves me when I think of it.

One day in the open country I met a peasant on the road, driving a laden donkey before him, while he followed, intently reading a book. I stopped him and said: 'Can you really read? What is it you're reading?'

He showed me the book, which was a greasy, tattered French grammar. He was about twenty-two or three years old, burnt brown by the sun, rough and ill-spoken; but he looked at me with an intelligent, mournful glance, very different from the wild, animal look usual in men of his sort in the Roman countryside. He told me he had taught himself to read and had started to learn and educate himself; and at the moment was studying French. He told me he loved music, but had never had the chance to study it. He had, however, made a sort of violin for himself, and God knows what witch's squeaking he got out of it!

He had managed to acquire some idea of a keyboard; so I invited him to the house and tried to help him.

You can't imagine how grateful this poor young man was. I lent him books and let him come and practise on the spinet. As he had a brutal father who understood nothing beyond the spade and mattock, he used to slip out in the evenings after work, to come for his lessons. I often found him with his head fallen on the spinet, so tired that he had gone to sleep.

One day he came to me downcast and told me his father, finding that art and letters were distracting him from his work, had ill-treated him, then taken an axe and smashed that abortion of a violin, fruit of so much labour and study and his great joy. Poor young man, I felt terribly sorry for him.

I would have given anything at that moment to have had my clutches on one of those young hopefuls who are surrounded by tutors, good examples, all the facilities for learning and getting educated—all to no purpose; they are born asses and asses they live and die. I should have put my peasant in their place and set them to dig.

I had soon to leave this poor peasant; and I fear, after all, that I did him more harm than good. I had shown him a gleam of light that would only have embittered the darkness to which he was inexorably condemned.

Not that I had illusions about what one can reasonably hope in such a case. It is not every day one finds a Giotto in a shepherd boy. But don't you agree? What a sad spectacle it is to see the hopeless efforts of an obscure, unknown peasant towards a moral emancipation, that he glimpses, that he longs for, and from which he is mysteriously debarred by an unrelenting force.

Towards autumn, because of either overwork, moral suffering, or the climate, which is far from ideal in that neighbourhood astride the Roman Campagna, my health sensibly deteriorated. The Roman climate was always like a slow disease for me. However, as I am still alive today, it is plain my constitution suffered no lasting effects. One can, of course, feel very ill without really being so; and such was my case.

I do not wish to boast, but brainwork and brushwork, both on canvas and horse, while one is faint and has pains and palpitations enough to feel one's heart in one's mouth, need a good deal of determination. Things got to such a pass that even my friends advised me to see a doctor and get treatment. When one suffers at Rome from the sort of illness that does not put one to bed with a temperature, but drags on without special symptoms, the panacea is invariable: try the Naples air.

I, who have never in my life had much fear of dying, but have been terrified of being neither dead nor alive, immediately resolved to undergo treatment and I agreed to go to Naples.

I forget if the gold-bearing waters of the Pactolus ran as a river or mountain torrent. I well know that for me they ran swiftly and those that fed my purse were at the time a mere trickle. The horse, a dapple-grey, went first; there was no question about it, but it was a pity! That was not enough. Money was required for a journey to Naples. As I did not want to apply to anyone, I did my utmost and scraped together the bare sum necessary. I don't remember how; by selling things probably. Then I adopted the great expedient of those who haven't enough and can't increase their income; I cut down my expenses. Let the Italian Finance Minister in office when this book appears take note!

There was a certain driver who had reduced the time of the journey to Naples so that he did it with really miraculous speed. He got there with only a single night's stop and with one lot of horses. Another entered into competition with him and did it without changing horses and without stopping for the night. It seems an unlikely tale—about one hundred and eighty miles—but it was really true. He didn't keep going all the time, but took two hours' rest every six or seven hours of travelling. The horses got to Naples alive, though they were only fed on oats.

I did this. I found one of these coaches just leaving, and I travelled 'boxed', that is to say on the box seat. I had the company of a German student or young professor, whose name was Westphall or something similar.

We were both short of cash, which kindled a certain sympathy between us, and we hadn't got as far as the Tor di Mezzaria when we seemed like brothers.

I reached Naples and put up at the sign of the Speranzella, the house kept by my old friend, Signor Giacomo Rotondo, in Afflitto Street. Sor Giacomo was an old gouty fellow with a great fondness for the young. His house was always full of homeless people, and therefore of artists, for whom he was a blessing. He welcomed me with pleasure, and my companion and I established ourselves in the coolest part of the house. Nevertheless the heat was insufferable. A doctor I consulted at once told me that I had need of protracted treatment of a special kind, but it was not possible in that heat; I should therefore return when it was cooler. Thank you very much! Two months to pay for in Naples! '*Pazienza*,' I said, we'll make use of the time by studying. So, puffing and palpitating, I began to go out to paint from nature.

I linked up with several artists living in the house. There was the brother of Père Enfantin, who later died of a chronic disease at Paestum; there was a certain Joinville; there were the Piedmontese father and son Storelli; Romegas, a Catalan painter of seascapes, a good chap with whom I went out sketching. Youth is a wonderful time! One is pliable and adapts oneself to everything and everybody and always seems to be in one's element!

So time passed, as I worked away, along the beaches of Mergellina, Regina Giovanna, and those picturesque coves with their great tufa cliffs and ancient grottos from which they had excavated the material for the building of Naples. My trouble grew no better: in fact I grew worse. I remember one day I had gone a long way from Naples, alone. After working all the morning I had eaten at a fisherman's inn where there was nothing to eat but that dark, thin macaroni, as tough as string. After dinner I set off towards Naples, with my gear round my neck. After half a mile, what with fatigue and that indigestible food, my heart seemed to be bursting and for a moment I thought my end had come. I really thought I had an organic disease. I then got furious, thinking that at the age of twenty-eight I couldn't go a few miles with thirty pounds on my back. 'Better dead, than feeble,' I said, and went forward in a charge; and my anger carried me through. I got to Naples without breaking a blood vessel and felt better. The secret, of course, was that my activity had helped me to digest that blessed macaroni.

It often happens that imaginative, highly-strung, impressionable young men think they have something wrong with their heart or some other major ailment, because of appropriate symptoms, which are really caused by nerves. If you asked me what I meant by 'nerves', I should answer: ask your doctor, and if he doesn't know, let him find out. I know some of my contemporaries who had such fears and couldn't get peace of mind or do anything for years. I myself first imagined I was consumptive, then had the stone; finally I thought I was doomed on account of an organic disease. I used to spend a long time listening to myself and feeling my pulse. I got so tired of these boring proceedings that, one fine day, I said: 'Either you have an aneurism, or you haven't; if you have, the Pope himself won't be able to cure you; if you haven't you're making yourself miserable for nothing.' This brilliant logic convinced me. I gave up feeling my pulse and started to fence and go in for jumping at a riding school; in fact I took up the most rigorous gymnastics. I never stopped to think about, or pay any attention to, my supposed ailments. Finally the whole thing faded and was forgotten and I gave it no more thought. Here I am, not far short of seventy, with a heart that jogs along as usual, without giving any cause for serious complaint.

Young men, therefore, who find themselves in a similar case must be persuaded that, even in matters of health, knowing how to make a decision and sticking to it firmly is a very good thing and saves one from serious consequences. What more terrible consequence than to be reduced to nothing by continual fears, doubts, and visits to specialists? Health may not be the first blessing, but, without it, all the rest are of little good. Let every young man take care of his body, strengthen it, and exercise it if he wants to be something in the world; in the same way that a man who goes to war sees that he has a good horse to carry him. Quite apart from saving your life, a good horse can sometimes save your honour. A strong, healthy body can enable you to become a great benefactor to your country and mankind.

For my sins, I know something about it, for I have always had to work like those poor pack animals who are loaded over a galled back. Believe me, therefore, I have had experience in the matter.

The great heat was now over and Romegas and I decided to go to Sorrento where it should be relatively cool. We left in one of those large open boats, which have a lateen sail as high as a house and a jib at a kind of bowsprit; they ply between the villages along the bay.

We were some eighty passengers with baskets, sacks, chickens, and animals of all kinds and ages.

When you go on board, the ship's boy comes along with a large wooden cup painted with the usual moving scene of a number of naked people, who seem to dislike living in the midst of slices of salt tongue: or to describe it otherwise, souls in the midst of the flames of Purgatory.

The boy shakes the cup in front of every passenger, calling out 'O *Priatorio!*', and he must pay tribute. I asked for an explanation and was told that our offerings were to procure the assistance of the said souls, when we were out at sea; or at the worst some refrigeration to our own, in case. . . . As one knows, those who go to sea don't know how they will land. So, off we went, with Romegas and myself next to the captain, as representatives of the vessel's ruling class.

Then came one of those thunderstorms one only sees at Naples: overcast sky, sudden gusts, and a high sea, black as ink.

Rain or snow, the boats of the bay manage to sail. Master Aniello has no intention of being later than Master Gennaro.

So not a hundred yards from shore, then: 'Oars inboard! Hoist the mainsail!' Up went the big canvas and we were thrown into the scuppers to leeward. Baskets, chickens, baggage went tumbling; the women screeched. All rushed to the opposite side so that we shouldn't turn turtle; the boat steadied and away we went like an arrow.

I had my own particular reasons for observing Master Aniello, now so close to me. He was an old chap, tanned by wind and sun, with wrinkles and furrows on face and neck. I saw him keeping a close eye on the crests of the huge waves, his gnarled hand on the tiller, ready to cry out as a gust came: 'Ease the sheet.' The sailor holding the sheet, with his eyes fixed on the captain, let it run, and the boat, which was shipping water on the lee side, righted herself, but still continued at the same furious speed. The women were all praying and crying out in chorus every time the boat lurched, and I very much regretted I'd only put a small coin in the *Priatorio* cup.

If I had the choice, I think I should end by agreeing with the Duke of Clarence rather than with the father of Theseus, in preferring Malmsey to salt water. I was, therefore, quite glad to see, after three hours, the sail slacken from time to time, the boat go on a more even keel and sail in a way that, if it had been a horse, you would call a steady gait. Finally, after some twenty miles, we came into calm water; the sailors lowered the sail and took to the oars; and so we came to the Sorrento shore, where our boat was run up on the sand, making a furrow as it did so.

I must ask the reader to forgive me for having used so many words to describe such a trivial incident as the crossing of the Bay of Naples under a strong wind. But you mustn't forget that I am an artist and that I love nature, trees, skies, and waters; that I love them as one loves good friends who have kept one company on a long journey and who have never fallen out with one, but have helped one a thousand times and given countless hours of happiness. When at times images of real pictures come vividly into my mind, images dormant for forty or fifty years, I cannot resist repainting them with fresh colours so that I can see them as they first appeared to me. It may be a fault, but I can't help doing it.

The town of Sorrento stands some two hundred metres above the sea, crowning the top of perpendicular cliffs. Sorrento by the sea is a small suburb peopled by fishermen, down on the shore. There is a lesser and a greater beach. We landed on the latter.

I will not describe the place further. I don't want to rob the tourists' guides of their daily bread. My stay there allowed me to produce a great many studies. I painted also on Capri, that bare, parched crag, sticking up out of the water, as desolate as a region of hell, but despite this ... it may be due to the sky, the sun, the view, the sea, the half-naked inhabitants, the memories, the ruins, but one ends by finding it beautiful and romantic; even remembering the second great iniquity of the imperial period: Tiberius. The first and greater iniquity was the Roman Senate who flattered him.

When the intolerable heat had ceased, even in Naples, we went back there. I changed my lodgings, however, and established myself in an inn, where two Roman families of my acquaintance were staying.

One of these had the practice of organizing a gaming table. It was all above-board, but all the same it was gambling. They played *monte*. One cannot deny that anyone who makes this their principal occupation is somewhat tainted. Fortunately, I have never felt any inclination towards gambling, but the Roman proverb says: 'For the sake of company the friar took a wife', and for the sake of company I gradually took to betting. But as I have the greater luck to be unlucky at cards, I began simultaneously to take note that the contents of my purse were visibly dwindling. One's natural desire in such cases is to see them increase, and one generally has recourse to methods which lead to the opposite result. I staked higher in order to recoup my losses and I lost more still. 'The loser loses nothing till he tries to recoup' is a grand proverb.

The best society in Naples frequented this house. People danced to a piano accompaniment in one room; and I myself, more often than not, provided the orchestra. In the next room the money danced with no need of music at all; sometimes it vanished in a way difficult to explain and not very pleasant for the player. It often happened that I staked something with twenty or thirty people playing. If I won, I thought it was impolite to throw myself on my winnings, but I observed that politeness was not appreciated. I got there last, and found the harvest gathered, without knowing to whom I was beholden. In the times of Louis XIV, according to de Grammont, this kind of behaviour was the thing. It is odd to observe that for a gentleman to cheat at play was not a disgrace. Yet those people were always talking about honour. It is a good thing that ideas have changed; and should there be someone in Paris or Naples who cheats at cards, let us hope he is called a thief, rather than a gentleman.

In the meantime I went on with my system of always winning less than I lost. My finances dwindled and I began to be hard up and had to think of my daily expenses. Early and late I was always doing sums, totting up accounts, subtracting by mental arithmetic. One evening it was so much won; another so much lost; a third it broke even. Then losses again; another win; calculations, totals, probabilities, hotel bills, etc., etc. In fact I was always restless, peeved, and tormented. 'I am a silly fool!' I finally said one night after tossing on my bed for two hours without a wink of sleep. Gambling does not amuse me; I am distracted; my head is always full of winning or losing; the long faces of the players bore me; even if I win I don't like seeing the agonized face of the loser. It would certainly give me no satisfaction to be broke to the world. And this is the pleasure for which I spend long nights at the *monte* table. Courage! I resolve here and now to cut it out. No more gambling! And I've never gambled again. It is true that it wasn't much of a sacrifice, so I can't be very proud of it.

Conversion is a saintly thing, but it doesn't pay bills. I had, certainly, always paid my losses on the spot, without leaving anyone waiting a minute; but I had small debts of another kind and my purse was not long enough to settle them.

This was the only time I had recourse to the generosity of my father, who most kindly provided what I needed, so I was able to honour my debts without further worry.

To moralize about the vice of gambling is really too stale a subject, and I have no intention of spending time in so doing, especially as it would be wasted breath, I mean ink! One can say at least that in no other case does the sin and the penance coincide so closely. But the inveterate gambler will reply: 'But my penance would be not to gamble.' Yes! at first this may be true. But balance the pleasure and pain you have experienced over a period of ten years, the loss of money, time, health, and reputation you have suffered; and can you sincerely say that this habit is to your advantage? I appreciate that there may be one of many who will have won a lot at the end of ten years; who will have felt no concern at seeing people driven to desperation on his account; who will consider that his time could not have been better spent; who may be as healthy as a King; and who will relish his rather doubtful description as a 'fortunate player', although it is his sole claim to fame. I know such types are to be found, but they are as rare as white blackbirds. Tell me! Would you like to be one of these white blackbirds? I don't want to be sentimental, or parade humanitarian enthusiasm. I know of nothing more objectionable than artificial philanthropy. But let's be just; it is only necessary to have the feelings of a gentleman to come to certain conclusions. Among all the things rich people do, one haunts me like a spectre. It is, as we are speaking of gambling, the sight of piles of gold and silver on those cursed green cloths, raked about from one to another at the whim of the cards; and of the sad faces and furrowed brows of the people watching this damned game in sinister silence. Not a smile; not a serene expression among the lot of them; no indication of a worthy thought or sentiment! And to think that not far away, perhaps in the same house, there are people sobbing and sighing for want of help, which the smallest of these coins could provide. One must think of this and, if one is not a block of wood, it will be a salutary thought, for gambler or non-gambler.

Real socialism, the most holy agrarian law, is that of the Gospel : *quod superest date pauperibus*. Otherwise you might well hear the fierce cry *'à bas les riches, et la propriété c'est le vol'*. So he that hath, let him waste less and give more. In this way they won't come and take it.

I fear I have been preaching too much; even ending with alms-giving! Well, I've done now and won't transgress again for a time.

In the meantime the cool weather had come, and I returned to see the doctor. I shall not name him, although he deserves it, as he was either a great ass or a rogue. He subjected me to a long, expensive, troublesome treatment, which did me more harm than good, so that I went back to Rome three months later in a worse state than before. The doctors I consulted later told me that there was not the slightest need for such treatment.

While I was under the doctor I couldn't continue studying from nature, so I worked at home. I took to revising my knowledge of anatomy. I then began to feel a great rush of ideas, which had been previously imperfectly conceived, but never abandoned. They had been dormant under my art activities. I felt an impatient longing to write; but what? Prose, poetry, history, novels, epics, lyrics? I didn't know myself.

I was not then aware that, apart from Dante, Petrarch, Ariosto, Manzoni, and a few others, who did well to write poetry—and even these not always—other authors would have been well advised not to do so. In my opinion there should be no second-rate poets. Anything short of the sublime is intolerable. Some think differently, but this is my view of the matter.

I began to write verses myself and from the depths of my inner ferment came certain stanzas in triple-rhyme, deploring the woes of humanity. If not new, the subject was vast. Many years later I showed these verses to Grossi, who, after reading them with great interest, said: 'They can't really be said to be good.' If at the time I had need of being cured of the poetic infection, this short, limpid remark from one of the most talented men in Italy, and a dear friend of mine, should have been a complete panacea. But I had no need of further treatment when, three or four years later in Milan, we got to know each other.

A good half of the population of Italy (the lower half of our boot-shaped peninsular) have much need of such treatment. It is remarkable that the first début of the Youth of southern Italy is a greater or lesser quantity of so-called verses. In our mechanical age this is most odd. It comes from the bad governments who kept those poor populations down. With roads, schools, and liberty protected by law, much will go, bad poetry into the bargain.

After the triple-rhyme, I had the notion of writing a little romantico-archaeological poem with the scene at Pompeii, and the destruction of the place as the finale. At the dead of night the angel-destroyer evoked the demon of Vesuvius and pointed out the city condemned to destruction. I've forgotten why, but it must have been the usual 'wicked world'. The fiery spectre rose up from the crater at the angel's summons, waist high like Farinata in Dante's *Inferno*. While he forked out lava from the volcano with his trident, he scattered ashes over the doomed city with the other hand. This was the introduction. The main interest of the story was based on filial love. A sailor of the Roman fleet wants to ransom his slave mother. A sum, sufficient for the ransom, was the prize offered to anyone who could overcome a famous gladiator in the circus. The son deserts, disguises himself, conquers his opponent, receives the prize, frees his mother. But he is discovered and his centurion claps him in irons to await sentence. The mother is at his side, comforts him, embraces him, and informs him he is to be freed after a short punishment. Meanwhile night falls, a dull rumble is heard, increases in volume; there are shrieks and cries; the earth shudders under foot; the walls topple, and down comes the whole bag of tricks, smashing, crushing, and burying the city.

The poor mother, begged and urged by her son to fly, tries to free him, but he is fettered to heavy beams, all hope is lost, etc., etc., etc. As can easily be imagined this plot gave ample opportunity to beat the big drum in all possible ways.

I wrote and told my father about these literary projects and he encouraged me to go on. But posterity will wait in vain for these moving pages. The poem remained in the realm of ideas. Meanwhile my troubles did not grow less; and I had now got a worse one—homesickness. My home, at that time, was Rome, with all its misery. This certainly did not help my doctor's prescriptions.

Up to then I had been able to live tolerably without her. Now I felt I couldn't do so any longer. I felt sinister, gloomy presentiments. I do not remember why, but all sorts of doubts rose in my mind; I seemed to notice a change of tone in her letters. I tortured myself and cursed the moment when I let myself be caught, but I still remained faithful and my life, my whole being seemed to hang on that single thread, which I should never, never have the strength to break. But there was someone who was going to do it for me.

11

HALF-WAY through the winter I returned to Rome. Everything seemed normal to me and I took up my foolish life with incredible satisfaction. As I have frequently stated, I have no intention of writing about love-affairs. But as we have reached the last chapter, thank God, of my long, wearisome romance, and as the catastrophe brought about a change of direction in my affairs, it is necessary to say something about it. The catastrophe occurred in such an unnatural, implausible way that at the time I simply couldn't understand it. What happened later gave me an explanation which I will place before the reader and we shall see what effect it has on him. The fact is that, one fine day, without my knowing why, hostilities opened with a scene of furious jealousy. I who for six years had not, I will not say tried, but been able, alas, to hold any image in my heart but hers, I who couldn't imagine that any other woman existed in the whole world, suddenly found myself accused and convicted of conduct that would have put Don Juan in the shade.

This fury turned into a kind of convulsive frenzy. You may imagine—on such occasions few have scruples in swearing what is false—if I exhausted all the possible formulae of oaths, as I was, in fact, actually swearing what was true. I will not describe the scenes and frenzies, etc.; you can imagine them. At first, as it was all about nothing, I imagined they were passing ebullitions, and I was not unduly worried; but as I gradually realized I was unable to persuade her, and seeing where things were going, I took the matter seriously and I passed anguished hours, which I pray God may be spared to any other human soul. The family, the relations began to notice things, to suspect, and inquire what had so disturbed her. Fearing that she might get into trouble and ready to spare her at any sacrifice to myself, I consulted one of her sisters-in-law and placed myself in her hands. She could do what she liked as far as I was concerned, as long as no harm or unpleasantness came to the lady. She was a sympathetic woman, wise in the ways of the world and well acquainted with my friend.

She promised to settle the matter. I came back in two days and I received the following charming communication : 'She thinks you are having an affair with G——. It is impossible to rid her of this idea. I have done my best. In the end she replied: "If it's not true let him give me a proof by leaving Rome at once." '

Much obliged ! Thanks very much !

I had, as I said, come back from Naples in a worse state of health than ever; I had, moreover, got a bad cough; it was midwinter; and I had my home, studio, all my affairs under way in Rome. With all this, do you know how it ended? It ended by my leaving the Porta del Popolo in the Florence coach, two days later. I, who remember the journeys I went when a child of six or seven, remember absolutely nothing about that particular journey, I give my word of honour. Except that I think I got to Turin at night, in a diligence packed with hay, freezing cold and my cough cured or nearly so, despite all. I remember too that going in to my father, he asked me who I was. Imagine in what a state I must have been ! After two or three months I heard from a friend in Rome that the Duke of L—— was my most fortunate successor. This was the end of the romance. Now, my dear reader, tell me if you think all that furious jealousy was sincere, or an ingenious trick in order to get rid of me? If the Duke of L—— had just come in brand-new, or had he been privately destined for the part? You must decide what you think the more probable. Meanwhile I have made up my mind about two things : first that if Baron Auget de Monthyon, who founded a prize for virtue, or anyone else, had founded

U

one for heroic stupidity, I should have deserved it; secondly, of the two sides in the dispute I prefer mine. I have the memory of having performed an action of great self-sacrifice, and this sort of memory becomes more gratifying as one grows older, even if one was a stupid dupe.

As you may imagine, all my ideas and projects in regard to Rome changed. I believe if things had gone according to plan I should never have changed my ways or habitat. Probably, month after month, I should have spent my life in that abasement. God plucked me from it, roughly it is true, but I recognize it was an act of far-seeing kindness. I therefore made up my mind to give up Rome and settle in Turin in my people's house. I cannot say that the plan attracted me. The reign of Carlo Felice was neither barbarous nor tyrannical, in the worst meaning of the words. It was certainly complete absolutism, with all its consequences; but after all it was not a foreign government, nor a foreign dynasty as those of Naples, Modena, Parma, and Florence. The customs, traditions, and reciprocal relationships, all peculiar to Piedmont, sweetened much that was bitter, and blunted many thorns. That is something, though not enough. It must be confessed that for anyone with the seeds of liberty in his heart—however limited, measured, organized, and disciplined, as much as you like—but after all, liberty and the wish to be free; for anyone who could not resign himself to eating, drinking, and sleeping, without raising his eyes from the trite life of everyday, it was an atmosphere of leaden dullness, a kind of indescribable lack of breathable air.

A little anecdote will illustrate this condition of moral suffocation, better than a long explanation. The King loved music, and was in his Number 1 Box, second row on the right, every evening from the first note. He took a frugal supper, consisting of a few rusk biscuits which he swallowed with dexterity, holding them one by one by the ends and nibbling away very quickly. Provincial visitors looked on this performance as one of the sights of Turin and used to stare at him open-mouthed. One evening I was seated on the farther side in a box of the first row on the left, near the entrance to the pit. There were two ladies with me and three or four others and we were chatting according to the practice of the person who, inviting a friend with whom he had business, said: 'My wife will be having music, so we can discuss our affairs.' All of a sudden an officer of foot guards appeared at the door of the box, saluted, and said: 'On behalf of His Majesty, I ask you to be quiet.' We stared at each other, exchanged bows with the officer, and the conversation languished, as you may imagine.

This was the sort of thing that happened in the Turin of those days, and you may well believe it wasn't to my taste. However, I adapted myself to the conditions and, in any case, I had first of all to attend to my health, calm my feelings, extinguish memories, and finally find some peace, after so many desperate thoughts. My father and mother, who partly knew and partly guessed the cause of my sad state, did not worry me with advice or inappropriate consolation, not even with overmuch attention. A real proof of their sensitive natures and their knowledge of the human heart. I could, however, read in their looks and in the affectionate gentleness of their behaviour towards me what their feelings were, and remembering their goodness now, I feel I should have shown myself more grateful than I did.

The winter passed and I began slowly to pick up. The shock had been such that I do not think I was ever quite the same again. At least, it took many, many years. I used to pass my time at the castle of Rivalta with my friend Benevello, whom I have already mentioned. We arranged a trip to visit the Abbey of San Michele, situated on the top of a crag at the mouth of the Susa Valley. It struck me as marvellous, and I felt the art demon stir within me.

This resurrection was very pleasant; I had become as one dead, I felt so old (I was not yet thirty); now I realized that I was alive. I took fire, as often happens with me. Courage! Up! and I produced a book about the Abbey of San Michele; text, engravings, sketches done on the spot, etc. I set about doing it with some enthusiasm, and my parents were very happy, as they saw that nature was helping to cure me in her own way. I went and took up my quarters in a little hamlet called Sant' Ambrogio, plumb under the Abbey, at the foot of the ascent. I lodged in an incredible inn; but I had an object, something to do, and I felt a new man.

I rose before dawn and climbed up the mountain with my gear. I spent the day drawing various views and went down to Sant' Ambrogio at night.

In this way I got together a good number of sketches of the exterior, the interior, architectural features, cornices, columns, capitals, etc. I took them back with me to Turin where I put them in order and organized my projected edition. I soon set to work on the lithographs.

This Abbey, of the ninth or tenth century, was built by a French baron called Hugues le Décousu, and is one of the most original and picturesque buildings I have ever seen. A mountain, or rather crag, is topped by a great mass of stone shaped like a sugar-loaf. It is completely covered by numerous irregular buildings, which encircle the summit, on which stands the church. The general appearance is half religious half military, owing to the battlements and turrets such as were usual in monasteries in those days. Curious tales are told about this place. For example, they say that Hugues le Décousu had begun to build on the mountain opposite, but every night angels transported the building material to the other side of the valley, so that the Abbey rose where it is now. One can understand the operation for the first day's construction work. The first stones laid for the foundations disappear; but later on when they have put up footings, columns, arches, they can't find what they built the previous day? . . . There must be a small discrepancy in the tale! Another story is about a beauty pursued to the monastery by some tyrant or other. She poses the usual alternative in such cases: he must unhand her or she will throw herself out of the window. The tyrant—one sees his point—thinks she will not do what she says, and advances. But the lovely Alda means it, and down the precipice above Sant' Ambrogio she goes. But angels bear her up and she comes to no harm. The tyrant is left gaping, robbed of his prey. Alda—and this too one can appreciate—is rather proud of the way her jump turned out and says she can repeat it at will. But, instead, she fell down to Sant' Ambrogio, and, as the tale says, 'The biggest bit they found was her ear.'

This monastery enjoyed feudal rights. It owned land throughout Lombardy, and still today there's a church in Milan, San Michele alla Chiusa, an ancient chapel of ease of the Abbey. The Chiusa, where the Abbey is, is the place where the Lombards under Desiderius blocked Charlemagne's way. Coming over the southern yokes of the Susa Valley, he got into the next valley of Giaveno, and attacked and broke the enemy on the flank. These skirmishes are to be found described in a chronicle which, because plain facts are given in simple words, you can understand at once without re-reading; and because it contains anecdotes of real life which carry you straight back to that age and explain it, would be called the 'crude' Novalesa Chronicle by those who treat others as ignoramuses and bore them thoroughly in the name of the 'dignity of history'. It is very curious, for example, to read of the bargain by which Charlemagne discovered the unknown pass which gave him the victory.

A certain man presented himself to the Emperor and offered to show him the way to get down to the plain, asking as reward, on fulfilment of the bargain, to be permitted to climb a hill and sound his horn and that all those who heard it should become his vassals. Charlemagne, who thought he was soft in the head, agreed at once. When the man had done what he promised, he blew his horn—you can just imagine with what a blast—and then came down from the hill. He asked everyone he met—'Did you hear it?' If the other said 'I heard it', he boxed his ears and said, 'You are now my vassal.'

Another anecdote! Before Charlemagne's invasion the country was infested with brigands and the Novalesa monks didn't know what to do to protect themselves. One of these was a certain Arimanno, previously a terrific soldier, now a humble penitent. The Abbot called him before him and charged him to go to the bandits and persuade them to respect the Abbey. He not only sent him without arms, but ordered him to put up with everything, for the love of God. Should he be mocked or stripped, he was to offer no resistance. The monk, having had his instructions, said: 'I will do so, if they strip me of my habit, my shirt, and my hair-shirt, but what if they take off my *femoralia* (under-pants)?' The Abbot, struck by the argument, said that he gave no instruction about his pants. Off went the monk on his old charger, which now worked for the convent, and found the ruffians who began to make fun of him. Not a word! They strip off his habit and his shirt; not a word! I imagine he simply longed for them to get going on his pants. Which in fact they did, and he wanted nothing better. As he had no arms, he unbuckled his iron stirrups and began to lay about him. He did it to such effect that he got back to the monastery with his own clothes, their clothes, and their arms. As for them, he left them in the wood for the benefit of the crows and wolves.

This episode later gave me the idea of introducing Fanfulla into the convent of San Marco in my novel *Niccolò de' Lapi*. I recognize, however, that the monk is the better man of the two.

'Who knows', will cry the 'dignity of history' gentlemen, 'whether your horn-blower or monk have even existed? How is it possible to introduce such fables in writings destined to hand down to posterity, as far as one can, the true and exact record of what happened?' Very true. But if they will allow me, I will tell them to what use such fables can be put. They help us to get to know what kind of men there were in certain periods of the past, their ideas, habits, virtues, vices, and inclinations, about whom we only know what the 'dignity of history' has allowed to be written. This has consisted of the deeds of Emperors and Empresses, Kings and Queens, Popes, Princes, and nobles, whom historians parade before us in gala dress and crowns, without deigning to tell us about how their contemporary inferiors lived and felt; in a word, about the conditions of humanity. So much so that we are often reduced to a state of astonishment in the face of historical events, victories, defeats, enthusiasms, and disasters which all seem inexplicable. The motive force and reason for such things would be found precisely in those social strata, which the 'dignity of history' considers beneath it. History for some time has been the history of the great; it is time it became the history of all. Such is partly the aim of the modern historical movement.

I have not finished with my little anecdotes. There is finally one which depicts the age so well that one seems to be there. Serious history tells us that, after the Lombards had been conquered, Desiderius retired and died in the island in the lake of Orta(?); and that Adalgiso took ship at Pisa and found refuge at the Court of Constantinople.

But the crude chronicle tells us something different. Charlemagne was holding court at Pavia. He was seated at table with his followers and also, it seems, with someone else who had pushed in and found a seat.

After he had finished dinner the Emperor, on leaving the room, saw a great heap of bones of stags, boars, and other game, on the ground beside a place at one of the lower tables. He inquired which of his guests had devoured so much, but all they could tell him was that an unknown, *miles fortissimus* by his looks, had ground up the bones with his teeth (I envy him, as I haven't got any) just as though they had been hempen threads. He it was who had made the pile on the floor.

Charlemagne was not considered a noodle by his contemporaries, although he is by Italian novelists. The chronicler tells us that he soon cottoned on and said: 'This can be no one but Adalgiso,' and ordered one of his men to run and find him. He took off his gold bracelets and told the man to give them to Adalgiso and invite him to return. The messenger found him just as he had embarked in a boat and pushed off on the Ticino. He called to him and gave the King's invitation and showed him the bracelets, telling him to come nearer the bank so as to take them, should he refuse to follow him back to the Emperor. Adalgiso came in nearer and the man proffered the bracelets on the point of his spear. This way of giving a present did not please the young man. He donned his cuirass and, taking off his own bracelets, he too proffered them on the point of his spear, saying: 'If you proffer the King's gifts with deceitful intention, then I too proffer mine on the point of my spear.' The man saw he had been discovered, took Adalgiso's bracelets, and carried them to Charlemagne. The Emperor wanted to wear them, but they fell up his arm as far as his shoulder. He said: 'We cannot be surprised at this man's great strength.'

Let us look into this. When serious history tells me that Charles came down in aid of the Pope, won a battle at the Chiusa, took Pavia, and destroyed the Lombard kingdom, it narrates a series of facts which resemble all others of the same kind. They could have happened before or after or in other countries, and they leave no special impression on my mind. When, on the other hand, the chronicler tells me the things I have just quoted (even if not true, they describe what is real), he carries me straight into the middle of the Carolingian period, which I cannot confuse with any other. I manage to form some idea of the causes and consequences of historical events, because I know what sort of men they were who gained or lost by them. I thus get to know, not only a few individuals in exceptional positions, but the great mass of humanity and their true history. Excuse this digression: I now return to my subject.

The book I wrote described the Abbey's origins with various pieces of information and many details, and also the story of a monk. The latter was a little tale of my own invention. It was received with benign indulgence. I really liked a long passage from the chronicle, from which I have taken the above anecdotes, and which I included in a note, side by side with a translation. The public understood. Just imagine! My opening was as follows: 'For many, many centuries Italy held the sceptre of the universe....' You can understand what they read into the book. Luckily my nature is quite opposed to anything like walking on stilts, so that I soon realized the situation. I learnt my lesson and have never sinned again (at least I think so) in anything I have written.

By and large, my work met with undeserved success in the restricted society of Turin. The text, as I say, was in a stilted style; rather as when some journalists try to write like gentlemen. Nor were there many facts and ideas of great interest. Thanks to my hard work, the lithographs produced a certain effect, but there was little artistic about them. However, the work was immensely valuable to me; it served to distract me and to provide me with a purpose for my thoughts and activities. It confirmed me in my idea of moving from Rome. As I still had pictures, books, drawings, furniture, and small interests there, I decided to return, in order to arrange things and wind up all my affairs.

The Marchese Crosa, our minister in Rome, was going back to his post, so we went together. We left half-way through February in an open carriage in a cold that seemed to skin one.

I should much like to say that, after a year's absence, and in the knowledge of the tales about the Duke, I adopted a cold attitude of dignified civility when I met that lady again. Should I be writing a novel I should say so in order to show what a fine fellow my hero was. But I am writing a true story, and I am concerned with a far from heroic person. I must therefore confess that when I found her as lovely as the sun, with her eyes swimming with the joy of seeing me again, all my jealousy, all my good resolutions, dignity, and heroism (that cannot really prevail when one is young) flew out of the window at a single glance from a beautiful woman. I remembered nothing any more; it seemed to me, and I'm certain also to her, that I'd never loved her so much, and I felt myself lifted to highest heaven. But it was all a phantasmagoria of imagination and the senses. My heart was ashes and so it remained. After the first delirium had passed, I knew it, and my resolution stood firm.

I don't want my last word about her to be a bitter one, however. She had good gifts, but little intelligence and less judgement. No one had taken any trouble to train her heart and sentiments: she lived in the midst of a society where all sense of what is true, generous, and high-minded had been extinguished; what could one have expected? I hope that even in Rome, whether or not the Papal rule continues, they will finally appreciate that it is not enough to be born under the shadow of the Capitol hill, and that it is necessary to think of the instruction and education of those who live there.

I found Rome in the gay confusion of a vacant Papal throne. Leo XII had died, to the incredible joy of his faithful Romans. The satires emanating from the statues of Marforio and Pasquino were numerous. I remember one:

> *Tre danni ci facesti, o Padre Santo:*
> *Primo accettare il manto*
> *E poi di campar tanto,*
> *Morir di carneval per esser pianto.* [1]

In fact, his death had put a stop to theatres, balls, even the puppet shows. In March, Cardinal Castiglioni was elected and took the name of Pius VIII. I found myself near him when he was carried up the steps of St. Peter's in his state chair, with ceremonial fans and Byzantine pomp, which to unprejudiced folk seem in direct contradiction to the *servus servorum*. . . . However would they treat him if he called himself master? The new Pope, who was extremely fat, with drooping cheeks, thanked the cheering crowd. He wept, I suppose with gratifica-

---

[1] Holy Father, three bad things you've done;
Ascending the throne,
Living so long,
Dying at peak of our carnival fun!

tion, but to judge by the faces he made, they seemed more like the tears of a child undergoing punishment. I thought: 'You are not the man to reform this country; something more than tears is wanted.' In fact, his reign was short and undistinguished and left no mark behind.

While I was engaged in putting my affairs in order, something that needed a little time, I started work in the studio of one of our scholarship winners, son of a Turin blacksmith. He was a friend of mine, a very competent painter. Moreover, he was an excellent companion, and a worthy young man, so that I got on very well with him. He was, as I said, there on a scholarship and one of the few who, if they did not distinguish themselves (none did), at least earned an honourable, mediocre competency. His name was Barne. The way they managed artistic matters at that time in Turin was really comic. There's not overmuch sense now, but as the arts have been recognized a little by the public, things are on a broader basis. In those days anything to do with art was solely under the Court, which meant the Chief Chamberlain and his satellites, who understood nothing about it. The Italian Courts never have understood art at any time, except for those of Milan, Venice, Florence, Parma, Ferrara, Urbino, Rome, and to some extent Naples, and only in the sixteenth century, or thereabouts.

As a first sample, Barne had sent to Turin two naturalistic half-length figures: the *Date obolum Belisario*, the latter with a child. Quite a decent picture: there was design, modelling, and a certain Spanish *bravura* in the brushwork. The whole thing was studied from life and the colouring was good, if you knew something about it; to suit the subject it was painted in a sombre, harmonious colour, little more than a chiaroscuro; colour without colours. Artists will understand what I mean. The picture had the same reception in Turin as dogs do in church. Poor Barne received a severe reproof: 'Was this a sample of the profit he was getting from his studies? Was this a suitable specimen to send, etc., etc.?' As he had been praised for the work at Rome, he had expected quite a different reception. He thought shrewdly to himself: 'They want gay things, colours, happy-looking people.' For the next year he chose an Apollo, complete with lyre and red cloak; he produced the most frightful thing I've ever seen: all curves, and with a besotted face with the straight nose usually given to the blond deity. The body looked as though it were made of pink ice-cream rather than flesh. The background was a bright green landscape, and as for the yellowish rays all round his head, they made you sick.

They loved it at Turin. Here let benefactors learn that to patronize without judgement is worse than not patronizing at all. Poor Barne, who, thanks to his own good sense, had started on the right road, rushed down a false one, as was only natural, solely because of the ignorance of those who supported him. This is the reason why high-placed asses do such harm: their breed multiplies, theoretically speaking, and they bar the way to those who would like to try not to be asses.

While I was with him, he was working on a large picture that should make him or break him, according to how it was received. Just imagine how the poor young man had racked his brains to hit it off. First of all, in order to pick a subject that would please, he had chosen the great battle in which an anonymous Duke of Savoy is said to have beaten an anonymous Turk and thus liberated the island of Rhodes. The joke is that there is a tradition in Piedmont which explains the four letters of the grand collar of our Order of the Annunziata as F(ortitudo) E(jus) R(odam) T(enuit). The founder of the Order, Amedeus VI, did go to the East, and he liberated the Emperor John Paleologus, who was a prisoner of the Bulgarians, by taking Varna. But neither he nor any other Duke of Savoy was ever in Rhodes with an army, as far as one knows. The Knights of St. John, from the year 1309 when they occupied the island, having been expelled from Palestine, up to 1522, when they exchanged it for Malta, knew very well how to defend themselves without any help from us.

This is interesting in showing how traditions of even stranger events could, little by little, take on the authority of history in the old days. It also teaches us to look with a very critical eye at all ancient narratives, and modern ones too.

Poor Barne, who wanted to please high circles, would have nothing to do with historical criticism and bravely painted Amedeus VI on horseback by the sea-shore, with sword raised over a great bearded Turk lying on the ground. Remembering perhaps the fiasco of his Belisarius and the favourable reception given to his Apollo, he had introduced a stripling page or son of the Turk, who with a graceful movement raised his little white hand to ward off the Duke of Savoy's huge cutlass. You can just imagine how true such an episode was to the martial practices of the fourteenth century! But patrons wanted the pathetic and as 'To dine or not to dine' depended on patrons, one had to heed them rather than good sense. So I repeat once more: better no patrons than asinine ones.

Apart from this absurdity, it wasn't a bad picture and perhaps it would have been followed by better ones, had not the poor young man fallen ill and died, a short time after we parted. May he rest in peace!

My departure from Rome was, this time, quiet enough; certainly not so dramatic as the previous one. I left *her*, my friends, and the place with some regret, but I had the inner conviction that Rome was not, and could never be, the place for me.

After I had got back to Turin with all my stock of studies, I occupied two rooms looking towards Piazza Carlina, which my father had had fitted up for me in the house. Here I was quiet, isolated, and could work. I was full of the desire to do something worth while at last, with mind at peace. Now that I was calm again and finally free of the image which had never left me a quiet moment for so many years, I felt a new man. Before settling down to work, as it was summer, I spent some months making expeditions in various parts of the country. I was at Viú above Lanzo and there, walking along a ridge of that mountain chain, I had the rare experience of feeling a severe earthquake shock. You have no idea how much grander and more terrible it is among high mountains. It seems almost natural that houses should shake; but to witness those immense crags shudder gives one the idea of some fearful power hidden in the bowels of the earth. I was impressed by the sense of a completely new manifestation of nature. When November came I retired to my studio and began work.

I too felt I had to produce something that people would like, working all by myself in Turin : so that they couldn't say that the picture I had brought with me from Rome had been painted for me. I too searched, first of all, for a good subject. I found it in Italian history of the year 1503, in the Challenge of Barletta. I decided to paint the moment when they were fighting, with the judges and spectators intently watching the fray. After many rough sketches and trials, I settled on the composition, which is well-known to all, as it has been splendidly engraved by Boselli and Cornacchia of Toschi's school at Parma. The subject permitted a lovely sky, rich vegetation (if today there are no fine trees between Andria and Corato, who can say they haven't been cut down since 1503?), arms, rich dresses, a varied crowd. Moreover, it had the great merit, the condition *sine qua non* of all I have done that is any good, of serving the Italian cause. Working feverishly, striving for beauty and poetical feeling, and above all with faith that I should do well (blessed youth! I never get these fevers now!), I had progressed so far in a month with my work that it already began to look good. I was, modestly, very pleased with it, and worked away diligently to get it finished. One day, I remember it as though it were yesterday, I was putting the finishing touches to that group of battling horses in the middle, when the idea came to me that, considering the importance of the event and the opportunity it gave to stir up the Italians, it would really achieve its purpose better if narrated, rather than painted. 'All right, let's tell it,' I said. 'But how? A poem? Oh no! Prose, it must be prose if one is to speak so as to be understood by the man in the street and not on Mount Helicon!' I flung myself into my new task and to the enthusiasm of painting there was added the enthusiasm of writing. Where could I undertake the historical research into the period, the topographical and artistic research about the locality; or better still, could I go there, see the place, make it mine, so that I could describe it? I hardly had the patience to read the relative pages of Guicciardini, but immediately started to describe the scene in the Piazza of Barletta at sunset, without the shadow of an idea what was going to come out of it. What did I know of those places? I estimated, on the first map of Italy which came to hand, the distance from Barletta to Monte Gargano and I seemed to think one could see it from there, and into my description it went as gospel truth. I then manufactured a Barletta, a Rocca, a Sant' Orsola island to suit my purpose, and on I went, as bold as brass, creating a new character every day and, indeed, giving birth to a larger family of persons than I really needed. For example whatever good did the character of Zoraide do me? However, the proverb 'the load adjusts itself on the road' never found better illustration than in the writing of my novel, whatever its literary merits!

I can never express in words the intimate pleasure and the deep happiness I experienced in painting and describing those characters and living the life of the chivalry of those days, in complete forgetfulness of the present. It was certainly one of the best times of my life. I was, for the most part, alone with the creatures of my imagination. I went to bed early and the morning never seemed to come, so impatient was I to get into action with them again. I had no need of entertainment. I have always been bored by parties and so on (except for a good theatre when there was singing). Off once more then to Barletta and its Knights! I should just think so! Many people are sometimes surprised that one doesn't like parties, balls, and dinners: the so-called amusements. If only they could experience for half an hour the pleasures of imagination, of conceiving and creating a world of fantasy, they would no longer be surprised when they saw what a difference there is. A thought comes to me: how is it that these really divine joys don't produce equally divine works? What, indeed, are even the least imperfect creations of man in comparison?

Nevertheless, despite all my enthusiasm, at the very bottom of my heart I heard the terrible voice that, at one's best moments, mocks and freezes one with the cursed doubt: 'It all seems wonderful to you, but who knows what rubbish you are writing?' Some natures never doubt. Blessed are they! Others, alas for them! are assailed by doubt in the very act of creation. I am one of the latter. To resolve the matter I said to myself: 'The only thing is to show what you've done to an expert who won't deceive you.'

As adviser and censor, I chose Cesare Balbo, the son of my father's sister, that is to say my first cousin and devoted friend. He was one of the finest, most generous characters seen for many years in Piedmont. If you will allow me I should like to stop a moment to say something about him.

His ancestors came from the charming town of Chieri, about six miles from Turin, in the hills behind Superga. The place was once a republic of which there is mention at the time of Barbarossa's invasion. From ancient days there were three families, known as the three B's of Chieri. The Bensos di Cavour, of whom Camillo was one; the Bertones of Sambuy, of whom one branch settled in France and produced the *brave* Crillon; the Balbos, who gave us Cesare and his father Prospero, he too a man of lofty mind, vast learning, and untarnished honour. Cesare had a very varied career, like most of our generation who had to pass through all the vicissitudes which began with the tyrannical foreign dominion of Napoleon and ended with the legal, national reign of Vittorio Emanuele II.

Those who now live in peace and quiet may thank God, but let them sometimes consider what others went through in toil, sorrow, and blood.

At eighteen Cesare was snatched from his family and sent to Paris to work in the legal department of the Council of State. Then occurred the invasion of Tuscany, and Rome; the eruption into the Quirinal; the imprisonment of the Pope; the violent, ignobly executed annexation of the Papal State to the Empire. Cesare, who was already in Florence as secretary of the new Tuscan Government, was transferred to Rome under the Miollis administration.

These events restored the basis of temporal power and infused new life into all its abuses; so much so that they exist today and will last for some time yet, thanks to those who shout *Rome or Death* ...; but let us speak of Balbo. He was then very young and full of fire and fine feelings. He must have felt how iniquitous and foul the actions of Napoleon were, the man who without being aware of it raised the Pope and the clergy in public esteem and covered his own name with ignominy. I speak of the esteem of honest men of good sense whom you can prevent talking, but not thinking. Of course, with the majority and to all appearances, Napoleon triumphed; but when the world saw all heads bowed before his throne, and only Pope, Cardinals, and clergy refuse obeisance, it began to form an opinion, which turned into something to his detriment. The Emperor shared this opinion and preserved an impression which was never erased and was the cause of the partial, emotional attitude he always adopted afterwards towards the Papacy and the Roman Government, both as a politician and a writer. If it was a mistake for him to do so, it was one with a generous origin.

Balbo was later appointed to various missions in Illyria and Germany. After the Russian disasters he was involved in the collapse of the campaign of 1813, not as a soldier but as a courier sent to the Emperor with a portfolio containing the current papers of the Council of State. To meet the French army, retreating to the Rhine in a disorderly rout after the battle of Leipzig, dressed as a civilian with a portfolio under his arm, was not something likely to appeal to many. Balbo's courage was equal to this and more. You should have heard him relate, with his habitual warmth, the story of those macabre days, when every thought or feeling of good seemed extinguished in those miserable hordes; when there was a total collapse of all moral and material order, such as always accompanies the defeat of great armies. There were ditches full of dead and wounded, overturned ambulances, sick men hardly dragging themselves along, sowing the roads and fields with corpses. Then those hosts of still vigorous infantry and cavalry, who swept past like a whirlwind, pitilessly trampling down the weak whom they knocked over and the half-dead whom they finished off. . . . He told me that at a point where the road was full of dead men, a long train of artillery and ammunition boxes had to pass. When they had gone, the bodies in the road were reduced to bloody pulp.

If only this had happened in defence of a right, to defend one's country from disaster or from foreign invasion, then that blood and misery would be hallowed. But it happened so that Napoleon could close the Russian markets against English sugar, and so that he could make his whim the law of the world. Perhaps it is for this that the world, as grateful as it is intelligent, has called him 'the Great'.

In fact, when one re-reads the history of such massacres and of the misery suffered by millions of innocent people, it would be impossible to go on (I speak for myself) did one not think of St. Helena. Even in this world justice is sometimes done. I do not call down curses on Napoleon, or on anyone else, living or dead; but I am moved to pity by the huge number of victims of the passion, the indomitable egotism of a man who, after all, acted in the intoxication of pride and ambition. What, therefore, really infuriates me is the foolish sanction men give in cold blood to those who trample on them and scorn them and whom they call 'great'!

I beg the reader's pardon for having got worked up, but never, never could I speak calmly on such a subject should I be reborn a hundred times. Of course I could cut out this page, but not on your life! As what I have written is what I think, it shall remain. As long as people won't understand, one must keep on hammering away.

Count Prospero Balbo went to Spain as minister, after the restoration, and took Cesare with him. When the 1821 revolution took place, the latter shared the fate of all honest, high-minded men in factious times. Disapproving of both sides he was assailed by both; and although he had taken no part in the movement (he was not the type of man to have anything to do with a military revolt), he was, on the one hand, a friend of some of its principal instigators and, on the other, he disapproved openly of the blind stupidity of the restored monarchy. When therefore the brief struggle was decided, he remained under suspicion, particularly by the government. No gentleman must, and can, tolerate being suspected, so he retired to one of his villas called Camerano, in the Asti region. He busied himself with his studies, chiefly learned historical researches, from which grew the books he later published. I will not speak of them, because now the fame and name of Cesare Balbo are recognized by all. It is enough to have introduced him and his general characteristics into my narrative. We shall find him again more than once and there will be more important reasons for introducing him than as a censor of the early stages of *Ettore Fieramosca*.

I asked him to listen to the first chapter of my book and he readily agreed. One evening he visited me and, after he had seated himself by the fire, I began to read, with some trepidation as I was in my phase of doubt and discouragement. But he soon cheered me up and, after he had listened to some twenty pages, impassive, he turned to me and said: 'But this is very well written.' No music by Rossini or Bellini ever sounded sweeter in my ear than those words. Finally he declared he liked my beginning and, being very fond of me, he told me with such warmth, that it seemed a triumph for him too. The next day I set to work more furiously than before and I plucked up courage enough to speak to my father about it, and he wanted to see what I had done. But he was starting to be troubled by that illness which the following year carried him off, so that the slightest mental effort tired him. This really exceptional man, worn out before his time by his sorrows and the struggle between his virtue and his impetuous character, although he felt his strength failing, was not to be persuaded to give up certain useless tasks. So much had self-sacrifice become a second nature with him that he continued his work for the principles he considered good for Italy and the sole basis of society, until the total exhaustion of his vitality.

The day came when his strength failed and he had to take to his bed. His illness caused terrible bouts of suffocation, painful to bear, and to witness for a spectator who could not relieve the suffering. For years he had been used to moral and physical battle, which he was taught by his life-long faith to be the painful road towards an ineffable happiness. He therefore bore his sufferings with a serene, unshakeable faith in the future.

Those who claim that we should open people's eyes and show them the truth (as though we had it in our pocket!) by shaking the faith of those poor souls who in present pain see the promise of a future joy, will tell me that truth must be revealed at all costs. I reply: 'First settle the criterion by which truth can certainly be known, and then snatch the last hope from the heart of the forsaken to leave despair in its place.' They will be cruel but logical. But until such a criterion be settled, until they can answer the terrible question: *Quid est veritas?*, they are cruel and ridiculous. Therefore the afflicted, that is to say the majority of men, still prefer—cruelty for cruelty and absurdity for absurdity—the teachings of that political Jesuitism, now called catholicism, to all the pantheisms, all the atheisms, all the speculations and systems of the many, who, if they had a little less vanity and a little more charity in their hearts, would think twice before robbing people for whom they profess such tender feelings of the only real comfort they have: that of believing that their present sufferings are the price of an immense future happiness.

I should be careful not to rob a poor savage of his faith in the efficacy of some puerile rite, supposed to procure him a better fate than he had at present, if I were not sure of being able to substitute another more comforting one. What right have I to make 'an immortal spirit' more miserable than God made him.

My father's illness had given him a little respite. He was able to get up, and was even so much recovered that he was able to accompany my mother to Genoa, where she went to escape the bitter winter climate of Turin. He had some days of improvement, then he became worse and we had the news at Turin that there was no hope. Roberto and I left for Genoa. My mother recorded as follows: 'At midnight his sons

Roberto and Massimo arrived from Turin, he embraced them tenderly, gave them some mementos, recommended their mother to them, enjoined them to live in peace and concord, and gave them his blessing with paternal love. . . .'

He died on November 29th 1831, at the age of sixty-seven years and nine months. I shall not say more on this subject. Family grief can only rouse luke-warm sympathies in the reader; very naturally. The secrets of one's heart must only be revealed to those who share them. I shall only say that this was a great, abiding grief for me. Not even now can I write of it with eyes entirely dry.

12

As long as our father and mother are alive we are sure of having someone who loves us for ourselves alone. When they have gone, there is no longer certainty, only the possibility. It is for this reason that the loss of parents marks one of the most important milestones of life. Only minds incapable of dwelling on thoughts of serious things, or hearts devoid of all nobility of feeling, can go through this experience with indifference. In my domestic situation, the case was still more painful and the loss irreparable. If I have been able to give the reader some idea of the father I was never to see again, it will not be necessary for me to write many words to convince him of the feeling of loneliness and painful loss which filled me at his death.

Although a pompous funeral was not something desired by him or by us, yet who can see a loved one carried to his grave without feeling the natural wish to pay him honour? We therefore had to undergo the sad, repugnant discussion with the parish church about the tariff which is concerned with the smallest details of a funeral. Without asking, one has to hear the enumeration of all the charges: so much for bells, so much for candles, for a plain coffin coverlet or for one with silver lace ... the whole thing with the evident intention of taking advantage of the distraction and compliance of those whose minds are full of other thoughts, in order to make profits which would make a usurer blush.

The honour we pay to the memory of our dead, the love, free of all egotism, we still feel for them, comes from the depths of our heart. No

x

people in any known period has ever been indifferent to such sentiments. Yet we 'civilized folk', must we at such painful moments have
our hearts rent by the claws of these birds of prey? Among the hundred
reforms needed by the Catholic religion, put funerals on the list! They
are, at present, shameful!

After a proper period of mourning, my brother and I returned to
Turin. I passed the winter in a state of melancholy, which I dare not
compare with the period I went through owing to what happened in
Rome; it would seem disrespectful to too revered a memory. I can say,
however, that my present grief had moral consequences, which had
been, so to say, started by the other grief, and gave it a more decisive
and lasting form. Affliction, which most people consider anathema, is
really a blessing from God. From affliction comes meditation over the
past; the discovery of forgotten or ignored faults; the salutary reproof
given by the better part of us to the worse; serious resolutions; grievous
but irrevocable changes.

Appreciating that I had now reached a new phase in my life, I insen-
sibly began to feel the need to compare the past with the new horizons
opening before me. A desire was born in me to contemplate the general
tenor of my life; to define its periods and phases; to divide it, as it were,
into chapters, as one does a biography. What had I achieved so far? I
had, it is true, studied with sufficient constancy, I had entered on a
certainly not blameworthy career, many at my age would have done
worse ... but let us be more precise; what I had done was to make
love and paint: I was thirty-two. I might live another thirty or forty
years; was this all? Making love and painting? It seemed little; not
enough (I could not know then that, in regard to changing professions,
fate was later to provide me with all the change I could desire); so I
began making plans and considering possibilities of doing better, but
without hitting on anything that satisfied me. I was like a man groping
in the dark for something solid to hang on to, but who finds only a
void. I passed a bad winter. When spring came I thought it would be
a good thing to have a look at the modest property left me by my
father. I went to spend some time at the castle at Azeglio. The village
has some two thousand inhabitants. It lies at the foot of a little hill on
which stands the castle. It is about five miles to the east of Ivrea, at the
mouth of the Aosta valley.

The tradition is that in Roman times it was a kind of penitentiary
colony with special privileges, an *asilum*: hence Azeglio. Now it is a
village of good, excellent folk; full-blooded and somewhat irascible, as
all we Canavesani profess to be. I am perhaps claiming too much in

boasting that I am one of them because, as I have said, my people come from Savigliano in the centre of Piedmont. But I am linked to the population of Azeglio by so many good memories and they are so fond of me, that I'm sure they won't object if I describe myself as one of them. My family, however, has only owned the castle for a few generations, and it came to them from the distaff side.

The good memories are based on the love and esteem my ancestors earned while they held feudal sway. What the old people of the village used to remember with emotion was the building of the beautiful church with its fine belfry at nearly the entire expense of my grandfather. As a boy I remember talk about the difficulties encountered in hauling certain huge columns to the village. I imagined it as such a feat that I saw this grandfather as though he were one of the pyramid-building Pharaohs.

That summer I paid visits to my friends in their holiday retreats in the mountains, with my manuscript of *Fieramosca* with me, adding to it as I went. When the cold weather began I returned to Turin, where my brother and I had to sign the instrument which finally regulated the division of our father's property. While the lawyer was drawing this up, I made my will. Death is possible at any moment and I have always considered it a right and proper thing not to leave confusion behind one. Furthermore, the funeral orations pronounced by the general public over those who die intestate, leaving their families in a predicament, did not appeal to me. 'What a silly fool,' they say, 'he thought he would hasten his death by making a will and now look at the squabbles, the lawyers, and the cost of it all! ... What a goose!' I have chanced to see more than one case, where a foolish hesitation in pronouncing the words 'I bequeath' and in admitting the fact of mortality has led to a great deal of misfortune. One simply must have heirs!

As far as I was concerned, after having signed the deed with my brother, I had my own will in my pocket. I was only intestate during the half-hour it took me to walk from my house to the office of the lawyer where I deposited it. I think this procedure was good in my case, and the reader must allow me to think it good for him, should he not already have considered the matter.

Another piece of advice, which I have proved good by experience, is not to be too romantic in one's domestic arrangements. As long as the father is alive, the family home can contain all the sons. Directly the father dies, the house is no longer a home. In fact, there are as many homes in it as there are brothers to share it. At the moment of loss, the family is in an emotional state and decisions are made which do not always work out right in practice. This may be so through no one's fault, but simply by the facts of the case.

A difference of character is quite enough: one person is gay and carefree; the other is serious and particular; one likes warm rooms, the other cool rooms, etc., etc. Such trifles are quite enough to cause trouble and disturbance among equals which can give rise to serious quarrels. I do not deny that there are instances of brothers happily living together. Lucky people! The exception, however, does not make the rule. It is prudent not to make such an arrangement at the time when one is under the sway of emotion, but one should look well into it and make suitable arrangements calmly, under the guide of reason.

I experienced the truth of this. My brother and sister-in-law were models of every worthy moral quality. The name they left was that of real benefactors of the people. Both of them ran schools for poor children at their own considerable expense. The money they provided I do not consider a great merit. What I think is wonderful is that they personally spent many hours every day in teaching the children to read, to be clean, honest, and good; to correct the bad tendencies of a class to whom no one had paid any attention, except to send to prison those discovered to be law-breakers. No one had done anything to prevent them being so. In one word, I consider personal service a much greater merit than giving money. I remember sometimes in winter having been in my brother's house after dinner, when a person no longer young feels heavy and needs repose. The school bell rang and Roberto said to his wife: 'Time we were off.' One read the effort it was in the good woman's face; but she would get up with a little sigh and go out in all weathers, whether in fog, or snow, or rain, to shut herself up all the evening in the close, and far from sweet-smelling, atmosphere of the school. This is real merit! At the death of both of them, their coffins were accompanied to the cemetery by a host of children and their parents; all poor people, who came out of love, not self-interest, to pay what honour they could to those who had felt concern for them when they were alive. They, therefore, had the rarest of earthly rewards: gratitude from those who had benefited; not forced or paid, but entirely spontaneous. Let us hope they now enjoy a still greater one at the hands of God.

Notwithstanding this, I had to recognize that it would be well for me to set up my own house; so I resolved to move my household goods to Milan. There I found the Austrians; not very pleasant circumstances, but was it worse than under Carlo Felice, who was glad to rule through their auspices? As I wanted to study and follow the profession of art, I should have faded away in Turin, where the arts were tolerated like Jews in a Ghetto. In Milan, however, various circumstances had combined to produce a real artistic movement. Many distinguished artists had assembled there. It was fashionable to buy modern pictures. The rich were acquiring collections for their galleries; those who were not rich sometimes suffered all sorts of strange deprivations in order to acquire a little picture by some special painter. The shoemaker Ronchetti is celebrated for having made boots and shoes for the best artists, and getting payment in the form of sketches, pictures, statuettes, little models, etc., etc.

Making money was not, and never has been, my principal aim. I intended, nevertheless, to follow art as a profession and to sell my pictures for a different reason : because it is the best way of classifying them; because it is the best way to discover if they are liked; finally, because feeling that one is capable of earning a decent living by one's own efforts flatters one's self-esteem and that need for independence which is the basis of my character. It is for this reason that sloth debases and work ennobles : because sloth brings men and nations to slavery; while work makes them strong and independent. These are not the only good results. The habit of work diminishes all excesses and induces the need and taste for good order. Material order leads to moral order; work therefore is to be considered one of the best auxiliaries of education.

The need for order is second nature in me : the circumstances of my life and a series of bitter experiences had increased it and the reflections I had made during hours of sadness had made it quite irresistible. In deciding to leave Turin and go to Milan, my art was not the only object. I felt a strong desire to regularize my life and, thinking over the phases and vicissitudes of my blessed love-affairs, I had to confess that, all in all, I had done much harm to myself, much to others, and had had little good to show for it all. These thoughts did not arise from any renewal of religious sentiments, but were the sole effect of a sense of natural fairness, by which I considered myself to have been unjust and blameworthy towards others and myself; I regretted it and wanted to change my habits. I understood very well that a feeling for religion, quite apart from a real positive faith, would have been a valid support in such a decision; I wished I possessed it, I don't know what I shouldn't have done to possess it; but of what use are wishes in such a case? Man believes, as I have said, not what he wants to, but what he can.

My mind has always refused to accept the dogma of original sin as an explanation for the origin of evil. Therefore all its consequences fall to the ground. They were days of bitter, painful struggle for me. But I felt the aspiration towards a new life so strong within me; and to persist in a state of irresolution was, as always, so contrary to my nature that I decided to escape from it by embarking on a course which will appear strange to the reader. This was to adopt the outward forms of a religion before being able to persuade myself of the truth of its doctrines. I planted the shoot, hoping it might take root later, and I started to put into practice the precepts of the Catholic cult, trusting that with time my mind would understand and accept its fundamental beliefs. I don't know if it would be possible to provide a greater proof of good will in this sort of thing.

It is plain that if one wants to give an entirely new direction to one's life, changing one's domicile, if one can, facilitates the matter considerably. It was this consideration, together with my art plans, which took me to Milan.

I took up my abode there, spent twelve years in the place, married, and founded a family. I held it very probable that I should live there for the rest of my life. Then unforeseen circumstances arose for me: to this must be added the whirlwind that convulsed Europe and which has still not yet finished its work: and I was catapulted into the vortex of a restless career, as I shall presently relate. Those twelve years were passed by me in home and family life. Under such circumstances, every act, question, incident loses its purely individual character and involves the complicated interests of two or more persons. If a man be allowed to reveal his own feelings without reserve, he should not—as the philosopher said—make the walls of his home of glass for all to peer in. If one desires that the privacy of the home be respected one must be the first to give a scrupulous example. Avoiding speaking of things of little interest, I shall restrict myself to writing about the work I did in Milan, both artistic and literary, during that period, and to giving some account of the things, the men, and the times.

Although the Emperor Francis the First had said to a deputation of citizens: 'He could do nothing now but try to let Milan slowly decay', Milan had not wanted to decay. Certainly the foreign, despotic government did what it could; but one was yet to see what effects a few years of free, independent governments produced on the cities of Italy. Not even the Austrians were able to reduce Lombardy to too bad a state. At the moment of my arrival in the city, the recent changes in France, the independence of Poland, the revolt in the Papal States had stirred the blood of all. The arts, letters, industry, the whole of society shared in this increased vitality. The slack moral fibre of the country was hardening; one breathed freer; everyone worked harder and with a greater will. This state of excitement gradually grew less, as the House of Orleans consolidated its power in France, and after that government allowed those Italians who had been deceived by the French occupation of Ancona to fall into the hands of the Austrians. Poland too, partly through her own fault, but more through the fault of others, had to hear the announcement in the French Chamber that: 'Order was restored in Warsaw.' The people of Lombardy had recourse to their old consolations of eating, drinking, and amusing themselves. All that remained in being was the apparatus of the secret societies and the Giovine Italia, which being *giovine* (young) one could not expect to have good judgement—of which indeed it had very little.

Long oppression, by making lies and pretence necessary, profoundly corrupt the character of peoples. Unfortunately Italy is an example of this; there is alas! a tendency to walk privily, the subterranean mole instinct: and God knows when we can correct it. It is a mistake and a fault even under foreign tyranny; but it is a mistake, a fault, and an absurdity under a free government such as ours today. Owing to this, without considering the societies which hatch assassins and, it is said by many, organize colossal thefts, I should not wish to see even Masonic lodges in Italy. Not that I should want to close them or forbid them, if I had the power; but I should like them to close themselves, at least for fifty years. I am the first to recognize that there is nothing more innocuous than the Grand Orient, King Iram, Prince Cadoc, the apron and hammer, etc. I well know that the 'Perfect Light', that is to say the great secret, is not the frightful thing it is supposed to be by some. I know too that in many countries various local advantages derive from this society. Their affectation of always stressing charitable works as their principal object, however, smacks somewhat of pious humbug. But in Italy, gentlemen! in the classic land of factions and political chicanery, where everything degenerates into coteries, cliques, and underhand arrangements; for goodness sake give us air and take your 'Grand Orient' farther to the orient, or occident, if you prefer it. Do not put temptation in our way of becoming sectarians; for with all your good works, mutual help, and hospitals—all excellent things—you cannot prevent, on our corrupted soil, your humanitarian society becoming a real faction or political secret society, with its deceptions, exclusions, and clerical persecutions; with its intrigues, its manipulations to provide a job for one person or oust someone else, its directing and ordering, by flattery or fear, under the cloak of darkness. It becomes, in a word, a substitute for the honest, open, public action of the political power and of society, in which the sectarian element, rather than reforming, persists and becomes more evil, not having now any pretext or excuse.

I ask you! Whatever idea, opinion, or point of view can't be spoken, discussed, published, or debated in present-day Italy? What absurdity, crankiness, or stupidity can't be offered to the good public in a lecture-room or from the stage of some little theatre (paying the rent, of course) with chairman, chairman's bell, vice-chairman, speakers, seats of honour, lights, gilded candlesticks, etc., etc. As long as you keep clear of the civil and criminal law, you can hold meetings as much as you like, and air your views; be they political, theological, social, artistic, or literary. Who will object? Why, therefore, do you need all this secrecy? Here you are in a quandary, for you must either admit you are playing a childish game to enhance your own importance as children do when they set up toy altars; or that you wish to get round the law and undermine the house in which we all live. Or it may be you want a hand in getting jobs, influential support, or cash: you therefore obstruct or favour, not those who are useful or harmful to society, but those who are for or against you in your private schemes. For this, we might just as well have kept the Jesuits!

A free country wants no mysteries. In Italy, more than elsewhere, if we are to get out of the mire quickly, we must be very careful to avoid everything that tends towards pretence and working in the dark.

This moral disease of ours is similar to many epidemics. For example, in a country where there is cholera, anyone who falls ill gets cholera; in Italy everything degenerates into secret societies.

The Giovine Italia was a bad example and a bad school for Italians, with the absurdity of its political principles, the foolishness of its proposals, and the perversity of its methods. Finally there was the bad example of its leaders who, themselves staying in safety, sent to the gallows those generous noodles who did not understand that their heads were not sacrificed for Italy but to water her parched soil with the blood of martyrs.

Yet you still find people today who believe that our present liberty is largely due to these secret societies. In the same way, some believe that without the Terror of 1793, the world would never have been reborn. They do not understand that terrorism and murderous secret societies have put such fear into men's hearts, that it is only now, after long years, that they began to have less fear of liberty and to prefer it to despotism! The fact is that those horrors have not hastened, but retarded, our liberation.

During my residence in Milan, most young men spent their time in drinking and with chorus girls—they often married them!!! They cursed the Austrians and kept apart from them. They lived in sloth and profound ignorance. A few of the more daring involved themselves in all the secret, useless intrigues of the Giovine Italia, which meant passing letters, documents, newspapers, passports; concealing emissaries, helping those on the run, smuggling messages to prisoners, etc. What for? They had no idea, and I defy anyone to understand it!

I did not share the opinions of the Giovine Italia, as I recognized that all the activity of its most faithful members was perfectly useless. What is more, I detested the practice of continual falsehood (I make no mention of daggers), and so I kept aloof from it all. My view was, and still is, that we must concern ourselves with the national character; that is, if we want an Italy we must make Italians. When they are truly made, then Italy *farà da se*, will act independently. I therefore formed a plan to influence people through a patriotically inspired literature, and *Fieramosca* was the first step I took in that direction. In fact, during the whole time of my stay in Milan, the Austrian police had no occasion to concern themselves with my affairs. If they ever had the idea that I was so cute as to avoid their vigilance, they would have made a big mistake. It is true that I was hard at work to get at them in a different way, which would not be of advantage to them, so that I have no right to their gratitude.

This then was the political condition of the country. In regard to art, there was a new vitality which lasted for about ten years, and sometimes had the character of real enthusiasm. I had brought a few pictures with me: the large one, *Challenge of Barletta*; *Inside a Fir Wood*; and the *Battle of Legnano* of smaller size. They didn't seem bad to me; but as I suffer, as I have said, from diffidence to a superlative degree, I really trembled at the thought of the moment when I should have to exhibit them to the public in the rooms of the Brera Academy. As happens to people of lively imagination, I saw, if I closed my eyes, my three poor pictures surrounded by fine big landscapes, so true and real that one could almost see the leaves moving in the wind and the birds fluttering through the branches.

Before saying anything to anyone I thought to myself: 'Let's have a glance round and see what they can do.' So I began to visit studios and get to know the principal artists and amateurs and exchange confidences. They naturally wanted to know who I was. They got information and so found out what they wanted, and I was warmly welcomed. By degrees they began asking: 'Do you too draw and paint?' And I modestly replied that I amused myself a little in that line.

Modesty is the best attitude to adopt and I recommend it in all such circumstances. If you don't show off, you get about one-third more appreciation than you deserve, if you have any merit. If you have none, you have not pretended to any, so nobody minds. Let young men starting their careers take good note of this.

The result of my reconnaissance was to boost up my courage and I did not tremble so much, though I still felt nervous. It wasn't that I did not find competent artists; but I did convince myself that the leaves on their trees did not stir in the breeze, but were painted just like mine. The great day came at last. Pictures began to be taken into the Brera Academy, and I too hired carpenters, hangers, and porters, and had mine carried to the place allotted to me, one of the best, thanks to the courtesy of the people there.

I have never so closely scanned the looks, gestures, and expressions on the faces, not only of the dilettanti, but of the attendants, porters, and boys who helped to set up my little shrine, to see what effect my pictures had on them. The result seemed to tremble in the balance and I hung between hope and fear. As long as a work of art is passable on the whole, because most people think it so and stop to look at it, one then has to hear the opinions of others. The opinion of a friend of mine, Cattaneo, director of the Brera numismatic department, induced me to have confidence. He had studied art in Rome before the time of the French; he was a contemporary of Bossi, Appiani, and all the best landscape painters of the day: Denys, Woogd, Hackert, and so on. I put great trust in this worthy man, who was fond of me yet no flatterer; he kept on saying I should get a favourable reception, so that I plucked up courage.

The exhibition opened on the first of September. Cattaneo had guessed right and my success was far more than anything I could have hoped. The *Fir Wood* was bought by the Viceroy; *Barletta* by Count Porro; *Legnano* by somebody I don't remember. In two or three days I had placed all I had to sell. I was rather scared that the picture of the victory of the Milanese over the Emperor (*Legnano*) might get me into trouble. Poor Barbarossa with his horse—white of course as all painted heroes' horses—was down in front of the Milanese *carroccio* in a very poor way. If in fact he had been as I painted him, I very much doubt that he could have reappeared three days later in Pavia, where they had thought him killed.

In any case, as the police and the government well knew that— alas!—it was the *carroccio* that came down and the Emperor who got up again, they did not cloud my success with any silly nonsense.

After such a success, commissions poured in from all sides, and I always had plenty as long as I stayed in Milan. So much so, that one winter I painted twenty-four pictures, all more or less commissioned.

While I was doing my best to establish myself firmly in the art world of my new domicile, I continued to work away at the novel *Fieramosca,* which was now nearly finished. In those days literature was represented in Milan by Manzoni, Tommaso Grossi, Torti, P. Litta, etc. Memories were still fresh of the period of Monti, Parini, Foscolo, Porta, Pellico, Verri, and Beccaria. Although the literati and scholars lived a life of their own, entrenched in their houses with the gruffness of men not wishing to be disturbed, yet if one really wanted to and knew how to do it, there they were and one could get to see them. As Manzoni's son-in-law I found myself, naturally, in their midst. I knew them all, but I got on especially well with T. Grossi, with whom I had a close, lasting friendship until his, alas! premature death. I particularly wanted to show my novel to him and to Manzoni and ask their advice, but once again I was overtaken by nervous anxiety, this time literary rather than artistic. Still I had to make up my mind to be bold, and so I did. I revealed my secret and begged for patience, advice, and *not indulgence.* I wanted the naked truth. Better to be trounced by a couple of friends than by the public at large. I think both expected it to be worse than they thought it, to judge by their looks of rather surprised approval, when I read them the novel.

Manzoni said smiling: 'Literature's a strange trade; anyone takes it up from one day to the next! Look at Massimo: he feels an itch to write a novel and he really doesn't do half badly.'

This expert opinion gave me the courage of a lion. I set to work once more with renewed resolution, so much so that in 1833 I could undertake publication. Thinking it over now I am sure I was exceedingly impertinent, as a newcomer who had never done or written a thing, to have come in among all these pundits with my little tale and published it without a qualm. But things turned out well and that excuses it all.

At that time there was a printing office in Via San Pietro all' Orto run by a man called Ferrario, a big, fat fellow. He was an old Jacobin dating from the Cisalpine Republic, of good reputation; so much so that at the time of Franco-Italian depredations he had been held blameless in the matter of a difficult mission on which he had been sent by the government to mop up the famous treasure of the Loreto Madonna.

As no one had offered me a penny for my manuscript, I had to put my hand into my own pocket if I wanted to publish. This excellent man took the responsibility of printing, asking only to be reimbursed for his outgoings; anything over and above this was to be mine. I could very easily have lost my labour and my money; but it turned out reasonably well and I made 5,000 *francs* profit from *Ettore Fieramosca*. I don't want to boast, but had I been able to take one per cent. of what others have gained from the book, I should have been able to keep a carriage. And though all things in the world are vanity, as Solomon said, he did exclude this from his anathema, probably owing to the fact that he was an old man, as I am now.

The day I took my parcel of manuscript to San Pietro all' Orto, I was full of trepidation, worse than before. As the poet Berni says:

> Having found
> A man who printed rather well
> I said: 'Print this and go to hell.'

However I suffered the worst nervous anxiety I ever experienced on the day the book was published. When I went out that morning and saw my respected name in large letters, stuck up at all the street corners, I thought I was dreaming. Here was really the case of the die being cast, and myself being sunk.

You can consider this great fear of the public as modesty; but I think, at bottom, it is nothing more than vanity. Of course, I am referring to sensible, intelligent people of discretion. With foolish men, vanity takes the form of an impertinent faith in themselves. Hence the many stupid things published here, which would present a curious picture of us throughout Europe; but for the fact that, luckily for us, Europe doesn't understand Italian. In our own affairs, the two extremes of vanity are equally harmful. In Parliament, for example, those who feel a *timid vanity* could speak out more boldly to the general advantage, and if those who show an *impertinent vanity* were not always raising their voices, discussions would be more cogent; they would take less time and things would get done quicker and better.

One could apply the same reasoning to other branches, journalism, literature, society, etc., etc. Unfortunately vanity is the weed that sucks the goodness from the soil of our political life. As it is a persistent plant which flourishes all the year round, it is not a bad thing to guard against it.

Timid vanity was terribly much in evidence in me on the day I published *Fieramosca*. I heard nothing for twenty-four hours. A whole day is necessary for even the keenest readers to form their opinion about a book. The following day, directly I went out, I ran into a friend of mine, young then, now a middle-aged man, who has never guessed the fatal blow he dealt me, without in the least intending to. I met him in Piazza San Fedele where he lived. After we had greeted each other, he said: 'Well! well! So you've published a novel? Splendid!' Then, quite uninterested, he went on to talk of quite different things. I felt that I had been drained of my life-blood and thought: 'Mercy! Help! Serves me right! They're not even talking about *Fieramosca*.' It seemed impossible that my friend, who was a member of a large family, connected with all the rich, aristocratic people of the city, would not have heard something about it if it had been mentioned. As he was an excellent young man and a friend, it seemed equally impossible that, had there been mention, he would not have told me. So it was a fiasco, the worst possible sort of fiasco: silence! I left him with a bitter taste in my mouth and I don't know where I went. It wasn't long, however, before I felt very much better.

Fieramosca had such an enormous success that I was simply amazed. I could really say: *'Je n'aurais jamais cru être si fort savant.'* The success kept on growing more and more. It spread from the newspapers to the male half of society and then to the female; it reached the studios and penetrated behind the scenes of the theatres. I was the *vade-mecum* of prima donnas and tenors, the hidden joy of schoolgirls; I took up my abode under the mattresses of seminarists and I was read by the cadets of the military academies. My highest peak was to be compared in certain newspapers to Manzoni himself. Needless to say, such an idea could only have occurred to people who understood nothing about it. Those who did, did not make such howlers. It would be like confusing a Cesare da Sesto with a Raphael.

To sum up, it was a howling success. Did I deserve it or not? Here a curious question arises about the fate of books, which is often the least understandable and the most anomalous of proceedings. On the whole, in speaking, for example, of *Guerrin meschino, Paris e Vienna, Colo-andro fedele,* the *Reali di Francia, Bertoldo,* one says: Trash! Certainly trash; but, from time immemorable, they have persisted, first in manu-script, then printed, reprinted, and they keep on being printed. So they must have appealed to men's hearts and minds; they must have some merit. You can say it is not a literary merit and perhaps you are right. But, I ask you, what is the purpose of literature? In certain countries, at certain periods, it has no purpose or fulfils an evil one. What should the purpose be? A great and good one. Therefore, a literary work, even should it be worth little from the artistic point of view, can be worth a great deal from another. As long as it serves a useful purpose, it will have a value of another kind and cannot be considered quite worthless.

If one considers the matter like this, I believe that *Fieramosca* has real merit. Let's forget modesty once again!

My aim and object was to initiate a slow work of regeneration of the national character. I only wanted to rouse lofty, noble sentiments in Italian hearts. If all the literati of the whole world had agreed to condemn me according to the rules, it didn't matter to me a jot, provided that, without rules, I could succeed in inspiring one single person. I will add this: Who can say what moves, and continues to move, people is against the rules? It may be against some of them and consistent with others; and the rules which appeal to the heart and animate the mind do not seem to me to be the worst.

I have always found it interesting and instructive to analyse success and popularity and the reasons for them. To work on men in order to guide them towards the good is the highest object of all, higher than wanting to be the first writer or poet in the world. The best of studies is, therefore, to discover what moves and persuades men most. This discovery can be made by observing the most ordinary people. I have often heard peasants telling some tale of woe, some poor mother speaking of the idleness of a son, or perhaps his goodness towards her, and I have felt deeply moved. Even from the cheapjacks in the streets, there is something to be learnt. Not everyone knows how to hold the attention of an audience of one or two hundred for several hours. If they don't move away, there must be a reason, and it would be interesting to discover what it is. I don't want to overdo these considerations, and I leave it to the reader's curiosity to follow them up. I only say that in Milanese literary circles of the day, they were debating whether the historical novel was an acceptable literary genre. I had brought out *Fieramosca*; a few years before, Manzoni had published his *Promessi Sposi*, one of the best books ever conceived by the human mind. Meanwhile T. Grossi was writing *Marco Visconti*. The question was a burning one therefore. Manzoni was induced to settle the question against us and himself, with arguments of such good sense and good taste that they were difficult to contradict. But I said that my object was to galvanize my characters into life and, if I can succeed in doing so in the framework of the historical novel, what does it matter to me if it is not in accordance with the rules? No one understood and accepted this argument more than Manzoni.

In conclusion, I claim that *Fieramosca* had something that could serve a useful purpose at the time and this suffices.

I do not wish to omit a few facts about how it passed the censor, sufficiently interesting and odd to those who have never had to come to grips with the strange creature. The problem to be settled was just this. Admitting the fact of an Austrian censorship, one wanted to publish a book written with the object of inciting the Italians to attack the foreigner. Was this a trifling difficulty?

The censor was a good Christian soul without malice, an excellent individual, fat, heavy and therefore averse to hard work. He was, as a censor, a real treasure. His name was the Abbé Bellisomi. I started on him patiently, studying his likes and dislikes, and his usual habits. I became friendly with his servant girl and got information through her as to whether he had slept, dined, digested well; whether he was in a good or a bad mood, etc., etc. All this was in order to choose the right moment to come and discuss controversial passages, explain them, soften them without altering them, and so on. I had to use all the theological and cardinal virtues to keep on a level keel, and not lose my patience and spoil everything. By the help of God, I carried away the *Imprimatur* up to the very last page, and on leaving the house I said: 'Now it's up to you to excuse yourself in Vienna.' In fact Vienna understood the book perfectly and took it damnably seriously. Poor Bellisomi got a terrible wigging, and not only from the government side. He also got into trouble with the bigots on account of the letter from Alexander VI to Cesare Borgia. In his defence he pleaded: 'It is a question of a historical document, how can you wish to prohibit it?'

The good Bellisomi didn't know that I myself had written the historical document. I must confess I was not a little proud of his error. What happened was that he left, or was removed from, his post. The book ran up and down Italy. Catch it if you can!

13

THE very favourable reception of my novel was likely to have the immediate result of inciting me to write another, and this is precisely what happened. As I said before, I had struck up a close friendship with Grossi. Our characters and dispositions went well together. He encouraged me to undertake my new book. Everything now proceeded on velvet, and I went at it with a quite different self-confidence from when I still had to make up my mind about myself and my public.

Having decided to do it, I began to search for a subject, which, of course, had to be in the spirit of Italian liberalism. One had, however, always to keep the Austrian censorship in mind.

Before continuing, I must say a few words about Grossi, that rare friend of mine, whose loss none of his circle, and I least of all, have been able to get over. I say nothing about his works and literary merit. The former are well known; the latter is rated high as it should be and cannot be dimmed. I will speak of the man, who was worth more than his poetry, however excellent it is. Tommaso Grossi came from Bellano, a large and lovely village on the banks of Lake Como at the entrance to the Val Sàssina. He was born of honest but poor parents. An uncle who was the parish priest of Treviglio, a jansenist of the school of Tamburini, took an interest in him, supported him at school in Milan and afterwards at the University of Pavia. It was there that he began to write poetry. All good men, of course, do likewise in adolescence, but noodles, destined to turn out engineers, clerks, and apothecaries rather than poets, get over their poetic rash by producing an ode to the nymph Phyllis, lacrimose cogitations on the moon, or blank verse epistles to a friend, informing him that mankind is corrupt; in fact they cook up stale stuff for the millionth time. Grossi, however, who had a spirited, enterprising, realistic nature, chose subjects he could see, touch, and feel. He clothed them with his own discriminating ideas and, from the start, proved to be original, himself, a man who would go far. There was a professor of law at Pavia, a very odd person who gave eccentric lectures, partly in Italian, partly in dialect, partly in Latin, at which everyone laughed. Grossi put him into verse, so realistically and so true to life that the poem was a real gem.

I don't know how old he was exactly when he was sent to the Oblate school, near Lecco. It was a rough and ready, almost brutal, education of little Latin and poor food, with beating to enforce discipline. Grossi's nature, which was ardent and impetuous, was here somewhat embittered and he was always fighting with his companions. He was, however, of slender build and had more courage than strength, so that it is inconceivable what knocks he had to take. His skull had to be seen to be believed; there were scars and cuts all over it. Finally, having had enough of these Oblates, whom he never afterwards forgave, he ran away one day with a fellow pupil, and they heard nothing more of them until, quite a long time afterwards, they were discovered at Magenta.

He told me a curious tale, which proves how greatly he loved his schoolmasters. It was during the time when the French, no longer led by Bonaparte, were in retreat, pursued by the Austrians and Souvaroff's Russians.

One summer afternoon [he told me] we were in the class-rooms facing the cloisters of the entrance courtyard. All of a sudden there was a noise at the main gate, which was opened, and in burst a whole troop of Cossacks on their rough little horses, all lances and beards. They spread over the grass of the quadrangle. We were simply delighted at the novelty. Lessons stopped, and then I simply can't tell you what pleasure, joy, delirium it was to see the self-assured, overbearing faces of our tyrants turn pale, become confused and conciliatory, and adopt an almost deprecatory mien towards those barbarians. They feared they would at any moment blow up the college, the friars, and the boys as well. The Cossacks themselves seemed decent people. They found us an odd assortment, and they laughed and strolled about and enjoyed a good meal, which fear produced for them and which was better than what we got. When I saw the terror of one of the Oblates, whom I particularly hated [said Grossi] I thought we might make the most of the opportunity. I took hold of the hem of the coat of one of those great bearded fellows. While I pointed out my Oblate with the left hand, I made urgent signs with the other to indicate that I should like him well and truly beaten. The Cossack split his sides with laughing but, to my great sorrow, left the friar alone.[1]

[1] Massimo d'Azeglio's death cut short his Memoirs at this point (tr.).

Y

POSTHUMOUS ADDITION
authenticated by d'Azeglio's daughter[1]

I WENT to visit my good friend Michelangelo and we soon agreed to go on an expedition to Fiumicino. I knew the steamer left in the morning: I packed my bag and a couple of hours before daylight my friend and I had arrived at the Ripa Grande. I thought it odd that the steamer left at such an unusual hour, which must have scared more than one passenger, especially female passengers. When I got to the Ripa I saw that the company had not gone out of its way to make things convenient.

As the moon was on the wane, in its last quarter, it only gave a gleam of light and the river was in darkness. 'Where is this boat?' I asked one of the crew. 'Over there,' he replied. 'Where is over there?' 'In the middle of the river.' 'How do you get aboard?' 'Why, here.' The 'here' was a narrow plank, twenty foot long, which led to a coal barge. From this there was a similar plank to the steamer. Both planks were as springy as elastic. This was the facility offered to passengers. I, who am famous for getting giddy, had to get the sailor to go first, hold on to his shoulders, and pray God to keep him straight. Luckily my prayer was heard and, step by step, we got aboard. Two hours after sunrise we were at Fiumicino.

Fiumicino is a row of houses stretching along the right bank of the Tiber, which is there confined and controlled within embankments so that boats can find bottom. Near the sea is a big old watch tower, one of those which guarded the coast against Barbary pirates. The shore is low, in parts covered by woods, in part by dwarf scrub or meadows. It is a district more or less similar to all the *maremma* (marsh-land) from Pietrasanta to Terracina. The air is good in March and the passage of the quails attracts sportsmen and sportswomen. The first want quails, the second amusement. And with the good will Roman ladies never fail to show in the pursuit, even at Fiumicino they find their diversions. They go boating, riding, driving, fishing, shopping; they organize dinner-parties, suppers, dances, gambling. All this variety of occupation is based on the inevitable sport of love-making.

[1] See p. xi. The material that follows is taken from the Feltrinelli Edition, 1963, pp. 514-49.

Altogether, the country holiday turns out animated, lively, and pleasant; of course for those who have no need of good fare, a good bed, and a good lodging to be happy.

It must be said that when Romans of both sexes are born into the world, they bring with them the firm intention of being happy; and they succeed, despite their government, which seems resolved on precisely the opposite.

This optimism, or heedlessness, is perhaps the most attractive quality of that group of people, who often have no home, no shelter, no means, no certainty of anything for the morrow; yet they sing, laugh, and enjoy themselves. They're always on the go, and after all reach the end of the year just as well as careful people. They benefit by never worrying and they never die of the spleen like the English. Poor Romans! God knows what makes them so thoughtless; were they not so, they would indeed be in a bad way.

I spent a month with these people. There I found Peppe Sartori, Nanna, and Checchina. I spent my time with them, and by their aid and my own I got along. But I was still not cured of my spiritual malady.

I had a picture to do for Paolo Datta. I only got forty *écus*, but in times of scarcity, oaten bread must do. I painted it. It wasn't bad.

At that period I came across a man whom I thought worth studying. As I have always thought it worth while to study men rather than books, I wanted to get to know him. He was the butcher of Fiumicino, a celebrated anti-liberal, about whom they told a tale of some mad prank in the Ghetto. I wanted to hear it at first hand.

At the café one evening, where nearly everyone forgathered, I had him pointed out. I attacked him on the side by which all men, great or small, are vulnerable—his vanity—something which is part and parcel of the human creature. Soon I had him seated at a table with a brimming half-litre glass before him, in the most expansive condition you could want.

I had already given him to understand that I considered him a celebrity, and following this line I said: 'Sor Pietro, I hear that when you were young you were pretty hot-blooded—and I have heard tell of something that happened in the Ghetto when you had it out with the Jews. How was it?'

'What is it you want to know? Certainly, there was a bit of a bother. You know, I was the shop-boy of the butcher at the corner going to Trinità de' Pellegrini.'

'Yes, I know.'

'Well, one day I was taking meat into the Ghetto. There had been some talk before then: the Jew who comes to inspect how the animal is killed must have had a bribe from some other butcher and wanted them to change shops. If it was beef he would say the animal had died of some disease; if it was buffalo meat he would say that we had included the hind quarters; in fact he was making trouble. One morning after I had gone into the Ghetto with the meat, I was walking down a street when one Jew after the other came up to me, with complaints, calling me a little rascal, until finally one of them boxed my ears. Just imagine! Slapping me, Sor Pietro! I didn't wait for more; I took hold of the big butcher's knife and I laid about me, and those to whom it was coming, got it! I was as good as a regiment. They all took to their heels and I after them. One, I remember, ran down into a cellar and he got a thrust right under his trouser belt. I was really furious. After a bit, I saw that there was a crowd of about two hundred round me, but this didn't worry me much. However, I thought I saw the police squad coming, so I nipped off in the opposite direction and in a couple of shakes I was at home. My mother saw me coming in like a wild animal and said: "What have you done, my son?" I replied: "I don't know what I've done, but it's something big." Without further ado she gave me eight *paoli* she had with her. I changed my clothes, took a flannel waistcoat and the knife, and out by the San Giovanni gate I went and cut across country; before dark I was in Pantano di Borghese. I should just like to see the Chief of Police get me from there!' etc., etc.

It must be said that, though the immunity of the Roman Princes has ceased according to law, it exists in practice. At least it existed at the time Master Pietro, following in the steps of Samson, but minus the jawbone of an ass, without being aware of it, took revenge on behalf of the Philistines.

I have forgotten the end of his adventure, as it is so similar to all similar tales. That is to say, find a protector, stay quiet until the thing blows over, and then reappear one day, and he who has had the dirty end of the stick must keep it.

After a short time, Fiumicino having begun to bore me and feeling more cheerful, I packed my bag, and went back to Rome. I found my little lodgings on the Corso free. I found my landlady, Signora Angelina, still more faithful portrait of Alcina, the witch described by Ariosto, after Melissa, with a magic ring, had showed her as she was to Ruggero. I took up my humdrum life once more, but soon saw it wasn't going to work.

I felt the need of some major activity of brain and heart. But where should I find it?

Fate provided. I soon had more than I had bargained for. During the winter I had made the acquaintance, in the Paris's house, of a Signora Clelia Piermarini, once, for many years, lady-in-waiting to Christina of Spain in Madrid. Ill-treated and then deserted by her husband, and dismissed from the Queen's household owing to palace intrigue, she had remained without support with two grown-up daughters to maintain. She was typically Italian, good, expansive, imaginative, always ready to believe everyone honest and true. In politics it was 'Kill the tyrant, out with the barbarians, free the people' and so on, without bothering to find out how this could be made possible.

By degrees I had got friendly with Clelia and her daughters, who were really excellent people and as unfortunate as they were good. At their house, where all the keen pro-Italians were received with open arms, whether mad or not, rascals or not, I had got to know a number of them. Among the rest, two seemed to me to be practical men: Adolfo S. from Pesaro and Filippo A. from Cesena. I had come to an understanding with them. They showed me much kindness. The former had a brother in prison because of the events of 1832, if I am not mistaken. By the grace of God he was finally liberated and they went back home together.

The latter told me one day he wanted to have a long, serious talk with me, and it was fixed for the next evening in Clelia's house. I understood that it was a political matter, so I went prepared as I did not then know Filippo for the great gentleman he was.

After we had met and sat down, I began as follows:

'Signor Filippo, I must tell you I have suffered for many years from a chronic pain under the ribs on my left side, accompanied by difficulty in breathing, and sometimes by palpitations; as you are a doctor I should like to consult you. Will you feel my pulse, examine me, feel me, and then give me your opinion?'

It was true that I had periodically suffered in this way; but I had never thought it serious and had treated it as a nervous disability of little moment.

Filippo, who had other things on his mind, paid scant attention to what I was saying and felt my pulse in a half-hearted way. I then burst out laughing and, taking away my hand, I went on: 'Let's take the consultation as over for the moment; but as you, a Papal subject, could be taken and subjected to an interrogation, rather than I, please remember, in such an event, that our meeting this evening in a private room of Clelia's house has been to enable me to consult you about my pain, and that you have judged it to be a purely nervous symptom and told me I shouldn't take it seriously and that after the consultation we parted without further talk.'

Here I will make the observation that, of all the evil effects produced on the characters of those living under governments such as the Papal, perhaps the worst of all is that of extinguishing sincerity in their hearts and making duplicity and simulation a necessary condition of life; forcing those who don't want to run the risk of imprisonment at any moment to make a system of deceit.

Filippo smiled and then began to talk of what was of greater concern to him. As I am not able to remember his exact words, I will repeat the substance of his remarks. He said that Pope Gregory was failing and couldn't last long; that, as I knew, Romagna was tottering; that level-headed people had all they could do to hold back the population from breaking out in one of the usual Mazzinian revolts, which were always idiotic and always fatal; that one must seriously think of what would happen at the death of the Pope, and try to prepare people's minds for the event; that influential people should use all their authority to persuade the populace against innovations, even at the Pope's death; that the usual revolutionary violence would only lead to Austrian intervention, with prison, exile, and death for many and the worsening of the conditions of all.

He then added: 'All sensible people in Romagna are tired of secret societies, Carbonari plots, and Giovine Italia plots, and are convinced that all they achieve is to send poor young men into exile or to the gallows.'

'Do you mean to say there are no more secret societies in Romagna?'

'They hardly exist among the common people and they are not functioning; anyone with a grain of sense laughs at them. Now many of the most influential people have had the idea that, it being of the greatest importance to forestall the troubles that will surely break out on the death of Pope Gregory, there is need of a new man, not stale as they are, a man who would inspire faith and try to bring to a point, lead, and restrain, if necessary, the many longings and ideas now undisciplined and contradictory; and they think, my dear Signor Azeglio, that you are the man!'

I so little expected this nomination as general in command of the more or less moribund secret societies of the Papal State—all the stranger because, as was well known, I had not only belonged to none of them, but had never even met anyone who had thought I looked enough of a conspirator to ask me to join—that all I could say was: 'I?' in amazement.

'Certainly! You are considered to be a man of integrity by all, and no one suspects you.' He then added the short panegyric usual in such cases and I too replied with broken words and an expression on my face meaning *Domine, non sum dignus*. After a moment's reflection I said:

'But I am not, and never was, a Carbonaro or a Calderaro or anything of the sort. I don't agree with any of the ideas of the Giovine Italia, except that of independence for Italy. I don't hold with plots and the sort of up-risings you people of Romagna indulge in from time to time. Do you really think it is possible that they would pay any attention to me when I speak in a language none of them understand?'

'The fact that you are not a sectarian is all to the good, and, as I told you, nearly everyone has given up that tomfoolery. The fact that you hold views opposed to those of Mazzini will be all the more effective on minds tired of what has happened and uncertain of what is to come.'

So, from one thing to another, he kept on pressing the suggestion of the prominent liberals in the Papal State, that I should take over the leadership of the party, and in the first place that they should meet me and get to know me personally.

At first sight, the thing did not displease me. Not that I could see any basis in it for helping Italy; but because I felt the need for something to do which would fully occupy my mind and expel my tormenting thoughts. It seemed I could not find a better for the purpose. Nevertheless, following my usual laudable practice of always taking time to think, I said to Filippo:

'I have understood you, and I do not see overwhelming obstacles, but I must have time to think it over and I will then tell you what I think.'

So the thing rested and we parted.

I thought it all over during the next few days from all angles.

Now it seemed the start of something important; now a mere escapade; now a method to get to know Italy and Italians better; now something to get involved in and then end in prison and nothing useful done. Actually I think it was a mixture of all these things.

Finally I decided to do it, for several reasons. The principal one was the desire, I should say the sense of duty, which prompted me to leave nothing possible undone to prevent the disorders which, without any doubt, would break out on Pope Gregory's death, to the detriment of Italy and the Italians and to the sole and certain advantage of Austria. Then came the other reason, that of having the chance of curing myself of melancholy, and finally my taste for a life of adventure and action.

When I met Filippo after a few days I told him I was disposed to try it.

At that period of my life I had got to know, how I do not recall, an individual from Umbria who was half man of letters, half politician. He was one of those candid, credulous people of whom Italy is full. As he was leaving for his village near Spoleto, it was decided that we should go so far together.

One September morning (the first or second, if I am not mistaken), we started out through the Porta del Popolo, driven by one of those *vetturini* from the Marches, who alone maintain the true poetical traditions of travel, now destined to be swept away in the general corrupting influence of the railways. It is true that the Papal Government has so far saved itself from, at least, this form of corruption; and it is likely, I think, to continue to do so. It will be a great attraction which will cause all those in Europe with poetical natures to visit Rome.

Antonio had a couple of those horses which, from their looks, seem hardly likely to move their legs, but in practice keep going all day like demons. The same with his vehicle; it looked like a split open corn-cob. On the way to the Porta del Popolo it went all lop-sided with a noise on the cobbles like a barrow of old iron, yet it did the whole journey like an arrow, as tight as a drum. This sort of carriage is called, for some reason, a 'Sant' Antonio', in the Papal States.

Out we went gaily by the Porta del Popolo; Antonio cracking his whip and Pompili, my Umbrian companion, and I arranging ourselves so as to have all the little conveniences of carriage life handy.

Pompili was in the great secret of the reason for my reconnaissance. When we had begun to discuss things, I soon saw that I had a test case with me, whom I could try to convince in the far from easy business (so I then thought) which awaited me along the road. 'I can judge the whole lot from this sample,' I thought. 'I shall have a difficult job.'

I thereupon began to follow with him the plan I had formed for all future interviews with the liberals who awaited me.

This plan was twofold. The first thing was to destroy the old ideas; the second to propose new ones, in regard both to the general Italian situation and to the special conditions of the Papal State.

The arguments against the system of secret societies, plots, street-risings, etc. have been so often repeated that it serves no useful purpose to discuss them: therefore the destructive first part was not difficult, and everyone can imagine the reasons I was to give.

The constructive part was a thornier problem.

As long as one says to a people suffering in all possible ways the spiritual and physical tortures of the worst of all known governments: 'The way you have hitherto taken cannot lead to any good', you can, more or less, get them to see reason. But when you reach the point of what is to be done; when they ask you to show them the best thing to do, and you are forced to reply: 'For the present, do nothing', or 'What you must do, is to sit tight', then they may easily send you to the devil. To speak the truth, if those who suffer and are reaching breaking-point do send you to the devil, it is excusable.

It is true that it was not my idea that nothing should be done; but the man who does not look far ahead, who must sow in the morning and reap before night, does not take kindly to being told that some things, especially in politics, cannot succeed without being long prepared by influences whose connexion with the results is not sufficiently apparent to be grasped by those without some intelligence, education, and the habit of reflection.

However it was clear that I could not exert any beneficial influence unless I could succeed in getting this truth into their minds. I therefore started to put my plan into effect, in the first place, with my travelling companion, chiefly making use of similes anyone could understand. I have always noticed that there is nothing which persuades the average mind more than a well-chosen simile.

I therefore said to my ingenuous friend: 'Let us speak clearly. What do you people want, and I too? Do you want to turn the Austrians out of Italy, and priestly government out of your own house? If you ask them to go, they will probably say no. It is therefore necessary to force them to go; to force people you need force; and where is yours?— If you haven't got it, you must find someone who has. Who has any in Italy? Even some? Piedmont: because at least she leads an independent life; she has money in reserve (she had then), an army, a navy, etc.'

At the word 'Piedmont', the man to whom I was speaking made a grimace (during my whole journey every single one of them did the same), and added ironically: 'Do you mean we should pin our hopes to Carlo Alberto?'

'If you don't want to hope, give up hope; but you must reconcile yourselves to hope in no one else.'

'What about 1821, 1832?'

'I don't like '21 and '32 any more than you do—although there is something to be said about what happened then—but I will admit the very worst construction you can put on those events, and I repeat that you must hope in him or no one. In any case let us consider the thing dispassionately and discuss it. If we asked Carlo Alberto to take on something against his interests, out of pure heroism, to benefit Italy, you, all of us, you could say to me: "What, you put trust in the traitor of '21, the executioner of '32!" And you might be right. But what is it that we are really asking him to do? To benefit us, it is true, but to benefit himself far more. We ask him, at the right moment, to let us help him to become greater and more powerful than he is now; do you think that there is any doubt, that he will not agree with you?' Here I added a very irreverent comparison, but I was jogging along between villages, miles away from Courts, and I did not reckon myself a courtier in any case; I said: 'If you invite a thief to become an honest man and he promises to reform, you can have doubts whether he will maintain his word; but if you invite a thief to steal, I do not see that you need fear he will let you down.'

Poor Carlo Alberto! Time has proved that he did not deserve to be judged so harshly; and when I remember my comparison I feel a twinge of conscience. But this is what happens to a ruler who doesn't follow the straight path, one who thinks he can make use of cleverness to his advantage! Poor Carlo Alberto, who thought he was cunning!

The good Pompili gradually agreed with what I was saying; but I spoke longer and with greater detail than I give here. He thought that the situation might be as I described. But at this point he, as all the others invariably did, wanted me to tell him when they could hope that something would be settled. Then another difficulty arose, that of inducing patience in those who are suffering; the greatest and most natural of difficulties, as I have already said. It was necessary to bring home the fact that, without some great European event, it was impossible, as things were, for Italy to be able to take action and for Carlo Alberto to help her. 'And when will this European event take place?'

'You must ask the Lord,' I replied.

Who would have said then, in 1845, that the good Lord had decided that this event, the greatest convulsion of peoples known to history, was to take place only three years later?

As for me, no prophet, I confess I did not expect to see it before my death. But the curious coincidence between my words and the events of '48 played a large part in the influence I had in Italy for some time afterwards.

Talking like this, we were put down at sunset by our Antonio at the village of Baccano. A fine place to spend a night! In the heart of the malarial district, at the worst season of the year. It was necessary to make a virtue of necessity, so I was prepared to stay awake. In September in those low-lying parts, even the toads get malaria.

I never fully understood so well before that evening the sonnet Alfieri wrote when he too stayed there in the :

> Vast unhealthy tract that calls itself a State,
> A place of bare, uncultivated fields.

There were a few groups of dirty, smoke-begrimed hovels falling to pieces, on both sides of the main road. The walls, roofs, and window-shutters were peeling; this was Baccano, a real picture of desolation.

No one lives there but the postmaster, his men, their families, and the inn-keeper. All their faces were yellow, tragic, evil. They were people debased by bad government, by malaria, by poverty and the coming and going of foreigners. It was a physical and moral slough.

I went into the kitchen, which also served as the inn parlour, and seated myself by the fire. I meant to add a page to my book of jottings about the animals of the human species, and luck would have it that I had come to a place where I was sure to find some specimens. I could not let such an opportunity slip, for they don't come every day.

There were postilions, cow-hands, and country people. I began, as usual, to start a conversation. Although I might be held to represent the aristocracy of that select society, my method of travel gave me a status which, though high, yet couldn't be considered beyond the reach of those I was talking to.

Two things remain stuck in my mind about the evening I spent talking to a postilion of Baccano, who had especially attached himself to my company. We took supper together, drank, and smoked. One was the really monstrous size of the mosquitos of that fortunate spot; the other was the total lack of any idea, of any inkling, of honesty to be discovered in my tavern companion. He told me with such candour about the various ways he swindled foreigners of a few *paoli,* that it was really impossible to consider him a rogue, even in my heart. Instead of this I mentally reeled off a series of objurgations against the government, the system, the priests, etc., and still more confirmed myself in the belief that the criteria of right and wrong have been completely lost, extinguished, dead and buried in the happy Papal dominions.

In fact the whole administration is nothing but a great society of thieves. How the devil could one presume that my postilion shouldn't rob when he got the chance, and still more not believe that honesty really consists in the frank avowal of dishonesty?

I dragged out the evening as well as I could, so as not to be tempted to fall asleep. Finally, however, now one, now the other vanished; the fire went out and I had to let the host retire. I went upstairs to a room with two beds, in one of which lay Pompili. I threw myself down on the other and we continued chatting as long as we could, until finally sleep overcame us both, and—fever or no fever—we fell asleep. We got away with it and did not catch fever.

I almost persuade myself that, having once had malarial fever very badly, my constitution, being very sound, if not robust, is immune. For I have several times slept in malarial districts with impunity.

Hardly had day come when Antonio put in his nimble steeds and away we went at full speed for Sette Vene, Monterosi, Nepi, Civita, and Otricoli.

Here we stopped for refreshment. I passed my time talking with the hotel waiter and led the subject to the revolution of '31 when Zucchi's bands had got as far as Otricoli.

'Who knows what damned rascals (I said to the waiter) they must have been and how much they made you suffer in the town here!' 'No sir!' he replied. 'To tell you the truth they were excellent young men and no one had any complaints against them.'

The waiter, replying in this way to an unknown stranger, showed more civil courage than I did, who had spoken in a very pro-government way to test the ground.

In this way, and I did so whenever I had the opportunity, I tried to get a true idea of public opinion in all the places we passed through. There is no other way to get to know the material in which one has to work. Those who decide the fate of mortals should really take the trouble of finding out at least what they would like and what their troubles and needs are.

By dark we were at Terni. This is where my trip (or rather my *via crucis*) started. Here is the reason.

The line of communication between the liberal elements in the State had originally been organized for the use of the secret societies; then when these had dwindled and almost vanished, it had remained as a great network spanning the country from end to end. In every village there was a trusted man who formed one link in the chain; this chain was known as the 'Trafila'. It was used for sending news, warnings, instructions, letters; sometimes persons such as fugitives, political commercial travellers, etc., etc. In fact one used the phrase 'to send something or somebody or other by Trafila'. At Terni, however, it went no farther in the direction of Rome, but entered the Kingdom of Naples over the Abruzzi mountains.

In those days Rome and its territory, maritime and rural, although containing isolated individuals concerned in political intrigues, did not have enough to warrant the honour and expense of the Trafila. One can see from this that the provinces held Rome and its neighbourhood in scant respect, nor would they have trusted the Romans much.

One single link of the Trafila, who turned traitor, would have brought disaster to a great many people. It is a notable fact that, during the many years that the mortal struggle between the Pope and his subjects lasted, never, never did the Roman police get to know of a single link in the great chain, and not one found his way into prison.

Poor Italian stock! How much virtue there still is in it, after all it has suffered from so many persecutors!

It was at Terni, therefore, that I picked up the first link of the Trafila.

After Pompili and I had brushed off the dust of travel and had a bite of supper, we went out late at night and, not without some difficulty, traced our man.

As we live in curious times and, as long as certain governments and certain police forces are still in existence, it is not a good thing to take liberties in writing, I will not give any slightest indication that could serve to identify this, or any other, member of the Trafila.

I shall content myself by saying that, where I had expected to find almost insuperable obstacles owing to angry political passions, ignorance, or shortness of view, I found in this first contact, as with all later ones, every imaginable facility in getting my ideas and their corollaries accepted.

I found all persuaded that the Giovine Italia was madness; secret societies, madness; the little aimless revolutions such as previous ones, madness. They thought it was necessary to adopt other measures. Those I proposed were at first received with grimaces, but soon, persuaded of the necessity that nothing could be done without force and not having it, they had to look for it from those who had, they ended up, after a good many contortions, in accepting the idea of Carlo Alberto. What clinched the matter was my famous impertinent simile of the thief, which seemed to each and all an unanswerable argument.

In all this unanimity of opinion I only found two exceptions, curiously enough in Tuscany; and still more curiously, in two men, one of whom is pre-eminent in every way, and recognized as such throughout Europe; the other, if not his equal, is distinguished for his

sentiments, intelligence, and culture; with a mind, however, occupied
with abstractions, as will later appear.

The first of these (neither had anything to do with the Trafila),
when I named Carlo Alberto, said: 'What? Carlo Alberto as leader of
the Italian liberals? Get along with you! . . .' He then changed the
subject.

The second exclaimed: 'That traitor!' I replied: 'In the first place
the title you give him can be disputed; but leave that on one side.
Traitor or no, he is the only man with the strength, money, ships,
soldiers. . . .'

Here he cut me short: 'The Roman soldiers,' he said, 'when they
discovered a certain General (I have forgotten which he mentioned) to
be a traitor, they killed him. What sort of soldiers are these of Carlo
Alberto who support him?'

I tried to excuse the poor Piedmontese soldiers for not having killed
Carlo Alberto, saying times had changed, customs were different, etc.,
etc. All to no purpose. That cursed Roman legion, with its expedient
of killing its commander, routed me too, and I had to leave without
having got anything useful from this worthy gentleman.

Next day the trusty Antonio, cracking his whip, drove us in the cool
of the morning through Strettura and Somma to Lombard Spoleto.
We recalled that the Spoletans came out against Barbarossa and all his
first-rate army, and were cut to pieces as was bound to happen.
I thought that when a people feels like this, sooner or later, it will
conquer. Blood may be lost, but not the example.

Pompili came from a village a few miles outside the city. He could
therefore consider his journey over. I stopped in the upper city, visited
the ducal castle and the great aqueduct, the work of Cardinal Egidio
Albornoz, and then we met for dinner.

He had been visiting his friends. I knew he had an old flame in
Spoleto, and I said a few jesting words to him on the visit I presumed
he had paid to her. He replied seriously, almost tragically: 'Now is
the time to think of one's country, not of women. I saw her indeed,
but we did not speak of love, but of our common hopes.'

I know this is trifling, but I record it with pleasure, because, as I
noted on a thousand occasions between '45 and '48, it was a striking
thing how the first, magnificent Italian movement, the first reasonably
based hopes of independence and national honour, had suddenly
roused fine, generous sentiments in all hearts; of which I, who had
gone up and down Italy for so many years, had previously seen little
sign.

I mention this now, but I shall have occasion to return to the same subject again, for it is worth considering.

I took my leave of Pompili, who accompanied me to the bottom of the long city of Spoleto. It is easily recognized that it was once rich, populous, and flourishing; though now it is reduced to the state of all cities under priestly rule.

I entered my little carriage alone and Antonio and his nimble steeds flew me along the fine, level road to Fuligno.

On the way I arranged my thoughts and determined on my plans and the methods I must adopt on my pilgrimage so as not to compromise myself and others.

Here I will relate what I did successfully wherever I went.

My first precaution on leaving Rome was not to take a servant with me. I was thus certain of not having a spy. I took some painting equipment so that I could stop wherever I wanted, without rousing suspicion.

To every place I went, I had with me the one name of the person who was the Trafila representative, which had been given to me at the previous place. Having arrived and put up at a hotel, I never asked for anyone. I went out and, according to circumstances and the people I met, judging by looks, I made my inquiry, and I ended by discovering the man whom I was looking for.

I arrived at Fuligno with the name given to me at Terni, and soon found my man. After a day's stay and having to make for the Marches, I really had to visit Perugia so I made a trip there. I found Cavalieri, the celebrated professor and my old friend, with Serafinetta, one of my numerous cousins. I spent a very jolly evening with them. I didn't say a word about politics to Cavalieri. He held a government post and had never concerned himself with anything beyond science and art. I have always loathed traitors, at first or second-hand, and it never entered my head to implicate him in political matters, not even in an ordinary conversation about them.

The next day I returned to Fuligno and took leave of my friends there. That night I left for Colfiorito and the Marches. The trusty Antonio had asked permission to take another passenger; I had consented, so I was not alone.

About one o'clock a.m. I jumped into the carriage and began to arrange myself as comfortably as possible. I couldn't see who my companion was. Each of us settled down in his corner and there mused or slept, waiting for sunrise.

Dawn's rosy fingers at length drew back the veil which concealed my fellow-traveller. I saw the figure of what appeared to be a kind of college youth. He was lanky and yellow-complexioned, with the impertinent face of a young gentleman and a loud contralto voice. He was certainly leaving college and home for the first time. I could presume that from the newness of his kit and all the little things he had with him: presents, such as fond mamas and ancient aunts provide at the moment of parting, as a reminder of their advice and an addition to their last blessing. He had a new bag, a smart hat, something or other slung round his shoulders, all brand-new stuff. He even had a box of sweets (a kind of almond-paste such as nuns eat). The lad offered me some, which I refused. I had a feeling that we were not going to get on, and I did not want to be beholden to my future hypothetical foe.

We started to talk and, without being asked, he told me all about his affairs. After having finished his education in a Jesuit college he had obtained a post, and he was now proceeding to Ancona, where he was to join his corps. Good heavens! I thought, have I got hold of a budding Papal warrior!

He then told me that he had been enrolled as a cadet in the revenue corps. I therefore had to move him down a peg in my estimation.

As there was nothing better to do, I thought I would study this customs calf and see what he had learnt in college.

From one thing to another I drew him on to talk of politics. Do you know what he came out with? Nothing more or less than the belief that all those who wanted change were madmen, rogues, etc., etc. So far so good; it is an opinion like any other; but he added in a tone that raised his contralto to a treble squeak: 'Ah, the government is too lenient; heads, heads, that's what's wanted.'

At first I didn't understand this 'heads', so, reading my face, he assisted my tardy intelligence.

'Certainly, if the government cut off a few heads instead of being so mild, you would soon see that everything would settle down.'

'Well! Well! Well!' I thought. 'Who would have imagined that there was a Robespierre in this infant?' But I added to myself: 'We haven't parted company yet, my child! Before we do I shall pay you out, in one way or the other, for these "heads" of yours.' I was angry to see such venom in a youth and I was also surprised. I had been led to believe he was a creature of the Jesuits, but I recognized none of their mellifluous character in his policy of 'heads'.

The far from amiable intentions I was harbouring towards this undergraduate *coupe-tête* were confirmed by his dominating manner.

He acted as though the world had been invented for him and for his convenience alone.

My penal code, however, was less Draconian than his, and I had no intention of meting out capital punishment for the crimes I have mentioned. I only wanted to inflict a penance that would teach him a lesson; but however much I racked my brains, I couldn't think how to do it.

'Let's leave it,' I thought. 'We'll get on, and things will settle themselves. Opportunities are never lacking for those who recognize them and know how to exploit them.'

The opportunity did come; and very soon.

We got to Camerino at noon; it had clouded over and was drizzling. As we alighted the inn-keeper came towards me, beaming, and gave me a welcome fit for an old acquaintance. I had never seen him before, so I showed some surprise, and he, as though at fault, said: 'Excuse me, please, I mistook you for someone else.' He said no more, but most politely waited on me inside.

I imagine he must have known something about my journey and, thinking I was goodness knows what masonic big-wig, placed great reliance on my influence; hence the effusive welcome.

'When are we off?' I said to Antonio.

'At three o'clock.'

'Very well, be punctual, as I am always on the tick myself.'

The fledgling Robespierre also heard the time of leaving, and perhaps thinking I would feel worried if I did not see him at the inn, thought good to inform me that he would be taking lunch at the Jesuit convent.

'I don't envy you,' I thought, and went in. Meanwhile, the weather had thickened. A cold wind was blowing everywhere, and the rain came pouring down in squalls.

I ate very well. Before three, Antonio had already harnessed the horses and was ready waiting. He had to drive us to San Severino by evening, and he didn't want to be caught by darkness in that filthy weather. Punctually at three, I was in the carriage; but where was our young gentleman? The young gentleman was not to be seen.

I knew that Heaven had kindly handed me the disciplinary cane with which to punish the bouncing boy and teach him a little about life. I grasped it with the utmost pleasure.

After a couple of minutes I began to get impatient and protest to Antonio: 'I say, I was ready at the appointed time, and I'm not one to be kept waiting by that gentleman.'

z

Antonio looked in all directions and didn't know what to do. He asked where he could be and if he had been seen. I knew where he could be found, but perfidiously kept mum. After a little I said: 'Let's start slowly; we may meet him.'

Antonio obeyed and the jingle of the carriage bells announced our departure at walking pace. We went for about a hundred yards down the steep street of that precipitous city, when Antonio's conscience pricked him and he stopped, to stare about on all sides. Nothing!

Meanwhile, the wind was getting stronger, and I said: 'My dear Antonio, to keep the horses standing in this downpour won't do them any good, for they are still sweaty from this morning's run. Do as I say, it's nearly half past three; so much the worse for those who are unpunctual. Get on, if you want to reach San Severino this evening. There are plenty of horses at Camerino; he'll hire a trap, and will be along in no time.'

I know the drivers of the Marches through and through, and touched him in his most sensitive spot. It was, in fact, true enough; tired horses standing in a side wind soon begin to feel pain in their shoulders.

Antonio, now persuaded, gave another glance round for the look of the thing, shrugged his shoulder, mumbled some final remark between his teeth, and uttered the 'gee-up' which meant 'forward march' for the animals, and, for my victim, a good wetting and seven or eight *paoli* to be added to the cost of his journey to the Corps.

As the road was nearly all downhill, descending as it does from the Appenines to the Adriatic, we simply flew.

By the time the Angelus bell was tolling, I was already under the roof of the inn of San Severino.

There was a great hubbub there, owing to the crowd of strangers who had arrived for the fair at Loreto, which was taking place at that time.

As I did not feel like supper, I saved the hostess the trouble of attending to me; she had her hands full in any case. I did not need my room at once either, so I hung about in the kitchen, chatting with all and sundry and learning from my usual teacher, Man, who can be studied whatever the age, sex, or circumstances.

At least two hours passed, it was well into the night, and it was simply pouring with rain. Then came the sound of a trap stopping at the door, and in another moment our young gentleman stormed in. He first found Antonio and began to abuse him up and down; no longer in contralto but in a definite treble, such was his just wrath. Antonio, who did not feel greatly alarmed and knew he had a faithful ally in me, stood up to him very well. So much so that our gentleman came rushing into the kitchen, and came straight up to me with the expression of a young master who has been badly waited on by his servant. I gave him the kind of look which warns children that they had better stop it, and replied to his complaints as follows: 'Are you addressing me? Speak to the driver.' I then turned my back on him and took myself off. Seeing he would get nothing out of me, he went back to Antonio; but after some more storming, he could do no more than remove his luggage from the carriage, renounce our company, and leave us with his cordial malediction.

So next morning at sunrise I left for Loreto, very pleased at being once more on my own.

I found the place *en fête* for the fair. I visited the sanctuary and spent the whole day there. I started a conversation with an old café proprietor and began to get an idea of the place and its inhabitants. I'm sorry to say it was not a very favourable idea.

I have always noticed that towns and villages where there is a famous shrine are worth very little. In looking for the reason for this I have come to the following conclusions. It is because the people have for long been accustomed to live, not by labour which really deserves its reward, but rather by cozening the vast crowds who flock to the shrine. The mass of the inhabitants have little faith in the legend which maintains and fructifies their vineyard. They therefore grow accustomed to live in an atmosphere of constant pretence and not so much in idleness as in trickery, deceit, or worse, actively waging incessant war against the visitors. The small villages where there is a regular invasion of visitors are always the worst.

My café proprietor innocently deplored, not so much the falling off of devotion to the Holy House in general, but rather the scarcity of pilgrims who came with their cloak pockets well stuffed with good money. In fact the only people I saw were peasants, herdsmen, and Neapolitan hill-dwellers. My new friend would certainly not make much out of them.

Here I said farewell to Antonio, and having agreed to go to Ancona with another *vetturino,* I got into his carriage and there found a fine specimen of a Franciscan.

As these friars have the reputation of being rather liberal, perhaps owing to the tradition of their founder having come down to our time, I amused myself by cracking up the Papal Government to the skies. Finally his liberalism could stand no more and he said all the bad things about the government which it well deserves. So amusing myself in this way I got to Ancona.

Here, coming out of my inn room one morning, I found a gendarme standing by the door. As in those days they were my political foes— I had not yet fought side by side with them as I did in '48, and proud of it, seeing that they did so honourably at Vicenza and elsewhere—I imagined I was in for a visitation and perhaps a little walk in police company. I was, however, mistaken; he was on the look-out for somebody else and nothing more happened.

After Ancona, I pursued my way through the various cities of Romagna, with the usual stops, the usual discussions, and the usual facility in persuading people to my way of thinking. But as it is not possible to convince everybody, I had to persuade myself that one of the old-style outbreaks was imminent. Perhaps I succeeded in restricting it to a limited number of incorrigibles. Only a month afterwards a revolt broke out at Rimini and at the Fratte or Grotte, or whatever the place is called, and another parcel of poor youngsters was packed off to prison or exile, without any good coming of it.

Having gone round Romagna, through the Terra del Sole, Rocca San Casciano, and Dicomano, I crossed the Appenines and reached Florence. I only stayed for a short time in this city and in Tuscany. I visited the friend I mentioned with reference to the 'Roman legion' and his remark that the Piedmontese troops should have imitated their judicious example. Then, with a renewed appreciation of the level-headedness of certain good Italians, I left for Turin, via Genoa.

Now came the best of it: the moment had arrived to bell the cat; the bell was all ready, it only needed to be attached.

My role was not an easy one. I had received no mission from the King to undertake that journey and inquiry. The whole thing had been my idea. Whether I should be well received, or put ungraciously outside the door, entirely depended on what faith he had in me, and equally whether he considered it wise or not to reveal what he thought. I knew nothing of this.

I asked for an audience. It was granted at once, and this I took for a good augury. As was Charles Albert's practice, the audience took place at six o'clock in the morning. At the time fixed I entered the palace, all lit up and functioning, while the city still slept. My heart was beating. After a short wait in an antechamber, the equerry on duty opened the door for me and there I found myself in an audience chamber in the presence of the King. Carlo Alberto was standing up straight near a window; he replied to my bow with a courteous inclination of his head, and indicated that I should sit down on a chair in the embrasure of the great window. He sat opposite me.

At that time, the King was a mystery; and although his later conduct has been plainly intelligible, he will perhaps remain partly a mystery, even for history. At that time, the principal events of his life, those of '21 and '32, were certainly not in his favour: no one could reconcile his grand ideas for Italian independence with the Austrian marriages, his and his sister's; his inclination to aggrandize the House of Savoy with his courting of the Jesuits, or keeping round him such men as l'Escarena, La Margherita, etc.; his display of piety and his old-womanish penances with the loftiness of thought and firmness of character demanded by bold enterprises.

No one, therefore, trusted Carlo Alberto. A great evil for a ruler in his circumstances. Trying to keep the support of the two parties by guile, you end by losing that of both.

His very looks presented something inexplicable. He was very tall and slender, with a long, pale, habitually severe face. When he spoke, however, he had a sweet expression; his voice was charming, and his words were familiar and friendly. He exercised a real fascination on those to whom he spoke. I recall that when he began to talk to me about myself, whom he had not seen for some time, with a typical courtesy all his own, I had to struggle all the time not to be conquered by his winning ways and words, and I kept on repeating inwardly: 'Massimo, don't trust him.'

Poor gentleman! He had much that was good and noble in him; why would he believe in the use of guile?

In speaking politely of myself, he chanced to say: 'And where have you come from now?', which was a remark on which I could hang what I had to say. I did not let it slip, and I spoke as follows. If I do not repeat the actual words, I certainly give their sense.

'Your Majesty, I have been travelling through a great part of Italy, city by city; and the reason for my having asked to be admitted to your presence is precisely because, should your Majesty deign to permit it, I should like to give you an account of what I have found the present state of Italy to be, of what I have seen, and what I have said everywhere to men of all conditions with regard to political conditions.'

C.A.: 'Oh certainly! I shall be pleased to hear what you have to say.'

I: 'Your Majesty is not ignorant of all the unrest, plots, and little revolutions which have occurred since 1814. You are well aware of the influences which stimulate them; the discontent which promotes them; the foolishness of the leaders; the sad consequences resulting. The uselessness, indeed the harm, of such activities, which only serve to denude the country of its best men and exacerbate the foreign influence, has now struck the more intelligent people in Italy, and they want to discover a new path to take.

'Some months ago I was in Rome, where I have considered and discussed with others possible remedies for this sad state of affairs. Pope Gregory is old and failing; at his death, if not previously, something big will happen. Romagna will go up in flames and the inevitable result will follow: another Austrian intervention, another series of executions and banishments, a worsening of all the evils which oppress us. It is therefore a matter of urgency to find a way out.'

Here I told him at length of the disgust of all honest, sensible men at the Mazzinian foolishness and wickedness; of the suggestion made that I should start to do something or other to try to give a new and better direction to the people's activities; of the excellent disposition I had found, with few exceptions, wherever I went. I continued as follows:

'Your Majesty, I have never belonged to any secret society; I have had nothing to do with intrigues and plots; but as I have spent my childhood and youth in various parts of Italy so that all are acquainted with me, they know I am no spy and therefore no one distrusts me; I have, therefore, known about their secret affairs just as though I had been one of them. They still tell me everything, and I think I can assure you, without fear of deceiving myself, that the majority of them recognize the absurdity of what has hitherto happened and want to change their policy. All are persuaded that without force nothing can be done; that the only force in Italy is that of Piedmont; but that they cannot count even on this as long as Europe is peaceful and organized as at present. These ideas are sensible and give proof of a real advance in political understanding. Your Majesty will ask: "How long will they last?" I myself confess that there is no certainty about this. I think I can say that I have a good deal of influence on the men who count in those regions at the moment. I have succeeded in convincing the majority; but the revolt at Rimini, which broke out a fortnight after I left Romagna, is a proof that I did not persuade all. Or, even if the leaders were persuaded, those immediately under them were not. In such a hierarchy, where the discipline is not obligatory and only relies on trust, obedience is always fortuitous. Sometimes passions and interests of all sorts determine actions not generally approved. Finally one must bear in mind the sad conditions which oppress the people. Where arbitrary actions, violence, corruption, deceit, suspicion, etc., are seen in those above, it is only natural that those below rely on the same methods. Where the general material and moral conditions are so bad, without a hope of improvement, one cannot foresee up to what point or for how long prudence and reason will be able to restrain desperation and rage. Those who suffer are the only ones who can decide the great question as to how long they can endure. Men are made like that: a wise, far-seeing policy must be based on things as they are, and accept the situation, if it doesn't wish to take the wrong road.

'This is why I have tried to restrain a new outbreak of desperation with a new idea, and for this purpose I have gone about to spread it, as I have reported. I think, despite the case of Rimini, my efforts have borne some fruit. Perhaps your Majesty will tell me if he approves, or not, of what I have done and what I have now said.'

I stopped and awaited the reply, which, to judge by the King's expression, did not seem likely to be hostile. But I guessed that, in regard to the essential, it was likely to be sibylline, and that it would not leave one any the wiser. Instead, he said quietly but firmly, without any hesitation or turning his glance away, but looking me straight in the eyes: 'Let those gentlemen know that they should remain quiet and take no steps now, as nothing can be done at present; but they can rest assured that when the opportunity arises, *my life, my children's lives, my arms, my treasure, my army; all shall be given in the cause of Italy.*'

Expecting something quite different, I remained for a moment speechless. I almost thought I had not heard aright. I pulled myself together at once, but perhaps the King noticed my surprise.

The intentions he had so resolutely revealed to me, especially the phrase 'let those gentlemen know', had so surprised me that they did not yet seem real. It was essential for me to understand them right. Then, as always, I thought that all the cards should be on the table and that any equivocation and—above all—miscalculation could only do harm.

Thanking him and showing how moved I was (as indeed I really was), captivated by his frankness, I was careful to repeat his own phrase in which I said: *Farò dunque sapere a quei signori,* etc. He nodded to show I had understood him, and then dismissed me. We both got up; he placed his hands on my shoulders, and offered me his cheek, first on one side, then on the other.

However, this embrace seemed somewhat studied, cold, almost funereal, so that I felt chilled. An inner voice repeated that terrible phrase: 'Don't trust him'. It is a tremendous punishment for those who are professedly astute, to be suspected, even when telling the truth.

He had really spoken the truth, poor gentleman: events proved it.

Who would have said then, as we sat at that window on two gilded chairs covered with green and white flowered silk (and every time I see them again they make me shudder); who would have said that when, through me, he offered his arms, treasure, and life to the Italians, I was unjust in not being immediately fully convinced? Who would have said that the great moment, so far beyond any expectation in 1845, and which both of us must have despaired of ever seeing, had been ordained by God to come three years afterwards? And that in that war, an impossible war as it then seemed to us, he was to lose his crown, his country, and then his life: and to me, as his son's Prime Minister, was reserved the sad duty of burying him among the royal tombs of the Superga, officially attesting the act in person?

Poor humans, who imagine they control events!

* * *

As may well be believed, I left the palace with my mind in a whirl. A great and splendid hope flew before me with beating wings.

I returned to my little room on the top floor of the Trombetta hotel, and sat down at the desk to write at once to my correspondents, who had to pass on the reply to all the others.

Before parting from them I had invented a code, quite different from all the usual ones. It was absolutely secure and, in my opinion, proof against breaking, but very tedious to use. I therefore could not write the letter quickly. It gave the exact purport of Carlo Alberto's reply; but to be scrupulously exact and in order not to give as certain what was really my own impression, I ended my letter thus: 'These are his words; God alone knows his inner thoughts.'

I have never, as the saying goes, wanted to sell a pig in a poke to anyone. I have always considered it essential, when you induce men to risk their substance, their liberty, their life, and the peace of their families—their whole existence in fact, to get them to know and see quite clearly what they are doing and why. I have never had to repent of this policy and I recommend it with all possible warmth to those who live in this poor Italy, so open to temptations, and where so many act otherwise and put people to every kind of jeopardy, by confusing their judgement with illusions and lies.

I shall now repeat something which, on thinking it over, seems certain; but at some moments leaves me with a shadow of doubt. I think, during the course of our conversation, that the King said: 'It would be a good thing for you to write something', and that I replied: 'I have already considered doing so', as I really had.[2]

I was turning over in my mind a plan to be put into effect, as far as possible, throughout Italy; a kind of non-secret daylight conspiracy, without concealment, disguise, or seeking to protect oneself from whatever dangers there might be from police or sectarians.

This was my plan and Balbo shared it. I couldn't say who invented it, he or I.

This was our general idea.

No revolutions: we've had enough! No war: we have no means or force (don't forget this was in '45). The question, then, must be debated where every individual has some influence, if he is not an idiot and doesn't mind risking his neck, that is to say in the field of public opinion.

Balbo had the greatest spirit and intelligence of anyone I have ever known. He had great spontaneity of feeling and sincerity of speech, without a shadow of that circumspect reserve and cold calculation so common among the Piedmontese. I too was against all these inhibitions, and inclined by nature to call a spade a spade, so that we were reciprocally congenial. We were first cousins, yet we always felt more like friends than relations. When, after my long absences, I returned more often to stay in Turin, our friendship became even closer. He certainly had a hot-blooded character and sometimes he made scenes . . . but I was very fond of him. There was no bitterness, no shadow of low or ugly sentiments. In fact, I could not have had a better friend, nor could our mutual attachment have been closer.

To pass from the greater to the lesser: he had such feeling for material and spiritual beauty, for the arts and literature. He felt such ingenuous enthusiasm for all noble, generous ideas; for all brave, honourable actions! Poor Cesare! A nature such as his is unique and I shall never see the like again.

We continually talked over the new direction to be given to the work for the resurgence of Italy and, for hours on end, we continued our discussions. He was living in his little Rubatto villa, on the banks of the Po, facing Valentino, where I too had established myself.

Those were good days! There was something in the air which announced a better time coming; which inspired hopes, presentiments undefined, but of which the heart felt certain.

---

[2] *Author's Note.* The doubt is whether the initiative was his or mine; and if, in the first supposition, he said it in person, or sent someone to tell me afterwards.

The Italian cause, which had become so depressed and decrepit from what it had gone through, now seemed rejuvenated and renewed. It was full of the charm and promise of youth, augury of vigorous manhood.

The problem of what form the government should take, the exclusive policies of the secret societies, all vanished before the idea of a general redemption from foreign domination of all Italians through-out the peninsula. Balbo's *Porro unum necessarium* was not yet written, but all felt it in their hearts.

The memory of those days now, after the sad series of events which has brought us where we are, produces the same effect in me as thoughts of his robust youth produce in a decrepit old man. But we must never despair. Who knows what treasures of vitality God has placed in the human heart? Who can gauge what strength has been lost or what remains? Who can distinguish, in the bundle of dry cuttings the husbandman plants in the earth, those which will strike root and flourish and those which will wither and die? After all, what inexhaustible vitality must there not be in the Italian people!

Our discussions usually turned on the need to prepare the minds and characters of the Italians, before starting to act (this is the key to the whole problem and little good can be achieved until it is done); on the impact and influence which our light-of-day conspiracy could exert to this end. History provided us with examples of excellent results obtained by open, persevering protests of the weak against the strong. So that, having discussed the matter thoroughly, we resolved to start work.

First, a book had to be written.

The aim we already knew; we now had to find the subject, or shall we say the occasion and pretext. I had the idea of writing about the recent up-rising at Rimini, and without taking sides speaking out plainly without any reserve. Balbo approved and I set to work.

As this was a complete change of liberal strategy, I did not wish to proceed without, I do not say getting their permission, but at least advising the friends with whom I had consorted for the last six months. I wrote to them about it.

After a few days I received a general cry of disapproval. They said I would be thrown out, exiled; that I was cutting my own throat; that I should be useless, powerless to do more, etc., etc.

My own opinion was that I was useless, powerless, and tied by the legs under present conditions; while if I could be expended with some hope of doing good, now was the chance. Balbo also persisted and I therefore wrote again. I said: 'So be it! I'm going on with it; and you will see that, instead of losing me, you will have me with redoubled strength.' I asked for all possible information that could be got on the Rimini up-rising. After a couple of months I received a fair bundle of notes in which somebody or other had described the whole thing. I then wrote my narrative. The unfortunate thing was that it was not very accurate, and therefore my little book on the Romagna rising, in so far as it is an account of what happened (I only mean with regard to events in Rimini, not the more general part about the Papal State and Italy), is inaccurate too, as I later discovered. But as the most important part was in the reflections I made, in the home truths given impartially to both sides, and especially in the publication of my name as responsible author with my full permission, this defect spoilt nothing.

My little book *Degli ultimi casi di Romagna* was ready in little more than a month. I wanted to know the opinions of my most intimate friends; so I invited them to meet one evening at Balbo's house. Lisio, Luigi Provana, Sauli, naturally Cesare, and others I forget, came along. I read my book aloud to them, and after agreeing to a few corrections, I had my censors' approval.

Then the question of printing arose. For us, Turin would have been the best place; as if the government permitted it to appear, it would be the same as accepting its principles and Carlo Alberto's political position would be clearly defined.

Whether the King would have done well to take up such a definite position at that time, is arguable. The truth is that such decisive decisions were not natural to him. In any case, I took my work to Promis, one of the censorship committee, for him to examine it and see if it would be possible for me to get permission to have it printed in Piedmont. I then awaited his decision.

In order to make use of the eight or ten days which I found difficult to wait for, I thought I would go to Milan to inspect my things there. I had so to arrange matters that I should not need to attend to them for a long time. I knew that once my book came out I had to forget about Milan.

After having arranged things as best I could, I returned to Turin.

I hurried straight to Promis, who handed me back my manuscript with a smile, pronouncing a 'No' as round as the mouth of a well! This is what I thought would happen, so, saying, 'I'll try elsewhere', I too smiled, and took my leave. I then packed my bag and started for that great *refugium peccatorum* of the time, called Tuscany.

This charming country presented a phenomenon I have never rightly been able to explain.

Tuscany lived under an unwritten constitution, without any backing of force, yet as generally respected and observed as the English constitution. This could really be called the Magna Carta of Tuscany. Even the Grand Duke was, willy nilly, subject to it; should he disobey it he found himself ignored by everybody. There was no official formulation of this law. It was understood and obeyed without it being stated in words. If I had to formulate it I should do so in these few words: 'Let it slide'. The application of this maxim to individuals, private persons, or to the government was continuous and frequent. If a young man went over the rails, if a girl had an *affaire;* if a woman was a flirt, after some fuss to keep up appearances . . . let it slide! If a family got into arrears, if bailiffs and peasants stole things, you complained for a time then . . . let it slide! If the police made a regulation which no one heeded, there was twenty-four hours of strict application, then—let it slide. If someone without too serious a crime on his conscience was thought to be a public danger, he was expelled, but if he did not clear out but went for a little tour and settled in Florence again . . . let it slide. And so on and so forth. One can say this arises from the gentleness of the Tuscan nature. It may be. But they were a long way from being gentle, three centuries ago; in fact there was something fierce in the Tuscan character; witness the last siege of 1530.

To cut a long story short, the *Casi di Romagna* was published in Florence. It is not for me to speak of the effect it had. Not now daring to return to Milan, as it would have been an absurd piece of audacity, I arranged things so that I could divide my time between Florence, Genoa, and Turin.

FINIS

APPENDIX

D'AZEGLIO'S RECORD OF HIS WORKS EXHIBITED AT THE BRERA PALACE OF MILAN.[1]

THE list of my Brera exhibits from 1833 to 1843 is so short that I can give it here, in case it should be useful to any of my good readers.[2]

1833

Battle at the Garigliano between the Spanish and French.
View of Cadenabbia on Lake Como.
View of Maiolica on the same lake.
View of Cernobbio as above.
Fishing boat.
The mouth of the Gresio near Cernobbio.
The Castle of Azeglio.
View of Grianta on Lake Como.
Bay of the Lake of Como near Balbiano.
Fountain of Perlasca, near Balbiano.
The Challenge at Barletta.
Seascape near Sorrento.
San Pietro d'Acqua Acetosa.
Seascape.
The Port of Cernobbio.
Houses at Perlasca.
Fieramosca arriving at the Island of Sant' Orsola.

In the Exhibition of 1834

View of Tremezzina.
Imaginary village with the episode of Argalia's ghost appearing to Ferraù.
The toast of Francesco Ferruccio, General of the Florentines, to his soldiers before the battle of Gavinana. Commissioned by the Marchesa Visconti d'Aragona.

[1] From the material supplied after the author's death by Giuseppe Torelli (see Introduction, p.xi above).
[2] Feltrinelli Edition, pp. 506–8.

Peasant woman pursued by pirates. Commissioned by Count Mazè.

The Challenge at Barletta. Commissioned by Cavaliere Paolo Toschi.

Battle of Gavinana. Commissioned by the Marquis Antonio Visconti.

Fight between Diego Garcia di Paredel against a great number of French on the bridge of boats over the Garigliano. The property of Signor Carlo Galli.

Bradamante fighting with the wizard Atlante to free Ruggero from the enchanted castle.

A vendetta. Presented to the church of San Fedele.

A pause in the hunt.

Defence of a bridge. Property of Signor Pietro Tron of Turin.

Ferraù and Argalia's ghost.

A fight. Commissioned by Signor Baldassare Ferrero of Turin.

1837

Funeral of Duke Amedeo VI (Conte Verde).

Flood in an Alpine valley.

View of the Castel dell' Ovo.

Fight between Ferraù and Orlando.

Astolfo in pursuit of the Harpies.

The Dora Falls near Saint Didier.

Landscape with animals.

View of the Roman Campagna.

Small landscape.

1838

Great flood.

Bradamante, having overthrown Atlante, demands Ruggero's liberation.

Soldiers on the march.

Napoleon addressing the army of Egypt.

Macbeth and Banquo meet the three witches.

Ippalca, messenger of Bradamante to Ruggero.

1839

Fight between Gradasso and Rinaldo.

Duke Amedeo VI receives Michele Paleologo as a prisoner.

Zerbino and Isabella.

Ferraù and Argalia's ghost.

Sacripante and Angelica. From Ariosto, Canto 1.

Mill near San Pellegrino. Property of the Provincial Delegate of
   Bergamo.
The defence of Nice against Barbarossa and the French. Commissioned
   by H.M. King Carlo Alberto.

1841

Rest during a hunt.
Thunderstorm.
The battle of Turin.
The battle of Col d'Assietta.
Imaginary landscape.

1842

Nothing exhibited, although I painted and sold not a few pictures.

1843

The Roman Campagna.
Peasant woman whose ass has fallen down.
G. Sforza in the act of throwing his axe at a tree to read the omen
   whether he should become a soldier.